Christi

Psychotnerapy

in Context

Christian Psychotherapy in Context combines theology with the latest research in clinical psychology to equip mental health practitioners to meet the unique psychological and spiritual needs of Christian clients. Encouraging therapists to operate from within a Christian framework, the authors explore the intersection between a Christian worldview and clients' emotional struggles, drawing from sources including both foundational theological texts and the "common factors" psychotherapy literature. Written collaboratively by two clinical psychologists, an academic psychologist, and a theologian, this book paves the way for psychotherapeutic practice that builds on Christian principles as the foundation, rather than merely adding them to treatment as an afterthought.

Joshua J. Knabb, PsyD, ABPP, is the director of the PsyD program in clinical psychology and an associate professor of psychology in the College of Behavioral and Social Sciences at California Baptist University.

Eric L. Johnson, PhD, is a professor of Christian psychology and counseling at Houston Baptist University and founding director of the Society for Christian Psychology.

M. Todd Bates, PhD, is a professor of theology and dean of the School of Christian Thought at Houston Baptist University.

Timothy A. Sisemore, PhD, is a clinical psychologist and president of the Society for the Psychology of Religion and Spirituality (APA Division 36).

"*Christian Psychotherapy in Context* equips mental health practitioners to meet the psychological and spiritual needs of Christian clients. This truly collaborative work draws on a theologically conservative Christian world-view to conceptualize how to understand and help Christians who struggle psychologically. Rather than champion one evidence-based practice in psychology, it draws on evidence-based common factors, Scripture, and classic and modern theologies to help struggling Christians. This is a great resource."

—**Everett L. Worthington, Jr., PhD**, Commonwealth Professor Emeritus of Psychology at Virginia Commonwealth University and co-editor of the *Handbook of Humility*

"I am grateful for this incredibly insightful scholarly and clinical resource. This book offers an important bridge between theology and clinical best practices while respecting the foundational importance of both. It will help practitioners address the very real, significant spiritual needs their Christian clients are facing with care that is informed by both Scripture and evidence without sacrificing either."

—**Jamie D. Aten, PhD**, founder and executive of the Humanitarian Disaster Institute and Blanchard Chair of Humanitarian and Disaster Leadership at Wheaton College

Christian Psychotherapy in Context

Theoretical and Empirical Explorations in Faith-Based Mental Health

Joshua J. Knabb, Eric L. Johnson, M. Todd Bates, and Timothy A. Sisemore

Routledge
Taylor & Francis Group

NEW YORK AND LONDON

First published 2019
by Routledge
52 Vanderbilt Avenue, New York, NY 10017

and by Routledge
2 Park Square, Milton Park, Abingdon, Oxon, OX14 4RN

Routledge is an imprint of the Taylor & Francis Group, an informa business

Library of Congress Cataloging-in-Publication Data
Names: Knabb, Joshua J., author.
Title: Christian psychotherapy in context : theoretical and empirical explorations in faith-based mental health / Joshua J. Knabb, Eric L. Johnson, M. Todd Bates, and Timothy A. Sisemore.
Description: New York, NY : Routledge, 2019. | Includes bibliographical references and index.
Identifiers: LCCN 2018054140 (print) | LCCN 2018055648 (ebook) | ISBN 9781351235143 (eBook) | ISBN 9781138566651 (hardback) | ISBN 9781138566828 (pbk.) | ISBN 9781351235143 (ebk)
Subjects: LCSH: Psychotherapy–Moral and ethical aspects. | Psychotherapy–Religious aspects. | Psychotherapy patients–Religious life.
Classification: LCC RC489.A32 (ebook) | LCC RC489.A32 K529 2019 (print) | DDC 616.89/14–dc23
LC record available at https://lccn.loc.gov/2018054140

ISBN: 978-1-138-56665-1 (hbk)
ISBN: 978-1-138-56682-8 (pbk)
ISBN: 978-1-351-23514-3 (ebk)

Typeset in Minion
by Integra Software Services Pvt. Ltd.

To my wife, Adrienne, who helps to refine my ideas as we walk, talk, laugh, and cry together on the winding roads of life.
J.J.K.

To Warren Watson, my first real therapist, who helped me turn a corner on my own healing journey, and who started out as a therapist who was a Christian, but has become a Christian therapist.
E.L.J.

To fellow travelers of the way.
M.T.B.

To my patient and supportive wife, Ruth.
T.A.S.

Contents

Figures

Tables

Acknowledgments

First of all, I would like to thank my co-authors, who have helped to strengthen my ideas, as well as provide many of the building blocks required to construct this complex architectural design. Also, thanks to my wife, Adrienne, and children, Emory and Rowan, who motivate me to "take my own medicine" each and every day as I humbly try to live out the central tenets of the Christian faith, psychologically and spiritually. Moreover, I would like to acknowledge Anna Moore at Routledge, who helped to bring this book to print, as well as the reviewers, Fernando Garzon and two anonymous reviewers, who offered helpful feedback in order to strengthen this writing project. Finally, thanks be to God for his perfect, trustworthy guidance: "your hand will guide me, your right hand will hold me fast."

J.J.K.

I would like to thank my co-authors for their work evident in this book. Co-authoring is a complex process, since each author sees the world from a different vantage point. Our common conceptual and therapeutic commitments brought us close together, but the actual writing creates an opportunity for dialogue that, at its best, is mutually transformational. I know that was my experience for I was deeply enriched by this process. May our combined efforts help point the way towards a distinctive Christian psychology literature.

E.L.J.

I would like to thank my collaborators on this project. The personal inter-action and exchange of ideas that took place was incredibly life enhancing and affirming. To each of you, thanks. To my children, you are mirrors of grace and deepest of friends—love to you. To Cathy, your love has revealed to me the most profound truths of the Trinity, without which I would be but a child.

M.T.B.

Thanks to my co-authors, who cast quite a vision for this work and for a coherent Christian psychology, both intellectually and clinically.

T.A.S.

Introduction

Psychological Interventions throughout History

For millennia, the major world religions have offered a clear, focalizing lens through which to view psychological suffering and healing. For those who identify with the Christian faith, a comprehensive worldview organically emanates from the Bible, answering a wide variety of existential questions on the causes of, and solutions to, human suffering.[1] In fact, at least four overarching, pressing questions naturally flow from a given worldview, organized around the "who," "where," and "what" of humanity: "who are we, where are we, what is wrong, and what is the solution?" (Wright, 1992, p. 123).

For followers of Jesus Christ, humans were created in God's image to be in relationship with both him and others, with God originally creating this world as "good," offering a vast, open space for humankind to interact and live. Yet, due to the fall of humankind, brokenness entered the world, resulting in a wide variety of ailments, diseases, and disorders. Although these experiences are ubiquitous, intricately intertwined with what it means to be human, Christians believe that Jesus Christ entered into the human experience to redeem a fallen world, reconciling those who put their faith in him as they wait with hope and endurance for God's eventual restoration of the world.

Christians have historically sought psychological and spiritual insight—that is, a psychospiritual understanding of the human predicament—from the characters and teachings in the Bible, with Scripture offering a coherent, comprehensive Christian metanarrative. Within this Christian metanarrative, there exists at least four stages, including creation, fall, redemption, and restoration (Beale, 2011). Although God's creation is broken because of the fall, Christians believe in a healing redemption offered by Jesus Christ, leading to an eventual restoration on the part of God.

In the Old Testament, the lament psalms reveal a common series of therapy-relevant actions, including crying out to God, requesting for God to help, expressing frustration or anger, thanking God, and recognizing that

1

God has heard the plea (Brueggemann, 1984). In the New Testament, both Jesus Christ and the Apostle Paul offered keen psychological insights into chronic, ubiquitous human struggles, ranging from worry (Matthew 6) to endurance in the face of unavoidable suffering (2 Corinthians 12), illuminating the ways in which Christians can improve and grow in life.

In addition to the Christian Bible, the Christian tradition has produced countless philosophical and theological works that reveal a well-developed psychospiritual framework for understanding humankind, including the most salient experiences that lead to suffering and healing. The early desert Christians often recited Scripture as a way to focus their attention on God, pivoting away from tempting, compulsive thoughts while battling a range of inner experiences in the desert (e.g., boredom, worry, sadness) (Harmless, 2004). Augustine of Hippo illuminated the reality of inner conflict, arguing for a healing relationship with Jesus Christ as the remedy (Foster, 2005). Thomas Aquinas wrote on both the cardinal and theological virtues (Wawrykow, 2005), presenting seven well-defined moral behaviors to guide the Christian life. Contemplative writers such as Theresa of Avila, John of the Cross, and the anonymous author of the *Cloud of Unknowing* offered strategies for surrender, detaching from worldly concerns so as to cultivate a deeper relationship with God (Bangley, 2006; Kellenberger, 2016). Thomas Kempis wrote on the importance of surrender in the Christian life (Creasy, 2007), and Jesuit writers such as Claude de la Colombiere (1980) and Jean-Piere de Caussade (2011) focused on surrendering to God's providence as a way to find peace in the midst of trials.

Among Protestant writers, the Puritans wrote heartfelt meditations that captured the struggles inherent within Christian living, providing an outlet for followers of Jesus who have guilt and shame, are in pain, and feel alienated from God (Bennett, 1975). Jonathan Edwards (1959) wrote about healthy Christian emotions in *Religious Affections*, arguing that focusing on God (rather than the self) is central to human flourishing. Søren Kierkegaard's writings covered a broad range of topics that are part of the human condition (e.g., anxiety, despair), offering profound psychological, philosophical, and theological analysis. In each of these instances, Christian writers have developed clear, coherent frameworks for understanding *both* psychological *and* spiritual functioning, which are deeply interrelated throughout human life.

Still, in the last 150 years, many suffering individuals in Western society have turned to modern psychology—rooted in an ontological materialism—as a way to make sense of the human condition. As Sigmund Freud offered an alternative, psychosexual theory to understand the human experience, a different lens was presented for ameliorating suffering; in doing so, a rift developed between the psychology of the Christian faith and the burgeoning modern version of psychology, despite the fact that Christian thinkers throughout the ages have offered psychologically astute conceptualizations of both the inner and outer worlds (Johnson, 2007; Welsh & Knabb, 2009).

Although these seemingly combatant, warring approaches have historically struggled to get along, there have been more recent efforts to work together in an attempt to better understand and treat human suffering (Johnson, 2010). Some of these approaches start from a secular orientation, attempting to fit Christianity into an already-established psychological framework (see, e.g., Free, 2015). Other contemporary efforts strive to cultivate a distinctly Christian psychology, turning to the Bible and Christian philosophical and theological works throughout the ages as a foundation to better understand what helps humans improve, grow, and successfully respond to suffering in modern society (see, e.g., Knabb & Frederick, 2017).

Interestingly, these attempts within the Christian psychology literature to commence with a Christian worldview parallel current efforts in clinical psychology to develop therapy models that begin with a Buddhist foundation, including a Buddhist view of concepts such as suffering, clinging, impermanence, and no-self (see, e.g., Schuman, 2017). In other words, there are many current efforts underway to start from a Buddhist worldview, enhancing mindfulness meditation by converting it into a coherent delivery system for ameliorating suffering in the 21st-century therapy room (see Grabovac, Lau, & Willett, 2011). Although, in many cases, meditation has been stripped of its Buddhist influences (Benson, 2000), some authors have pointed to the importance of strengthening scientific explorations of meditation by making its roots more explicit (Walsh & Shapiro, 2006).

Recent Developments that Necessitate a Distinctly Christian Approach to Psychotherapy

Several recent developments have taken place within the psychology literature in recent years, paving the way for a distinctly Christian approach to psychotherapy. First, there has been an increasing emphasis on cultural diversity, including recognition of the importance of taking clients' worldview into consideration in clinical practice. Rather than merely tolerating a religious framework in the therapy room, recent guidelines have advocated for the necessity of working from *within* clients' cultural framework. As an example, the American Psychological Association's *Guidelines on Multicultural Education, Training, Research, Practice, and Organizational Change for Psychologists* (2002) explains that clinical psychologists are to view "clients-in-context," striving to understand their unique worldview as they intervene to ameliorate suffering. To offer an additional example, Josephson and Peteet (2004) published an edited book on working from within clients' spiritual worldview, with Peteet (2004) noting there is often an overlap between "clinical concerns" (e.g., psychiatric symptoms, impaired functioning) and "existential concerns," resulting in the need to explore a variety of worldview issues (e.g., meaning, morality, self-identity, hope) in the therapy room. Although Peteet explained that worldview issues can sometimes be addressed by solely focusing on the psychological experience of clients or relying on a religious leader to help make sense of the issue, more deliberate strategies involve operating from within the "patient's own philosophy of life" or working with the client from a "shared perspective" (p. 54).

Second, decades of psychotherapy outcome research have revealed that no one theoretical orientation has the "monopoly" on the change process. Rather, a range of common factors seem to be at play when examining the amelioration of suffering within clinical psychology. For example, a supportive relationship, learning through cognitive insight and emotional processing, and developing a set of healthy new behaviors (Lambert, 2013) are ubiquitous within the clinical psychology literature, regardless of the theoretical orientation. In a recent review of the literature, Laska, Gurman, and Wampold (2014) found that common factors accounted for a higher percentage of variability in psychotherapy outcomes than specific ingredients, with the top three including collaborating on common goals (12%), empathy (9%), and building and maintaining a therapeutic relationship (8%). Many of these common factors, certainly, are embedded within the Christian tradition, threaded throughout the pages of the Bible and included in other important philosophical and theological works within two millennia of Christian writings (Frank & Frank, 1993).

Third, based on epidemiological studies, both clinical psychologists and psychiatrists are increasingly coming to grips with the reality that psychiatric disorders are pervasive and enduring, explicating that psychological pain is a ubiquitous, inevitable part of life (rather than something that can be fully eliminated with either coping skills or medicine). For example, roughly one in three adults will suffer from an anxiety disorder in their lifetime, with one in five experiencing a mood disorder (Kessler, Petukhova, Sampson, Zaslavsky, & Wittchen, 2012). This understanding of the human condition is highly congruent with a Christian view of the world, given Christianity's emphasis on the fall of humankind and its consequences. Thus, Christian writers over the last 2,000 years have frequently presented astute insights into the psychospiritual resources that help humans to "suffer well" (Keller, 2015).

Fourth, the psychology of religion literature has revealed that religion can be a source of comfort, encouragement, and improvement for clients. A meta-analysis of 34 published studies revealed a positive association between religion and mental health (a small effect size) (Hackney & Sanders, 2003). A separate meta-analysis of 49 published studies found a positive correlation between religious coping and the ability to adjust to stressful life events (a medium effect size) (Ano & Vasconcelles, 2005). Christians throughout the ages have consistently written on the protective benefits of a committed, unwavering Christian faith in the midst of stressful life events and other forms of suffering.

Fifth, given that mindfulness-based interventions and an emphasis on self-compassion have permeated the clinical literature in the last few decades, increasingly drawing from Buddhist roots (Grabovac et al., 2011), it seems only natural for Christian clients to turn to their own religious heritage in response to suffering. Instead of translating Eastern philosophy into Christian language, Christians can rely on the rich philosophical, theological, and psychological perspectives that make up a Christian understanding of health, dysfunction, and positive change.

Finally, psychiatry has continued to struggle to establish the validity of many DSM-5 diagnoses, suggesting psychological pain may be more complicated than merely pointing to a biological condition that requires a medical intervention. Although field trials were employed to establish the reliability (i.e., consistency) of DSM-5 diagnoses (APA, 2013), diagnostic validity has yet to be established among many highly prevalent disorders. As Paris (2015) recently noted, the majority of disorders within the pages of the DSM-5 rely on symptoms and signs to arrive at a diagnosis, rather than well-established medical tests like other branches of medicine (e.g., genetic testing, blood work, imaging results). In fact, there continue to be a plethora of "unresolved problems" within psychiatry, such as (a) difficulties understanding the dividing line between normal and abnormal (which means psychiatrists sometimes pathologize what is normal, with drugs to "improve" functioning); (b) a lack of biological markers to identify disorders; (c) comorbidity between diagnoses; and (d) arbitrary cutoffs when listing the symptoms required for a diagnosis (Paris, 2015; see also Greenberg, 2013). Interestingly, the DSM-5 is quick to point out that clinicians must conceptualize psychopathology in the context of clients' given culture, acknowledging that what constitutes distress varies from culture to culture (APA, 2013). In fact, the definition of *distress* (the cornerstone of diagnosing in the DSM-5, along with symptom counts and clients' report of their own perceived level of impaired functioning) may even vary between cultures, suggesting that the diagnostic process can be culturally biased (APA, 2013). As a parallel, the Christian tradition most certainly makes room for at least a partially biological cause for many psychiatric disorders, given the fall of humankind. Yet, a Christian worldview illuminates the reality of psychological, social, and spiritual suffering, too. Based on these developments, the world religions are being re-invited to the conversation, recognizing they play a vital role in understanding suffering.

Building a Case for a Distinctly Christian Approach to Psychotherapy for Emotional Disorders

Based on these six developments within the clinical literature, a few key points are worth making so as to build a strong case for a distinctly Christian approach to psychotherapy for emotional disorders in the 21st century. To begin, clinical interventions in psychotherapy must be sensitive to the needs of culturally diverse clients, which includes meeting the religious and spiritual needs of devout Christians in the therapy room. As the cultural diversity literature has revealed, most psychotherapy models were originally developed based on a secular, materialistic worldview, divorced from the perspective of the religious clients they sometimes seek to serve. In fact, Miller (2012) recently argued that materialism "can no longer suffice as the exclusive rubric through which we view the human psyche" (p. 2), with Katonah (2006) advocating for an expanded view of psychological functioning:

> Within the paradigm of scientific materialism we cannot consider the realm of spirit as a reality and investigate how spirituality is related to health, healing, and the development of the person. We desperately need access to human processes that restore our capacity to address the whole person.
>
> (p. 70)

Although materialism has dominated psychological science in the 20th century, "zooming out" to take into account a broader history illuminates the reality that thinkers from diverse disciplines throughout the ages have acknowledged the more transcendent, spiritual aspects of human functioning (Miller, 2012). Therefore, newer models that *start* from clients' religious worldview seem to make more sense, especially since a theoretical orientation in clinical psychology often functions like a worldview—surely, why ask clients to somehow change their worldview to make room for clinical psychology? Instead, maybe clinical psychology can make room for clients' religion and spirituality. When this happens, a religious framework can be utilized as a source of resilience for devout clients, buffering the negative effects of human suffering.

Second, because there is no one framework in clinical psychology that fully explains mental health, dysfunction, and healing, the common factors literature illuminates the reality that there are a plethora of general ingredients that account for psychotherapeutic improvement. These factors, to be sure, often overlap with well-developed psychospiritual writings within the Christian tradition, revealing that secular clinical psychologists have not so much "discovered" something new, but recaptured what has already been present for thousands of years. In Frank and Frank's (1993) innovative, pioneering book on common factors in psychotherapy, they make a similar case, outlining several elements of healing practices across cultures. Referring to *demoralization* as the reason clients seek services from psychotherapists, Frank and Frank argue that individuals feel alone, hopeless, and helpless as they reach for another to help them with their pain. In their efforts to get help in ameliorating their distress, clients enter the psychotherapeutic encounter, which provides them with several ingredients for effective change: (a) a safe, supportive relationship that emphasizes clients' emotional experience, (b) a familiar location from which to work towards improvement, (c) a lens through which to conceptualize both the problem and solution, and (d) an agreed-upon strategy to work together to impact change (Frank & Frank, 1993). In this important relationship, the therapist ameliorates clients' loneliness, cultivates a restored sense of hope, offers new forms of learning, supports client efficacy, and creates the necessary space for practicing new behavior (Frank & Frank, 1993). From our perspective, *both* the evidence-based psychotherapy models of contemporary clinical psychology *and* the Christian tradition can be effectively synthesized to offer a comprehensive framework of improvement. Such an outcome would help Christian clients change in their own proverbial country, rather than traveling to a distant land to interact with strangers who do not share their view of the world.

Third, psychotherapy clients with chronic mental disorders must be prepared to face the inevitability of recurrent symptoms. For Christian clients, drawing from the Christian faith can help them to do so, especially because of Christianity's emphasis on the reality of suffering. Interestingly, Keller (2015) recently noted the following with reference to Christians' ability to endure suffering when faced with tremendous pain:

> Early Christian speakers and writers not only argued vigorously that Christianity's teaching made more sense of suffering, they insisted that the actual lives of Christians proved it. Cyprian recounted how, during the terrible plagues, Christians did not abandon sick loved ones nor flee the cities, as most of the pagan residents did. Instead they stayed to tend the sick and faced their death with calmness.
>
> (p. 41)

Also, because Christians believe that Jesus is the "suffering servant" mentioned in Isaiah 53, he has led the way to provide his followers with a trustworthy example of perseverance. To be sure, given he lived a fully human life, he is able to empathize with human struggles (Hebrews 4:15).

Fourth, a Christian framework can be a resiliency factor for suffering clients. For religious clients, there is empirical support for the notion that faith can be protective, enhancing clinical work as a foundational element of treatment (rather than merely serving as an add-on to a secular understanding of the world). To offer a recent example in the clinical psychology literature, Knabb, Frederick, and Cumming (2017) found that positive views of God's providence were linked to the ability to surrender to God, with surrendering to God's providence correlated with less worry. The surrender–worry link, moreover, was mediated by the ability to tolerate uncertainty. These findings emerged among both college students and a community sample of Christian congregants, with the study's theoretical framework flowing from a 17th-century Jesuit writing, entitled *Trustful Surrender to Divine Providence* (Colombiere, 1980).

To conclude, a view of psychopathology must be culture-dependent, and clinical psychiatry by no means has the monopoly on understanding suffering in the 21st century, especially considering a purely biological conceptualization does not fully explain the complex nature of mental disorders. In fact, in the more recent clinical psychiatry literature, there have been a variety of emerging critiques of the DSM-5 (Frances, 2014; Paris, 2015; Paris & Phillips, 2013). Although the DSM-5 is certainly useful as a tool to help clinicians utilize a common language for organizing symptoms and planning treatment options that help clients heal, many disorders have yet to be fully validated in the same way as diseases like cancer (e.g., there is a clear line dividing a benign versus malignant growth of cells in the body). As a result, clients' religious framework for understanding suffering should not be regarded as inferior to clinical psychiatry; instead, religion needs to be honored as an important way to make sense of the human experience.

"Neighbors in Different Countries": A Metaphor for Understanding the Relationship between Christian and Secular Versions of Psychotherapy

The notion of neighboring countries can be a useful metaphor to highlight the prioritization of Christian (i.e., theistic) and secular (i.e., naturalistic) worldviews in psychotherapy.[2] In other words, in general, psychotherapy can be seen as one big structure, like an entire geographical region, whereas Christian and secular versions of psychotherapy can be seen as opposing directions within that structure, similar to two countries existing side by side (Wolters, 2005). Given secular psychotherapy's emphasis on an onto-logical naturalism, Christian clients struggling with emotional disorders who see secular clinicians are commonly required to adopt a secular perspective (a theoretical orientation functions much like a worldview, with a view of human nature, development, dysfunction, and healing) to make sense of their psychological struggles. This can feel like being asked to pack up and move to a neighboring country to live, disavowing Christians' culture of origin in favor of the cultural beliefs and practices of a different geographical location. In that Christian clients are in pain as they seek out psychotherapeutic services, having to pack up and move in the midst of their suffering to a country with a different culture can be scary and confusing, exacerbating an already difficult experience.

Rather than having to actually move to a different country, we believe Christian clients are best served when they can receive psychotherapeutic services "within their own country" from psychotherapists who have learned the best of what is done in other countries, but who are working from within Christians' culture of origin as the starting and ending point of treatment—a distinctly Christian psychotherapy. This is especially important when considering that Christians believe God is the author of creation.

Continuing with the metaphor, God is the creator of all lands, with each country developing the gifts of God. Because Christians know God, all archi-tecture (whether local or foreign) can be appreciated and rightly interpreted for what it is. From this viewpoint, Christians passing through secular cultures can enjoy the local cuisine because they know the chef, who is the source of "every good and perfect gift" (James 1:17). Walking along a beautiful bridge, Christians in a different country can appreciate its intricate design, given they know the structural engineer, who shares his wisdom with those made in his image (Genesis 1:26–27; Daniel 2:19–23). At the same time, when Christians know God, they are also able to view different cultures critically through the lens of their own worldview, given this worldview serves as the foundation for life. By doing this, Christians can benefit from the best of what neighboring countries have to offer, recognizing God as the author of all the good in other lands, while remaining committed to the worldview beliefs of their own culture.

To apply this metaphor to the relationship between Christian and secular forms of psychotherapy in the 21st century, these two worldviews—theistic and naturalistic—in psychotherapy are like two different countries. In the Christian country, there is a spiritual focus on issues of transcendence, whereas the secular country is largely devoid of this perspective. Both countries, moreover, have their own ways of making sense of psychological health, dysfunction, and healing, drawing from their respective worldviews. Given these two countries are neighbors, "sharing a border" (which represents a common interest in understanding and responding to suffering), they ought to become familiar with each other and be willing to learn from each other.

In one country are residents who embrace the Christian tradition (having lived there for millennia), which emanates from the Christian Bible; these citizens have been actively discussing human functioning for roughly 2,000 years. In this country, Christians embrace a theistic worldview, recognizing that reality involves both psychological and spiritual functioning. From their viewpoint, a personal God exists, who intimately interacts with humankind. Residing in the other country are materialists, who officially formed their own version of psychological change about a century ago (although materialists in disciplines such as philosophy have lived there for centuries). These occupants have conducted empirical research for decades on what can improve their country, believing that reality is best understood by looking exclusively to the material, natural world for answers.

Both countries have their own respective views on what constitutes healing, and each actively strives to ameliorate psychological pain in a suffering world. Although these neighboring countries get into regional disputes from time to time, such as where the border begins and ends and whose responsibility it is to ensure the geographical region is taken care of, they pursue answers to very similar questions and need to learn how to peacefully co-exist. The country of materialists can begin to recognize that some of their ideas are by no means "new," in the sense that the Christian country has been attempting to understand human functioning for roughly twenty centuries. On the other hand, the Christian country can learn to appreciate the ways in which materialists have utilized the scientific method to carefully break down psychological functioning into measurable components. From a Christian perspective, although the country of materialists often has identified useful building blocks, they do not possess the Christian blueprint. Because of this, perhaps both countries can learn how to work together as they attempt to respond to a suffering world, with the materialist country elucidating certain information within this world, and the Christian country illuminating a more transcendent understanding of health, dysfunction, and healing.

In light of recent developments within the psychotherapy literature (especially an emphasis on the limitations of embracing purely Western, secular models when working with diverse clients), a pressing question within this book is as follows: how can the Christian faith be a central part of the conversation already taking place in clinical circles about the change process, especially in a Christian-sensitive professional context that embraces both a spiritual and empirical understanding of the human condition?

For the last several decades, secular clinical psychologists have been busy integrating a variety of treatment approaches (referred to as the "psychotherapy integration" literature) in order to understand how clients heal, drawing from a naturalistic worldview in the process. Unfortunately, integrating religion and spirituality has rarely been introduced into the conversation. These efforts have been inspired by the notion that no one approach fully captures healing within the therapy room, leading to the need to amalgamate different approaches to best meet the needs of clients. From our viewpoint, the psychotherapy integration literature can offer a fitting heuristic for our current book, providing a way to reconcile the Christian faith as a foundational framework with the best science contemporary clinical psychology has to offer. As a result, what follows is a brief overview of the four types of clinical integration, including an exploration of which of the four approaches can best meet the needs of Christian psychotherapy clients by fully embracing a Christian worldview. In drawing from the psychotherapy integration literature, we believe both clinical psychology and Christianity can benefit. Clinical psychology can benefit from an expanded view of human functioning (beyond materialism as the be-all, end-all), and Christianity can benefit from a contemporary delivery system through which to inject its most helpful healing ingredients.

Psychotherapy Integration—Four Distinct Views

Within the psychotherapy integration literature, there are at least four ways in which authors have advocated that different therapy models can be integrated (Norcross & Goldfried, 2005). With the *theoretical integration* model, efforts are made to combine the actual theoretical underpinnings of the various modalities, which includes the amalgamation of techniques that flow from well-developed theories (Norcross, 2005). As another option, *technical eclecticism* is highly pragmatic, relying less on theory to guide treatment;

rather, eclecticism draws from the best possible interventions, without emphasizing a need to integrate theory into psychotherapy (Norcross, 2005). As a third approach, the *common factors* view explicates that there is a shared space, filled with interventions that work across the various theoretical orientations. In this shared space, treatment approaches have significant overlap, regardless of the therapy model they flow from (Norcross, 2005). Finally, *assimilative integration* starts with a theoretical foundation, which serves as a beginning point; in turn, interventions from other models are "assimilated," recognizing that therapists rarely (if ever) utilize a pure model (Norcross, 2005). To be sure, although one model is used as a proverbial map, other approaches are utilized, as needed, so as to strengthen the foundational model.

When beginning with a Christian worldview, we believe the latter two are the most fitting options. The common factors approach has identified ubiquitous strategies for therapeutic improvement, which are embedded in both contemporary psychotherapy models and the Christian faith. As Frank and Frank (1993) have revealed, there are a plethora of interventions within clinical psychology that extend back much further than the more recent era of psychological science in the 21st century. From our perspective, these treatment methods are threaded throughout the vast collection of Christian writings (such as philosophical and theological works, in addition to the Bible) throughout the ages. What is more, assimilative integration begins with the Christian faith, allowing clinical psychologists to work effectively with Christian clients according to a shared Christian framework by assimilating empirically supported treatments (ESTs) (as well as theoretically grounded interventions) into a Christian approach that views health, dysfunction, and healing in a Christian-sensitive manner.

On the other hand, the other two—theoretical integration and technical eclecticism—do not seem to be particularly sensitive to a Christian worldview. Theoretical integration requires a "synthesis," which leads to the development of an approach that is "better than the constituent therapies alone" (Norcross, 2005, p. 8). For Christians, though, there is no need to somehow improve the Christian faith, given Christians believe it is both a starting and ending point. Rather, clinical psychology can help to frame Christianity in such a way as to offer a contemporary vehicle through which healing can take place. With technical eclecticism, moreover, there is no real effort to draw from a unifying theory, which poses problems for Christians in that the Christian faith naturally leads to a comprehensive worldview for making sense of the human condition.

Why a Distinctly Christian Psychotherapy for Emotional Disorders?

Survey research has recently revealed that psychotherapists tend to be much less religious and are less likely than non-therapists to view religion as a central part of life (Post & Wade, 2009). We believe a distinctly

Christian approach to psychotherapy for emotional disorders is important for (at the very least) one overarching reason—Christian psychotherapy clients are deserving of ethical, competent, effective, and sensitive client care in the 21st century, which requires clinicians to take the Christian worldview seriously as the main dish, rather than some sort of condiment or lightly sprinkled seasoning upon a secular, materialistic dinner plate. In other words, Christian clients have a set of mental health needs, given their worldview, which emanate from the Christian Bible. Although prevalence rates for psychiatric disorders among Christians are likely similar to non-Christian populations (based on the fact that over two-thirds of individuals in the United States identify as Christian [Pew, 2015]), Christians are sometimes an underserved population because of their reluctance to fully embrace secular views in psychotherapy, which emanate from a naturalistic, materialistic worldview.

Rationale for the Outline in This Book

Within this book, we believe there are at least four pillars that uphold a Christian worldview, stabilizing the proverbial Christian house. Because we start with a Christian framework (rather than add on Christianity to a secular model, *post hoc*, as an afterthought), we have elected to organize the book around these four pillars, which include (a) theology, (b) ontology and epistemology, (c) biblical anthropology and axiology, and (d) redemption.

We start with theology as the first pillar because, from a Christian perspective, all of creation flows from God, who is sovereign. As a result, a distinctly Christian approach to psychotherapy begins with a firm understanding of God, who intimately interacts with the world that he created. Next, the pillar of ontology and epistemology is explored, providing a Christian lens through which to view reality and knowledge when employing a Christian psychotherapy approach. As a third pillar for this book, biblical anthropology and axiology are presented, since both play a central role in understanding Christian mental health and treatment, revealing a Christian view of humanity and values. As the final pillar, redemption offers a Christian conceptualization of healing, which we believe is unique, differing significantly from secular models.

Each of these pillars holds up the proverbial Christian house, functioning as a coherent framework for understanding the human condition. As we suggested above, Christian clients do not have to leave their own country to attain change in a secular country; rather, we argue that improvement can best take place when clients draw strength from their own meaning-laden framework. Therefore, we utilize the common factors model, recognizing that many of these basic building blocks of psychotherapy have been present within the Christian tradition for millennia, long before the clinical psychology literature "discovered" them. However, precisely because we are Christians, we value the science of psychotherapy research and believe that studying the clinical literature is an essential requirement for developing interventions that work.

Worth mentioning, in the clinical application chapters (Chapter 3, 6, 9, and 12) for each pillar, there is certainly some overlap (in terms of common themes), given we present a variety of goals and interventions for each of the "support, learning, and action" phases, all in the context of treating emotional disorders from a Christian worldview. Yet, we believe these common themes (e.g., God's providence; the balance between contemplation and action, captured by the story of Mary and Martha in Luke's gospel; the importance of both *kataphatic* and *apophatic* meditation in the Christian life) actually strengthen a Christian-sensitive approach to psychotherapy, based on the notion that the goals and interventions in each treatment pillar are viewed through a slightly different lens and involve a somewhat different focus, all in an effort to help Christian clients attain the familiarity and consistency necessary to impact change.

A Balanced Approach

This book covers theological, theoretical, and empirical considerations for psychotherapists working with Christian clients. In four sections (which serve as four distinct "pillars" and include three chapters each), we explore a range of overarching themes within a uniquely Christian worldview: (a) theology, (b) ontology and epistemology, (c) biblical anthropology and axiology, and (d) redemption.

From a clinical psychology viewpoint, we draw from the psychotherapy outcome literature (rather than only certain theoretical orientations), especially the psychotherapy integration literature (generally) and the "common factors" and "assimilative integration" models (specifically) (see Norcross & Goldfried, 2005).

As a result, common therapeutic factors, embedded within a Christian worldview, are emphasized throughout the book. Based on recommendations by Laska et al. (2014), we argue for a common factors approach in Christian psychotherapy that is (a) supported by decades of psychotherapy outcome research, and (b) consistent with Frank and Frank's (1993) observations on the overlap between universal healing practices (which we believe include the Christian tradition) and Western secular approaches to ameliorate suffering. Common factors that we believe are best understood within a distinctly Christian psychotherapy approach are drawn from Lambert (2013) and unfold in a sequential order: (a) support (e.g., the therapeutic relationship), (b) learning (e.g., insight, a corrective relational experience, cognitive reframing, emotional processing), and (c) action (e.g., healthy new behaviors). See Table I.1 for a list of "common factors," most of which we draw from in each chapter on psychotherapy for Christians (adapted from Lambert, 2013).

As the literature on a distinctly Christian psychotherapy for emotional disorders continues to grow in the coming decades, we believe there is additional

Table I.1 Common factors in psychotherapy. Adapted from Lambert (2013)

Support-Related Goals	Learning-Related Goals	Action-Related Goals
Verbalize Painful Affect	Give Advice	Confront Fears
Reduce Isolation	Process Emotions	Master Thinking Patterns
Provide a Framework for Understanding Health, Dysfunction, and Positive Change	Attain Insight	Practice Healthy Behaviors
Offer an Encouraging Relationship	Offer a Corrective Relational Experience	Take Risks
Offer a Safe Relationship	Provide Feedback on Thoughts, Feelings, Behaviors, and Relationships	Achieve a Sense of Self-Efficacy
Offer a Collaborative Relationship	Explore the Inner World	Model New Behaviors
Develop and Maintain a Working Alliance	Attain Realistic Expectations	Test Assumptions of Reality
Explore the Inner World	Reframe Views of Self and Others	Work Through Ingrained Patterns
Offer Therapeutic Qualities (Authenticity, Warmth, Empathy, Acceptance)	Accept Difficult Experiences	Practice Affect Regulation

room for specifically Christian empirically supported treatments (ESTs). In the meantime, beyond merely drawing from the "common factors" literature, we use an "assimilative integration" approach, presenting empirically supported techniques (as well as theoretically grounded interventions) from a distinctly Christian perspective. However, rather than beginning with secular theory, we employ an inverted "assimilative integration" model (see, e.g., Morgan, 2001), starting with a Christian worldview as the core framework, then suggesting well-established techniques that have been used among Christians over the centuries and adding techniques from empirically supported treatments (ESTs) and other theoretically grounded interventions in the clinical psychology literature to effectively work with Christian clients.

Interestingly, when discussing attempts by secular psychologists to research meditation, Walsh and Shapiro (2006) noted that efforts to fit mindfulness into a Western scientific framework have led to a sort of chipping away of the "richness and uniqueness" of meditative experiences; consequently, the authors advocated for an improved relationship between meditation practitioners and Western scientists that is "mutually enriching," consisting of a more "comprehensive, coherent, and holistic conceptual framework, adequate to both meditative and psychological traditions" (p. 228). Consistent with Walsh and Shapiro, we argue that starting solely with a secular clinical perspective, then "adding on" a Christian worldview, may also undermine the "richness and uniqueness" of the fertile, life-giving soil that is the Christian tradition.

In line with Morgan's (2001) "assimilative integration" effort some 15 years ago (beginning with Buddhism as the foundation, then adding on Western psychotherapy), we have elected to start from a particular religious tradition as an organizing framework, assimilating clinical psychology into a well-developed Christian worldview. Although we believe that recent attempts to integrate religion and spirituality with psychotherapy are well intentioned, they ultimately fall short in that they do not seem to fully consider the worldview implications of starting with a secular model, only to "add on" religion and spirituality as an afterthought.

Thus, "spiritually integrated psychotherapy" (e.g., Pargament, 2007), along with "integrationist" models within the Christian psychotherapy literature (e.g., Free, 2015), may not *fully* capture the "richness and uniqueness" (Walsh & Shapiro, 2006) inherent within the Christian tradition as a distinct worldview. Rather, these well-intentioned efforts sometimes end up "[feeding] the global 'colonization of the mind' by Western psychology that 'undermines the growth and credibility of other psychologies'" (Marsella, as cited in Walsh & Shapiro, 2006, p. 228) in that they often begin with a secular perspective, adding on a Christian worldview *post hoc*. By contrast, we firmly believe a distinctly Christian psychology needs to be included among the "other psychologies."

Almost two decades ago, Marsella (1998) advocated for a new emphasis on non-Western psychologies (we take "Western psychologies" to mean secular, ontologically materialistic orientations that do not view the world through a spiritual lens), given the reality of an increasingly global society. In this book, we argue that a distinctly Christian psychology, utilizing an inverted assimilative integration model to enhance clinical practice, is needed, and that secular models often fail to address the unique psychological and spiritual needs and worldview considerations of Christian clients. By doing this, we believe we are offering a sensitive approach for therapists working with Christian clients with emotional disorders, striving to ameliorate suffering by viewing psychological struggles through a distinctly Christian lens, consistent with other attempts to start from a particular religious framework (Morgan, 2001).

In each of the four "pillar" sections, we start with a chapter on a Christian view of the topic, drawing from the Bible and other Christian writings that are accepted within Christian orthodoxy. In the second chapter of each section, we provide a theoretical and empirical exploration of the topic, drawing from the contemporary psychology literature. As the third chapter within each section, we apply the topic to a distinctly Christian psychotherapy for emotional disorders, integrating a Christian understanding with both a "common factors" and "assimilative integration" approach.

Returning to the "neighbors in different countries" metaphor, the first chapter in each section reflects the Christian country, beginning with a

Christian foundation by reviewing traditional Christian beliefs that are grounded in the Bible and Christian theological works. Within the second chapter of each section, we consider the psychological implications of our country of origin and travel to the country of secular psychology, exploring relevant theory and research within the psychology literature. In these middle chapters of every section, we primarily focus on psychology of religion and clinical approaches that emanate from relational (e.g., attachment and psychodynamic perspectives), experiential and emotion-focused, and cognitive (e.g., traditional and acceptance-based cognitive behavioral perspectives) models, given these tend to be the more popular models in the clinical literature. We discuss these contemporary theoretical and empirical frameworks in the context of the four pillars and emotional disorders. Finally, in the third chapter of each section, we offer a Christian approach to psychotherapy, recognizing that a distinctly Christian understanding of life can help Christian clients to experience healing. From our perspective, traveling to the country of secular psychotherapy is important, but doing so requires a recognition that God is the creator of all lands, ensuring Christians are firmly anchored to their homeland in a sensitive manner.

Since emotional disorders are common in Western society (see Kessler et al., 2012), we have elected to more narrowly focus on depressive and anxiety disorders, rather than attempting to cultivate a Christian psychotherapy for *all* possible psychiatric disorders. See Figure I.1 for a visual of our model. Notice that everything good flows from God, who has revealed himself to humankind by way of the Christian Bible. In turn, the four "pillars" make up a Christian worldview, with empirically supported treatments (ESTs) and the "common factors" contributing to positive change in psychotherapy in a top-down (rather than bottom-up) manner. Above all else, we start with a Christian foundation (a bottom-up approach), recognizing that the "common factors" in the psychotherapy outcome literature have existed within the Christian tradition prior to their scientific validation within the field of clinical psychology.

"The Cast": A Metaphor for Christian Healing in Psychotherapy

Before concluding this introduction, one additional metaphor may be helpful for better understanding our vision for this book. When someone fractures a bone, a common medical intervention involves wearing a cast for a period of time. In doing so, the individual is relying on a cast to provide protection and reinforcement, utilizing the passage of time for the body to naturally repair the broken bone. At the most basic level, a cast provides the necessary support for the healing process to organically unfold. Of course, sometimes surgery is needed, and the fracture needs to be properly set for the bone to heal correctly; yet, the fundamental healing process involves relying on the body's innate ability to heal the bone.

In our efforts to draw from a Christian worldview, the "common factors" in psychotherapy function in the same way as a cast, offering the support

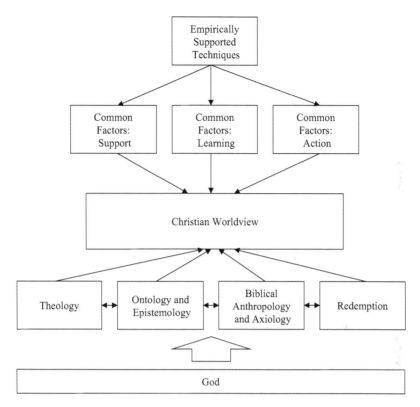

Figure I.1 Relationship between God, the four "pillars," worldview, the "common factors" in psychotherapy, and empirically supported techniques

and stability necessary for positive change to occur. As the psychotherapy outcome literature has revealed, a safe, consistent relationship is ideal for clients to learn and grow as they gain insight into their struggles. Along the way, this working alliance helps them to balance acceptance and change as clients practice new, healthy behaviors that contribute to authentic living.

We believe that Christian clients can naturally ameliorate their psychological pain when they are able to employ their own religious, theistic worldview, reminiscent of relying on the body's innate ability to heal, utilizing psychotherapy's "common factors" as the proverbial cast so as to attain the stability necessary to impact change. By establishing a therapeutic alliance, filled with trust, support, and safety, clinicians working with Christian clients are able to offer a protective reinforcement, relying on Christians' own change process so as to gain new insights and take action by adopting healthy behaviors that are consistent with their own faith tradition.

The Intended Audience and Informed Consent

Before concluding this chapter, it is important to note that we have at least two audiences in mind for this book. First, this book is written for *Christian* graduate students, psychotherapists, professional counselors, and pastoral counselors who are working with *Christian* clients. This primary audience may identify as Evangelical Protestant, who make up about 25% of Christians in the United States, or Catholic, who make up about 21% (Pew Forum, 2015). As a secondary audience, this book is for *secular* graduate students in clinical programs and mental health professionals in general who want to learn more about their *Christian* clients, meeting their religious clients' needs by operating from within a Christian, theistic worldview. In either case, we advise mental health professionals (whether Christian or non-Christian) using this approach to secure informed consent, thoroughly explaining to their Christian clients the goals and techniques within this distinctly Christian treatment model. In addition, therapists and counselors are advised to adhere to the ethical principles and code of conduct of their professional organization, reviewing the literature on legal and ethical considerations when utilizing psychospiritual interventions in psychotherapy (see, e.g., Chappelle, 2000), honoring client self-determination in the process.

Notes

1 Throughout the book, we use several synonyms for "worldview" (e.g., "framework," "background," "lens"), with the aim of capturing the need for a Christian "blueprint" for making sense of the human condition. In other words, although we believe psychological science has many of the requisite "building blocks" for assembling a Christian psychotherapy model, only orthodox Christianity possesses the right "blueprint" for making sense of the "who," "where," and "what" (Wright, 1992) for Christian clients in psychotherapy. Ultimately, a Christian "worldview" offers the much-needed context for our Christian-sensitive model.
2 In this chapter, naturalistic and materialistic worldviews are presented as synonymous.

References

American Psychiatric Association (2013). *Diagnostic and Statistical Manual of Mental Disorders* (5th ed.). Washington, DC: APA.

American Psychological Association (2002). *Guidelines on Multicultural Education, Training, Research, Practice, and Organizational Change for Psychologists*. Washington, DC: APA.

Ano, G., & Vasconcelles, E. (2005). Religious coping and psychological adjustment to stress: A meta-analysis. *Journal of Clinical Psychology, 61*, 461–480.

Bangley, B. (Ed.) (2006). *The Cloud of Unknowing: Contemporary English Edition*. Brewster, MA: Paraclete Press.

Beale, G. (2011). *A New Testament Biblical Theology: The Unfolding of the Old Testament in the New*. Grand Rapids: Baker Academic.

Bennett, A. (Ed.) (1975). *The Valley of Vision: A Collection of Puritan Prayers and Devotions*. Scotland: Banner of Truth Trust.

Benson, H. (2000). *The Relaxation Response*. New York: Harpertorch.

Brueggemann, W. (1984). *The Message of the Psalms: A Theological Commentary*. Minneapolis, MN: Augsburg Publishing House.

Caussade, J. (2011). *Abandonment to Divine Providence*. San Francisco: Ignatius Press.

Chappelle, W. (2000). A series of progressive legal and ethical decision-making steps for using Christian spiritual interventions in psychotherapy. *Journal of Psychology and Theology, 28*, 43–53.

Colombiere, C. (1980). *Trustful Surrender to Divine Providence: The Secret of Peace and Happiness*. Charlotte, NC: Tan Books.

Creasy, W. (2007). *The Imitation of Christ: A New Reading of the 1441 Latin Autograph Manuscript*. Macon, GA: Mercer University Press.

Edwards, J. (1959). *Religious Affections*. New Haven, CT: Yale University Press.

Foster, R., & Smith, J. (Eds.) (2005). *Devotional Classics: Selected Readings for Individuals and Groups*. New York: HarperCollins.

Francis, A. (2013). *Saving Normal: An Insider's Revolt against Out-of-Control Psychiatric Diagnosis, DSM-5, Big Pharma and the Medicalization of Ordinary Life*. New York: HarperCollins.

Frank, J., & Frank, J. (1993). *Persuasion and Healing: A Comparative Study of Psychotherapy*. Baltimore, MD: Johns Hopkins University Press.

Free, M. (2015). *CBT and Christianity: Strategies and Resources for Reconciling Faith in Therapy*. Malden, MA: John Wiley & Sons.

Grabovac, A., Lau, M., & Willett, B. (2011). Mechanisms of mindfulness: A Buddhist psychological model. *Mindfulness, 2*, 154–166.

Greenberg, G. (2013). *The Book of Woe: The DSM and the Unmasking of Psychiatry*. New York: Blue Rider Press.

Hackney, C., & Sanders, G. (2003). Religiosity and mental health: A meta-analysis of recent studies. *Journal for the Scientific Study of Religion, 42*, 43–55.

Harmless, W. (2004). *Desert Christians: An Introduction to the Literature of Early Monasticism*. New York: Oxford University Press.

Johnson, E. L. (2007). *Foundations for Soul Care: A Christian Psychology Proposal*. Downers Grove, IL: InterVarsity Press.

Johnson, E. L. (Ed.) (2010). *Psychology and Christianity: Five Views*. Downers Grove, IL: InterVarsity Press.

Josephson, A., & Peteet, J. (2004). *Handbook of Spirituality and Worldview in Clinical Practice*. Washington, DC: American Psychiatric Publishing.

Katonah, D. (2006). The felt sense as avenue of human experiencing for integrative growth. In L. Hoshmand (Ed.), *Culture, Psychotherapy, and Counseling: Critical and Integrative Perspectives* (pp. 65–90). Thousand Oaks, CA: Sage Publications.

Kellenberger, J. (2012). *Dying to Self and Detachment*. New York: Routledge.

Keller, T. (2015). *Walking with God through Pain and Suffering*. New York: Riverhead Books.

Kessler, R., Petukhova, M., Sampson, N., Zaslavsky, A., & Wittchen, H. (2012). Twelve-month and lifetime prevalence and lifetime morbid risk of anxiety and mood disorders in the United States. *International Journal of Methods in Psychiatric Research, 21*, 169–184.

Knabb, J., & Frederick, T. (2017). *Contemplative Prayer for Christians with Chronic Worry: An Eight-Week Program*. New York: Routledge.

Lambert, M. (2013). The efficacy and effectiveness of psychotherapy. In M. Lambert (Ed.), *Bergin and Garfield's Handbook of Psychotherapy and Behavior Change* (pp. 169–218). New York: John Wiley & Sons.

Laska, K., Gurman, A., & Wampold, B. (2014). Expanding the lens of evidence-based practice in psychotherapy: A common factors perspective. *Psychotherapy, 51*, 467–481.

Marsella, A. (1998). Toward a "global-community psychology": Meeting the needs of a changing world. *American Psychologist, 53*, 1282–1291.

Miller, L. (2012). Introduction. In L. Miller (Ed.), *The Oxford Handbook of Psychology and Spirituality* (pp. 1–6). New York: Oxford University Press.

Morgan, D. (2001). Assimilation from the East and the spectrum of consciousness. *Journal of Psychotherapy Integration, 11*, 87–104.

Norcross, J. (2005). A primer on psychotherapy integration. In J. Norcross & M. Goldfried (Eds.), *Handbook of Psychotherapy Integration* (2nd ed.) (pp. 3–23). New York: Oxford University Press.

Norcross, J., & Goldfried, M. (Eds.) (2005). *Handbook of Psychotherapy Integration* (2nd ed.). New York: Oxford University Press.

Pargament, K. (2007). *Spiritually-Integrated Psychotherapy: Understanding and Addressing the Sacred*. New York: The Guilford Press.

Paris, J. (2015). *The Intelligent Clinician's Guide to the DSM-5* (2nd ed.). New York: Oxford University Press.

Paris, J., & Phillips, J. (Eds.) (2013). *Making the DSM-5: Concepts and Controversies*. New York: Springer.

Peteet, J. (2004). Therapeutic implications of worldview. In A. Josephson & J. Peteet (Eds.), *Handbook of Spirituality and Worldview in Clinical Practice* (pp. 47–62). Washington, DC: American Psychiatric Publishing.

Pew Forum (2015). *America's Changing Religious Landscape*. Washington, DC: The Pew Forum on Religion and Public Life.

Post, B., & Wade, N. (2009). Religion and spirituality in psychotherapy: A practice-friendly review of research. *Journal of Clinical Psychology, 65*, 131–146.

Schuman, M. (2017). *Mindfulness-Informed Relational Psychotherapy and Psychoanalysis*. New York: Routledge.

Walsh, R., & Shapiro, S. (2006). The meeting of meditative disciplines and Western psychology: A mutually enriching dialogue. *American Psychologist, 61*, 227–239.

Wawrykow, J. (2005). *The Westminster Handbook of Thomas Aquinas*. Louisville, KY: Westminster John Knox Press.

Welsh, R., & Knabb, J. (2009). Renunciation of the self in psychotherapy. *Mental Health, Religion and Culture, 12*, 401–414.

Wolters, A. (2005). *Creation Regained: Biblical Basics for a Reformational Worldview* (2nd ed.). Grand Rapids, MI: William B. Eerdmans Publishing.

Wright, N. (1992). *The New Testament and the People of God*. Minneapolis, MN: Fortress Press.

CHAPTER 1

The Doctrine of God in Christian Theology
God's Nature within the Christian Tradition

Introduction

The knowledge and love of God are central to Christianity and the Christian tradition. They are at the heart of Christian revelation, which tells Christians who God is and how all created things relate to him. Foundationally, God is triune, personal, and transcendent. These frame and qualify all descriptions of God's nature. The belief that God is personal and loving begins with the intra-Trinitarian relationship between God the Father, Son, and Spirit, which shapes and analogously models not simply human relationships, but the relational nature of all creation. Further, God as personal assures the Christian that God is not somehow weighing options and making decisions far removed from those affected by such decisions. As personal, the Christian tradition believes God has a loving relationship with each Christian, and his knowledge (omniscience), power (omnipotence), and goodness (omnibenevolence) invite, sustain, and apply to every Christian *personally*. In other words, because God is good, he has the best interests of his creation, especially humans, in mind; in that God is all-knowing, he lovingly makes decisions knowing the best possible outcomes; and due to his power, he directs each and every life event for their good (Romans 8:28). Combined, these show God's all-embracing providential care for his people, including Christians with depression and anxiety.

God's personal presence in the daily life of every Christian is possible through God's transcendence. It is precisely God's complete otherness that affirms his absolute presence. The classical Christian view of God's transcendence holds that he is Lord of time and space (he is eternal and omnipresent). This does not mean that he is far away, however. Rather, because he is not limited to time and space (as humans are), God can be everywhere fully present. So, the personal goodness, power, and knowledge of God is relationally present to every one of his people, wherever and whenever they live. Even in the midst of emotional disorders, when isolation and loneliness seem to press in, the Christian can be assured that God is there. Based on this personal awareness of God's perfect characteristics, Christians struggling with psychological pain can more confidently express their pain to him, accept and reframe challenging inner and outer experiences, and engage in healthy new behaviors.

God's Nature within the Christian Tradition

In the Christian tradition, all that exists is viewed as a gift. It was created by a personal God who made us to relate to him personally and enjoy him gratefully in and through the good world he created. Indeed, one of the great ways this has been stated is found in the Westminster Catechism,[1] which says that the chief purpose of human life is "to glorify God and enjoy him forever." For a Christian, then, the overall purpose of life is not attainments to be amassed, but a relationship with God, the maker of heaven and earth, who is active and present in his world and with his people, even in the midst of psychological pain.

As we will see in the coming chapters, within the Christian tradition, to know and love God is the best means of coming to know and understand ourselves. John Calvin, the great 16th century pastor and theologian, opens his work, the *Institutes of the Christian Religion*, stating the following:

> Nearly all the wisdom we possess, that is to say, true and sound wisdom, consists of two parts: the knowledge of God and of ourselves. But, while joined by many bonds, which one precedes and brings forth the other is not easy to discern. In the first place, no one can look upon himself without immediately turning his thoughts to contemplation of God, in whom he "lives and moves" [Acts 17:28].
>
> (Calvin, 1960, p. 35)

Beginning this way, Calvin articulated a long tradition within Christianity. Humans, created in God's image, are now alienated from that image through sin and struggle to properly understand ourselves. When reconciled with God through the work of Jesus, Christians have a restored relationship with God and can understand more clearly who we are and what we were created to be. Further, as our knowledge and understanding of God increases, so does our knowledge and understanding of ourselves.

To rightly understand Christianity in its proper context, we must begin with the source of all being—God himself. Because of its importance to understanding the context of Christianity, this chapter will cover God as *triune, personal,* and *transcendent* in successive order, ending with a section joining them together in God's *providence* and discussing why this is important for psychological functioning. The discussions below will be brief and, as such, incomplete. We make no claim to full treatment, but will offer general descriptions of key doctrines that inform the context for Christian psychotherapy. Because our effort is to give a general description, we will focus on what is held in common within these great doctrines of the Christian intellectual tradition and not on the contentious points. Much fuller treatments are available on each of these rich, and at times controversial, doctrines (many of the sources will be mentioned along the way). Our hope, however, is to join the doctrines together in a way that is faithful to the tradition and helpful to those who are working with Christian clients with depression and/or anxiety in psychotherapy.

God as Triune

The doctrine of the Trinity sets Christianity apart from all other monotheistic religions and serves as a central part of Christian Scripture. Throughout the Christian tradition, many great thinkers have held that natural reason can arrive at the conclusion that God is one in his divine essence, but that God as a trinity of persons would remain unknown if he had not revealed it. The critical transformation comes about in the revelation of Jesus Christ. Theologian Gerald Bray (1993) explained, "The Trinity belongs to the inner life of God, and can be known only by those who share in that life. As long as we look at God on the outside, we shall never see beyond his unity" (p. 119). It is in Christ, the Son of God, that God reveals to us the inner life of God.

Biblically, Christianity shares Judaism's emphasis on God's unity. In the book of Deuteronomy (6:4–5), we read, "Hear, O Israel: The Lord our God, the Lord is one. Love the Lord your God with all your heart and with all your soul and with all your strength." But Christians hold this in tension with the life and teachings of Jesus and the belief that he is truly God. In John 10:30, Jesus stated, "I and the Father are one." In Colossians 2:9, Paul wrote, "For in Christ all the fullness of the Deity lives in bodily form." Thus, God the Father is understood as the source of all things, and God the Son—sharing in his full deity—is understood as lovingly carrying out his Father's plan. This scriptural teaching is affirmed in the Christian tradition, as the Nicene Creed put it:

> We believe in one God, the Father almighty, maker of heaven and earth, of all things visible and invisible. And in one Lord Jesus Christ, the only Son of God, begotten from the Father before all ages, God from God, Light from Light, true God from true God, begotten, not made; of the same essence as the Father. Through him all things were made. For us and for our salvation he came down from heaven; he became incarnate by the Holy Spirit and the virgin Mary, and was made human. He was crucified for us under Pontius Pilate; he suffered and was buried. The third day he rose again, according to the Scriptures. He ascended to heaven and is seated at the right hand of the Father. He will come again with glory to judge the living and the dead. His kingdom will never end.

Further, the belief in the Holy Spirit as God is also taught in Scripture and affirmed in the same creed. In John 14:26, Jesus said, "But the Advocate, the Holy Spirit, whom the Father will send in my name, will teach you all things and will remind you of everything I have said to you." Matthew 28:19 stated, "Therefore go and make disciples of all nations, baptizing them in the name of the Father and of the Son and of the Holy Spirit." Here, the Spirit is given the same significance as the Father and the Son, which would have been unthinkable if Jesus and his disciples did not accept the Spirit as equally God. The scriptural teaching of the divinity of the Spirit is affirmed in the Nicene Creed: "We believe in the Holy Spirit, the Lord, the giver of life, who proceeds from the Father and the Son.[2] With the Father and the Son he is worshiped and glorified." With the passage of time and distance from the original setting, the significance of the claims that Jesus and the Spirit are God is easily missed. The early disciples were faithful adherents to Judaism and committed monotheists. It was not abstract reasoning or philosophical arguments that made them convinced Trinitarians; it was being confronted with the living reality of the Trinitarian life in the incarnation of the Son of God and the living presence of the Spirit of God, given to believers at Pentecost.

Being introduced to the inner life of God through Christ and the Spirit caused Christians to significantly shift how they understood the God of the Old Testament, which now is understood as the activity of one God in three persons. Theologian Gerald Bray (2011) stated,

> It was only with the sending of the Holy Spirit at Pentecost that God began to dwell in the heart of every believer, revealing to him the secret of his own internal relations. Thus it is now possible for Christians to think in terms of the person and work of the Father, the person and work of the Son, and the person and work of the Holy Spirit.
>
> (p. 202)

With the incarnation of Christ, the inner-life of the Trinity is revealed, as is God's extraordinary grace. In Christ, God made a way for people to share in that life, and by faith in Christ we may approach God with freedom and absolute confidence. Christ, then, fulfills God's purpose in creation, redemption, and the ultimate consummation of all things, which will be accomplished in the tri-unified work of Father, Son, and Spirit.

It is important, here, to see how this directly relates to Christians struggling with psychological pain. Because we have been invited to share in the life of God, his triune presence is with us, and together they already know the pain with which we struggle. The triune God is not surprised by our pain, so we can openly express it to God. Because of God's presence in our lives, Christians can confidently know that every act of God in our lives involves the Father, Son, and Spirit. Such knowledge allows us to reframe challenging experiences in light of God's capable, loving presence, which can foster healthy responses to such experiences.

To understand God's relational presence in the life of Christians more fully, we need to first discuss how the persons of the Trinity relate to each other. The inter-Trinitarian relationship is a difficult idea to understand. To ask the question simply: "How can *one* God be *three* persons and *three* persons *one* God?" The traditional way the Trinity is described can be summarized as follows:

> God is one in essence and three in persons (or hypostases). An essence is simply something with characteristics—that is, an entity about which something can be said. A person (or hypostasis) is a distinct bearer of an essence. Applied to the Trinity, it means that the Father, the Son, and the Spirit are distinct persons, each with his own personal attributes, while each also shares equally the attributes of deity (i.e., the divine essence).
>
> (Horton, 2012, p. 97)

One in essence, three in persons is the basic Trinitarian life. Though difficult to grasp, the importance of the Trinity for understanding Christianity in context cannot be overstated. Practically, it is to understand that every divine action entails the Father, Son, and Spirit, and to know that when God acts in the life of the Christian, the triune God is acting on the Christian's behalf.

The inter-Trinitarian life also helps us think more deeply about what it means to be a person and relate to other people in ways that do not take away from their personhood, but enrich it. Gerald Bray put it this way:

> Far from asserting themselves at the expense of the others, each of the divine persons manifests perfection whilst containing and manifesting the perfection of the others. This doctrine of co-inherence is perhaps the most important single teaching of the Bible in an age which finds it hard to reconcile individual freedom and dignity with corporate commitment and responsibility.
>
> (Bray, 1993, p. 242)

We will see in the pages to follow how, from a clinician's perspective, this doctrine impacts not only our relationship with God, but our relationship with other persons and the Christian community. This is foundational for the task of Christian psychotherapy, especially in the context of recurrent psychological pain and emotional disorders.

The shared nature of the divine life has been given a technical name, *perichoresis*, and speaks directly to the relationship of oneness shared between the persons of the Trinity. These terms, both "Trinity" and "perichoresis," while not found in the Bible, are intended to communicate the dynamic, self-giving, and indwelling communion of the Father, Son, and Spirit. This mutual self-giving and indwelling guarantee that each Person of the Trinity is involved in all divine activity and has implications for a distinctly Christian psychotherapy.

The concept of the interpersonal relations involved in *perichoresis* grew out of close readings of Scripture. In the Gospel of John, particularly Chapter 17, the mutual indwelling of *perichoresis* is clear. In 17:21, Jesus prayed to the Father for his followers that they may be one, "just as you are *in* me and I *in* you" (italics added). Again, in 17:22–23, Jesus asked that "they may be one as we are one—I in them and you in me."

In John 16:13–15, we are told of the mutual possessions shared between Father, Son, and Spirit:

> But when he, the Spirit of truth, comes, he will guide you into all the truth. He will not speak on his own; he will speak only what he hears… He will glorify me because it is from me that he will receive what he will make known to you. All that belongs to the Father is mine. That is why I said the Spirit will receive from me what he will make known to you.

The last verse captures what is meant by co-inherence. The Spirit of truth will speak of what is his, namely truth. Still, the truth the Spirit speaks is from the Son—"the Spirit will receive from me what he will make known to you." What is the Son's is the Father's.

The self-giving nature of the mutual indwelling of *perichoresis* is communicated in a word that, at its best, captures perfectly the inter-Trinitarian relationship: love. Returning to John 3:34–35, Jesus said, "For the one whom God has sent speaks the words of God, for God gives the Spirit without limit. The Father loves the Son and has placed everything in his hands." In John 17:24, this love is said to be shared "before the creation of the world." The eternal being of God has always existed as a loving communion of Father, Son, and Spirit.

Efforts by the early church to formulate the scriptural teaching of *perichoresis* still resonate today. One of the most formative was developed by St. Augustine (AD 354–430). Without going into great detail about his doctrine, Augustine drew from the above passages the description of the Trinity as a loving relationship (Augustine, 1991). For Augustine, the Father is the Lover, the Son is the Beloved, and the Spirit is Love. The language itself communicates the co-inherent relationship. Without each person singularly, none would be what they are communally—Lover and Loved entails an indwelling and mutual Love.

While helpful, this analogy is not perfect. Theologian Timothy Ware helps us see why:

> There is a decisive difference between the infinite and uncreated love that unites the three divine persons, and the finite love that we human beings show towards God and each other; and this difference is

rendered all the greater by the fact that we human beings are not only finite but fallen.

(Ware, 2010, p. 113)

Because of the inadequacy of our love—we do not always love people we should, in the way we should, for the reasons we should—we easily misunderstand God's inter-Trinitarian love and his love for us. So, although Augustine's description has been helpful and rightly emphasizes the *perichoretic* relationship of love, it is not fully adequate.

What is not in doubt, however, is the importance of *perichoresis* and the love shared between each person of the Trinity. Further, in the psychotherapy context, the Christian who struggles with emotional pain can take comfort in the eternally loving, mutual relationship within the Trinity. Moreover, through the work of Christ, each Christian is taken into their loving relationship—as we abide in the Son, the Son abides in the Father, and the Spirit abides in us. So, the unending, unbreakable love between the persons of the Trinity is the unending and unbreakable love with which each Christian is loved. Pain, while very real, cannot "separate us from the love of God that is in Christ Jesus our Lord" (Romans 8:39).

All that God is—in all his fullness—acts *for* us and *sustains* us in and through all of life. This means that the Trinitarian life of love is extended to Christians through God's providential care, even in the context of depression and anxiety. This notion can bring comfort to Christians suffering from a profound, seemingly paralyzing sadness and deep sense of loss, as well as uncertainty, worry, and anxiety about an unknown, ambiguous future. In other words, in spite of difficult psychological experiences, God, and all that he is, is intimately involved in the apparent messiness of life.

Thus far, we have discussed the Trinity within the Christian tradition—simply and incompletely as it may be. Why discuss such a topic in the context of Christian psychotherapy? Only from within the inner Trinitarian life of God and the *perichoretic* indwelling can we truly see that God is *personal*, but also *transcendent*. It is here that Christianity speaks to the human condition and struggle with psychological pain.

God as Personal and Transcendent

As curious as it may sound, it is precisely because God is so very different from everything else (his *transcendence*) that he can be so very close to us, which is why his *personal* relatedness is exactly what suffering Christians need so they can confidently press forward on the precarious roads of life.

Though it is a difficult and complex topic, the Trinity establishes the personal-relational nature of God. For the Christian tradition, God is the ultimate reality and source from which all reality comes. This directly influences how Christianity views God's relationship with all other aspects of reality, that is, everything not-God. While God, as personal, relates personally to all things (including Christians suffering from depression and anxiety), he also transcends all things. God is fundamentally different from all things he creates.

The Christian tradition holds that God created the universe *ex nihilo*, that is, out of nothing. God is not an extension of the universe, but exists independently of it. He *transcends* it in existence, power, goodness, and so on. In emphasizing God's utter transcendence from all reality, that does not mean God is distant or in tension with the rest of reality. While God transcends all things, he stands in relationship with creation personally and lovingly.

God personally calls creation into existence and invests himself personally in shaping humankind in his image. God's free personal action as creator means that the natural order and each created thing is known to him. God has shaped, ordered, and continually sustains all things, and all created things lie open to, and stand in personal relationship with, God. Indeed, it is only through a personal relationship with God that anything has its existence and identity. Further, a created thing's identity can be rightly understood only when it is understood in relationship with God.

Because all creation lies open to the personal and transcendent God, he relates to all creation in a personal, life-sustaining way that is without constraints or external limitations. Christians struggling with depression and anxiety can find comfort in this notion—God is not restrained in his ability to lovingly engage with Christians who experience recurrent pain. In fact, because all things stand in relationship with God, the pain can now be interpreted in light of God's loving relationship with us. In relationship with him, the pain can be reframed and seen as God's active work in shaping each Christian's life, though clinicians working with Christian clients recognize that such reframing is easier for some than for others.

Rather than viewing God as somehow removed from the immediate experience of emotional disorders, unable to fully understand the gravity of human pain, God is very present, free to create and interact with and bring comfort to humans by way of his perfect attributes. Nevertheless, to fully grasp the importance of God's personal transcendence, more needs to be said of each separately.

Transcendence

Throughout the Christian tradition, there have been many ways of discussing God's transcendence as it relates to his personal nature. Some contemporary examples describe God as being infinite (Grudem, 1994) or supernatural (Olson, 2017). A more traditional way of describing transcendence is God's *aseity*—from the Latin *a se*, which means that God's existence is from himself. His existence does not come from another source, only from who he is as God. This term is used to affirm God's independence: "aseity refers to God's self-existence or independence from creation. There is God and there are creatures.... Creation exists as a result of God's word freely spoken, not as a necessary and external extension of God's being" (Horton, 2012, p. 76). While there are a number of terms that describe transcendence, and each term carries technical, nuanced meanings—nuances we do not want to diminish—central to each is the establishing of God's nature as fundamentally distinct from his creation. Indeed, it is only when we come to appreciate God's utter transcendence that we can truly marvel at his presence with humankind.

The Incommunicable Attributes of God

One of the ways to further illuminate God's utter difference and independence from his creation is to explore God's *incommunicable* attributes. Attributes are ways of talking about God's nature, as it is revealed in Scripture. In the Christian tradition, a common classification of God's attributes draws a distinction between those that are *incommunicable* and *communicable*; that is, those characteristics that God does not share or "communicate" with humans and those God does share or "communicate" with humans (Grudem, 1994).

While this distinction is not absolute, it can be helpful. So, in thinking about God's wisdom or goodness, Christians know what they are because they have experienced wisdom and goodness in others and themselves—they are communicable, or shared. But in considering God's nature as unbound by time and space or being completely unchanging, Christians have no frame of reference or personal experience because we are always bound by time and space—it is incommunicable, not shared.

When discussing the attributes of God as a whole, and incommunicable attributes in particular, we are dependent on God's self-disclosure in Scripture—God is using words and meanings we can understand. So, while the words communicate truly, they do not—indeed, they could not—capture all that God is. (Imagine, for example, an expert in quantum physics trying to explain "quarks" to a middle schooler.) God speaks of his transcendent nature in terms and concepts that are used to describe non-transcendent things—like rocks, shepherds, fortresses, and so forth. These are common to our experiences and understandable. The words used in biblical descriptions, however, should not be taken to exhaust what is described. Indeed, Horton suggested the following:

> a helpful distinction was drawn between God's essence [who God is or his nature] and God's energies [God's works or actions]... As Basil expressed it, "The energies are various, and the essence simple, but we say that we know our God from his energies, but do not undertake to approach near to his essence. His energies come down to us, but his essence remains beyond our reach."
>
> (Horton, 2012, p. 75)

The incommunicable attributes, then, are pointers to God's essence, which can be glimpsed but remains beyond our reach, and, thus, not fully communicable. Because of this, in the Christian tradition, there has also been a strong commitment to God's incomprehensibility and a healthy strand of *apophatic* theology.

Traditionally, *apophatic* describes the way the "glimpses" of God's essence are revealed. They are often conveyed through negation. This way of communicating tells us what God is *not*, rather than positively stating what he is. So, terms like independence and immutable/unchanging begin with the negation—God is "not" dependent, God is "not" mutable/changing. Terms like God's omnipresence and other "omni's" can also be understood negatively—namely, God is *not limited* by constraints of time/space, nor constraints on his knowledge and power.

Immutability and Omnipresence

To understand God's transcendence, and why it matters for the Christian context of psychotherapy, two additional incommunicable attributes need to be set out more fully: God's immutability and God's omnipresence. Each is best understood as an extension of God's independence. While it is fairly easy to state that God's nature is unchanging, the implications are more difficult to work out in detail.

Basically, if God is independent from the world, then nothing in the world can force a change in God. God's character and eternal purposes are stable: "if we are faithless, he remains faithful, for he cannot disown himself" (2 Timothy 2:13), and "God is not human, that he should lie, not a human being, that he should change his mind. Does he speak and then not act? Does he promise and not fulfill?" (Numbers 23:19). The importance of this will become clearer below when God's goodness is discussed. For now, consider this in light of Romans 8:28: "And we know that in all things God works for the good of those who love him, who have been called according to his purposes." When God commits himself to the wellbeing of his people, God will never change, and his good purposes for them cannot be thwarted by anything.

God's omnipresence can likewise be stated fairly easily. It simply means that God is not bound by time and space, so his presence is everywhere. This attribute is a good example of why the distinctions between communicable and incommunicable cannot be absolute, and also an example of how negative theology works. We can all understand what it means to be present. We have stood face to face with others, that is, experienced their presence. We have also talked with people over the phone and, when we hung up, were acutely aware of their absence. Being constrained by space is one of the basic limits humans face. Further, all of us have experienced the wish to go back and change some action we regret, but cannot. Being constrained by time is another limit humankind faces. Because we keenly experience these limits, to comprehend omnipresence, we need to mentally "remove" these constraints when we think about God's nature.

Biblically, the idea of God being present to the whole of creation is taught in many places. In Jeremiah 23:23–24, we are told:

> "Am I only a God nearby," declares the Lord, "and not a God far away? Who can hide in secret places so that I cannot see him?" Declares the Lord. "Do not I fill heaven and earth?" declares the Lord.

This is echoed in Acts 17:24–28, where Paul declared to a gathering of Greek philosophers that:

> "The God who made the world and everything in it is the Lord of heaven and earth and does not live in temples built by human hands. And he is not served by human hands, as if he needed anything. Rather, he himself gives everyone life and breath and everything else. From one man he made all the nations, that they should inhabit the whole earth; and he marked out their appointed times in history and the boundaries of their lands. God did this so that men would seek him and perhaps reach out for him and find him, though he is not far from each one of us. For in him we live and move and have our being."

These passages suggest that God "is present with his whole being in all places: 'whole and entire in every place but confined to none'" (Bavinck, 2004, p. 167).

Though these concepts can be difficult to grasp in detail, the significant point for understanding the Christian context in psychotherapy is the emphasis on God's faithful presence with his creation. When God declared, "'I know the plans I have for you,' declares the Lord, 'plans to prosper you and not to harm you, plans to give you hope and a future'" (Jeremiah 29:11), his promise will never change, for he is unchanging. When pain and struggle are present and the clouds of suffering take away a sense of God's presence, the Christian tradition declares that God is still present: "'Never will I leave you; never will I forsake you.' So we say with confidence, 'The Lord is my helper; I will not be afraid'" (Hebrews 13:5–6).

These powerful ideas about God are established by God's transcendence. It is because God is independent from all of reality that God can be fully present to all reality, as Karl Barth observed, "precisely because God is free from creation, he is free for creation" (Barth, as cited in Horton, 2012, p. 77).

This notion of God's presence, from our perspective, can bring comfort to Christians with depression and anxiety, given that a common struggle with depression involves social withdrawal, and anxiety can lead to efforts to avoid others for fear of scrutiny and embarrassment. Since God is everywhere, Christians with depression and anxiety can find consolation in the notion that they have a friend in close proximity to them all the time. Indeed, it is precisely when things seem so silent that we can meet God in the most profound ways.

Personal

The personal nature of God is rooted in the very identity of the triune God of Christianity. The inner-Trinitarian life revealed in Scripture grounds Christianity's belief in God as the ultimate personal Being. After considering God's transcendence, it might be easy to think of God in more abstract ways as simply "ultimate reality," or the "ground and source of all being," that is, somehow removed from his creation. While God certainly is all of these things, God is no "generic deity," but rather a particular personal Being who is also transcendent (Olson, 2015). Namely, the Triune God reveals himself to his creation as personal and stands in personal relationship with all he creates. To speak of God as transcendent does *not* make God impersonal. Rather, it elevates personhood profoundly. God is irreducibly personal; as such, he relates to us personally (Olson, 2015).

When considering beliefs about God as ultimately personal, two questions arise. First, if something is truly ultimate, can it be personal? Second, if we claim that the ultimate is personal, are we not just projecting our own personhood onto the universe?

The first question suggests that if anything is truly personal, then it must be human, and if something is human, it must be limited. So, something may be ultimate or it may be personal, but it cannot be both. The second is closely related to the first and may be seen as an implication of it. Because to be a person is to be limited, if personhood is ascribed to the transcendent, it must be a projection of human traits onto the cosmos.

For the sake of brevity, a few comments must suffice. Both critiques actually illuminate something very important to Christianity, namely, there is a fundamental relationship between human personhood and divine personhood. From a Christian perspective, however, the order is reversed. It is the personal God who projects his image into humans, since they are created in the image of God (Vanhoozer, 2010). Far from projecting personhood on the cosmos, the Christian tradition believes that we are persons and understands personhood *because* we were created by a personal God. Again, the inter-Trinitarian persons-in-relationship is foundational to rightly understanding the Christian context.

Though it is difficult to understand how God can be both transcendent ultimate reality and fully personal, it is important to see these beliefs as thoroughly grounded in Scripture, not simply a result of abstract reasoning. Olson (2017) suggested that, despite the difficulties an unbiased reader of the Bible can see, Scripture depicts ultimate reality as someone who freely thinks, relates, and responds to others, which are personal actions. Further, Scripture reveals that ultimate reality is the source of nature, but not a part of nature. Olson concluded, "What words are better suited to describe such an ultimate reality than personal and supernatural (transcendent)—even if they are inadequate and problematic" (p. 54).

Thus, while God is truly ultimate, God is also truly personal. Instead of defining persons in light of humans, perhaps it would be better to see humans in light of the truly personal God. The result would not be a lessening of God or humans, but a more profound insight into God's loving nature and the privilege of existing in God's image.

As the personal transcendent, God freely acts within time and in nature and totally involves himself in his creation; yet, he remains unbound by it and totally distinct from it. By relating closely to the world, God further reveals his character. Here, we move into consideration of God's communicable attributes—elucidated in his works and actions—and how they can help Christians with depression and anxiety in the context of psychotherapy. It is precisely because God is personally present in his creation that his active work illuminates the ways in which he can bring comfort to suffering Christians.

The Communicable Attributes of God

Before moving into the communicable attributes, two things should be kept in mind. We are now dealing with the personal *works* of God, rather than the *essence* of God. These are revealed "positively" in Scripture; thus, they are known *kataphatically* (positively), as opposed to *apophatically* (negatively).

Take knowledge, as an example. In Psalm 139:1–2, we are told, "You have searched me, Lord, and you know me. You know when I sit and when I rise; you perceive my thoughts from afar." Because knowledge is something we have and can experience—we, too, can know things—when Scripture speaks of God's knowledge, we understand this "positively" in the sense that we similarly experience what knowledge of things is like.

Second, though we can relate to God's communicable attributes in part, we cannot relate to them wholly. God, while personal, is still transcendent. The characteristics that God shares or communicates with humans will be like ours, but always *more so*.

Omniscience

God is *omniscient* (all knowing), that is, God knows everything there is to know and his knowledge is without limit. Again, consider the Bible verses mentioned above. It is only God who can truly and exhaustively know us—indeed, he knows us better than we can know ourselves (Jeremiah 17:9).

Seen in this light, God's knowledge is closely related to his transcendence. As such, it differs from our knowledge in several important ways. Just as his presence is not constrained by limits, neither is his knowledge. God is the transcendent Creator of all things and holds the beginning fully in his mind before it ever existed, as Isaiah 46:9–10 revealed, "'I am God, and there is no other; I am God, and there is none like me. I make known the end from the beginning, from ancient times, what is still to come."' Therefore, he is able to also know the end towards which creation is unfolding—the end is contained in the beginning, as it were. This is also why God's good purposes, though sometimes mysterious to us, will always be accomplished. In God's mind, the beginning, end, and all things in between are always already known, even if to us they seem perplexing, confusing, and painful.

Further differences between our knowledge and God's are detailed by Berkhof (1994), who notes that God's knowledge is *immediate*, by which he means God's knowledge is not a result of an investigative process; God's knowledge is also *simultaneous*, not successive, which means God knows all things all at once, not one after another; and God's knowledge is *complete*, that is, God knows fully and infinitely, "every bit of God's knowledge is always fully present in his consciousness; it never grows dim or fades into his nonconscious memory" (Grudem, 1994, p. 191). This follows from God's omnipresence—God is present everywhere and in all fullness.

When the Christian tradition speaks of God's omniscience, it extends to all areas of his creation, which includes the future actions of his creatures. While this is an extremely complex, and controversial, issue (which cannot be resolved in this brief treatment), a few clarifying comments might be helpful. God's knowledge should *not* be seen as impeding humankind's ability to choose. St. Augustine held that God has given humans "reasonable self-determination" (Augustine, 1993). What Augustine meant is what we take to be true in our own experiences, namely, that normal humans usually give thought to, and are intentional in, their course of action. This does not preclude influences on our decisions—things such as culture, family, and technology—but it is we who choose and act on such choices. In affirming we have personal agency, we are simply affirming that our choices matter—they determine what happens. Some events do not occur regardless of our actions, but because of our actions (Grudem, 1994).

Being made in God's image means a great many things; minimally, that we are personal agents capable of genuine action. Yet, because we are reflections of God (and not God), our actions are often incomplete, inadequate, and can go awry. Nevertheless, as God's images, we act in relation to the God who knows us.

A significant implication of God's omniscience is his truthfulness. The Bible teaches that God is true and cannot lie (Numbers 23:19; Romans 3:4; Hebrews 6:18). All truth, then, literally is God's truth. Truth is seen in his creation. Truth is seen in his actions. Truth is seen in his words. Thus, God is reliable in all of these ways, but especially important for the Christian context in psychotherapy—God is reliable in all his relationships. This is the point of Jeremiah 9:23–24:

This is what the Lord says: "Let not the wise boast of their wisdom or the strong boast of their strength or the rich boast of their riches, but let the one who boasts boast about this: that they have the understanding to know me, that I am the Lord, who exercises kindness, justice and righteousness on earth, for in these I delight," declares the Lord.

God is reliable, faithfully relating to his people with all that he is and in all of our need. The term translated "kindness" is a very important word in the Old Testament and often translated "steadfast love." It refers to God's covenant faithfulness and can be loosely translated to mean God's "unfailing devotion" to his people. God literally pledges himself to those with whom he stands in relation, and there is *nothing* that can prevent him from offering, or cause him to withhold, his steadfast love.

Omnipotence

There is a common saying: "knowledge is power." If this is true, then absolute knowledge means absolute power. Indeed, these two are one thing in God's nature. The Christian tradition holds that God not only possesses knowledge, he has the power to act on that knowledge. God's sovereignty over creation is an expression of God's power as he governs through his absolute knowledge. It is, like much of our discussion, a great mystery how and why God allows certain things to occur in his creation, but the Bible frequently affirms that God is all powerful: "Ah, Sovereign Lord, you have made the heavens and the earth by your great power and outstretched arm. Nothing is too hard for you" (Jeremiah 32:17), and "For since the creation of the world God's invisible qualities—his eternal power and divine nature—have been clearly seen, being understood from what has been made, so that men are without excuse" (Romans 1:20). Finally, and poetically, we read in Job 9:4–10:

> His wisdom is profound, his power is vast. Who has resisted him and come out unscathed? He moves mountains without their knowing it and overturns them in his anger. He shakes the earth from its place and makes its pillars tremble. He speaks to the sun and it does not shine; he seals off the light of the stars. He alone stretches out the heavens and treads the waves of the sea. He is the Maker of the Bear and Orion, the Pleiades and the constellations of the south. He performs wonders that cannot be fathomed, miracles that cannot be counted.

This last verse is particularly telling because of Job's circumstances. Job experienced overwhelming suffering—the stuff of the mystery just mentioned—and, while he struggled, often wondering what God was doing, it was precisely through the struggle that he came to say to God, "My ears had heard of you but now my eyes have seen you" (Job 42:5). In one of life's great paradoxes, we often perceive God with the greatest clarity at moments when pain seems to cloud everything else.

While God is all powerful and Scripture teaches that "with God all things are possible" (Mathew 19:26), that does not mean that God can do things that are inconsistent with God's nature and character. The Bible also clearly says that God cannot lie, cannot be tempted to sin, and cannot deny himself. Traditionally, these types of actions that God cannot do have been understood as expressions of weakness—e.g., one lies because of a weakness of character. Indeed, Anselm, an Archbishop of Canterbury (AD 1093–1109), used God's omnipotence to argue that God is the only truly free being. Freedom, then, is not the ability or power to do anything, but the power to do the right thing—"'the ability to sin' does not belong in the definition of freedom of choice" (Anselm, 2002, p. 33). So, since God is so powerful, he has no need to turn away from the right thing to lesser things for he cannot fail to do the right thing—and this includes his care and direction in the Christian life.

Omnibenevolence

At this point, it is important to reflect on God's moral character, which is always inseparable from, and involved with, his actions. So, God's knowledge and power are always extensions of, and never in opposition with, his goodness. Horton (2012) captures the connection by saying, "God's knowledge, wisdom and power are inseparable from his goodness and, further, whatever goodness we discern in creation—including each other—is but a reflection of its source" (p. 87). In conjunction with the above discussions of God's power and knowledge, God's goodness is never the result of naiveté. God's reliable knowledge means that his goodness is always rightly informed—in proper measure, proportion, and timing. Likewise, because of God's power, there is never any impediment to God exercising his goodness as he wishes in its proper measure, proportion, and timing. So, when Christians are struggling with painful emotional experiences, they need not doubt God's goodness. For example, a Christian client might ask, "If the God who controls all things is good, then why am I experiencing such pain?" While such questions are honest and appropriate, a fuller understanding of God's good nature can allow the painful experience to be reinterpreted accordingly. God knows we are struggling because he is walking with us in our pain. He is also the same God whose powerful goodness acts on our behalf, preparing us for, working in, and seeing us through all our painful experiences. While those who have experienced chronic trauma may have extra difficulty with this, growing in the knowledge of God's goodness can enable Christian clients to reframe their suffering, especially as they learn to trust more deeply in him.

To adequately understand God's goodness in divine action, however, his goodness needs to be seen more fully in light of his unchanging nature. When we think of goodness in other things—a good book, a good meal, or a good vehicle—they are considered good because they do what each is supposed to do. So, a good vehicle is good because it starts, runs, and stops when it is supposed to. Now, it is possible to imagine a vehicle that is not good, so goodness is not inherent in a vehicle. For God, however, goodness is not something separable from who he is. Indeed, God is good in himself; goodness is not something God *has*, it is something he *is*. As we argued above, we can understand what it means to be a person because God is personal and made us in his image; so, too, we can know goodness only because God is good and shares his goodness with his creation.

As the ultimate good, there is nothing "better" than God. Goodness *is* God's nature, not something God has attained. Christians call God good not because he has "risen through the ranks" or met a standard of goodness higher than anyone or anything else. So, there is no goodness higher than, or outside of, God. He is the supreme Good and the source of all good; therefore, all other goods are from him, and whatever is good is measured by him. Consequently, God's goodness overflows into all that he does, beginning with creation itself. The Bible gives us God's commentary on his creation, reminding us that everything he created is "very good" (Genesis 1:31). The nature of creation is invested with the goodness of God and, while now fallen and fragmented, still reflects the goodness of God. God's goodness is also seen in his relation to his creation. Psalm 145:9–10 says, "The Lord is good to all; he has compassion on all he has made. All your works praise you, Lord." These verses describe God's mercy to all that he has made, which adds another dimension to God's goodness. Traditionally, God's goodness has been such a rich idea it required other terms to communicate its fullness—mercy, patience, and grace. These terms indicate aspects of God's goodness applied to different situations. "God's mercy is his goodness toward those in distress, his grace is his goodness toward those who deserve only punishment, and his patience is his goodness toward those who continue to sin over a period of time" (Grudem, 1994, p. 198).

Combined, God's knowledge, power, and goodness in the context of emotional disorders means that God (a) knows everything there is to know about Christians' suffering, (b) is in control of each and every moment, holding Christians' experiences in his hands, and (c) has Christians' best intentions in mind, even as Christians struggle with psychological pain. This unique combination of attributes means that the difficulties of life that can contribute to a profound sense of loss and uncertainty, that often accompany depression and anxiety, are by no means random occurrences for Christians traversing along the trails of life. Instead, God knows all about human pain—including its causes, its symptoms, and the course it will take. God is the perfect surgeon, if you will, who knows just the right intervention and balances his knowledge and power with an unwavering goodness and love that is entirely what Christians need in the midst of suffering. At the same time, one of the challenges of the Christian life (and Christian psychotherapy) is that learning to trust the biblical portrayal of God is a process, especially for Christians who have been exposed to abuse and neglect. The journey of deep, inner healing is usually much slower than simply being educated in biblical truths about God.

The combination of the attributes discussed above tells us much about the character of God. These attributes are how God wisely acts in the world—how he sustains and governs creation and, ultimately, will bring to a close all history. In the Christian tradition, God's personal and caring actions in relation to creation are referred to as his *providence*.

God's Providence

Simply stated, God's providence refers to God's governing of his creation; that is, his active sustaining and preserving of creation and careful and attentive administration of it, by which he is working all things according to his divine purposes. "God not only created the world with its own inherent potential for fruitfulness, but continues to work in the Son, and by the Spirit to enable creation to bring forth fruit" (Horton, 2012, p. 112). Added to this is often a third component that refers to *how* God preserves and administers his care, which is through *concurrence*. This means God's power often works in and through creation as he designed it. So, while the tree is sustained by God's power, God created the tree to grow, bloom, and produce fruit—the productive power of created things is concurrent with God's sustaining power. Another way of saying this is that God uses certain means to accomplish his purposes. The means God chooses to use, however, are never accidental, but providential. This extends particularly to the part of his creation that bears his image.

For the purposes of Christian psychotherapy, we will focus on God's providential relationship with Christians. This means that each Christian is the object of God's active sustaining and attentive care. Further, God administers his caring providence to accomplish his purposes in our life by way of our actions and experiences—God's power is operative concurrently in and through our life experiences and healthy actions. This simply means that God uses everything we experience to accomplish his good purposes for our lives, even those things that are painful or confusing. So, what are his purposes and some of the means he uses in our lives to accomplish this?

One of the clearest declarations of God's careful and loving providence is Romans 8:28: "In all things God works for the good of those who love him, who have been called according to his purpose." Further, verse 29 describes God's purpose toward which he is working all things in the lives of Christians: "to be conformed to the image of his Son." This teaching can assure Christians that God has always been good towards them—a stance that began before the creation of the world—for it furthers their salvation until the return of Christ (Schreiner, 2008). This is truly comprehensive coverage. God's care for us began before we were born, has continued to sustain our lives—whether we are aware of it or not—and will continue all the days of our lives and beyond.

Of course, therapists working with Christian clients have to be mindful of the difficulties of those who have had severe and chronic trauma, especially in childhood. Simply reciting such verses to trauma survivors can be harmful and, if not done with great care, even traumatizing, for such verses raise puzzling perplexities for those who have endured horrific relational pain, sometimes for years. Too often, well-meaning, but unempathic, Christians have used such teachings to promote a quick Christian fix, not realizing that the healing internalization of such teachings, while a core part of the Christian therapy journey (Johnson, 2007), is often a very gradual process, somewhat analogous to the chemical process of *titration* (Levine, 2010). This is the slow introduction of one chemical into another that gradually changes the latter's chemical composition, but without a destructive reaction. Wise therapists working with Christian clients will similarly promote the appropriation of teachings about God's good providence with trauma survivors in session with lots of questions, in empathic dialogue, and in homework through practices like *lectio divina*, meditative prayer, and guided imagery (discussed in subsequent chapters), allowing it to drip into the soul little by little. (Further exposition of the clinical implications of Christian theology will be found in the coming chapters. For a more thorough discussion on the careful Christian treatment of trauma, see Gingrich [2005] and Langberg [2015].)

At the same time, in the context of Romans 8:28, Paul showed he was very aware that God's good providence encompasses suffering. Previously, in Romans 8:18, he wrote, "I consider that our present sufferings are not worth comparing with the glory that will be revealed in us." Later in the chapter, he argued that nothing can separate believers from the love of Christ, not even "trouble or hardship or persecution or famine or nakedness or danger or sword" (8:35). Yet, "in all these things we are more than conquerors through him who loved us" (8:37), since his love accompanies us through all our difficulties (8:38–39). So, while such experiences—past or present—are not pleasant, they can be productive, because, coming from the hands of God, they have meaning. This should not imply that the Christian will always understand why painful experiences have happened or are happening, but it does establish that the pain is not meaningless, and God can bring good out of it. The term used in Romans 8:28 for "work" carries the sense of "collaboration." God's concurrent power is at work in and through our experiences, lovingly creating conditions for a greater good, which is forming us into the image of his beloved Son.

God is present in the life of Christians, even in the midst of significant loss, walking alongside those who experience a range of depressive and anxiety-related symptoms. Although it is easy during these difficult times for Christians to believe God has somehow turned away from us in our state of depression, struggling with ruminations about the past, negative self-judgments in the present, and hopelessness about the future (among other symptoms), God has been guiding the process, holding us in his loving arms all along. So, too, with anxiety; although Christians may struggle with repetitive, worrying thoughts about a catastrophic future that seemingly lies just around the corner, God knows what tomorrow will bring and has Christians' best intentions in mind. It is easy to forget in the midst of painful circumstances that God's loving care and protection is not synonymous with a life free of suffering. Jesus, after all, is the Suffering Servant, who invites Christians to follow him.

Though we are not promised easy circumstances, we are promised God's constant and loving presence. Because of this, Christians can trust that our pain has a purpose and God is with us—he is the master physician, who knows all about our symptoms and sufferings, and offers a caring, loving relationship along the way. God allows bad things to happen in order to collaborate with Christians to enable them to be more like Christ. In other words, God's method, timing, and process of change is good, given that he is infinitely wise, loving, and powerful. Admittedly, life on earth is fraught with mystery. There is so much about God's providential purposes that we do not know and will not fully understand in this life. But what we do know can help Christians learn to surrender to God's providential care, confident in the fullness of his goodness and grace in our time of need (Hebrews 4:16)—including Christians with emotional disorders.

Christian psychotherapy, then, begins with God. To properly understand the life of God is to become aware that all God is—the vibrant inter-Trinitarian life from which all things come and to which all things will return—is *for* us personally, powerfully, and providentially.

Notes

1 The Westminster Catechism was originally created in 1646–1647 and teaches the Christian faith in a question and answer format.
2 "The phrase 'and the Son' was added after the Council of Constantinople in 381 but is commonly included in the text of the Nicene Creed as used by Protestant and Roman Catholic churches today. The phrase is *not* included in the text used by Orthodox Churches" (Grudem, 1994, p. 1169, italics added).

References

Anselm (2002). *The Three Philosophical Dialogues* (T. Williams, Trans.). Indianapolis, IN: Hackett Publishing.
Augustine (1991). *The Trinity* (Edmund Hill, Trans.). New York: New City Press.
Augustine (1993). *On Free Choice of the Will* (T. Williams, Trans.). Indianapolis, IN: Hackett Publishing.
Bavinck, H. (2003). *Reformed Dogmatics* (J. Vriend, Trans.). Grand Rapids, MI: Baker Books.
Berkhof, L. (1941). *Systematic Theology*. Grand Rapids, MI: Eerdmans Publishing.
Bray, G. (1993). *The Doctrine of God*. Downers Grove, MI: InterVarsity Press.
Calvin, J. (1960). *Institutes of the Christian Religion* (F. Battles, Trans.). Philadelphia, PA: The Westminster Press.
Gingrich, H. (2013). *Restoring the Shattered Self*. Downers Grove, IL: InterVarsity Press.

Grudem, W. (1994). *Systematic Theology.* Grand Rapids, MI: Zondervan.

Horton, M. (2012). *Pilgrim Theology.* Grand Rapids, MI: Zondervan.

Johnson, E. L. (2007). *Foundations for Soul Care: A Christian Psychology Proposal.* Downers Grove, IL: InterVarsity Press.

Langberg, D. (2015). *Suffering and the Heart of God: How Trauma Destroys and Christ Restores.* Greensboro, NC: New Growth Press.

Levine, P. A. (2010). *In an Unspoken Voice: How the Body Stores Trauma and Restores Goodness.* Berkeley, CA: North Atlantic Books.

Mounce, R. (1995). *Romans: The New American Commentary.* Nashville, TN: B & H Publishing Group.

Olson, R. (2017). *The Essentials of Christian Thought.* Grand Rapids, MI: Zondervan.

Schreiner, T. (2008). Study notes in Romans. In the English Standard Version Study Bible. Wheaton, IL: Crossway.

Vanhoozer, K. (2010). *Remythologizing Theology.* Cambridge: Cambridge University Press.

Ware, T. (2010). The holy Trinity: Model for personhood-in-relation. In J. Polkinghorne (Ed.), *The Trinity and an Entangled World* (pp. 107–129). Grand Rapids, MI: Eerdmans.

CHAPTER 2

The Doctrine of God in Christian Theology
A Theoretical and Empirical Exploration

Introduction

In each section, as a bridge between the chapter on Christian doctrine and the chapter on clinical practice, we will consider relevant psychological theory and research, including contributions from the Christian tradition. Given the explicitly religious nature of a Christian worldview, much of our reflection on contemporary work will be focused on the psychology of religion. Over the past few decades, this subdiscipline has identified a wide range of information about the nature of religious thought and experience, and because of where it was conducted (the United States), most of the research has been with Christian participants. Nevertheless, this body of literature has two limitations from a Christian psychology perspective.[1]

First, contemporary psychology of religion, like most modern psychology,[2] assumes methodological naturalism, so its investigations do not consider the actual existence and influence of God. Modern psychologists of religion act as if they are impartial observers of religious phenomena and do not consider the ontological reality of the supernatural object of religious experience. Such research has value, as we shall see. However, by starting with a Christian worldview, we utilize a Christian interpretive framework that assumes (a) the God who created all things has revealed himself pre-eminently in Jesus Christ and secondarily in the Christian Scriptures, (b) God is personally involved in the Christian life, and (c) God is the one in whom all humans live and move and have their being (Acts 17:28).

Second, most modern psychology of religion studies have only considered the religious experience of simple theism (or monotheism), not the Trinitarian theism of Christianity (for an exception, see Sharp, Rentfrow, & Gibson, 2017), even though much of the research has been conducted on Christians. We believe the contemporary psychology of religion literature is, in a sense, too ecumenical, preferring to paint with broad strokes, rather than recognizing the differing details within each faith tradition (as well as Christian denominational affiliations). This broad strategy is seldom—if ever—supported when considering other domains of cultural diversity (e.g., ethnicity, age, gender).

Because of these two limitations, modern psychology of religion research is not as helpful for our purposes as it could have been, had it been conducted assuming a Christian worldview. Nevertheless, we are grateful for its findings, and we will simply do our best to interpret it according to a Christian worldview. In doing so, we are attempting to offer Christian clients an empirical understanding of psychological functioning, while acknowledging the current literature's limitations in fully revealing the Christian experience in a Christian-sensitive manner.

The Knowledge of God and the Knowledge of Oneself

As we trace the relevance of the doctrine of God to Christian psychotherapy, we remind ourselves again of Calvin's (1559) classic opening statement in his *Institutes of the Christian Religion*:

> Nearly all the wisdom which we possess, that is to say, true and sound wisdom, consists of two parts: the knowledge of God and of ourselves. But, while joined by many bonds, which one precedes and brings forth the other is not easy to discern.
>
> (p. 33)

This statement provides a sound basis for a Christian psychology. Knowing mere doctrines about God is not sufficient for wisdom or the Christian life. To become truly wise, humans need to know both God and themselves in a mysterious interrelationship. There is an interpersonal, interactive, and experiential quality to this knowing that constitutes genuine psychological wisdom. Obviously, a Christian understanding of self-knowledge differs profoundly from a secular version at this most foundational level (see Harter, 2012). This is why we began this psychotherapy book with the doctrine of God.

Yet, as important as Calvin's insight is for a Christian psychology in the therapy room, we should point out two incomplete ideas in Calvin's definition of wisdom. First, the necessary involvement of the knowledge of others in the knowledge of God and self was not addressed by Calvin, though it seems obvious to us today. Such involvement is not surprising, when we consider that the Christian God consists of three persons. Second, knowledge is essential to wisdom, but love is also necessary, in the Christian scheme of things, so a more comprehensive Christian psychology will be based on an interrelated knowledge and love of God, self, and others. These two elaborations result in a triangular relational model of human life, as represented in Figure 2.1 (adapted from Johnson, 2007).

The Worship of God and Its Psychological Benefits

As we saw in the first chapter, from a Christian standpoint, God is the supreme being and highest value there is. Christians believe further that

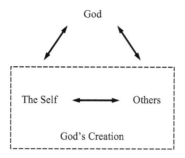

Figure 2.1 The relationship between God, God's creation, the self, and others. Adapted from Johnson (2017)

humans are made in God's image (Genesis 1:26–27). The notion of the image of God is a whole-person construct with a number of significant psychological implications (Adams, 1999; Johnson, 2015; Johnson, 2017). First, being made in God's image means that God is supposed to be the most important being in a mature human's relational universe (signified by God being at the top of the triangle in Figure 2.1); second, it suggests we are made for a unique kind of relationship with God; and third, human flourishing is found in increasing correspondence to the form of God (his goodness, love, righteousness, and so on).

According to Taylor (1989), all humans have to be oriented towards some ultimate good (what he called a hyper-good), and "the assurance that I am turned towards this good gives me a sense of wholeness, of fullness of being as a person or self, that nothing else can" (p. 63), and research has confirmed that pursuing one's ultimate good is correlated with personal and marital wellbeing (Emmons, Cheung, & Tehrani, 1998). This makes sense, because the pursuit of one's ultimate good will presumably integrate all of one's personal strivings, which itself contributes to a sense of unity and wellbeing and reduces the distress associated with conflict among one's values and goals (Adams, 1999; Emmons, 1999; Johnson, 2017). Therefore, the more thoroughly and consistently that God is regarded as one's greatest good, the more all other values are subordinated to, and reorganized around, God and his will.

From a Christian standpoint, there is no more important therapeutic consideration than the ultimate good that a worldview community posits, whether explicitly or implicitly (Johnson, 2017). Religious communities are usually explicit about their ultimate good, whereas matters have become more obscure in modernity. Nevertheless, in writing about the modern worldview community (e.g., Western secular society), many authors have variously argued that its ultimate good (and that of its psychotherapy) is the self (Lasch, 1979; Rieff, 1966; Twenge & Campbell, 2009; Vitz, 1994; Welsh & Knabb, 2009). Christians value the self, since humans are made in God's image. The issue is what is the *ultimate* good in the therapeutic system, and from the Christian standpoint, given the infinite greatness of God, one cannot conceive of a greater difference in ultimate goods than that which distinguishes the Christian and modern therapeutic communitiess.

We turn now to consider the therapeutic value of having God as one's ultimate good. Christians have assumed for centuries that human wellbeing is best promoted thereby. Indeed, flourishing in a Christian framework entails such a relationship (Edwards, 1989; Johnson, 2017; Pieper, 1979). Such pre-eminence, or ultimacy, is especially reflected in acts of worship. Research has begun to document a number of psychological benefits of such worship, including connecting with God's purposes, the promotion of gratitude, and the experience of God's presence and divine forgiveness (Abernethy, Kurian, Rice, Grannum, Rold, & Jones, 2015; Abernethy, van Oyen-Witvliet, Kurian, Brown, Uh, Rice, & Rold, 2016). Further Christian reflection might add that worship is meaningful because it affords the opportunity to identify with God as his children, servants, and lovers; to experience the love of the greatest being there is, and to perceive God's beauty, which is intrinsically joyful (Johnson, 2017). God, according to Edwards (1989b), is "infinitely the most beautiful and excellent being" (p. 550) and "the foundation and fountain of all being and all beauty" (p. 551). What kind of beauty does an invisible God possess? The glorious attributes that make up his being and character—his infinity, omnipresence, omnipotence, omniscience, holiness, justice, righteousness, love, compassion, mercy, and so on—some of which we considered in the previous chapter.

God is "infinitely happy in the enjoyment of himself" (Edwards, 2003, p. 113); indeed, such happiness is one of his attributes. Being made in God's image, then, involves the capacity to perceive God in worship, praise, and adoration, and to focus on various aspects of his beautiful character— all of which allows us to participate in his happiness. So spending time in meditation, contemplating on any of these attributes, must also be good for the human soul. Such human experiences will presumably lead to temporary, and in some cases long term, brain changes, particularly as they are repeated (Blevins, 2016).

There are other psychological benefits from having the triune God as one's ultimate good. Knowing that God is perfect and omnicompetent, combined with knowing that God is our advocate and friend, relieves humans of the pressure to be perfect and omnicompetent ourselves. This frees us from the illusions of our fallen pretensions.

> We live in a world of unreality and dreams. To give up our imaginary position as the center, to renounce it, not only intellectually but in the imaginative part of our soul, that means to awaken to what is real and eternal.
>
> (Weil, 1951, p. 159)

As a result, shame becomes less a core motivation, and less psychic energy has to be spent hiding one's limitations from others, as well as oneself. In addition, one can take greater risks opening up to others and engaging in self-examination, reflection, and journaling, becoming more aware of one's defenses and learning how to relinquish them in the process.

Modern psychology and psychotherapy has been based on naturalistic methods and rules of discourse since its founding in the late 1800s (see, e.g., James, 1890, Vol. 1, p. 183), and, therefore, its discourse can only refer to natural entities and processes; with regard to therapy, this means the resources of the therapist and client. Furthermore, because the self is assumed to be the ultimate good, the therapist is officially constrained to work within the current value set of the client. But what if the client's values are contributing to his or her problems?[3] A more enlightened Christian psychotherapy system would be open to the wise and careful introduction of therapist values, including transcendent values (so long as both the therapist and client identify as Christian and have agreed to this framework within the informed consent process). Sharing such values has been a normal part of human dialogue from time immemorial, particularly when a person is seeking greater enlightenment from a "sage." Because of its naturalistic and individualistic biases, modern psychotherapy is often ill-suited to identify and challenge the contemporary crisis of having comparatively meager ultimate goods, particularly when that good is oneself. At the same time, we acknowledge that secular clinical psychology and psychiatry advocate operating from within the client's culture/worldview—in terms of defining abnormal behavior according to what is considered normative in a given culture and honoring client "self-determination"—when it comes to diagnostic (see American Psychiatric Association, 2013) and treatment (see American Psychological Association, 2002) considerations, which formally legitimates the introduction of Christian values to Christian clients in psychotherapy.

A Transcendent Therapy Intervention

Another way in which Christian psychotherapy differs from modern versions is the Christian assumption that God is an actual being who transcends this creation and can make a difference in human life. The majority of world religions have similar assumptions (except Buddhism, which is one reason why theorists and researchers may be more accepting of Buddhist psychology in current psychotherapy models). Most human beings sense a need for a source of goodness and help outside this visible world and beyond one's own resources (Adams, 1999), and psychological wellbeing has been found to be enhanced with a focus on the transcendent (Muller, Creed, & Francis, 2004; Piedmont & Leach, 2002; Tomcsányi, Martos, Ittzés, Horváth-Szabó, Szabó, & Nagy, 2013). More specifically, belief in the reality of God, in contrast to God as an abstraction, has been found to be correlated with positive psychological outcomes (Testoni, Visintin, Capozza, Carlucci, & Shams, 2016).

Christian psychology, in particular, suggests that the triune God has made himself available as a transcendent resource for psychospiritual transformation: omniscient, omnipresent, and omnipotent, righteous, as well as loving and compassionate (omnibenevolent). He has provided a transcendent remedy in Christ's life, death, and resurrection for humanity's greatest hindrance to flourishing: the shame and guilt that comes from sin,[4] keeping us from reconciliation with God, our truly greatest Good. As a result, this God can become a meaningful and impactful part of one's social system, a loving, wise father-figure and friend who provides assistance and support for all other aspects of the psychotherapeutic process.

Attachment to God

According to Christianity, humans can form a close personal relationship with God through faith in Christ. Such an ideal is made even more meaningful with the knowledge that the Christian God is triune and seeking the ultimate wellbeing of humans by drawing them into their Trinitarian communion (Ephesians 3:16–19; 1 John 1:3).

Based on attachment theory, many researchers have begun to consider human relations with God as a kind of attachment. "There is considerable evidence to support the notion that believers view God as a kind of exalted attachment figure" (Granqvist & Kirkpatrick, 2008, p. 908). Believers seek closeness to God and derive from him a sense of safety and security, both features of a healthy human attachment. Many studies now have investigated the relationship between early human attachments and God attachment, recognizing that the affectively loaded mental representation of self-and-other that is formed in childhood—which Bowlby (1969) called an internal working model (IWM)—provides the psychological basis for close relationships in adulthood, including one's relationship with God. Evidence has been found of both *compensation* and *correspondence* explanations for why people form an attachment to God (Granqvist & Kirkpatrick, 2008). With the former, individuals turn to God as an attachment figure to make up for the insecure attachment in earlier human relationships, finding in God the perfect relational safety and security that is especially needed because of a deficient IWM; whereas the latter characterizes individuals whose relationship with God matches the secure attachment of their family of origin due to the adult transfer of the relatively well-formed IWM to God (McDonald, Beck, Allison, & Norsworthy, 2005).

At the same time, because of deficiencies in their IWM, Christians who were insecurely attached in childhood will generally experience greater internal and relational conflict than securely attached individuals, leading to potentially more turmoil in their relational experiences with God (more on that below). For some, it is hypothesized that this insecure attachment can be remediated in some degree in adulthood in a relationship with an omnipresent and perfectly loving caregiver (Granqvist & Kirkpatrick, 2008).

Over time, it seems possible that the emergence of "earned secure attachment status" could result for those who have had repeated, significant experiences of God's love and care, similar to the mechanism of change in psychotherapeutic relationships (Hesse, 2008). However, such a process will likely be uneven and involve a gradual restructuring of one's IWM through the experiences of life, an engagement with biblical revelation, and an encounter with God in affective and contemplative prayer, meditation, and worship. Though earned secure attachment with God has been repeatedly anecdotally confirmed, research is needed to document more rigorously this pathway of healing. By contrast, Christians who grew up with secure attachment will likely more readily obtain a safe and secure relationship with God, one who stabilizes them through the inevitable stresses and challenges of adulthood. In principle, such "continuously secure" individuals (Hesse, 2008) would seem primed to be able to enter into an increasingly intimate relationship with God throughout adulthood. Thus far, there has been very little discussion in the psychological literature on attachment specifically with the Trinity (for an exception, see Miner, 2007) and how that might differ from attachment with a merely monotheistic God.

God Concept and God Image

A distinction has been made in recent years between a person's *God concept* (one's conscious, mental beliefs about God, shaped more by religious teaching) and one's *God image* (a deeper, affect-laden, often unconscious representation of God shaped more by one's early attachment history; Grimes, 2008), and this distinction may help illuminate troubled Christian experience. (A God image is generally interpreted as the application of one's IWM to God; see Granqvist & Kirkpatrick, 2008; Noffke & Hall, 2007.) These contrasting perspectives on God can be discussed in therapy with Christian clients, since most Christians are unaware of the possibility that their implicit experience of God may differ from their explicit understanding of God due to impoverished relational histories (Davis, Moriarty, & Mauch, 2013).

Spilka and other early researchers found positive relationships between positive views of self and images of God as loving and forgiving, as well as negative views of self and images of God as primarily wrathful and vindictive (Benson & Spilka, 1973; Spilka, Addison, & Rosensohn, 1975). This finding partly supports the contention mentioned above that one's views of God, self, and others are fundamentally interrelated.

Research has also found that depressive and anxiety-related symptoms tend to be correlated with insecure God attachment and negative God images (Braam et al., 2008; Exline, Yali, & Sanderson, 2000; Knabb & Pelletier, 2014), whereas positive psychological and physical benefits are associated with a positive God image (Krause, Emmons, & Ironson, 2015; Bradshaw, Ellison, & Marcum, 2010). In addition, some have found that Christians'

God attachment and God image can change in positive directions with cognitive, affective, and relational psychotherapeutic strategies (Cheston, Piedmont, Eanes, & Lavin, 2003; Thomas, Moriarty, Davis, & Anderson, 2011; Tisdale, Key, Edwards, Brokaw, Kemperman, & Cloud, 1997). However, again, research is needed on how the revelation and experience of the triune God (Father, Son, and Spirit) might impact one's God concept and God image.

One concern ought to be raised about the God image literature. Some authors have argued that humans only have access to their perceptions of God (congruent with much modern thought about God since Kant) and are, therefore, agnostic about whether those perceptions can count as knowledge that corresponds to their (noumenal) object (e.g., Jones, 2007; McDargh, 1983; Rizzuto, 1979). However, the classic Christian tradition has generally affirmed a realist epistemology regarding biblical revelation by means of the Holy Spirit and the Christian's consequent knowledge and experience of God (Plantinga, 2000). In a similar vein, some authors within the indigenous psychology movement have critiqued secular clinical psychology because of its emphasis on reductionism, scientism, and materialism (Marsella, 2009). In the present context, a therapeutic orientation rooted in the classic Christian tradition would suggest that, while one's God concept and God image can certainly be distorted by sin (e.g., alienation from God, broken communion with God) and poor socialization with malformed image-bearers, an important goal of Christian psychotherapy is the healing of such distortions so that one may know and experience God with increasing validity.[5]

Because of God's transcendence and infinitude, every human's perception and knowledge of God are more or less limited by finitude and more or less distorted by sin (Boyer & Hall, 2012; Frame, 2002). We perceive and know God only analogically. From a classical Christian standpoint, one's psychological representations of God—both one's God concept and God image—are the means by which one perceives and experiences the true and living God. Because one's God concept is easier to change, more accurate perception and knowledge begin *there*, as Christians come to conform their conscious *beliefs* of God to the divine self-revelation recorded in the Bible. Second, they can use their more accurate God concept to guide the restoration of their God image so that it, too, increasingly conforms to God's self-revelation in Scripture through multiple relational experiences with God via *lectio divina*, worship, and Christian meditation (e.g., contemplative prayer), profoundly reinforced by close personal relationships with humans who resemble God more than their early caregivers did (e.g., in therapy relationships).

Providence, Religious Coping, and Surrender

We saw in the previous chapter that, according to Christianity, God's omnipotence means he is mysteriously overseeing all that happens in the created order and has control over all that occurs. "God control" has been studied as a theistic attribution style (Welton, Adkins, Ingle, & Dixon, 1996), has been linked to wellbeing, and appears to serve as an active form of coping in the midst of Christian challenges (Krause, 2005). Rather than lead to passive resignation, studies have found God control is positively correlated with internal locus of control among believers (Jackson & Coursey, 1988; Silvestri, 1979). In fact, the collaborative religious coping style, in which believers assume an active role in resolving problems while relying on God's activity, is associated with numerous indeces of well-being (Pargament, 1997).

However, there are also times when wisdom dictates that direct human action is not warranted (e.g., dealing with the slow death of a loved one, accepting psychological symptoms that will not go away). In such cases, knowing that God is providentially guiding all that occurs for good is important (Romans 8:28), leading to another religious coping style: *surrendering to God*. Within the last few decades, surrender has been operationalized, and its psychological benefits for believers have been examined (Cole & Pargament, 1999; Wong-McDonald & Gorsuch, 2000). Drawing from a 350-year-old Jesuit writing called *Trustful Surrender to Divine Providence*, a recent study has empirically confirmed that deeply held, positive beliefs about God's providence are linked to the ability to surrender to him as a form of religious coping (Knabb, Frederick, & Cumming, 2017). Also in the Knabb et al. study, surrender was negatively associated with worry, mediated by the ability to tolerate uncertainty. In Knabb et al.'s theoretical model—which was confirmed with path analyses in separate college and church samples—surrendering to God's providence was related to less worry, with the surrender–worry link explained by the ability to accept the uncertainties and ambiguities in life.

Based on this theoretical model from the Christian tradition, Knabb et al. conducted a pilot study on an eight-week group therapy for chronic worry—primarily utilizing contemplative prayer (e.g., the Jesus Prayer and centering prayer based on the *Cloud of Unknowing*) as a way to help practitioners surrender to God during instances of worry, uncertainty, and anxiety. Results elucidated medium to large effects pre- to post-treatment when examining changes in views of God's providence (conceptualized as a type of God image), surrender as a form of religious coping, worry, intolerance of uncertainty, and depression, anxiety, and stress.

Surrender is also related to higher intrinsic religiosity, religious and existential wellbeing, and belief in God control (Wong-McDonald & Gorsuch, 2000), lower stress levels (Clements & Ermakova, 2012), less depression, better quality of life, and stress-related growth (Koenig, Pargament, & Nielsen, 1998), and lower depressed mood among childhood sexual abuse survivors (Gall, 2006). Surrender to God is also distinguishable from a deferring religious coping style, which cedes to God complete control over one's problems, promotes passivity, and has been found to reduce the quality of life of cancer patients (Pargament, 1997; McLaughlin, Yoo, D'Angelo, Tsang, Shaw, Shah, Baker, & Gustafson, 2013).

In what appears to be the first published randomized trial on contemplative prayer for psychological problems, researchers recently found that the daily practice of the Jesus Prayer—"Lord Jesus Christ, Son of God, have mercy on me"—decreased perceived stress among a sample of Christian college students, as well as increased their ability to surrender to God as a form of religious coping (Knabb & Vazquez, 2018). In a two-week time period, the authors also found a dose–response effect, suggesting that increasing the frequency of practice was linked to a higher score on a measure of surrender as a form of religious coping at the conclusion of the study.

It seems likely that having a strong view of providence, when combined with a benevolent view of God, helps believers negotiate difficult life circumstances, as well as address depressive and anxiety-related symptoms. Christians in therapy may also benefit from understanding the difference between the deferring and surrender religious coping styles and learning how to surrender themselves and troubling aspects of their lives to God, based on God's perceived support and care in light of his omnipotence.

As revealed in the aforementioned studies, Christian meditation (e.g., *apophatic* prayer without words and images, such as centering prayer; *kataphatic* prayer with words and images, such as meditating on Scripture [Davis, 2012] and Ignatius' "prayer of the senses") can help practitioners learn to surrender to God as a form of religious coping. This Christian-sensitive practice stands in contrast to the Buddhist-informed mindfulness and loving-kindness meditations that are currently popular in the clinical psychology literature (Germer, 2009; Kristeller & Johnson, 2005). With mindfulness meditation (referred to by Germer [2009] as "nonattached awareness"), practitioners typically focus on one thing at a time in the present moment (e.g., the breath, one of the five senses), relating to their thoughts and feelings with non-judgment. Loving-kindness, on the other hand, helps practitioners to cultivate compassion for themselves and others by repeating a mantra (e.g., "May I be free from suffering"). Both practices have been empirically investigated in the clinical literature, based on the operationalization of these Buddhist-influenced practices.

A meta-analysis of 24 studies on loving-kindness found it to be effective in improving positive emotions (Zeng, Chiu, Wang, Oei, & Leung, 2015). Moreover, among 39 studies, Hofmann, Sawyer, Witt, and Oh (2010) uncovered a medium effect pre- to post-treatment when exploring mindfulness as an intervention for mood symptoms and a large effect across four studies for depressive disorders. Although there is certainly some overlap between Buddhist-informed and Christian meditative practices (e.g., both tend to emphasize a single point of focus; cultivate focused, sustained attention; and help practitioners to relate differently to distressing inner experience), Christian clients may prefer to draw from their own religious heritage for meditative practices (e.g., the Jesus Prayer, scriptural meditation within the Puritan tradition, the *Cloud of Unknowing*, or the *Practice of the Presence of God*) that can help them change the way they relate to difficult inner experiences, with the added benefit of cultivating a deeper relationship with God along the way. In other words, in the clinical psychology literature, Buddhist-informed (or secularized) meditation is utilized for pragmatic purposes (e.g., to ameliorate suffering), whereas Christian meditative practices are about surrendering to God—via the virtue of Christian detachment, exemplified by Jesus in Gethsemane—so as to pivot from earthly preoccupations to an awareness of God's active, loving presence. Along the way, preliminary research suggests that Christians' God image can change (Knabb, Frederick, & Cumming, 2017).

Detachment from the Created Order in the Christian Tradition

In the last several years, researchers have identified non-attachment as a mediating variable that links mindfulness and positive mental health outcomes (Coffey & Hartman, 2008; Sahdra, Ciarrochi, & Parker, 2016). Drawing from the Buddhist tradition, recent attempts have been made to measure non-attachment as a reliable and valid construct, defined succinctly as "release from mental fixations" (Sahdra, Shaver, & Brown, 2010, p. 116). Buddhist non-attachment, however, is premised on a worldview in which belief in individual, existent selves is considered an illusion to be overcome (Epstein, 2007). As a result, for Christians, the benefits can come at a high cost: practitioners come to believe they are a "no-self," without personal existence and particular characteristics—assumptions that are controversial for most Christians because they are contrary to a biblical view of the human self.

Christianity, as we have seen, teaches that humans are made in the image of God. This implies that humans, similar to God, are existent selves with unique characteristics who are capable of becoming more mature, responsible selves. At the same time, because God is supposed to be the ultimate good of Christians, our maturation depends on adopting a stance towards the creation that involves a kind of psychological distance, leading to Christian concepts that are analogous to Buddhist non-attachment, but do not involve the same worldview assumptions, for example, denying one's self (Matthew 16:24), losing one's life for Christ's sake (Matthew 10:39), yielding (Romans 6:13), purgation (John of the Cross, 1935), and renunciation (Merton, 1961). One term of special interest is *detachment* (John of the Cross, 1935; Merton, 1961). Addressed by a wide range of Christians over the centuries, from the early desert Christians up to the Reformer John Calvin's (1559) "first rule of right prayer" (p. 853), detachment has been defined by the *Westminster Dictionary of Christian Spirituality* as "correcting one's own anxious grasping in order to free oneself for committed relationship with God" (Miles, 1983, p. 111).

In a recent study among Christian college students, researchers found that deeply held beliefs about God's providence were linked to the ability to surrender to God (Knabb, Vazquez, Wang, & Bates, 2018). In turn, surrender was negatively associated with repetitive negative thinking, with the surrender–negative thinking link mediated by a new construct in the psychology of religion literature, "humble detachment." The authors defined "humble detachment" as follows:

> A detached, flexible, humble ability to (a) let go of the tendency to clutch or push away a preoccupation with inner experiences and the self, and (b) pivot from a preoccupation with the self and inner experiences to a more transcendent awareness of God's active, loving presence.
>
> (p. 3)

Although the first study of its kind, this preliminary research suggests that spiritually humble detachment—arguably a virtue present throughout the Christian tradition—can play a role in the amelioration of repetitive negative thinking, which is a transdiagnostic construct that helps to describe emotional disorders.[6]

At any rate, knowing and loving the triune God, who owns the entire created order, provides a transcendent, interpersonal "wedge" between oneself and the created order that can make it possible for believers to distance themselves psychologically from unhealthy or sinful attachments to other creatures, including elements of one's inner life. Recognizing the authority, love, and grace of God allows one to reinterpret one's affective bondage to a sinful or inappropriate object, so that its hold is loosened and a new way of living can be fostered, which can become increasingly routinized over time. In these ways, therapists can train Christian clients with emotional disorders to distance themselves psychologically in distinctly Christian ways from stressful events and the hurtful actions of others (external triggers), as well as sinful desires and unhelpful emotions (internal conflicts). Contrary to the self-transcendent passivity promoted by Buddhist worldview assumptions, knowing God has created and has authority over everything, including oneself and one's internal world, can help enable one to detach from that created order and become more like Christ. We will discuss Christian detachment more fully in later chapters.

God and Identity Formation

As suggested in the opening section of this chapter, from a Christian standpoint, nothing is more important to the development of a Christian self than one's knowledge and love of God. Through one's relationship with God, one comes to see oneself in relation to God as a relatively insignificant and utterly dependent creature, as a sinner who resists the Creator, yet as one sought and loved by that same sovereign king of the universe. In turn, through faith in the Son of God, one discovers that one is God's child and on a journey of being drawn into Trinitarian communion, along with others. Such realizations can come to form the most influential components of a Christian's self-understanding and sense of identity—the answer to the question, "Who am I?" Over time, such a self-understanding contributes to the formation of one's narrative; impacts one's goals, strivings, imaginings, and actions; and forms one's future self, that is, the self one wants to become. Such materials can lead to a greater sense of inner unity, purpose, personal congruence, and integrity (Johnson, 2007, 2017; McGee, 1990).

God and Meaning-Discovery and -Realization

Humans were created to live meaningful lives, and being able to make sense of one's life has a positive effect on one's ability to cope with stressful life events (Park, 2010). Most authors researching and writing in this area refer to humans as meaning-makers. However, this implicitly reflects an anthropocentric orientation, since it assumes meaning is created by humans. By contrast, a theocentric orientation (which is highly relevant for a distinctly Christian psychotherapy) begins with God as the ultimate source of meaning. Indeed, for theists, God's glory is his infinite meaningfulness, and human meaning or glory is bestowed by God (Johnson, 2017). Everything and every activity, therefore, has meaning in so far as it participates in God's glory. Consequently, Christians might reframe this important dimension of human life as the *discovery* of divinely bestowed meaning or glory. This does not mean that humans play no role in this discovery. On the contrary, as images of God, we are especially equipped to reflect God's glory precisely in our unique and personal realization of divine meaning in our lives. This includes, of course, finding meaning in one's personal relationship with God, serving him, and fulfilling his will. But this also embraces the discovery of one's own particular callings, the realization of one's gifts, the acceptance and forming of relationships with others based on our unique qualities (family, friends, co-workers, and so on), the pursuit of one's vocational journey, the development into a more virtuous character (i.e., conformity to Christ), and even the use of one's free time. The late Trappist monk Thomas Merton (1961) succinctly captured this Christian reality with the following:

> Ultimately the only way that I can be myself is to become identified with Him in Whom is hidden the reason and fulfillment of my existence. Therefore there is only one problem on which all my existence, my peace and my happiness depend: to discover myself in discovering God. If I find Him I will find myself and if I find my true self I will find Him.
>
> (p. 36)

Of special note is how one approaches suffering, a ubiquitous, but more or less unpleasant dimension in human life. Yet, in the divine scheme of things, we can find meaning in suffering since in suffering well one resembles Christ (1 Peter 2:21–24) and one's character matures (Romans 5:3–5; Hebrews 5:8; James 1:2–4), an outcome which has now become well documented in the empirical literature (Emmons, 1999; Calhoun & Tedeschi, 2006). So, while all meaning is ultimately derived from God, it has to be personally realized by consciously receiving, appropriating, and participating in that meaning in everyday life, in order for its divine purposes to be most fully accomplished.

Insecure God Attachment, Distorted God Images, and Spiritual Abuse

We have focused most of our attention in this chapter on the psychological benefits of being rightly related to God as a real being in one's relational universe and how one's beliefs about God and experiences with him are the means by which one relates to God. Unfortunately, humans have significant obstacles to relating to God well (Johnson, 2007, 2017), which we will discuss in more detail in Chapter 7. But, before concluding the current chapter, something must be said about these obstacles with regard to our relation to God. Adults are not a blank religious slate, any more than they are in cognition. Original sin, genetics, and experience give humans predispositions that can distort their current perceptions, experience, and actions in relation to God. As a result, therapists working with Christian clients need to become knowledgeable about, and experienced in dealing with, these maladaptive influences.

To begin with, the Bible (Psalm 51:5, 58:3; Romans 3:10–18) and the Christian tradition have acknowledged that humans are born in a state that is alienated from God, so that as we develop we are predisposed to resist God and his purposes and pursue an autocentric agenda, until it begins to be mitigated by God's grace, especially through salvation in Christ. This "original sin" does not obliterate all awareness of God, but it blinds us to God's beauty and our fundamental dependence on him for everything.

Adding to this severe religious impairment are the tragic consequences of exposure to poor parenting and aberrant forms of religion, especially in childhood, since they can distort one's perceptions, beliefs, and experience of God. Through insecure attachment to parents who poorly represent God's form, one's IWM becomes relatively malformed. Depending on the quality of the interactions, such experiences lead to one of three kinds of insecure attachment: avoidant, anxious/ambivalent, or disorganized/disoriented (Ainsworth, Blehar, Waters, & Wall, 1978; Main & Solomon, 1990). Research on the corresponding quality of the parenting has been described by researchers as dismissive and emotionally unavailable, preoccupied and inconsistently responsive, and unresolved/disorganized and frightening or frightened, accordingly (Hesse, 2008; Wallin, 2007).

As children later become capable of forming a relationship with God, many will likely experience God correspondingly (Griffith, 2010; though we might call this a negative correspondence, in contrast with the positive correspondence mentioned above in the "correspondence hypothesis"). Because of this, some insecurely attached people will be especially disinclined to seek God, while those who become Christians will likely struggle with a God image that is more or less distorted. Those who perceive God through a dismissive-emotionally unavailable God image will likely perceive God as distant, uninvolved, and uninterested; those with an anxious/ambivalent attachment IWM will likely perceive God as inconsistently available and vacillate between feeling close to God and feeling unsure of God's affection; and those who perceive God from an unresolved/fearful perspective will likely feel that God is a threatening being who is inclined to punish (Noffke & Hall, 2007). Such more or less negative experiences of God can occur in spite of what Christians may consciously believe about God (Griffith, 2010).

Complicating matters further is childhood exposure to spiritually abusive families and churches, in which their teachings about God (God concept) and religious practices reflect a harsh view of God and a stern-minded, angry kind of Christianity that is at odds with the portrait of Christ in the gospels. Such experiences can come to contaminate the entire world of faith, compromising adult attendance at certain kinds of worship services, reading the Bible, and prayer, reflecting at least a temporary inability to personally engage with God. In these cases, a severely distorted God concept can tragically compound the insecurity of one's attachment to God and the distortion of one's God image.

Though the psychologically damaging effects of Christian fundamentalism may be more obvious, liberal versions of Christianity can contribute their own kind of spiritual harm by conforming to contemporary culture and softening the tenets of the Christian faith, providing little rationale for making God one's ultimate good. In the cultural diversity literature, this approach is called "assimilation," which involves distancing oneself from one's culture of origin in order to adopt the views of the dominant culture (Georgas, 2008). In an attempt to fit in with the culture in power, vital cultural traditions, values, and customs may be sacrificed.

So, in different ways, fundamentalism or liberalism may have had deleterious effects in the past on those seeking Christian psychotherapy in adulthood and, therefore, may need to be taken into account as part of its focus. Indeed, a kind and loving therapist can be a bridge back to an orthodox, consistent form of Christianity. However, in such cases, therapy may have to avoid much reference to Christian content for a time, because of psychospiritual contamination and inaccurate views of the Christian faith in the client's history, while the therapist's efforts are aimed at accepting such clients where they are at and working for as long as necessary on other, important biopsychosocial issues, until the client is ready for more direct engagement with the Christian faith.

Notes

1 There are several ways to reconcile psychological science and the Christian faith. The best of the "integration" movement typically starts with secular psychological science, then adds some Christian considerations, *post hoc.* A second option, the "biblical counseling" movement, tends to reject psychological science due to its secular assumptions, drawing solely from the Bible to understand the human condition. A third option, "Christian psychology," attempts to start with Scripture and the Christian traditions to make sense of the human experience, striving to utilize scientific methods common in the psychological sciences to operationalize and investigate biblical concepts; however, this perspective recognizes the value of secular psychological science as a gift of God's common grace to deepen our understanding of human functioning (just so long as it is not inconsistent with God's special revelation, the Bible). Along this continuum, which runs from drawing purely from secular science to solely using Scripture, we believe the Christian psychology perspective is optimal for devout Christian clients in psychotherapy, given Christianity is the starting point. Along the way, we are building in the flexibility to empirically investigate God's design so as to deepen our understanding of health, dysfunction, and healing.

2 Throughout this chapter, we utilize "modern" as a label for the psychology literature (both theoretical and empirical) based on the worldview of naturalism that originated in the formal founding of this movement about 150 years ago to the present day. Yet, this approach to human beings by no means has a monopoly on the study of the soul, as well as the investigation of thoughts, feelings, behaviors, and so on. Rather, the Christian tradition—often using philosophical and theological methods of inquiry—has a rich heritage of psychological understanding, especially in relation to God.

3 We see this as a major limitation in many secular theoretical orientations. For example, acceptance and commitment therapy (ACT) advocates for the use of client-generated, arbitrarily constructed values (i.e., principles for living) (see, e.g., Harris, 2009); although having a proverbial map to guide life is a useful starting point, from a Christian perspective, such values are not anchored to an unwavering, immutable source of the ultimate good. Instead, Christian virtues emanate from the Bible, were displayed by biblical figures throughout the Old and New Testaments, and were exemplified by Jesus Christ.

4 Unfortunately, the Christian notion of "sin" has rarely been explored (let alone operationalized and empirically investigated) within the psychotherapy literature (though for one attempt, see Watson, Morris, Loy, & Hamrick, 2007). Although it is beyond the scope of this book to offer a detailed exploration of the Christian notion of "sin," here, we wish to succinctly and foundationally define this biblical concept as turning away from God (i.e., idolatry"; see Exodus 20:3; Keller, 2010) in all of its forms. For a balanced, and more detailed, approach to sin and grace in psychotherapy, see McMinn (2008).

5 Interestingly, the Jewish psychoanalytic author Moshe Spero (1992) makes the same point.

6 The same authors of this study are currently planning a manualized preventative approach—a four-week program—for Christians with repetitive negative thinking,

using Christian meditation to help practitioners "humbly detach" from repetitive negative thinking so as to focus, instead, on God (Knabb, Vazquez, Garzon, Ford, & Wang, 2018).

References

Abernethy, A. D., Kurian, K. R., Rice, B. E., Grannum, G. D., Rold, L., & Jones, H. (2015). Corporate worship and spiritual formation: Insights from worship leaders. *Journal of Psychology and Christianity, 34,* 266–279.

Abernethy, A. D., van Oyen-Witvliet, C., Kurian, K. R., Brown, S., Uh, M., Rice, B., & Rold, L. (2016). Varieties of spiritual experience: A study of closeness to God, struggle, transformation, and confession-forgiveness in communal worship. *Journal of Psychology and Christianity, 35,* 9–21.

Adams, R. M. (1999). *Finite and Infinite Goods: A Framework for Ethics.* New York: Oxford University Press.

Ainsworth, M. D. S., Blehar, M. C., Waters, E., & Wall, S. (1978). *Patterns of Attachment: A Psychological Study of the Strange Situation.* Hillsdale, NJ: Erlbaum.

American Psychological Association (2002). Ethical principles of psychologists and code of conduct. *American Psychologist, 57,* 1060–1073.

American Psychiatric Association (2013). *Diagnostic and Statistical Manual of Mental Disorders* (5th ed.). Washington, DC: APA.

Benson, P., & Spilka, B. (1973). God image as a function of self-esteem and locus of control. *Journal for the Scientific Study of Religion, 12,* 297–310.

Blevins, D. (2016). Neuroscience and Christian worship: Practices that change the brain. In M.A. Maddix (Ed.), *Neuroscience and Christian Formation* (pp. 99–109). Charlotte, NC: IAP Information Age.

Bowlby, J. (1969). *Attachment and Loss*: Vol. 1, *Attachment.* New York: Basic Books.

Boyer, S. D., & Hall, C. A. (2012). *The Mystery of God: Theology for Knowing the Unknowable.* Grand Rapids, MI: Baker.

Braam, A., Schaap-Jonker, H., Mooi, B., Ritter, D., Beekman, A., & Deeg, D. (2008). God image and mood in old age: Results from a community-based pilot study in the Netherlands. *Mental Health, Religion & Culture, 11,* 221–237.

Bradshaw, M., Ellison, C. G., & Marcum, J. P. (2010). Attachment to God, images of God, and psychological distress in a nationwide sample of Presbyterians. *The International Journal for the Psychology of Religion, 20,* 130–147.

Calhoun, L. G., & Tedeschi, R. G. (2006). *Handbook of Post-Traumatic Growth: Research and Practice.* New York: Routledge.

Calvin, J. (1960). *The Institutes of the Christian Religion.* Philadelphia: Westminster.

Cheston, S. E., Piedmont, R. L., Eanes, B., & Lavin, L. P. (2003). Changes in client's images of God over the course of outpatient therapy. *Counseling and Values, 47,* 96–108.

Clements, A. D., & Ermakova, A. V. (2012). Surrender to God and stress: A possible link between religiosity and health. *Psychology of Religion and Spirituality, 4*(2), 93–107.

Coffey, K., & Hartman, M. (2008). Mechanisms of action in the inverse relationship between mindfulness and psychological distress. *Complementary Health Practice Review, 13,* 79–91.

Cole, B. S., & Pargament, K. I. (1999). Spiritual surrender: A paradoxical path to control. In W. R. Miller (Ed.), *Integrating Spirituality to Treatment: Resources for Practioners* (pp. 179–198). Washington, DC: American Psychological Association.

Davis, D., Moriarty, G., & Mauch, J. (2013). God images and God concepts: Definitions, development, and dynamics. *Psychology of Religion and Spirituality, 5,* 51–60.

Davis, J. J. (2012). *Meditation and Communion with God: Contemplating Scripture in an Age of Distraction.* Downers Grove, IL: InterVarsity Press.

Edwards, J. (1989). Dissertation II. The nature of true virtue. In *The Works of Jonathan Edwards.* Vol. 8: *Ethical Writings.* New Haven, CT: Yale University Press.

Edwards, J. (2003). *The Works of Jonathan Edwards.* Vol. 21: *Writings on the Trinity, Grace, and Faith* (S. H. Lee, Ed.). New Haven, CT: Yale University Press.

Emmons, R. A. (1999). *The Psychology of Ultimate Concerns: Motivation and Spirituality in Personality.* New York: Guilford.

Emmons, R. A., Cheung, C., & Tehrani, K. (1998). Assessing spirituality through personal goals: Implications for research on religion and subjective well-being. *Social Indicators Research, 45,* 391–422.

Epstein, M. (2007). *Psychotherapy without the Self: A Buddhist Perspective.* New Haven, CT: Yale University Press.

Frame, J. (2002). *The Doctrine of God.* Phillipsburg, NJ: P & R.

Gall, T. L. (2006). Spirituality and coping with life stress among adult survivors of childhood sexual abuse. *Child Abuse & Neglect, 30,* 829–844.

Georgas, J. (2008). Family and counseling with ethnic groups. In P. Pedersen, J. Draguns, W. Lonner, & J. Trimble (Eds.), *Counseling across Cultures* (6th ed.) (pp. 415–436). Thousand Oaks, CA: Sage Publications.

Germer, C. (2009). *The Mindful Path to Self-Compassion: Freeing Yourself from Destructive Thoughts and Emotions.* New York: The Guilford Press.

Granqvist, P., & Kirkpatrick, L. (2008). Attachment and religious representations and behavior. In J. Cassidy & P. R. Shaver (Eds.), *Handbook of Attachment: Theory, Research, and Clinical Applications* (2nd ed., pp. 906–933). New York: Guilford.

Griffith, J. L. (2010). *Religion that Heals, Religion that Harms.* New York: Guilford.

Grimes, C. (2007). God image research: A literature review. In G. L. Moriarty & L. Hoffman (Eds.), *God Image Handbook for Spiritual Counseling and Psychotherapy: Research, Theory, and Practice* (pp. 11–32). Binghamton, NY: Haworth Press.

Harris, R. (2009). *ACT Made Simple: An Easy-to-Read Primer on Acceptance and Commitment Therapy.* Oakland, CA: New Harbinger Publications.

Harter, S. (2012). *The Construction of the Self.* New York: Guilford.

Hesse, E. (2008). The adult attachment interview: Protocol, method of analysis, and empirical studies. In J. Cassidy & P. R. Shaver (Eds.), *Handbook of Attachment: Theory, Research, and Clinical Applications* (2nd ed., pp. 552–598). New York: Guilford.

Hofmann, S., Sawyer, A., Witt, A., & Oh, D. (2010). The effect of mindfulness-based therapy on anxiety and depression: A meta-analytic review. *Journal of Consulting and Clinical Psychology, 78,* 169–183.

Jackson, L. E., & Coursey, R. D. (1988). The relationship of God control and internal locus of control to intrinsic religious motivation, coping and purpose in life. *Journal for the Scientific Study of Religion, 27*(3), 399–410.

James, W. (1890). *Principles of Psychology.* New York: Henry Holt & Co.

John of the Cross (1935). *The Complete Works of Saint John of the Cross* (E. A. Peers, Trans. and Ed.). Westminster, MD: Newman Press.

Johnson, E. L. (2007). *Foundations for Soul Care: A Christian Psychology Proposal.* Downers Grove, IL: InterVarsity Press.

Johnson, E. L. (2015). Mapping the field of the whole human: Toward a form psychology. *New Ideas in Psychology, 38,* 4–24.

Johnson, E. L. (2017a). *God and Soul Care: The Therapeutic Resources of the Christian Faith.* Downers Grove, IL: InterVarsity Press.

Johnson, E. L. (2017b). The imago Dei: A folk psychology construct of the whole person. Paper presented at the annual convention of the American Psychological Association, Washington, DC, August.

Jones, J. W. (2007). Psychodynamic theories of the evolution of the God image. In G. L. Moriarty & L. Hoffman (Eds.), *God Image Handbook for Spiritual Counseling and Psychotherapy: Research, Theory, and Practice* (pp. 33–56). Binghamton, NY: Haworth Press.

Keller, T. (2010). *Gospel in Life: Grace Changes Everything.* Grand Rapids, MI: Zondervan.

Knabb, J., & Pelletier, J. (2014). The relationship between problematic internet use, God attachment, and psychological functioning among adults at a Christian university. *Mental Health, Religion & Culture, 17,* 239–251.

Knabb, J., & Vazquez, V. (2018). A randomized controlled trial of a 2-week Internet-based contemplative prayer program for Christians with daily stress. *Spirituality in Clinical Practice, 5,* 37–53.

Knabb, J., Frederick, T., & Cumming, G. (2017). Surrendering to God's providence: A three-part study on providence-focused therapy for recurrent worry (PFT-RW). *Psychology of Religion and Spirituality, 9,* 180–196.

Knabb, J., Vazquez, V., Wang, K., & Bates, T. (2018). "Unknowing" in the 21st century: Humble detachment for Christians with repetitive negative thinking. *Spirituality in Clinical Practice, 5,* 170–187.

Knabb, J., Vazquez, V., Garzon, F., Ford, K., & Wang, K. (2018). *Christian Meditation for Repetitive Negative Thinking: A Four-Week Program.* Unpublished manuscript.

Koenig, H. G., Pargament, K. I., & Nielsen, J. (1998). Religious coping and health status in medically ill hospitalized older adults. *Journal of Nervous and Mental Disease, 186,* 513–521.

Krause, N. (2005). God-mediated control and psychological well-being in late life. *Research on Aging, 27,* 136–164.

Krause, N., Emmons, R. A., & Ironson, G. (2015). Benevolent images of God, gratitude, and physical health status. *Journal of Religion and Health, 54,* 1503–1519.

Kristeller, J., & Johnson, T. (2005). Cultivating loving kindness: A two-stage model of the effects of meditation on empathy, compassion, and altruism. *Zygon, 40,* 391–407.

Lasch, C. (1979). *The Culture of Narcissism: American Life in an Age of Diminishing Expectations.* New York: W. W. Norton.

Main, M., & Solomon, J. (1990). Procedures for identifying infants as disorganized/disoriented during the Ainsworth Strange Situation. In M. Greenberg, D. Ciccetti, & E. M. Cummings (Eds.), *Attachment during the Preschool Years: Theory, Research and Intervention* (pp. 121–160). Chicago: University of Chicago Press.

Marsella, A. (2009). Some reflections on potential abuses of psychology's knowledge and practices. *Psychological Studies, 1*, 13–15.

McDargh, J. (1983). *Psychoanalytic Object Relations Theory and the Study of Religion.* Lanham, MD: University Press of America.

McDonald, A., Beck, R., Allison, S., & Norsworthy, L. (2005). Attachment to God and parents: Testing the correspondence vs. compensation hypotheses. *Journal of Psychology and Christianity, 24*, 21–28.

McGee, R. S. (1990). *The Search for Significance* (2nd ed.). Houston, TX: Rapha.

McLaughlin, B., Yoo, W., D'Angelo, J., Tsang, S., Shaw, B., Shah, D., Baker, T., & Gustafson, D. (2013). It is out of my hands: How deferring control to God can decrease quality of life for breast cancer patients. *Psycho-Oncology, 22*, 2747–2754.

McMinn, M. (2008). *Sin and Grace in Christian Counseling: An Integrative Paradigm.* Downers Grove, IL: InterVarsity Press.

Merton, T. (1961). *New Seeds of Contemplation.* New York: New Directions.

Miles, M. (1983). Detachment. In G. Wakefield (Ed.), *The Westminster Dictionary of Christian Spirituality* (p. 111). Philadelphia, PA: The Westminster Press.

Miner, M. (2007). Back to the basics in attachment to God: Revisiting theory in light of theology. *Journal of Psychology and Theology, 35*, 112–122.

Noffke, J. L., & Hall, T. W. (2007). Attachment psychotherapy and God image. In G. L. Moriarty & L. Hoffman (Eds.), *God Image Handbook for Spiritual Counseling and Psychotherapy: Research, Theory, and Practice* (pp. 57–78). Binghamton, NY: Haworth Press.

Pargament, K. I. (1997). *The Psychology of Religion and Coping.* New York: Guilford Press.

Park, C. L. (2010). Making sense of the meaning literature: An integrative review of meaning making and its effects on adjustment to stressful life events. *Psychological Bulletin, 136*, 257–301.

Pieper, J. (1979). *Happiness and Contemplation.* South Bend, IN: St. Augustine's Press.

Plantinga, A. (2000). *Warranted Christian Belief.* New York: Oxford University Press.

Rieff, P. (1966). *The Triumph of the Therapeutic: Uses of Faith after Freud.* New York: Harper & Row.

Rizzuto, A. M. (1979). *The birth of the living God: A psychoanalytic study.* Chicago: University of Chicago Press.

Sahdra, B., Ciarrochi, J., & Parker, P. (2016). Nonattachment and mindfulness: Related but distinct constructs. *Psychological Assessment, 28*, 819–829.

Sahdra, B., Shaver, P., & Brown, K. (2010). A scale to measure nonattachment: A Buddhist complement to Western research on attachment and adaptive functioning. *Journal of Personality Assessment, 92*, 116–127.

Silvestri, P. J. (1979). Locus of control and God-dependence. *Psychological Reports, 45*, 89–90.

Spero, M. H. (1992). *Religious Objects as Psychological Structures: A Critical Integration of Object Relations Theory, Psychotherapy and Judaism.* Chicago: University of Chicago Press.

Spilka, B., Addison, J., & Rosensohn, M. (1975). Parents, self, and God: A test of competing theories of individual–religion relationships. *Review of Religions Research, 16*, 154–165.

Testoni, I., Visintin, E. P., Capozza, D., Carlucci, M. C., & Shams, M. (2016). The implicit image of God: God as reality and psychological well-being. *Journal for the Scientific Study of Religion, 55*, 174–184.

Thomas, M., Moriarty, G., Davis, E., & Anderson, E. (2011). The effects of a manualized group-psychotherapy intervention on client God images and attachment to God: A pilot study. *Journal of Psychology and Theology, 39*, 44–58.

Tisdale, T. C., Key, T. L., Edwards, K. J., Brokaw, B. F., Kemperman, S. R., & Cloud, H. (1997). Impact of God image and personal adjustment and correlations of the God image to personal adjustment and object relations development. *Journal of Psychology and Theology, 25*, 227–239.

Tomcsányi, T., Martos, T., Ittzés, A., Horváth-Szabó, K., Szabó, T., & Nagy, J. (2013). Spiritual transcendence and mental health of psychotherapists and religious professionals in a Hungarian adult sample. *The International Journal for the Psychology of Religion, 23*, 161–170.

Twenge, J. M., & Campbell, W. K. (2009). *The Narcissism Epidemic: Living in an Age of Entitlement*. New York: Free Press.

Vitz, P. C. (1994). *Psychology as Religion: The Cult of Self-Worship* (2nd ed.). Grand Rapids, MI: Eerdmans.

Wallin, D. J. (2007). *Attachment in Psychotherapy*. New York: Guilford.

Watson, Jr., P. J., Morris, R. J., Loy, T., & Hamrick, M. B. (2007). Beliefs about sin: Adaptive implications in relationships with religious orientation, self-esteem, and measures of the narcissistic, depressed, and anxious self. *Edification, 1*, 57–67.

Weil, S. (1951). *Waiting for God*. New York: Harper & Row.

Welsh, R., & Knabb, J. (2009). Renunciation of the self in psychotherapy. *Mental Health, Religion & Culture, 12*, 401–414.

Welton, G., Adkins, A., Ingle, S., & Dixon, W. (1996). God control: The fourth dimension. *Journal of Psychology and Theology, 24*, 13–25.

Williams, D. L. (2018). Locus of control, god image, task value, self-efficacy and instrumentality as predictors of willingness to use faith-based health coaching. *Section B: The Sciences and Engineering, 78*(10-B)(E).

Wong-McDonald, A., & Gorsuch, R. (2000). Surrender to God: An additional coping style? *Journal of Psychology and Theology, 28*, 149–161.

Zeng, X., Chiu, C., Wang, R., Oei, T., & Leung, F. (2015). The effects of loving-kindness meditation on positive emotions: A meta-analytic review. *Frontiers in Psychology, 6*.

CHAPTER 3

The Doctrine of God in Christian Psychotherapy

Introduction

In this chapter, we present a Christian model of psychotherapy, embedded within the "theology" pillar. In particular, we offer a central theological theme in working with Christian clients with emotional disorders, along with goals for treatment and specific interventions from a distinctly Christian worldview. We draw from a range of Christian resources in this chapter, building on a theological, theoretical, and empirical understanding of emotional disorders from the previous chapters. Our hope is that mental health professionals will be equipped with a variety of Christian-sensitive interventions for depressive and anxiety disorders, integrating the "common factors" literature so as to enhance a Christian approach in the therapy room.

As noted in the introductory chapter, our presentation will draw from Lambert's (2013) review of the literature, utilizing an inverted "assimilative integration" model (see, e.g., Morgan, 2001) to inject the "common factors" literature into a Christian worldview as the foundation for treatment. By doing this, we are moving away from the implicit (and sometimes explicit) worldview assumptions threaded throughout the secular clinical literature, such as ontological materialism and arbitrarily constructed values for daily living. In conceptualizing the treatment process, we move from left to right within an adapted version of Lambert's model, beginning with the "support" phase, before moving on to the "learning" and "action" phases of treatment.

The Christian Tradition and Emotional Disorders

As we begin the first clinical application chapter, we offer a word on terminology. Though Christians have counseled since biblical times using our own terminology and constructs, science has helped us better understand what can go wrong with the soul in a fallen, fragmented world. Yet, contemporary diagnostic systems (e.g., the DSM-5, the ICD-10) are rife with problems and vagaries in that psychological problems lack clear etiologies and are less circumscribed than medical diagnoses (thus, the problems with conflicting and co-morbid diagnoses, among other limitations; see Francis, 2010; Knabb, 2016b; Paris, 2013). Moreover, they also lack attention to the spiritual dimension in their formulation, including God's providential role in the midst of suffering. To be sure, even the DSM-5 cautions clinicians against diagnosing a psychiatric disorder when behavior is considered culturally normative (APA, 2013). From a Christian perspective, if God is active and present in our suffering within a fallen world, labeling our psychological pain as a "disorder" is correct in one sense (we live in enduring brokenness due to originally turning away from God), but incorrect in another (if God is caring for us and refining us in the middle of our trials, his "afflictive providences" are by no means "disordered" [see Romans 8:28; Flavel, 2017]).

So, what are we to call the problems our Christian clients present with in the therapy room? Acknowledging the imperfections of diagnostic schemes, we realize that these are a dominant form of understanding and categorizing emotional suffering in the mental health field. Therefore, we have elected to use terms like "disorder" and "diagnosis" throughout the book—especially in the context of depressive and anxiety disorders—asking the reader to keep their limitations in mind.

Central Theme

In consideration of the previous two chapters in this section, a central theme in working with Christian clients with emotional disorders involves helping them to surrender to God's providence (giving control to God) because of his trustworthy attributes (God is relational, personal, and transcendent) and corresponding actions. In other words, because God is infinitely loving, wise, and powerful—and, thus, our ultimate good and source of meaning—suffering Christians can turn to him in the midst of daily distress. In the process, Christians are able to cultivate a secure attachment with God, viewing God as a "good object" (this terminology is grounded in an object relations perspective and need not imply a lessening of God's personal/relational character) so as to find rest in him in response to the recurrent symptoms of emotional disorders. As Christian clients modify their God image, they are able to relate differently to rumination (dwelling on the past), worry (catastrophizing about the future), experiential avoidance (an unwillingness to accept unpleasant inner experiences), and uncertainty (struggling to accept the uncertainties and ambiguities of life). In treatment, these transdiagnostic constructs—repetitive negative thinking, experiential avoidance, and intolerance of uncertainty—from the cognitive behavioral tradition are important to consider in the context of God's attributes and providential care. Drawing from relational (attachment theory) and cognitive (traditional and acceptance-based cognitive behavioral) models, we argue that Christians can balance acceptance (of symptoms they cannot change) and change (following Jesus in spite of pain) as they learn to surrender recurrent symptoms to God. In turn, they can increasingly rely on God as a secure base and safe haven for soothing comfort and relate differently to unpleasant inner experiences, consistent with acceptance-based models in the clinical literature (Hayes et al., 2012; Knabb, 2016a, 2016b; Sisemore, 2014).

Goals for Treatment

In applying the "common factors" domains of support, learning, and action (adapted from Lambert, 2013) to Christian theology, we offer the following overarching goals within the "theology" pillar of treatment (see also Table 3.1):

(a) *Support* involves the therapist modeling God's love, wisdom, power, and providential care, given that God is the ultimate good and source of meaning.
(b) *Learning* involves helping Christian clients to better understand and embrace God's perfect attributes and actions (even in the midst of pain).
(c) *Action* involves deepening a safe, trusting relationship with him in order to follow Jesus along the roads of life via living out his teachings. By doing this, Christians can work towards improving the avoidance, isolation, and loneliness that emanate from emotional disorders, as well as gently pivot from rumination, worry, and uncertainty to an awareness of God's active, loving presence.

Christian Resources

In the chapter, we utilize a range of Christian writings and strategies to develop Christian-sensitive interventions and techniques, including the following (in no particular order):

(a) Brother Lawrence's (2015) *The Practice of the Presence of God* to help Christians deepen their awareness of the supportive relationship available in Christ.
(b) Jean-Pierre de Caussade's *Abandonment to Divine Providence* (1921) and Claude de la Colombiere's *Trustful Surrender to Divine Providence* (1980) to help Christians "find God in all things" (the famous Jesuit saying) as a reframe for the symptoms of emotional disorders.
(c) *Lectio divina* to help Christians read about God's attributes in Scripture, meditate on his character, pray to God in order to deepen a relationship with him, and contemplate on his love (beyond words) by sitting in silence with him, surrendering to his providential care in the process (Benner, 2010).
(d) Puritan meditation (from a variety of sources) to shift from "earthly-mindedness" to "heavenly-mindedness" (Ball, 2016), focusing on God's

Table 3.1 Christian-sensitive common factors in psychotherapy for the "theology" pillar. Adapted from Lambert (2013)

Support-Related Goals	Learning-Related Goals	Action-Related Goals
Verbalize painful affect, reminiscent of the psalmists lamenting to God	Give Christian advice by drawing from biblical teachings on God's attributes and actions	Confront fears through *kataphatic* and *apophatic* meditation, inviting God into the process
Reduce isolation by building an alliance, modeling God's relational character	Process emotions (i.e., experiential acceptance) by writing a lament to God and surrendering to God's providential care	Master thinking patterns with *apophatic* meditation and Christian detachment
Provide a framework for understanding health, dysfunction, and healing in the context of God's providence and a deeper relationship with God	Attain insight on trusting in God in the midst of pain by reviewing Paul's thorn in the flesh (2 Corinthians 12)	Practice healthy behaviors by following Jesus' teachings
Offer an encouraging, safe, and collaborative relationship that models God, functioning as a secure base and safe haven	Offer a corrective relational experience by surrendering pain to God	Take risks by following Jesus' teachings
Explore the inner world, emphasizing that the fall has led to emotional pain, but God is active and present in the midst of suffering	Provide feedback on thoughts, feelings, behaviors, and relationships (i.e., repetitive negative thinking, experiential avoidance, intolerance of uncertainty), placing them in the context of God's providential care	Achieve a sense of self-efficacy by following Jesus' teachings in the midst of emotional pain
Offer therapeutic qualities (warmth, empathy, acceptance) that model God	Explore the inner world, emphasizing that the fall has led to emotional pain, but God is active and present in the midst of suffering	Model new behaviors by living out Jesus' virtues
	Attain realistic expectations, recognizing the fall has led to emotional pain; yet, God is active and present in the midst of suffering	Test assumptions of reality by practicing both the presence of God and "divine reading"
	Reframe views of self and others in the context of God's attributes and providential care	Work through ingrained patterns with *kataphatic* and *apophatic* meditation, inviting God into the process

Support-Related Goals	Learning-Related Goals	Action-Related Goals
	Accept difficult experiences (i.e., experiential acceptance) in the context of God's attributes and providential care	Practice affect regulation through *kataphatic* and *apophatic* meditation

attributes and actions in the midst of the symptoms of emotional disorders.

(e) The Jesus Prayer, originating out of the Orthodox tradition, which has helped Christians to focus their attention on God (*proseuch*), remember God (*mneme theou*), remain watchful over the inner world (*nepsis*), and cultivate a still, peaceful inner state (*hesychia*) (Johnson, 2010).

The Support Phase: Modeling God's Attributes and Actions

In the support phase of treatment (adapted from Lambert, 2013), we are attempting to accomplish several overarching goals when working with Christian clients, including reducing clients' isolation and building a solid therapeutic alliance that reflects (albeit imperfectly) God's attributes and actions. In this process, we are functioning as a secure base and safe haven, analogous to God's relationship with his children in the Bible. As we become a source of soothing comfort for Christians dealing with the pain of emotional disorders, we are modeling Jesus' empathy, as well as providing a framework for understanding emotional disorders from a Christian worldview. Finally, in the support phase, we are encouraging the verbal expression of psychological pain (to us as therapists, and also to God), reminiscent of the psalmists, so as to help Christian clients begin to explore the inner world with safety and confidence.

Building the Therapeutic Relationship and Reducing Isolation

Support within the "theology" pillar begins with entering into the therapeutic relationship by offering encouragement, safety, collaboration, and support, cultivating a working alliance along the way. In this process, reducing Christian clients' isolation is an important goal within the support domain. Because God is triune, personal, and transcendent, he understands Christians' pain—he pursues his creation, reminiscent of the lost sheep, coin, and son in Luke's gospel (15:1–32). In other words, we can work with Christian clients to better understand God's character as a loving father who protects his children, even in the midst of emotional disorders.

To do this, we want to model the pursuit that psychodynamic authors refer to as "optimal responsiveness" (Siegel, 1996). In these attempts to respond to clients' pain, we are offering just the right level of attuned engagement, empathizing with clients' sadness and anxiety as we build and maintain a stable, supportive relationship. In a similar vein, God offers us his care from moment to moment, knowing what we need as he responds empathically and redemptively to our pain in the here and now (Knabb & Emerson, 2013). At times, God pursues us (Luke 15:3–6); yet, at other times, he patiently waits for our return when we have wandered away (Luke 15:11–32). In either case, he knows what we need, loves us, and generously provides for his followers (Matthew 6:25–34). (Therapy for those who grew up in religious environments within which they experienced chronic trauma will have to address a deep skepticism towards God, to whom they may have frequently prayed to be released from their abusive situation [see Langberg, 2015]. Indeed, some people's atheism is a symptom of such abuse.)

As we offer these helpful psychological ingredients, we are striving to change our clients' God image, helping Christians to view God as trustworthy, loving, and caring. In support of this aim, research has revealed a correlation between our human relations and relationship with God, suggesting that the ability to trust in human relationships is related to a deeper view of God as loving and caring (Lawrence, 1997). One of the authors (T.S.) has a carving in his office shaped by an artist from Mali. It depicts a little girl leaning her head against a large hand, clearly intended to be the hand of God. This is a wonderful metaphor, as it could be easy to think how the girl could be crushed by the hand; yet, the placid look on her face makes the interpretation clear—she is at peace knowing such a powerful God holds her in his hand. This captures the shift we hope for in Christian psychotherapy.

Offering a Secure Base and Safe Haven

Upon building a therapeutic relationship with the client, we begin to function as a secure base and safe haven, which can serve as a stepping stone towards a similar dynamic with God (Knabb & Emerson, 2013). Based on attachment theory, a secure base is a person we can launch out from to confidently explore the world, with this same person functioning as a safe haven when we return to him or her for soothing comfort during dangerous or distressing moments in life (Mikulincer & Shaver, 2004).

Within the Christian tradition, God is described as a rock and fortress, someone we can "take refuge" in during the storms of life (Psalm 18:2). In Christian psychotherapy, we can point our clients to Jesus Christ, the "perfect attachment figure" (Kirkpatrick & Shaver, 1990), by offering ourselves as a source of stability, safety, and emotional responsiveness in the midst of their emotional pain (Knabb & Emerson, 2013). Unlike human attachments, though, God is omnipresent and, therefore, always with us, transcending the limitations of the secure base/safe haven dynamic within human attachment bonds.

Nevertheless, this corrective experience, to be sure, can help Christians to begin to reach for God during painful feeling states, building on the safe, supportive relationship that we offer. In other words, we are modeling Jesus, entering into a trusting relationship with our clients so as to serve as a transitional object towards a deeper, life-sustaining encounter with God.

In sum, while therapists cannot model the presence of God in every moment and circumstance (e.g., Isaiah 43:2; Matthew 28:20), we can strive to "be present" in each session, serving as a picture of God's constant presence and care. Certainly, the therapist models God by being there *for* the client, though he or she, unlike God, is not always there *with* the client (e.g., outside of weekly 50-minute sessions).

Modeling Jesus' Empathy, Acceptance, and Grace

In addition, therapists working with Christian clients can offer empathy, grace, and mercy, modeling *some* of Jesus' qualities (see Hebrews 4:15). (Unlike Christ, though, we do not serve as a perfect sacrifice for sins.) Because Jesus empathizes with our weaknesses, we can confidently approach his "throne of grace." Since he offers his mercy and grace when we need him the most, modeling these attributes of God can help Christian clients to move from the tangible to intangible. In other words, we can begin to help Christians bask in God's generous offer—mercy and grace to those who are inevitably suffering within the human condition—by first displaying these attributes in our therapeutic relationship.

Yet, what does it mean to model mercy and grace in the therapy room? From a Christian perspective, Jesus understands us because of his humanity, with Jesus' empathy capturing both compassion and a willingness to assist us in our moment of need (Schreiner, 2015). Stated differently, Jesus is both "transcendent" and "tender," reflected in his willingness to respond to our vulnerabilities (Schreiner, 2015, p. 154). Working in unison with his mercy, Jesus generously offers us grace, that is, "the strength and power to face every situation in life" (Schreiner, 2015, p. 154). With this being the case, we can model Jesus' mercy and grace through our accessibility, responsiveness, and offer of stability in our clients' ability to lean on us in the midst of their depressive and anxiety-related symptoms. Through this therapeutic accessibility, we can imperfectly reflect some of Jesus' most important relational attributes in the therapy room.

Providing a Relational Framework

A key support-based intervention is to provide a framework for under-standing emotional disorders in a Christian context. God is relational;

therefore, he enters into a relationship with humankind. In this relationship, God's providence extends to all of creation. As a result, he has a plan, even in the midst of suffering, and he incorporates this plan into the life of the believer for good and for God's own glory (Romans 8:28). God is active and present in the very pain of emotional disorders. Although pain is inevitable because of the fall of humankind, pivoting back towards him can help to strengthen Christians' ability to endure with hope and resilience. Healing, then, involves "walking with God through pain and suffering" (Keller, 2015), consistent with a "both/and" approach, *both* accepting painful inner experiences *and* recognizing that God is active and present in the midst of suffering.

Taking this conceptualization one step further, many Christian writers throughout the centuries have advocated trusting in God's providence in the midst of pain, suggesting that God is refining us in our most difficult life circumstances. The 17th-century Puritan author, John Flavel, referred to this dynamic as God's "afflictive providences" (e.g., physical and psychological pain), arguing that these distressing experiences can serve a useful purpose in the Christian life (Flavel, 2017). As an example, he pointed to the ubiquitous experience of a headache, noting that it can actually distract someone who is struggling with lust. Although by no means an easy task, this reframe of emotional disorders can help our clients to be more accepting of the symptoms they cannot change, which frees them up to boldly follow Jesus along the roads of life.

This trusting goes beyond checking the doctrinal box that God is in charge. Joseph Caryl (1644), another of the English Puritans, noted that when under duress we are to commit our cause to God. This is a way of saying:

> I will not strive or contend about, question or dispute his decision or judgement of my cause: I will lay my self down at his feet, and tell him how the case stands with me; then, let him do with me, what seems good in his eyes.
>
> (p. 228)

In a way, this perspective anticipates contemporary acceptance-based therapies—such as acceptance and commitment therapy (ACT)—that advocate for acceptance, given that attempting to avoid pain simply does not work in the long run. Still, from a Christian vantage point, acceptance is optimal if we can trust that the author of "afflictive providences" guides our suffering with his perfect love, wisdom, and power. Worded differently, shifting from an individual to relational (and a pragmatic to transcendent) understanding of suffering, we can help our Christian clients to see that a perfect God is walking alongside us as we experience the potholes, detours, and other blockades on the roads of life.

This notion of Christian acceptance can be illustrated by one author's (T.S.) story from his childhood. His parents and he were lost in a downpour of rain in a strange city when he was about 10 years old. His recollections of this event include the perceived coziness of the backseat of the car with the rain all around. Lost and in danger, he had peace. Why? He knew his father was driving; therefore, they would be safe. The relationship overruled the visible dangers. How much more so with God. Therapists might point anxious and troubled clients to Jesus, asleep on the boat during the storm (Mark 4:37). Accepting the storm is easier when we are oriented to our heavenly Father, who is greater than the storms and pains of life. A meditative exercise in therapy, where the client is encouraged to consider God's presence in a specific, difficult situation and how he has ultimate power and control, may encourage a reliance on the relational God. We often see God's job as to prevent or stop the storms, rather than to comfort us in the midst of them. This can lead to Christians pulling away from God in hard times, rather than savoring his companionship and sovereignty on our pilgrim journeys.

Exploring the Inner World and Verbalizing Painful Affect

Finally, support involves helping Christians with emotional disorders to explore their inner world and express their pain to God, reminiscent of the lament psalms in the Old Testament (e.g., Psalm 22) and Jesus' prayer to the Father in the Garden of Gethsemane the night before his crucifixion in the gospels (Matthew 26:36–46). Within the lament Psalms, the psalmists frequently pleaded with God, followed by offering some sort of praise to him (Brueggemann, 1984). In this process, they were able to hold together the tension of suffering before God and surrendering to his perfect care with hope and gratitude. More specifically, the psalmists regularly offered a complaint to God, pleaded for God's help, verbalized the painful experience, expressed gratitude before God, and thanked God for listening to the psalmists' lament (Brueggemann, 1984; Knabb, 2016a).

In the 21st-century therapy room, clients' laments commonly resemble this biblical strategy. With their presenting problem, Christian clients are offering a complaint (e.g., a regret, a loss, a tragedy, sorrow, pain), accompanied by a petition for help. Following this petition, there is some sort of expression of emotional pain, followed by relief and gratitude with verbalized appreciation for therapists' willingness to listen to the complaint. As we listen to our clients' laments, we can begin to help them direct these petitions to God (like Caryl's notion of committing their cause to God), inviting God into the process to hear them, respond to them, and comfort them in the midst of pain and suffering. Although helping clients to lament to God is practiced in the learning phase of this chapter, planting this seed is important within the support phase, given clients are already lamenting about their current predicament with the therapist.

The Learning Phase: Recognizing God's Active, Loving Presence in the Midst of Pain

As the next phase in this three-phase process (adapted from Lambert, 2013), Christian clients can begin to recognize that God is active and present in the middle of their suffering. Rather than somehow removed from the psychotherapy encounter, God is moving in the midst of their emotional pain. With the first phase—support—we are beginning to model God's attributes and actions, before transitioning to helping clients see that God is with them on the roads of life. Even as they enter and exit the therapy room, God is by their side. Instead of serving as a passive traveling companion, God is guiding the way, helping our clients to navigate the difficult terrain ahead.

Through expressing their pain to God, surrendering to God's protective care, gaining insight by trusting God in the midst of pain, working on accepting emotional pain, and situating their pain in the context of God's loving care, we are helping our Christian clients begin to take action as the concluding step within the "theology" pillar. Above all else, this phase involves returning to—over and over again in varying ways—the theme that God is present in the midst of Christians' struggle with emotional disorders. Yet, rather than relying on aloof, overly cognitive explanations, we want to begin to help Christians *experience* God's presence, reconciling their God concept and God image (Davis et al., 2013; Thomas et al., 2011), which can hopefully be realized in the action phase.

Processing Painful Emotions: Cultivating Experiential Acceptance

We begin by considering learning-based interventions and techniques. Christian clients can learn to explore their emotions by writing their own lament to God,[1] gaining insight into the "both/and" of emotional pain (it is *both* painful *and* part of God's providential plan) by surrendering to God's providence. As revealed in the learning phase, lamenting to God in the Bible typically involves two major steps and five minor steps (Brueggemann, 1984). To help Christian clients work on writing their lament to God so as to combine verbalizing their pain to God first and then thanking him for his providential care, please see Table 3.2.

Before completing the exercise, you may wish to review an example of a lament Psalm (e.g., Psalm 22), moving through the five steps so that your Christian client understands the ingredients. You may also wish to discuss the reason for lamenting to God. Essentially, the Psalms capture the human experience, with songs of orientation, disorientation, and new orientation; at times, we sing songs to God that reflect a time of celebration, instances of suffering, and the blessings of a new day (Brueggemann, 1984). Of course, the lament Psalms—fittingly sandwiched in the middle—reflect our need to accept the seasons of suffering, given they are wedged in between

Table 3.2 Lamenting to God. Adapted from Brueggemann (1984), Knabb (2016a), and Knabb (2018)

Verbalize Your Complaint to God	
Plead for God's Assistance	
Share Your Emotional Pain with God	
Express Gratitude Towards God	
Give Thanks to God for Listening to Your Heartfelt Lament	

life's celebrations and the inevitable changes that come from God's fulfilled promises (Brueggemann, 1984).

Surrendering to God's Providence: A Three-Step Process

What does it mean to surrender to divine providence? Given what we have covered in earlier chapters, we see that God is not only loving and supportive, but powerful as he implements his plan for his children. Not a hair falls from our heads without his awareness and consent (Luke 12:7). The context of Jesus' comment here is that we need not fear when we understand the degree of God's loving control. Often, our suffering is exacerbated by our misunderstanding of the Christian life (and, sadly, this is often attributable to shallow teachings in the Christian community). When we develop more of God's perspective, we move beyond seeing life as simply for our pleasure and convenience, and we see that he has a bigger purpose and plan—one that does not shy away from hard things (Moser, 2013). Like the workout motto of "No pain, no gain," God's plan to grow us and use us for his glory involves suffering and adversity (Romans 5:3–5). Certainly, there are a wide variety of ways that adversity grows us in the Christian life—it can reveal human pride or a lack of trust in God, as well as allow us to see God's nature more clearly and our need for God's mercy, among other benefits. The apostle Paul even embraced the notion of suffering for Christ as part of his life goals (Philippians 3:10). Our plight worsens, then, when we fight against his plan, even as we state that we endorse it.

An excellent introduction to learning to yield to God's providence can be found in the 18th-century classic, *Abandonment to Divine Providence*, by Jean Pierre de Caussade (1921). De Caussade makes clear that God's goal for us is not wealth, or success, or a fancy house. He simply wants us to rely on him as he leads us to the goal of a pure heart. "The wisdom of the just soul consists in being content with what is intended for it!" (p. 28). Unlike secular approaches to acceptance, for the believer, abandonment to God's providence is an "abandonment to the good pleasure of God" (p. 41). It is toward an ultimate value, grounded in God (similar to, but also in contrast with, acceptance and commitment therapy [ACT]). So, it is casting our cares on him and accepting his sovereign will, knowing it is ultimately good for us and will be used to better us and glorify God. In this way, our troubling emotions can be redeemed.

In a similar work, *Trustful Surrender to Divine Providence* (written in the 17th century), the Jesuit author Claude de la Colombiere outlined a three-step process for surrendering to God, including putting faith in God's providence, remaining hopeful in God's providence, and loving God's providence (even in the midst of pain) (Saint-Jure & Colombiere, 1980). To yield to God, of course, is possible because of God's infinite love, wisdom, and power, with the combination of these qualities meaning his protective care is good, is what we need, and extends to us from moment to moment. In this exercise (adapted from Knabb & Frederick, 2017; Saint-Jure & Colombiere, 1980), you might try to walk your Christian client through the three steps in the context of emotional disorders:

(a) Help the client to think deeply about God's active role in daily occurrences, which includes both big and small events in life, by placing his or her *faith* in the reality that God is exercising his loving control over his creation. Although the client may feel like God is distant as he or she is suffering, God is present in the midst of the depressive or anxiety disorder. This step may involve helping the client to come up with examples—of both larger and smaller events—wherein God is lovingly intervening in the world. Personal life examples are optimal.

(b) Next, assist the client in cultivating a deeper *hope* in God's providence, looking out into the future and anticipating that God will continue to hold the client in his or her distress, reminiscent of a parent whose protective care is inevitably available in the room next door. This step may involve helping the client to generate a range of scenarios in the future, all with the inevitable outcome that God will be there to care for the client in the midst of the ups and downs of life.

(c) Finally, help the client to visualize falling into God's outstretched arms, feeling God's *love* by thanking him for offering his perfect plan for life. Because he overlooks no detail, he is caring for the client as he or she thinks, feels, and behaves in the here and now. In this last step, try to help the client imagine being held and reassured by God, trusting that God's plan is ultimately for the client's good.

Perhaps the best way to summarize this is with a prayer attributed to Blaise Pascal (2017):

> I ask you neither for health nor for sickness,
> For life nor for death,
> But that You may dispose my health and my sickness
> My life and my death
> For Your glory...
> You alone know what is expedient for me,
> You are the sovereign master;
> Do with me according to your will
> Give to me or take away from me,
> Only conform my will to yours.

Attaining Insight: Trusting in God in the Midst of Pain

Paul's thorn in the flesh (2 Corinthians 12) can also be used to highlight a way recurrent pain can be reinterpreted through the lens of God's providence, accepting and reframing challenging inner and outer experiences (Knabb, 2016b). In his second letter to the Corinthians, Paul explained that God gave him a "thorn" (the Greek word, *skolops*, meaning a sharp, pointed affliction), with some speculating his affliction was some sort of physical, relational, or sexual problem (Matera, 2003). Although he asked God to take the annoyance from him three times, God declined Paul's request, with Paul eventually reframing this suffering as a way to receive God's grace and power more fully in the midst of his weakness. In other words, he was able to celebrate his vulnerabilities because they allowed him to function as a vehicle through which God displayed his strength.

For Christian clients with depressive or anxiety disorders, their "thorn" can be reframed as a medium through which God can display his grace and strength. In spite of the pain, God is active and present, offering soothing comfort to those who reach out for him. Consistent with Paul's "thorn," we can work with Christian clients to trust in God's providence, recognizing that he has a purpose and plan for human suffering. Gaining a deeper insight into this relationship with psychological pain is paramount, especially when our clients do not attain the emotional relief they seek from God through the traditional Christian activity of petitionary prayer.

Learning to Accept Emotional Pain

As another example, Christian clients can learn to *have* emotional pain, as detailed by Henry Krystal (1988):

> It is a matter of clinical commonplace that the patients who present with the request to be free of certain feelings, e.g., depression, in fact

need to *have* the depression. They come to us at the end of a vicious cycle of maladaptive handling of their emotion by becoming angry with themselves, or frightened, or desperate about having the depression, thus perpetuating it. By contrast, people who can comfortably experience a feeling generally feel secure that their state is justified by their life experience; that it makes sense; and that, having accomplished its purpose or run its course, it will stop. People who recognize the source and meaning of their intense affects, for example the reaction following a near accident or in bereavement, are much less likely to engage in maladaptive pattern, and the emotion runs its natural, short-lived course.

(p. 21, italics added)

For Krystal, a psychiatrist and survivor of the Holocaust, when we make room for our emotions and view them as an important signal, we can begin to relate differently to them and, thus, ameliorate our emotional suffering. Given that our emotions fluctuate and change, we can learn to notice them without simultaneously experiencing a critical meta-feeling. Stated differently, although we may not be able to fully rid ourselves of life's ubiquitous negative emotions (e.g., sadness, anger, anxiety, fear, guilt, shame), we can work towards changing our feeling about the feeling as we recognize our emotions are valid, God-given, and necessary. After all, God is the designer of the limbic system (though it, too, is fallen).

Still, a Christian understanding of pain is somewhat different from a more pragmatic, secular understanding, which Krystal (1988) and others explicate. For Christians, God's providence extends to all of creation, which means that God is sovereign over our inner world. Based on this understanding, Christians can find peace in "giving over" control to God, especially when it comes to painful inner experiences that might not fully go away. Rather than fighting against pain, which distracts our clients from following Jesus, Christians can learn to make peace with intrapsychic distress, recognizing that God may be revealing his will in the midst of suffering (Allender & Longman, 1993; Knabb, 2016a). As this happens, God is growing them through it, making them more Christlike. In fact, the life of a Christian disciple is to understand all things in light of Christ, growing in sanctification so as to deepen our relationship with God and close the gap between our God concept and image (Davis et al., 2013; Thomas et al., 2011; Johnson, 2017).

In this learning phase, we are working with the Christian client to experience a corrective encounter with his or her emotions, wherein he or she comes to recognize God's active, loving role in the midst of inner pain. This change, of course, is by no means easy, given our society's emphasis on biomedicalizing emotional pain and striving to eliminate it via psychotropic medication (Hayes, Strosahl, & Wilson, 2012). Yet, when we are able to move our clients in the direction of reframing emotional pain as part of

God's providence, we can help them to accept the things they cannot change, as the famous Serenity Prayer wisely suggests.

Providing Feedback: God's Providential Role

Also in this second phase, Christian clients are gaining insight into their thoughts, feelings, behaviors, and relationships, in that we are repeatedly situating them in the context of God's providential care. By helping our clients to explore the inner world, we are working with them to invite God into the process in the midst of their suffering. Along the way, they are gaining realistic expectations, given the fall of humankind has led to emotional pain. Yet, all hope is not lost, in that God is with us (*Emmanuel*; Matthew 1:23). This reframe of emotional pain is especially salient—God's presence helps us to understand our emotional pain, surrender it to him, and more effectively follow Jesus in the midst of our distress. An important part of this change involves accepting difficult inner experiences, based on God's attributes and actions. Because he is infinitely loving, he has our best intentions in mind; in that he is infinitely wise, he knows what we need; and because he is infinitely powerful, he is in control of the situation. These attributes lead to an awareness of God's providential care—he has a perfect plan to care for us in the middle of our pain.

When working with Christian clients with distressing thoughts, we can present an understanding of several types of negative thinking patterns. With repetitive negative thinking (Ehring & Watkins, 2008), we get stuck in ruminations about the past and worries about the future, which distract us from following Jesus on the roads of life. These perseverative thinking styles can be linked to mind wandering—the inability to stay focused on the task at hand throughout the day (Killingsworth & Gilbert, 2010)—resulting in the struggle to attend to what is in front of us. In the Christian life, this means we may have a hard time living the life God has called us to live, given our mind is distracted from moment to moment. With intolerance of uncertainty, our clients may struggle to accept the ambiguities of life, striving to engage in approach-related (e.g., compulsively checking) or avoidance-related (e.g., procrastination) behaviors so as to attain a false sense of certainty (Dugas & Robichaud, 2007; Mahoney & McEvoy, 2012). Finally, with experiential avoidance, our clients might struggle with accepting inner pain, striving to avoid inner distress through distraction, drugs, alcohol, procrastination, and other futile efforts to get rid of the innevitable distress of life (Chawla & Ostafin, 2007).

Yet, our emotions are important, given they serve as God-given signs or signals on the roads of life (Johnson, 2007; Knabb, 2018). For example, sadness helps us to recognize when we have experienced an important loss, with dysphoria allowing us to rest when we are unable to attain salient resources (Knabb, 2016b; Zettle, 2007). In the midst of sadness, God may be revealing something to us, communicating to us that we need to slow down to reach for him. What is more, anxiety is firmly embedded within the human condition, helping us to anticipate danger or catastrophe (Eifert & Forsyth, 2005; Knabb, 2016b), as well as revealing where our trust lies. When we experience anxiety-related symptoms, asking what God is communicating to us can be helpful in inviting him into the process, trusting that he is active and present in our pain.

What is more, when we begin to engage in ruminations, worries, and intolerance of uncertainty, these inner experiences can serve as a catalyst towards reaching for God (Knabb, 2018). Worded differently, we can help our clients to pivot from what the Puritans called "earthly-mindedness" (e.g., earthly preoccupations that pull our attention away from God) to "heavenly-mindedness" (e.g., focusing on God's plan for our life) when they notice they are engaging in thinking patterns that pull them away from an awareness of God's loving, protective care (Ball, 2016). This shift can take place through both formal and informal meditative practices within the Christian tradition, presented to Christian clients in the action phase of treatment. Each time we notice our mind has drifted away from God, we can celebrate in knowing we have the opportunity to focus on him again. To be sure, if God is sovereign over the inner world (Saint-Jure & Colombiere, 1980), he has a purpose and plan for even repetitive negative thinking and intolerance of uncertainty, especially if these inner events lead us back to his outstretched arms (Luke 15:11–32).

The Action Phase: Balancing Sitting at Jesus' Feet and Serving Him

Action-based interventions and techniques (adapted from Lambert, 2013) enable Christians to work towards engaging in healthy new behaviors (rather than avoidance) because of an awareness of God's personal, active, and loving presence. These behaviors, modeled by Jesus, can serve as a useful road map for life and help to develop personal agency. In that, by this time, we have hopefully helped Christians to attain much-needed support (from us, as well as from God) and insight, we are now ready to work with them to take action in the midst of pain, turning to God as the author of life. Certainly, by definition, the action phase involves taking deliberate steps to facilitate the change process; yet, equally important, we are helping Christians to know when to sit at the feet of Jesus, surrendering their inner world to him.

This balance between acceptance and change is captured in the story of Mary and Martha in Luke's gospel (10:38–42). Mary sat patiently at Jesus' feet, whereas Martha served Jesus. Although Jesus preferred Mary's posture, Martha's service was not the problem. Rather, her anxiously driven behavior served as a distraction to the most important task at hand—listening to Jesus while resting at his feet. Historically, Christians have looked to Mary to capture contemplation, whereas Martha represents a life of action (Cutler, 2003). As we move into the action-based stage, we want to help Christians balance sitting at the feet of Jesus and serving Jesus (Knabb, 2016b), surrendering the inner world to God and following Jesus by way of well-defined virtues for optimal living. (We will be referring repeatedly to this story throughout the book, believing that it has tremendous significance for Christian psychotherapy, as well as the Christian life in general.)

Confronting Fears with Christian Meditation

To begin with, Christian clients can learn to confront their fears through *kataphatic* and *apophatic* meditation. With Christian meditation, the goal is to notice the inner world, shifting from "earthly-mindedness" to "heavenly-mindedness" (Ball, 2016). Along the way, Christians are striving to master their thinking patterns in that there is a deeper awareness of unhelpful cognitive processes.

With *kataphatic* meditation, Christians are thinking deeply about God's attributes and actions, developing focused, sustained attention along the way. One form of *kataphatic* meditation, which uses words and images as a medium to draw closer to God, comes to us from the Puritans, a group of devout Christians from England in the 1500s and 1600s who aimed to radically follow the Jesus of the Bible in daily living. Puritan meditation can be defined as follows:

A focused, sustained cognitive process within Puritan Christianity, shifting from earthly- to heavenly-minded thinking in order to cultivate a corresponding feeling state for Christ-like behavioral action.
(Knabb, 2018, p. 86)

Or as Puritan Nathaniel Ranew, in his valuable book, *Solitude Improved by Divine Meditation*, added regarding the "sustained" aspect:

It is not the diving into the sea, but staying longer, that gets the greater quantities of pearls. To draw out the golden thread of meditation to its due length, till the spiritual ends be attained, this is a rare and happy attainment.
(Ranew, 1995, pp. 43–44)

In consideration of God's providential care in the midst of Christians' emotional disorders, the following two goals can be pursued: help our clients to (a) let go of problematic thoughts and feelings; and (b) cultivate focused, sustained attention on God by recognizing his active, loving presence (Knabb, 2018; Kristeller & Johnson, 2004).

Next, an eight-step process (adapted from Ball, 2016; Baxter, 2015; Beeke & Jones, 2012; Hall, 2016; Watson, 2012; quoted directly from Knabb, 2018, p. 87) can be employed to help Christians with emotional disorders shift their focus from depressive and anxiety-related symptoms to an awareness of God's attributes and actions:

1. Choose a biblical topic to focus all your attention on.
2. Say a short prayer to God, asking him for guidance during the next 20 minutes.
3. Shift your focus from "earthly-mindedness" to "heavenly-mindedness," letting go of rumination, worry, and self-criticism and shifting towards a single point of focus—a short passage in Scripture that reveals the biblical topic.
4. Repeat the passage in Scripture with focused, sustained attention.
5. Begin to move from your "brain" to your "heart," focusing on the feeling that corresponds with the biblical topic and short passage in Scripture.
6. Deeply experience the feeling that corresponds with the biblical topic and passage in Scripture.
7. As you conclude the meditation, make a commitment to act on what you have just focused all your attention on by extending love and compassion to others in a Christ-like manner.
8. Say a short prayer to God, thanking him for revealing himself to you via the biblical topic and short passage in Scripture.

In this formal practice, we can advise our clients to find a comfortable, quiet environment, sitting up straight in a supportive chair. During this time, Christians are advised to close their eyes and meditate on God's infinite love, wisdom, power, and providence by selecting a short passage in Scripture to focus their attention on.

Focusing on God with the Jesus Prayer

As another meditative strategy within the Christian tradition for relating differently to depressive and anxiety-related symptoms, Christians can gain a deeper awareness of the fluctuating states of the mind (what authors of the *Philokalia* call *nepsis*, or watchfulness), utilizing the Jesus Prayer to remember God, focus on God, and cultivate an inner stillness (Johnson, 2010). The Jesus Prayer, which comes from the Eastern Orthodox Christian tradition, likely developed in the first part of the first millennium, when Christians began to move to the deserts of Egypt, Palestine, and Syria to reject the societal comforts and materialistic tendencies they were accustomed to. Emulating Jesus' period of temptation in the wilderness (Matthew 4:1–11), they sought to face their inner experiences, often turning to the Psalms as a way to focus their mind on God. Eventually, they developed the Jesus Prayer, which is rooted in gospel accounts of individuals asking Jesus for mercy and Paul's instructions to "pray without ceasing" (1 Thessalonians 5:16–18).

Considered an *apophatic*, "non-iconic" form of meditation (see Bingaman, 2012; although an argument can certainly be made that it is characteristic of *kataphatic* meditation, given we are repeating a short phrase), the prayer itself goes as follows: "Lord Jesus Christ, Son of God, have mercy on me."[2] In this practice—which can take place formally during a designated period of time or informally throughout the day—we are striving to accomplish several goals (adapted from Johnson, 2010; Knabb, 2018):

(a) We are focusing on God (the Greek word, *proseuch*).
(b) We are remembering God (the Greek phrase, *mneme theou*).
(c) We are noticing our inner experiences (the Greek word, *nepsis*).
(d) We are developing inner stillness (the Greek word, *hesychia*).

In the context of psychological problems, recent research has found the Jesus Prayer can be effective in reducing worry and intolerance of uncertainty (Knabb, Frederick, & Cumming, 2017), as well as daily stress (Knabb & Vazquez, 2018).

To practice, simply instruct your Christian clients to find a quiet environment, free from distractions, closing their eyes and gently reciting the Jesus Prayer for a 20-minute period of time. With the in-breath, we can breathe (from the diaphragm),[3] "Lord Jesus Christ, Son of God," and then breathe out while saying, "have mercy on me" (Talbot, 2013). The idea is to surrender the inner world to God by breathing in Christ (as an embodied, metaphorical action) and breathing out our distress, handing it to him in the midst of our pain. Most people find it is an effective stress-releasing activity. (We will be recommending use of the Jesus Prayer repeatedly throughout the book, because we believe that a conscious, mindful, Christ-centered recitation of it will tend to promote positive psychological benefits; see Knabb, Frederick, & Cumming, 2017; Knabb & Vazquez, 2018.)

Learning to Follow Jesus

In the action phase of treatment, Jesus' teachings can be used as a guide, since many of his guidelines for living were recorded in the gospels. In other words, Christians can practice healthy new behaviors by following Jesus' teachings, taking risks in order to develop new patterns of living. Jesus' Sermon on the Mount can function as a proverbial map (Matthew 5–7), with Christians striving to follow Jesus' teachings in concrete steps. One such way to do so is to establish measurable, attainable, positive, and specific goals (*MAPS*; Chang, Scott, & Decker, 2013) that emanate from the Sermon on the Mount (Pennington, 2018).

For example, when Jesus instructs us to love our enemies (Matthew 5:44), we can view this command through the lens of *MAPS*, asking the following questions:

(a) How can we help the client to set a *measurable* goal, behavior-wise, to love his or her enemies in spite of the emotional disorder?
(b) How can we help the client to set an *attainable* goal, behavior-wise, to love his or her enemies in spite of the emotional disorder?
(c) How can we help the client to set a *positive* goal, behavior-wise, to love his or her enemies in spite of the emotional disorder?
(d) How can we help the client to set a *specific* goal, behavior-wise, to love his or her enemies in spite of the emotional disorder?

We may come up with a goal like the following:

(a) I will complement my co-worker once per day over the next week by mentioning a specific example of how he or she is performing well on our treatment team, regardless of my thoughts and feelings.

In addition, developing the fruit of the Spirit (Galatians 5:22–23) more intentionally can be a focus in Christian psychotherapy. The Christian virtues can be utilized to help Christians follow Jesus in spite of psychological pain (adapted from Gregory & Rutledge, 2016; Knabb, 2016b; Knabb, 2018):

(b) Chastity/purity
(c) Temperance/self-control
(d) Charity/love
(e) Diligence/hard work
(f) Patience
(g) Kindness
(h) Humility

Again, these virtues can be operationalized by turning to *MAPS*, shifting from an abstract notion of virtuous living to actually envisioning—in behavioral terms—how to live out these famous moral behaviors. In the context of Christian virtues, a central theme involves helping Christian clients to balance sitting at Jesus' feet and serving Jesus by following him on the roads of life, despite the pain that they carry with them as they walk with him. Balancing Christian meditation with action is especially important, given that experiential avoidance (Hayes et al., 2012) can get in the way of optimal Christian living. By learning to relate differently to the inner world by pivoting from "earthly-mindedness" to "heavenly-mindedness" (Ball, 2016), we are helping our clients to fill their mind with God's trustworthy attributes and actions, rather than unilateral attempts to make sense of the world on their own (Proverbs 3:5–6).

Testing Assumptions by Practicing the Presence of God

As another example of an action-based intervention, Christians can test assumptions—when deepening an awareness of God's presence, new opportunities open up to see the world from a more spiritual perspective, beyond a previously limited understanding because of ruminations, worries, intolerance of uncertainty, and experiential avoidance. Christians can gain a deeper awareness of God's presence in the here-and-now with Brother Lawrence's instructions in *The Practice of the Presence of God*, staying connected to what matters most—following Jesus from moment to moment and day to day.

Brother Lawrence lived a humble life as a Carmelite monk in the 1600s, working as a sandal-maker and cook during his short time on this planet (Lawrence, 2015). In his famous writing, he argued for the following:

> We must continually apply ourselves so that all our actions, without exception, become a kind of brief conversation with God, not in a contrived manner but coming from the purity and simplicity of our hearts.
>
> (Lawrence, 2015, p. 38)

He went on to explain that daily activities—even the smallest of tasks—can be performed "carefully and deliberately, not impulsively and hurriedly" so as to avoid the maintenance of a "distracted mind" (Lawrence, 2015, p. 38). Embedded within his succinct instructions, he recommended reciting a short phrase to remember God throughout the day, such as "My God, I am completely yours" (Lawrence, 2015, p. 44).

To help our Christian clients pivot from repetitive negative thinking and intolerance of uncertainty to an awareness of God's presence, we can work with them to develop a short phrase (either the one above or a different saying) to cultivate focused, sustained attention (adapted from Knabb, 2018; Lawrence, 2015). Then, we can help our clients to exercise God's presence in daily tasks, such as washing the dishes or mowing the lawn. Along the way, our clients are learning to bring God in to their experiences, which can be gradually extended to inner distress.

For example, when a depressed Christian client has the thought, "God will not forgive me for my sins," leading to depression and anxiety, he or she can practice God's presence with the following saying: "My Lord, I surrender my thoughts to you." Or, when experiencing anxiety in an uncertain situation, he or she can say, "When I am afraid, I put my trust in you" (Psalm 56:3). In either case, the goal is to invite God in to daily tasks and psychological experiences, recognizing he is active and present throughout the day. This "simplicity of heart," as Brother Lawrence revealed, can help with a wide variety of distressing experiences, given Christian clients are learning that they are not alone as they walk through life. This awareness of

God's presence, to be sure, fortifies our ability to persevere in the midst of adversities.

Working Through Ingrained Thinking Patterns

Along the way, Christian clients can work through ingrained patterns of rumination and worry, surrendering them to God. This state of surrender can be developed via *lectio divina* (i.e., "divine reading"). Within "divine reading," we are moving through four basic steps, leading to a silent still-ness in God's presence (adapted from Benner, 2010; Knabb, 2016a):

(a) Read: the client selects and reads a short passage in Scripture that relates to depression, anxiety, God's presence, and so on.
(b) Reflect: the client thinks deeply about (that is, meditates on) the passage in Scripture, moving beyond reading to better understanding God's intentions.
(c) Respond: the client prays to God, asking God to reveal himself to the client in the present moment.
(d) Rest: the client sits in silence with God, moving to a still state, reminis-cent of Mary sitting at the feet of Jesus.

In this exercise, the goal is to focus on God's presence, deepening this experience through moving from reading the Bible to resting in God's loving arms. Along the way, the client is cultivating focused, sustained attention, pivoting away from unhelpful thinking patterns. Upon "resting in God"—a description of contemplation coined by Gregory the Great—the Christian is learning to accept difficult inner experiences, given God is active and present in the moment.

Short passages in Scripture (some of which have been slightly adapted) that are applicable include the following:

(a) "I tell you, do not worry" (Matthew 6:25).
(b) "Trust in the Lord with all your heart and lean not on your own understanding" (Proverbs 3:5).
(c) "Blessed is the one who trusts in the Lord, whose confidence is in him" (Jeremiah 17:7).
(d) "Christ suffered for you, leaving you an example, that you should follow in his steps" (1 Peter 2:21).
(e) "For just as we share abundantly in the sufferings of Christ, so also our comfort abounds through Christ" (2 Corinthians 1:5).

Ultimately, we can help our clients to have a deeper conversation with God, first turning to his Word for guidance, followed by a more intimate reflection on his promises and the ability to rest in him in the midst of pain.

Affect Regulation with Christian Detachment

Finally, Christians can practice detachment as an active strategy for surrendering to God in the midst of emotional disorders. As the reader will recall, in contrast with Buddhist practice, Christian detachment involves surrendering to God's providence, letting go of the tendency to unilaterally grasp (or push away) inner and outer experiences. Through *kataphatic* and *apophatic* meditation—reviewed above—Christians are able to learn to let go of rumination, worry, experiential avoidance, and intolerance of uncertainty.

As noted in Chapter 2, Knabb, Vazquez, Wang, and Bates (2018) found that deeply held beliefs about God's providence were linked to the ability to surrender to him. In turn, surrender was negatively correlated with repetitive negative thinking, mediated by the ability to "humbly detach." To review, in the Knabb et al. study, "humble detachment" was defined as follows:

> A detached, flexible, humble ability to (a) let go of the tendency to clutch or push away a preoccupation with inner experiences and the self, and (b) pivot from a preoccupation with the self and inner experiences to a more transcendent awareness of God's active, loving presence.
>
> (p. 172)

Christian detachment is often referred to as self-denial, self-renunciation, self-forgetfulness, and so on (Lonsdale, 2004), reflected in the birth, life, death, and resurrection of Jesus Christ. Paradoxically, detachment can help Christian clients to find freedom, given they are letting go of the experiences that get in the way of deepening their relationship with Christ (Lonsdale, 2004).

One way to cultivate Christian detachment—"correcting one's own anxious grasping in order to free oneself for committed relationship to God" (Miles, 1983, p. 111)—is for our clients to imagine relinquishing their grip on whatever it is they are mentally holding on to. Their cognitive grasp may be firm, and they may be convinced they need to strive—on their own—to hold on to their preoccupations with an "earthly minded" perspective (Ball, 2016). Yet, detachment can help them to find rest in God, given they are no longer striving to unilaterally fix themselves, which leads to exhaustion and hopelessness. Rather, detachment is about trusting in God's hands, not our own, to carry us, cultivating a "heavenly minded" viewpoint in the process (Ball, 2016). This image of "letting go" may be followed by a simple utterance of the words, "let go," to remind our clients to relinquish the grip they have on their expectations apart from God's providential plan.

To fittingly summarize detachment, Martin Luther (2009) offered the following: "I have held many things in my hands, and have lost them all; but whatever I have placed in God's hands, that I still possess" (p. 50).

A Case Example

(This and subsequent case studies are not intended to reflect the specific experience of any known individual, but to capture some common concerns among Christian clients that present for psychotherapy.)

Elaine is a 29-year-old woman who was referred for psychotherapy by her church after she showed signs of being depressed when her husband of three years left her for another woman, despite his having stated he aspired to Christian leadership and their plan to go into ministry when he finished seminary. Though they had no children, Elaine was devastated, as she had moved away from her family when they married so she could support her husband financially as he finished his graduate degree. Since he left, she has withdrawn from a number of church activities, gained ten pounds, and has lost the "spark" of personality for which she was known.

The Support Phase

Elaine was open to coming for therapy, but her therapist quickly noted her frequent use of Christian clichés to cover her pain. "Sure, I'm hurt that he left, but all things do work together for good, right?" exemplifies her failing efforts to use her faith to cope with her pain. Jane, her therapist, was patient with this unhelpful strategy by gently affirming Elaine; yet, she also focused in on the pain itself, rather than the quick cognitive fix. She asked Elaine to read Psalm 42, but only the first 4 verses where the Psalmist laments, explaining to Elaine how the hope in God found in verse 5 came only after clearly pouring out his soul (in Verse 4) to God. Jane sought to be Christ's emissary as she invited Elaine to tell her more of how her abandonment by her husband impacted her emotionally, as well as express how it raised anxious feelings in her about God himself. Though it took some work, Elaine managed to trust Jane enough to share her lament.

The Learning Phase

Once Elaine could be honest about her pain, rather than bottle it up with Christian platitudes, Jane moved into helping her client better grasp the nature of God's providence. Romans 8:28 has to be more than just words; it needs to reflect a deeper, more restful appropriation of God's providence and surrender to it. Jane helped Elaine notice that her goal had always been to serve God; her husband was simply one avenue for her to do so. Her life goal was still intact, but how God's good pleasure was to be achieved would now be via a different path.

Jane led Elaine through the three steps of moving to abandonment to divine providence described earlier. She had her journal daily of the little providences she noted each day: the calls from supportive people at church, the strength she felt while praying, the affirming word of her boss, and so on. She began to see how Psalm 42:5 flowed from the first verses as she began to hope in God. While her loss was profound and not to be ignored, God's love was still evident around her. Finally, Jane supported Elaine as she quietly sought to be still and know that God is present in the here and now, watching over her and caring for her in the suffering, rather than preventing it.

The Action Phase

This phase, in a sense, began with the journaling as an exercise. But other actions may be helpful. Elaine continued to catch herself thinking negative thoughts about her ex-husband, and even God, whenever she felt pain. Jane guided her through a simple exercise to help with this. She asked Elaine to sit comfortably with a hand on each knee and relax by focusing on her breaths. As she did so, Jane encouraged her to notice the information coming to her brain from her five senses: things she noticed in the room with her eyes, ears, and nose, and sensations she felt from her body, such as the pressure of her back on the chair, the slight tickle of her hair over her ears, and the physiological experience of her emotions. Jane asked Elaine to slightly lift her left hand whenever she was noticing the current sensory information. But, like all of us, her mind quickly ran to think about her performance, or ask questions about what she could see or hear, or drift from the moment to things past or future possibilities. Jane instructed Elaine to raise her right hand slightly when she noticed herself moving from her senses to her "head." As the exercise progressed, Elaine's hand moved back and forth numerous times. Once finished, Jane explained how we constantly move back and forth this way, missing how a thought may trigger a feeling or vice versa. By inviting Elaine to practice this during the week, Jane hoped Elaine would learn to track unpleasant feelings and accept them (rather than being so quick to interpret them), and Jane wanted her to see how negative thoughts can produce negative sensations. In turn, Elaine practiced shifting from relying on her own understanding (which was sometimes flawed or inaccurate) to trusting in God (Proverbs 3:5) in the midst of painful emotions with *kataphatic* meditation. In other words, as revealed in a previous section of this chapter, she was able to work on (a) letting go of her over-reliance on problematic thoughts and feelings, and (b) cultivating focused, sustained attention on God by recognizing his active, loving presence.

While these steps helped Elaine, clearly there was much more to be done. Yet, as she shifted her eyes from her loss to her Lord, and learned to better recognize how she was moving from thought to feeling and vice versa, she began to experience hope that God would still use her, even if it was in a different way than she had long imagined, and would help her find in him the truest and most trustworthy relationship, helped by the alliance she built with Jane.

Conclusion

In this chapter, we focused on the "theology" pillar, moving from support, to learning, to action. Along the way, we offered a range of Christian-distinctive goals and interventions for therapists to operate from within a Christian worldview in the therapy room. In that the primary focus was on surrendering to God's providential care, we offered Christian meditative practices that can help Christian clients to pivot from repetitive negative thinking to God, deepening their attachment bond with him in the process.

With the next pillar, we will be focusing on the nature of both reality and knowledge, which naturally flow from God. In doing so, our hope is that Christian clients will come to embrace a relational understanding of reality, with God at the center of existence, given that God is active in the midst of emotional suffering. In this second pillar, a central theme involves Christians recognizing that a healthy dependence on God is vital for understanding reality and knowledge.

Notes

1 This exercise is adapted from Brueggemann (1984), Knabb (2016a), and Knabb (2018), and influenced by Dworsky et al. (2013). See also Card (2007) for a straightforward, pragmatic exploration of the lament.
2 One of the first references to the Jesus Prayer comes from Abba Philimon in the 6th or 7th century, recorded in the *Philokalia*: "Lord Jesus Christ, Son of God, have mercy upon me" (Pryne, 2015). Over time, variations of the prayer have been practiced, with the "a sinner" "added later by an unknown Russian *hesychast*" (Chumley, 2014, p. 83). Thus, the longest form in the contemporary Eastern Orthodox tradition is "Lord Jesus Christ, Son of God, have mercy on me, a sinner."
3 Research has found that diaphragmatic breathing can be an important part of relaxation therapy, reducing stress, anxiety, and sadness (Haslett-Stevens & Craske, 2011). The opposite kind of breathing—shallow and from the lungs—is actually a symptom of anxiety. So, clients should be guided in breathing that moves their stomach up and down and not so much their chest.

References

Allender, D., & Longman, T. (1993). *The Cry of the Soul: How Our Emotions Reveal Our Deepest Questions about God*. Colorado Springs, CO: NavPress.
American Psychiatric Association (2013). *Diagnostic and Statistical Manual of Mental Disorders* (5th ed.). Washington, DC: APA.
Ball, J. (2016). *A Treatise of Divine Meditation*. Crossville, TN: Puritan Publications.
Baxter, R. (2015). *The Saints' Everlasting Rest*. Louisville, KY: GLH Publishing.
Beeke, J., & Jones, M. (2012). *A Puritan Theology: Doctrine for Life*. Grand Rapids, MI: Reformation Heritage Books.

Benner, D. (2010). *Opening to God: Lectio Divina and Life as Prayer*. Downers Grove, IL: InterVarsity Press.

Bingaman, B. (Ed.) (2012). *The Philokalia: A Classic Text of Orthodox Spirituality*. New York: Oxford University Press.

Brueggemann, W. (1984). *The Message of the Psalms: A Theological Commentary*. Minneapolis, MN: Augsburg Publishing House.

Card, M. (2007). *The Hidden Face of God: Finding the Missing Door to the Father through Lament*. Colorado Springs, CO: NavPress.

Caryl, J. (2001). *An Exposition with Practical Observations upon the Book of Job* (10 Vols.). Berkley, MI: Dust and Ashes Publications.

Chang, V., Scott, S., & Decker, C. (2013). *Developing Helping Skills: A Step-by-Step Approach to Competency* (2nd ed.). Belmont, CA: Brooks/Cole.

Chawla, N., & Ostafin, B. (2007). Experiential avoidance as a functional dimensional approach to psychopathology: An empirical review. *Journal of Clinical Psychology, 63*, 871–890.

Chumley, N. (2014). *Be Still and Know: God's Presence in Silence*. Minneapolis, MN: Augsburg Fortress.

Cutler, D. (2003). *Western Mysticism: Augustine, Gregory and Bernard on Contemplation and the Contemplative Life*. New York: Dover Publications.

Davis, E., Moriarty, G., & Mauch, J. (2013). God images and God concepts: Definitions, development, and dynamics. *Psychology of Religion and Spirituality, 5*, 51–60.

de Cassaude, J. (1921). *Abandonment to Divine Providence*. St. Louis, MO: B. Herder Book Company.

Dugas, M., & Robichaud, M. (2007). *Cognitive-Behavioral Treatment for Generalized Anxiety Disorder: From Science to Practice*. New York: Routledge.

Dworsky, C., Pargament, K., Gibbel, M., Krumrei, E., Faigin, C., Haugen, M., Desai, K., Lauricella, S., Lynn, Q., & Warner, H. (2013). Winding road: Preliminary support for a spiritually integrated intervention addressing college students' spiritual struggles. *Research in the Social Scientific Study of Religion, 24*, 309–339.

Ehring, T., & Watkins, E. (2008). Repetitive negative thinking as a transdiagnostic process. *International Journal of Cognitive Therapy, 1*, 192–205.

Eifert, G., & Forsyth, J. (2005). *Acceptance and Commitment Therapy for Anxiety Disorders: A Practitioner's Treatment Guide to Using Mindfulness, Acceptance, and Values-Based Behavior Change Strategies*. Oakland, CA: New Harbinger Publications.

Flavel, J. (2017). *The Mystery of Providence*. Zeeland, MI: Reformed Church Publications.

Francis, A. (2013). *Saving Normal: An Insider's Revolt against Out-of-Control Psychiatric Diagnosis, DSM-5, Big Pharma, and the Medicalization of Ordinary Life*. New York: HarperCollins Publishers.

Gregory, E., & Rutledge, P. (2016). *Exploring Positive Psychology: The Science of Happiness and Well-Being*. Santa Barbara, CA: Greenwood.

Hall, J. (2016). *The Art of Divine Meditation*. Titus Books.

Hazlett-Stevens, H., & Craske, M. G. (2009). Breathing retraining and diaphragmatic breathing. In W. T. O'Donohue & J. T. Fisher (Eds.), *General Principles and Empirically Supported Techniques of Cognitive Behavior Therapy* (pp. 166–172). New York: Wiley.

Hayes, S., Strosahl, K., & Wilson, K. (2012). *Acceptance and Commitment Therapy: The Process and Practice of Mindful Change* (2nd ed.). New York: The Guilford Press.

Johnson, C. (2010). *The Globalization of Hesychasm and the Jesus Prayer: Contesting Contemplation*. New York: Continuum.

Johnson, E. L. (2007). *Foundations for Soul Care: A Christian Psychology Proposal*. Downers Grove, IL: InterVarsity Press.

Johnson, E. L. (2017). *God and Soul Care: The Therapeutic Resources of the Christian Faith*. Downers Grove, IL: InterVarsity Press.

Keller, T. (2015). *Walking with God through Pain and Suffering*. New York: Riverhead Books.

Killingsworth, M., & Gilbert, D. (2010). A wandering mind is an unhappy mind. *Science, 330*, 932.

Kirkpatrick, L., & Shaver, P. (1990). Attachment theory and religion: Childhood attachments, religious beliefs, and conversion. *Journal for the Scientific Study of Religion, 29*, 315–334.

Knabb, J. (2016a). *Acceptance and Commitment Therapy for Christian Clients: A Faith-Based Workbook*. New York: Routledge.

Knabb, J. (2016b). *Faith-Based ACT for Christian Clients: An Integrative Treatment Approach*. New York: Routledge.

Knabb, J. (2018). *The Compassion-Based Workbook for Christian Clients: Finding Freedom from Shame and Negative Self-Judgments*. New York: Routledge.

Knabb, J., & Emerson, M. (2013). "I will be your God and you will be my people": Attachment theory and the grand narrative of scripture. *Pastoral Psychology, 62*, 827–841.

Knabb, J., & Vazquez, V. (2018). A randomized controlled trial of a 2-week Internet-based contemplative prayer program for Christians with daily stress. *Spirituality in Clinical Practice, 5*, 37–53.

Knabb, J., Frederick, T., & Cumming, G. (2017). Surrendering to God's providence: A three-part study on providence-focused therapy for recurrent worry (PFT-RW). *Psychology of Religion and Spirituality, 9*, 180–196.

Knabb, J., Vazquez, V., Wang, K., & Bates, T. (2018). "Unknowing" in the 21st century: Humble detachment for Christians with repetitive negative thinking. *Spirituality in Clinical Practice, 5*, 170-187.

Kristeller, J., & Johnson, T. (2005). Cultivating loving kindness: A two-stage model of the effects of meditation on empathy, compassion, and altruism. *Zygon, 40*, 391–407.

Krystal, H. (1988). *Integration and Self-Healing: Affect, Trauma, Alexithymia*. New York: Routledge.

Lambert, M. (2013). The efficacy and effectiveness of psychotherapy. In M. Lambert (Ed.), *Bergin and Garfield's Handbook of Psychotherapy and Behavior Change* (pp. 169–218). New York: John Wiley & Sons.

Langberg, D. (2015). *Suffering and the Heart of God: How Trauma Destroys and Christ Restores*. Greensboro, NC: New Growth Press.

Lawrence, B. (2015). *The Practice of the Presence of God* (S. Sciurba, Trans.). Washington, DC: ICS Publications.

Lawrence, R. (1997). Measuring the image of God: The God image inventory and the God image scales. *Journal of Psychology and Theology, 25*, 214–226.

Lonsdale, D. (2005). Detachment. In P. Sheldrake (Ed.), *The New Westminster Dictionary of Christian Spirituality* (p. 234). Louisville, KY: Westminster John Knox Press.

Luther, M. (2009). *Luther Gold*. Alachua, FL: Bridge-Logos.

Mahoney, A., & McEvoy, P. (2012). A transdiagnostic examination of intolerance of uncertainty across anxiety and depressive disorders. *Cognitive Behaviour Therapy, 41*, 212–222.

Matera, F. (2003). *II Corinthians: A Commentary*. Louisville, KY: Westminster John Knox Press.

Mikulincer, M., & Shaver, P. (2004). Security-based self-representations in adulthood: Contents and processes. In W. Rholes & J. Simpson (Eds.), *Adult Attachment: Theory, Research, and Clinical Implications* (pp. 159–195). New York: The Guilford Press.

Miles, M. (1983). Detachment. In G. Wakefield (Ed.), *The Westminster Dictionary of Christian Spirituality* (p. 111). Philadelphia, PA: The Westminster Press.

Morgan, D. (2001). Assimilation from the East and the spectrum of consciousness. *Journal of Psychotherapy Integration, 11*, 87–104.

Moser, P. (2013). *The Severity of God: Religion and Philosophy Reconceived*. New York: Cambridge University Press.

Paris, J. (2013). The ideology behind DSM-5. In J. Paris & J. Phillips (Eds.), *Making the DSM-5: Concepts and Controversies* (pp. 39–46). New York: Springer.

Pascal, B. (2017). *Thoughts, Prayers, and Minor Works of Blaise Pascal*. Retrieved from https://archive.org/details/thoughtslettersm028185mbp

Pennington, J. (2018). *The Sermon on the Mount and Human Flourishing: A Commentary*. Grand Rapids, MI: Baker.

Pryne, R. (Ed.) (2015). *The Philokalia: The Complete Text*. Philadelphia, PA: The Great Library Collection.

Ranew, N. (1995). *Solitude Improved by Divine Meditation*. Morgan, PA: Soli Deo Gloria.

Sahdra, B. K., Shaver, P. R., & Brown, K. W. (2010). A scale to measure nonattachment: A Buddhist complement to Western research on attachment and adaptive functioning. *Journal of Personality Assessment, 92*, 116–127.

Saint-Jure, J., & Colombiere, C. (1980). *Trustful Surrender to Divine Providence: The Secret to Peace and Happiness*. Charlotte, NC: TAN Books.

Schreiner, T. (2015). *Commentary on Hebrews*. Nashville, TN: Holman Reference.

Siegel, A. (1996). *Heinz Kohut and the Psychology of the Self*. New York: Routledge.

Sisemore, T. (2014). Acceptance and commitment therapy: A Christian translation. *Christian Psychology, 8*, 5–15.

Talbot, J. (2013). *The Jesus Prayer: A Cry for Mercy, a Path of Renewal*. Downers Grove, IL: InterVarsity Press.

Thomas, M., Moriarty, G., Davis, E., & Anderson, E. (2011). The effects of a manualized group-psychotherapy intervention on client God images and attachment to God: A pilot study. *Journal of Psychology and Theology, 39*, 44–58.

Watson, T. (2012). *A Treatise Concerning Meditation*. Charleston, SC: Waxkeep Publishing.

Zettle, R. (2007). *ACT for Depression: A Clinician's Guide to Using Acceptance and Commitment Therapy in Treating Depression*. Oakland, CA: New Harbinger Publications.

CHAPTER 4

Ontology and Epistemology in the Christian Tradition

Introduction

The opening words of the Bible are as arresting in their brevity as they are in their profundity: "In the beginning God created the heavens and the earth." It rings the declaration of the world. God, existing from all eternity in the shared love of the inter-Trinitarian life, creates the world in his perfect freedom—he needs nothing and is dependent upon nothing. Yet, he creates, and in creating, he is the source of all existent reality. Nature is not an independent, self-existing, self-orienting entity, but is called into existence. God's voice knowingly and intentionally speaks the world into being, and its existence is a reply to God. Thus, all reality stands in relation to the God who knows and speaks, hanging open and attentive to the One who is the source of all things.

This understanding of creation gives the Christian tradition a formative view of existent things (ontology) and what it means to know such things (epistemology). The focus of this chapter is to consider the ontological and epistemological implications of God's triune activity in creation—specifically, how a deeper understanding of creation can offer support in the clinical context. The world need not be seen as a scary place, and our experiences in it need not be filled with uneasiness. We can approach it with confidence, knowing this is our Father's world. All things, including our painful experiences, stand before our Father and are responsive to his hand.

Reality as an Event of Communion

Within the Christian tradition, the inter-Trinitarian life establishes the personal and relational character of God. In creation, God's character is further seen as he personally creates the world, filling and ordering nature according to his wisdom and goodness, and granting life to the world from his infinite triune life. The fullness and order with which God invests in the universe is deeply unified and interconnected, which should not surprise us because the source of creation is the one God in three persons, Father, Son, and Holy

Spirit. Thus, creation reflects its source in its deep unity, as well as rich diversity. Physicist and theologian John Polkinghorne stated:

> Christian theology speaks of God as the One whose eternal being is constituted by the perichoretic exchange of love between the three divine Persons. Thus the deepest reality is relational, and this will surely be the character of all that originates from that divine source.
>
> (Polkinghorne, 2010, p. 12)

We can, then, given a deeply relational view of God, view creation itself as relational. First, all creation stands in relation to God. As we will see, the world does not exist independently of God; so, to the extent that anything exists, it exists in relation to God. Second, all creation is an inter-related whole. Each part exists in a sort of interconnected, perhaps entangled, way. In this sense, consistent with the Christian tradition, reality is relational; it is through this *relational ontology* that our world should be understood.

Relational ontology, or the inter-relatedness of reality, stems from a robust view of the inter-Trinitarian relations. Though the inter-related nature of creation should not be equated with the inter-Trinitarian life—remember God's transcendence—we can catch "signs" of God's essence through the unfolding of God's works in, and active sustaining of, the world. Creation is the most brilliant mirror of the divine majesty (Bavinck, 2004). The inter-relatedness, then, should be understood analogously, which means that there are genuine similarities, but also very distinct ontological differences. This even extends to our categories of thought, such as "relationship" and "substance," which are conceptions concerning the created order. While they are important and helpful, they, too, are used analogously. So, we should keep in mind Gregory of Nyssa's advice, "We say that every name, whether invented by human custom or handed down by Scriptures, is indicative of our conceptions of the divine nature, but does not signify what the nature is in itself" (Gregory of Nyssa, 1954, p. 259). Again, we must stay close to Scripture and attend carefully to how God discloses himself to us.

Being rooted in the inter-Trinitarian relations, relational ontology establishes that reality is a place of communion, "overflowing with the fatherhood of God, the mediation of Christ, and the tending of the Spirit" (Canlis, 2010, p. 54). In the Christian tradition, reality can only be truly understood when it is seen in its relation to God, who is its source, sustenance, and end toward which it strives. The deep connection between God and reality, however, should always be seen in light of God's personal transcendence that was enumerated in the first chapter. Keeping this in mind provides a way of avoiding two common errors—identifying creation and God in a form of pantheism or making creation independent and mechanistically self-perpetuating in a type of deism. Both of these tendencies stem from the same problem of improperly viewing the relationship between God and the world (Bavinck, 2004). To see more clearly the proper relationship between God and world, we begin our study with the biblical account of creation.

Creating Reality

God's involvement with creation is portrayed in Scripture as a deeply personal act. In Genesis, the Bible opens with these words:

> In the beginning God created the heavens and the earth. Now the earth was formless and empty, darkness was over the surface of the deep, and the Spirit of God was hovering over the waters. And God said...
>
> (Genesis 1:1–3)

Several things should be noted from this description. First, we are told that God was before anything else was. As we saw in the first chapter, God's *aseity* means he transcends all created things—he is independent from all other contingent and created things. God, though transcendent, is personally present and speaks creation into existence. Because of our familiarity with these ideas, the audacity of these words is easily missed. God personally calling reality into existence has profound implications, one of which is that God is unquestionably relational. Derek Kidner (2008), an Old Testament scholar and former Warden of Tyndale House, Cambridge University, commented:

> From the outset, Genesis confronts us with the Living God, unmistakably personal. The verbs of the opening chapter express an energy of mind, will and judgement which excludes all questions of our conceiving God in the category of "it" instead of the "Thou"... and the book continues to make this emphasis in its account of man's constitution in God's image, and of God's persistent concern for a personal relationship with his servants.
>
> (Kidner, 2008, p. 34)

The weightiness of our existence should also be seen in this light. If we have life, it did not just happen, and we are not accidental. We were called into existence for relationship by the Author of life. Humans, not just the rest of creation, stand in relation to God. When we experience pain—particularly when struggling with doubt, anxiety, and depression—it is easy to withdraw, which can enhance our sense of isolation and loneliness. To understand creation rightly is to understand that we are not isolated or alone. Both humans and nature stand before God, who called, shaped, and guides us in and through all things.

A second thing we can see in the opening words of Scripture is that, while God creates *ex nihilo*, out of nothing—stressing God's independence from creation—God lovingly cares for, and brings form and order to, his creation. The image is clear in the hovering of the Spirit of God. There is no tension or opposition between creation and God, as if God must somehow wrestle intractable nature into conformity. Rather, the Spirit, as often used in the Old Testament, is God's dynamic energy, creating and sustaining God's work (Kidner, 2008). God was intimately involved in forming his world, not in detached fiat, caringly hovering over it and bringing form to what was formless and fullness to what was void.

God's fatherly caring continues in every moment creation is sustained. One of the Psalms displays this care by saying:

> How many are your works, Lord! In wisdom you made them all; the earth is full of your creatures... All creatures look to you to give them their food at the proper time. When you give it to them, they gather it up; when you open your hand, they are satisfied with good things.
>
> (104:24, 27–28)

In echo of the opening words of Genesis and praise of God's generous provision, the psalmist continues, "When you send your Spirit, they are created, and you renew the face of the ground. May the glory of the Lord endure forever, may the Lord rejoice in his works" (104:30–31). The last phrase is revealing. God delights in what he has created. In the Genesis account, God declared that the world, including its fullness, is "very good." God not only creates and sustains all things, but delights in his creation. Moreover, his delight is its sustenance—John Calvin, commenting on this verse, said that the stability of the world depends on this rejoicing of God in his works (Calvin, 2003).

The inherent orderliness of creation that is communicated in Genesis is affirmed and deepened in the gospel of John. The opening words are an intentional echo of Genesis:

> In the beginning was the Word, and the Word was with God, and the Word was God. He was with God in the beginning. Through him all things were made; without him nothing was made that has been made. In him was life, and that life was the light of all mankind.
>
> (John 1:1–4)

The Word, or *Logos*, the second person of the Trinity, is the orderer of all that is created. Paul's words in Colossians 1:15–17 affirm the activity of the Son in creation:

> The Son is the image of the invisible God, the firstborn over all creation. For in him all things were created: things in heaven and on earth, visible and invisible, whether thrones or powers or rulers or authorities; all things have been created through him and for him. He is before all things, and in him all things hold together.

The clear and consistent message of the Bible is that creation, redemption, and final consummation (i.e., restoration) are the result of God's dynamic interpersonal activity and the constitution of reality; yet, our place in it will always be mischaracterized and misconstrued if this relational truth is not central. This holds also for the clinical context. As such, it is worth reflecting on the implications of a distinctly relational ontology for Christian psychotherapy.

Reality and Communion

The personal foundation of all of creation shapes how Christians understand and approach the world. Not only do all things exist in relationship to God, nothing has life in itself. To state this Christian understanding more directly, God *is* life, and everything else *has* life derivatively. Here, it is important to see that all created things are imbued with the power to exist, but this power should not be misconstrued as independence from God. Existence is a gift from God. Yet, not having self-existence is not an inadequacy in things, but makes a created thing a *created* thing. The inherent incompleteness that created things have can only find completeness in relationship with God.

At this point, a few things need to be considered. First, a lack of self-existence or autonomy does not mean a lack of integrity (Smith, 2004). Things that are created by God have a genuine goodness that is intrinsic because they have been made good by God. They have a goodness in how they are ordered, shaped, and exist. The particulars of each created object are integrated into a remarkable whole—in their particularity, and together as a whole, they have creaturely integrity. However, that integrity, while genuine, can never be separated from God. Consider this comment by theologian Lars Thunberg: "Being as created life is at the same time at every stage only a participation in what God gives to his creation out of his own being, goodness, wisdom and life" (Thunberg, 1995, p. 85). Recall in the first chapter where the image of God was said to be reflected in humans. Now, we can broaden this concept to the life and goodness of all creation. God gives to creation all its being, order, wisdom, and beauty.

Human efforts that attempt to elevate the material world by establishing autonomy from God often struggle with affirming the inherent dignity of created things. Ironically, without its proper orientation toward God, the goodness or power of created things can become a functional matter. Something may be good to the extent that it serves some utilitarian purpose—usually that of the self or others. When it ceases to function beneficially, it may no longer be considered good. The world can become full of disposable things to be used, neglected, or rejected based on their functionality. If, however, the dignity of created things is based on its relationship to God and his gifts to it, then all things have purpose and dignity beyond functionality. They have creaturely integrity. The worth of the world, including human worth, is not dependent upon what we do, but who we are as created by God and for communion with God.

Another implication of creaturely integrity is a positive view of the material world. The "stuff" of nature and our own embodiment are not errors. The matter out of which the world was made is not simply what happened to be on hand when God created; rather, it was called into existence by a God who invests himself in shaping and ordering it. The world, in all its fullness, should be approached with a deepened sense of communion with God (Canlis, 2010). Reality truly is a place of communion.

Because of the importance of the material world in the Christian tradition, our empirical interactions with the world have deep value. There is merit to empirical observations and studies that can yield important information that helps us live better, healthier lives. The benefits of attentive study of God's creation is what we might expect, given that

> God for our sake has so magnificently adorned the world, in order that we may not only be spectators of this beauteous theatre, but also enjoy the multiplied abundance and variety of good things which are presented to us in it.
>
> (Calvin, 2003, p. 169)

So, the merit of intensive study of the created order need not devolve into a myopic ontological materialism, where the material world is viewed as independent and autonomous—which, as mentioned above, can promote an "egocentric" functional view of the world. Creation in the Christian tradition supports a robust theory of empirical study without reductive materialism because, according to relational ontology, the study of the created order is an act of communion with the God who created it, whether the one who studies it recognizes it or not.

The inherent orderliness of creation supports both the pursuit and truth of empirical discoveries. It is easy to overlook this fact. God has created such a remarkably full and ordered world that even those who do not know God or receive his creational gifts with gratitude can still make extraordinary discoveries—discoveries that are true and genuinely beneficial to humankind. St. Augustine (1997) famously said that "a true Christian should realize that truth belongs to his Lord, wherever it is found" (p. 47). The person who discovers truth in the empirical world does not make it true, but, rather, points to a truth that is in the world due to it being created by a good and caring God. In the Christian tradition, the truth discovered in the world is a result of what is often called God's "general revelation" (although some contemporary authors prefer the term "common grace"). As Augustine mentioned, there is no truth independent of God. Thus, while empirical research can yield beneficial truths about our world, the world and truth can never be reduced to empirical research. The richness of the world bespeaks an extraordinary fullness; the depths of this richness, however, are only plumbed in communion with its Creator. It is the Christian's privilege to know the God of creation and commune with him while living, studying, and enjoying his good world; this is a privilege that we should not lose sight of in our preoccupation with otherwise good things.

One final point worth contemplating is an often unnoticed corollary of the creaturely integrity and physical dignity of the world. The very concepts of creaturely integrity and materiality require finitude. Unique objects are defined by their boundaries—boundaries literally make things what they are, in their uniqueness. This simply means that created things have limits. In addition, the existence they have is marked by dependence, first on God, then on other created things. This finitude and dependence are not a failure of creation—not a result of the fall—but the very definition of being created; thus, something other than God. As mentioned above, the world was never meant to be independent or complete in itself; it is complete only in relation with God. It is in communion with God, who is the fullness of all creation, that reality finds its completion.

The dependent nature of creation also indicates the direction toward which creation is oriented. God is the source of life, but he is also the end toward which life is directed. Thus, the incompleteness that comes from being a contingent, created thing also means that our life is directed toward God, and it is in relationship with God that we find the completion for which we were created.

While it sounds counter-intuitive, our being incomplete was not originally negative or problematic. We were inter-related parts in a larger whole, and this whole stood open to, and complete only in dependence upon, God —the very definition of relational ontology. Our incompleteness became problematic when humankind turned from God in sin. In alienation from him, we lost our orientation, and the whole became fragmented. Each part now, because it is only a part, cannot regain the whole. Because we were created as part of an inter-related whole, we struggle with our identity. We, as humans, now experience existential displacement.

Broken Communion and Fragmented Whole

As seen from Scripture, the origin of the world is from the loving, personal, relational acts of a good God. The world does not come about through strife or tension between light versus darkness or spiritual versus physical forces. God lovingly and caringly shapes and forms what he calls into existence and nurtures it in growth. God, then, entrusts his good creation to those created to care for it in faithful obedience. In obedience, both creation and its caretakers would experience the completeness for which they were made in communion with God. The dominion which Adam and Eve were to have over creation was to bring to actuality the inherent bountiful potential of God's fullness in the world—an expression of his generous riches.

When Adam and Eve turned away from God in disobedience, they removed themselves from communion with God and *dis*-placed themselves from the ordered whole directed toward God into *dis*-ordered fragmentation. The directedness toward order has not been destroyed, but broken. Adam and Eve give us a glimpse of the human effort to self-direction as they attempt to define for themselves how they will live in independence of God's will—they attempt to be like God. As finite, contingent, and inherently incomplete parts of a larger inter-related whole, humankind has ever since sought to define for ourselves how we will live. Yet, with the loss of proper orientation toward God, attempts toward order are now a human effort to "create" a meaningful whole from the fragmentation. Because of human finitude and *dis*-orientation, such efforts are inadequate and often lead to existential bewilderment, isolation, depression, and anxiety. Further, the very human impulse toward dominion over creation now issues forth as domination of creation, turning all things toward, and defining all things by, the self.

Though fragmentation and alienation are common human experiences in our fallen world, this does not mean creation ceases to be in relationship to God. The world is still God's and stands open to him as he sustains it and continually works toward restoration through Christ. Though strained through fragmentation, the interconnected and entangled universe remains defined by its relational ontology. Romans 8:19–25 reminds us that we live in a broken world, but not a world without hope. All of creation is now subjected to futility and frustration. As wonderfully bountiful as our world is (e.g., we encounter goodness and beauty every day), it is a pale comparison of what it once was and will one day be again. To the Lord's voice, creation still responds. The brokenness we encounter and alienation we experience is still under God's providential, fatherly control. He weaves our experiences together with his plan to conform us into the image of Christ. So, like creation, we await God's final act of redemption with a hopeful longing.

Our current existential displacement, however, remains painful, and we experience it in many ways. The effects of the fall extend to all of creation, including Christians. It extends to Christians with emotional disorders, who may struggle to understand the role that God played in their past and now plays in their daily experiences, including psychiatric symptoms and disordered functioning. Christian clients, for example, may view God as somehow distant and detached from their pain. Yet, because God created humankind to be dependent on him as the source of goodness, pivoting from self-sufficiency to a trusting, yielding stance before God is central to Christian mental health, even in the midst of pain and suffering. By drawing from a Christian relational ontology (rather than ontological materialism), therapists can help Christian clients to steadily move from an incomplete pseudo-autonomy and independence to completeness in God, emphasizing that reality understood in light of Christianity facilitates communion with God, the perfect source of all that is good.

Rather than revealing some sort of pathology, this healthy dependence on God as the source of goodness is part of God's original design for reality, which means Christians can find comfort in this innate, natural need for God. Although psychological suffering (e.g., depression, anxiety) is a by-product of the incompleteness and brokenness of humankind after the fall (via originally turning away from God as the source of life), cultivating a deeper relationship with him can help to buffer the negative effects of daily living (as Christians patiently and faithfully wait for God's eventual restoration of a broken world). In therapy, Christians can focus on (among other therapeutic goals) developing a deeper understanding of suffering and healing by drawing from a Christian relational ontology, finding comfort in knowing that God is actively calling us to return to communion with him as the supportive, stable, unwavering center of existence.

Indeed, because all reality stands in relationship with God, our experiences of brokenness in the world are used by God as a means of healing. Recall God's providence from the first chapter, including how his concurrent power is at work in and through our experiences by lovingly and mercifully applying only what is necessary for our good—which is forming us into the image of his beloved Son. Christian clients can gain insight into their own disordered functioning, recognizing their innate need for God in the midst of suffering, and begin to practice healthy new behaviors as they move towards relying on God for effective daily living. In relationship with God, then, humans come to know more deeply who we are and our deep need of him.

Epistemology within the Christian Tradition

Human knowledge can come from a variety of sources, including empirical research and special revelation (Entwistle, 2015). With empirical research, we can understand God's world through the various methods of science—operating on, and through, "general revelation," as well as God's "common grace," which is the source of all good science. We use our God-given minds to better understand the world God made. As we will see below, humans are embedded knowers, which means there are always beliefs about reality, knowledge, and humankind that shape and direct empirical research. Thus, while these two ways of knowing are commonly seen as antithetical, Christian researchers should be honest about what influences and informs their empirical research—namely, special revelation. These ways of knowing, for example, can work in unison when researchers in clinical psychology use deductive reasoning in quantitative research methods by generating hypotheses that are grounded in biblical truths about optimal psychological and spiritual functioning.

Though empirical research is certainly possible without special revelation, there will always be "background beliefs" that inform the researcher. Thus, ontological materialism, which informs much empirical research today, is no less a belief about reality, knowledge, and humankind. All genuine knowledge, as Augustine alluded, is a gift of God either in general revelation or special revelation, and learning obtained independently of Scripture is critiqued there if it is harmful and confirmed there if helpful (Augustine, 1997). Special revelation, then, informs Christian approaches to empiricism and must be taken into account when developing a Christian-sensitive psychotherapy model.

Knowledge as an Act of Communion

Human knowledge is, like reality itself, inescapably relational. Rooted in relational ontology, "knowing" entails interacting and coming to grips with our surroundings, or, rather, becoming attentive to the relations we have always been in. Relational ontology forms the context for, and conditions of, the development of all human knowledge. As such, knowing always involves the self in relation to other persons and things—knowing is always a knowledge "of." So, reality as an *event* of communion constitutes knowledge as an *act* of communion. Relational knowing, then, is not passive, but active, grounded in contact with the world, not as distant observers, but persons deeply engaged in the process with others. Scientist and philosopher Michael Polanyi put it this way, "into every act of knowing there enters a passionate contribution of the person knowing what is being known, and that this coefficient is no mere imperfection but a vital component of his knowledge" (1978, p. viii).

The dynamic nature of knowing involves the passionate contribution that we as knowers bring to our encounters, but knowing is far from one-sided. Philosopher Hubert Dreyfus argued that knowledge

> is the contact of living, active beings, whose life form involves acting in and on a world which also acts on them. These beings are at grips with the world and each other; this original contact provides the sense-making context for all their knowledge constructions.
>
> (Dreyfus & Taylor, 2015, p. 18)

The "original contact" Dreyfus mentioned is the relational context of knowing that makes it an act of communion.

For the Christian, the communion occurring in our acts of knowing should deepen our appreciation for our daily tasks and ennoble all the little interactions with creation that we experience. Christian philosopher Esther Meek (2003) pointed to this when she said:

> knowing God has unlocked the world for me. In knowing him I engage the world. To affirm: "I believe in God, the Father Almighty, Maker of heaven and earth; and in Jesus Christ, his only Son, our Lord..." opens vista upon vista. You can see a tree as a chance collocation of atoms, randomly evolved from a primordial soup. You can see

a tree as conforming to impersonal laws that regulate its behavior. But these come up short: neither tells us why the tree is there, why it is reliably there, and why I should respectfully get to know it. But see the tree as a thing made and moved by the utterly faithful words of an infinite person for his own delight, on whose ways we will know better as we explore the tree, and you have unlocked both the wonder of the tree and the majesty of God. Plus, you grasp yourself better, too: you are a knower who images and walks before God among the other things he has made. You are not God. They are not God. But you and they are made by him and thus fraught with significance and value.

(p. 144)

As dynamic personal knowers, we not only see the wonders of the created world, we are encountering nothing short of the glory of God, its creator. But if this is so, why do many of our experiences and encounters with the world seem so difficult and confusing? This salient question characterizes many of our very human interactions with the world. If we are encountering God's glory in all our encounters, why are they so perplexing? The answer needs to be considered in light of a few other aspects of the Christian tradition.

Knowing and the Loss of Communion

The short answer to why the world is so perplexing is the broken communion that occurs during the fall. But this is further complicated by two other factors—human knowers are embodied and embedded creatures.

Human embodiment is not an accident of creation. God created us as embodied beings to live in a "bodied" world, and he declared his creation good. Though our current embodied life is laden with disorder because of sin, our embodiment is not a mistake of creation—remember that God the Son became embodied to redeem our embodiment. Nor should our knowing in an "embodied" way be considered a misfortune, even with its consequent limits and finitude. Like our "incompleteness," this was not a problem in itself. Even in the Garden of Eden, human knowledge, while true, was not exhaustive. Knowing was unproblematic because communion was as natural as breathing. It becomes problematic after the fall—more on that below.

Because knowledge arises through our everyday embodied contact in a relational world, we are active knowers long before we are aware that we are active knowers. We grow up into knowing through our interactions with the world. This is what it means to be an "embedded" knower. We are embedded in all sorts of knowing relationships that operate in the background of all our focused engagements. Theologian John Apczynski (2017) wrote, "A knowing person always is engaged within a world, which includes the physical environment as well as the social and cultural features shaping the knower's relationship to the world" (p. 8). Our embeddedness is always involved in our daily experiences with the world. It forms the background or framework that informs and orients all our interactions. Due to our embeddedness as knowers, all human thinking and reasoning occurs within a framework, or "background beliefs," some of which include narratives. These background beliefs, including our narratives, order human experiences, giving them meaning by "placing" them in relation to larger and more fundamental beliefs and stories about the world. In other words, thinking always operates from a perspective.

Human rationality is a great gift of God, given so that we can commune with him and cultivate his creation as stewards and "sub-creators." Humans remain rational creatures after the fall, but because of the loss of communion, human frameworks lack the natural orientation toward God, and human rationality now turns back on itself—making the self the source and goal of all knowledge. Despite this, and because of God's goodness to all humans—sometimes called common grace—human interactions with the world still yield profound results. As mentioned above, while non-Christians may not know the Creator of the world, their deep study of the world through scientific investigation brings great discoveries that are beneficial to all (e.g., the "common factors" literature we draw from in this very book). Using inductive and deductive reasoning, for example, researchers in clinical psychology can better understand psychological phenomena through qualitative and quantitative research. To be sure, this should only deepen our amazement at God's grace and wonder of his creation.

In God's grace, though, he did not leave us to make our way with disordered frameworks. For Christians, God's revelation to us in the Bible explains the human dilemma of existence, how we got here, and what God has done for us. In the grand narrative of Scripture, we can understand God's original design (i.e., health), what has gone wrong (i.e., dysfunction), and how God goes about providing a remedy (i.e., healing). Although scientific exploration and reason can help us understand some of these phenomena, Scripture is Christianity's primary source of knowledge and interpretive guide, which informs and transforms our minds, while creating a framework by which all other knowledge is ordered.

As we turn to the Bible for guidance, we see a fairly candid picture about the current state of the fallen human mind, which is said to be "futile" (Ephesians 4:17; Romans 1:21). Interestingly, the same root word in the Greek is also used for creation in Romans 8:20, where we are told that "creation was subjected to frustration" after the fall. As we saw above, the fullness and beauty of the world, as wonderful as it remains, falls short of what it could be. It does not produce as it was originally intended to. So, too, with the human mind. Being alienated from God, the reasonable ordering of human experiences is turned back on the self as the ultimate arbiter of truth and goodness. The results are detailed in Ephesians 4:18, "They are darkened in their understanding and separated from the life of

God because of the ignorance that is in them due to the hardening of their hearts." The everyday experiences of God's world that are gifts of communion intended to turn us in gratitude toward God are, instead (by the alienated mind), turned toward the self, making the mind futile—making our thinking "vain." For this reason, a distinctly Christian psychotherapy emphasizes God's Word, the Bible, rather than solely relying on empiricism. In other words, due to the fall, our ability to fully understand psychological phenomena through reason and the scientific method will be flawed.

This understanding is confirmed in Colossians 1:16–17, "For in him all things were created; things in heaven and on earth, visible and invisible... all things have been created through him and form him. He is before all things, and in him all things hold together." This last clause is significant. It is in Christ that all things hold together, that all things are formed into the coherent whole we call creation. The common fragmentation we experience defies our attempts to develop a meaningful whole; and our finitude— that is, our being embodied and embedded—constantly frustrates the effort.

Though sin has fragmented the whole, Colossians goes on to tell of the healing that occurs in Christ. The writer of Colossians 1:19–20 said, "For God was pleased to have all his fullness dwell in him, and through him to reconcile to himself all things, whether things on earth or things in heaven, by making peace through his blood, shed on the cross." So, not only are all things created and held together in Christ, they are now healed through reconciliation in Christ. It is not simply the world that is reconciled, but humans, too. Again, the writer of Colossians offered:

> Once you were alienated from God and were enemies in your minds because of your evil behavior. But now he has reconciled you by Christ's physical body through death to present you holy in his sight, without blemish and free from accusation.
>
> (1:21–22)

Note that the fragmentation of the world in the fall shows up in humankind as alienation from God, which manifests itself in actions that are contrary to God and human good. The term translated as "mind" is a very full term in the Greek. It carries the connotation of disposition. So, humankind's whole disposition is against God with a determined, self-sustained attitude (Dunn, 1996). It is a self-declared independence from God and indicates humankind's effort to bring "completion" through human exertion. It is the same word used in Romans 12:2, where we are told not to "conform to the pattern of the world"—not to use the frameworks of the world—but to be "transformed by the renewing of [our] mind." In other words, we are to have a biblical framework by which we understand ourselves and the world in light of God's work in Christ. This is the means by which the gap in a person's "God concept" and "God image" can be bridged; in turn, our renewed mind can rest more fully in God's care shown to us in Christ.

Reconciliation in Christ brings healing to our minds and actions through reorienting us in Christ toward God. Reconciliation allows us to re-order our lives through Christ in a coherent and ordered way that is consistent with the world now re-ordered through Christ. So, in Christ, our knowing contact with the world can again be an act of communion.

While reconciliation has taken place in what Christ has done, the work of reconciliation is still being carried out and will be brought to full completion when Christ returns. It is in this hope that Christians can daily live. Though reconciliation can at times be hard to see, it begins as we consciously turn in dependent trust to God and allow him to heal and reconcile us to himself. It was for him we (and creation) were made, and only in him can we (and creation) experience the fullness and completeness for which we were made.

To conclude the chapter, it is important to keep in mind that understanding our created communion—how this communion has been fragmented and how it has been restored—may not abolish the pain and struggle we encounter in life, but it does offer a context by which it can be understood and have meaning. God is working in and through the difficulties to conform us to the image of his Son. Because God is all-knowing, all-powerful, all-good, and providentially guiding all things, we can know that he will allow only what is necessary for our good. Though in the darkness it may seem way too much, it is important to remember the lessons from the first chapter. God is *always* with us, and wherever God is, all of God is there.

Because Christian attempts to gain knowledge—including knowledge of the ongoing mental suffering that is ubiquitous in contemporary society—require communion, confusion and fragmentation can occur when we do not trace our experiences back to God as the source. This is why and how the task of interpreting our experiences can be frustrating and lead to psychological pain.

For psychotherapists who strive to make sense of their Christian clients' emotional disorders, a Christian epistemology takes into account empirical research, properly interpreted in light of God's special revelation—nature being God's creation (God's work), which he wants us to understand—for our purposes, for example, the etiology and maintenance of emotional disorders. Still, Christians are called to turn to the Bible (God's Word) as the foundational path towards a more transcendent understanding of reality, suffering, and healing. Ultimately, then, when conceptualizing emotional disorders among Christian clients, a Christian view of reality and knowledge can help to cultivate a holistic conceptualization of the problem and solution—biology, psychology, social functioning, ethics, and spirituality work together to form a coherent picture of health, dysfunction, and healing in the Christian life. By understanding the Christian framework, therapists can work more effectively with Christians to balance acceptance and change as their devout clients move from suffering to healing, drawing on communion with God as the ultimate relational source in the process.

Helping Christian clients to truly understand that this is our Father's world is paramount; all things, including painful experiences, stand before, and are responsive to, our Father's hand.

References

Apcyznski, J. (2017). A Polanyian epistemology manqué. *Tradition and Discovery, 43* (3), 4–13.

Augustine (1997). *On Christian Teaching* (R. Green, Trans.). Oxford: Oxford University Press.

Calvin, J. (2003). *Commentary on the Book of Psalms* (J. Anderson, Trans.). Grand Rapids, MI: Baker Books.

Canlis, J. (2010). *Calvin's Ladder*. Grand Rapids, MI: William B. Eerdmans.

Dreyfus, H., & Taylor, C. (2015). *Retrieving Realism*. Cambridge, MA: Harvard University Press.

Dunn, J. (1996). *The Epistles to the Colossians and to Philemon: A Commentary on the Greek Text*. Grand Rapids, MI: William B. Eerdmans.

Entwistle, D. (2015). *Integrative Approaches to Psychology and Christianity: An Introduction to Worldview Issues, Philosophical Foundations, and Models of Integration*. Eugene, OR: Cascade Books.

Gregory of Nyssa (1954). Introduction to Gregory of Nyssa. In E. Hardy (Ed.), *Christology of the Later Fathers* (pp. 235–250). Louisville: Westminster John Knox Press.

Kidner, D. (2008). *Genesis*. Downers Grove, IL: InterVarsity Press.

Meek, E. (2003). *Longing to Know*. Grand Rapids, MI: Brazos Press.

Meek, E. (2011). *Loving to Know*. Eugene, OR: Cascade Publishing.

Smith, J. (2004). *Introduction to Radical Orthodoxy*. Grand Rapids, MI: Baker Books.

Thunberg, L. (1995). *Microcosm and Mediator* (2nd ed.). Chicago, IL: Open Court.

Wrathall, M. (2014). *Skillful Coping*. Oxford: Oxford University Press.

CHAPTER 5

Ontology and Epistemology in Christian Mental Health
A Theoretical and Empirical Exploration

Introduction

In this chapter, we seek to extend our discussion of ontology and epistemology that began with Christian theology and philosophy into the realm of Christian psychology, serving as a bridge to the next Christian psychotherapy chapter. In so doing, our aim is to help therapists working with Christian clients better understand the crucial role that our view of reality and knowledge—sometimes overlooked in the clinical psychology literature based on unexamined assumptions—play in contributing to a Christian worldview in psychotherapy with Christian clients.

Worldviews and Psychology

As we have seen, according to Christianity, humans live in a transcendent relational universe, in which a triune God has created us for himself, to live in a fitting relationship with him and with one another as an image or sign of the triune God. As a result, humans exist and know and love in a relation of receptive dependence upon God, whether we are aware of this reality or not.

This relational ontology shows up analogously in human life; for human existence, knowing and (perhaps more obviously) loving are necessarily contextual. Especially early in life, we live with our caregivers in receptive dependence. As we develop into personal agents (who resemble the *persons* of the Trinity), our dependence matures into a healthy interdependence (which resembles the *communion* of the Trinity) (Johnson, 2017); only abnormally do we age into increasing isolation and alienation from others.

Our knowledge, too, is fundamentally relational, contextual, and dependent. We know something in relation to other things, and we are dependent on their "opening up" to us—especially the knowledge of persons (others and ourselves). As we age, our web of beliefs becomes increasingly complex and interdependent, with some beliefs providing the grounds for other beliefs. By the time humans reach adulthood, a set of basic or ultimate beliefs has formed—a "worldview." One of the paradoxes of adult cognition is one's set of ultimate beliefs cannot be proven to be true (except to those who already hold them); yet, it necessarily grounds the rest of our beliefs about reality, including human beings, and provides the "lens" through which we interpret it (Naugle, 2002) (interestingly, changing a worldview amounts to a cognitive conversion, and after age 30 they are relatively rare; Spilka, Hood, Hunsberger, & Gorsuch, 2003).

Worldviews also are a kind of cultural or subcultural phenomenon, since they are usually shared and disseminated by groups of people, which we might call "worldview communities." There is plenty of evidence that culture is an influential factor on psychological dynamics and functioning, such as intelligence, narrative, emotion and motivation, and psychopathology (Kitayama & Cohen, 2007), as well as positive aspects of human being, like happiness, the virtues, and definitions of wellbeing (McGrath, 2015; Tov & Diener, 2007). While worldview beliefs within single cultures have been less investigated, they also have been found to have similar influence (Lund, 2014; Magee, 2014). What is more, both culture and worldview need to be taken into account in psychology and psychotherapy (Utsey, Fischer, & Belvet, 2010; Slife, O'Grady, & Kosits, 2017). Someday, hopefully, the field of psychology will become more pluralistic with regard to culture and worldview (Johnson & Watson, 2012; Smythe & McKenzie, 2010).

All this is vitally important to both Christians in the mental health field and Christian consumers of therapy. Modern psychology and its therapies have largely accepted the worldview of naturalism, the belief set that only natural entities and processes exist and influence human life (Goetz & Taliaferro, 2008). Many worldviews agree with naturalism, as far as it goes, but it can be severely restrictive, according to a Christian worldview, when we move beyond the empirical world and accept the existence of transcendent reality. For, in addition to being biological and psychosocial beings (natural entities that function according to natural processes), humans are also ethical and spiritual beings, characterized by processes that are not reducible to nature alone (like human freedom), and we were created to live according to God's design plan for humanity and in eternal communion with him. However, because humans are alienated from God, we only obscurely know what we are missing and apparently many are satisfied with a truncated worldview. As a result, modern psychology has left out much that is relevant to a more holistic study of human beings, according to Christianity, including that which is foundational and most important.

Theism, by contrast, is a worldview that assumes the necessary existence of a supreme being who brought everything else into existence. Judaism, Christianity, Islam, and some forms of Hinduism are types of theism. As a result, theistic psychologies are versions of psychology that, in addition to assuming the existence of natural entities and processes, assume that God's activity is also involved in human life (Slife & Reber, 2007; Watson & Johnson, 2012).

Reference to God is, of course, a matter of spirituality and transcendence, both of which are now viewed as legitimate avenues of psychological inquiry (Piedmont, Ciarrochi, Dy-Liacco, & Williams, 2009; Sawatzky, Ratner, & Chiu, 2005) and dimensions of psychotherapy (Aten, O'Grady, & Worthington, 2011; Pargament, 2007). As a result, there is greater openness to challenge the hegemony of naturalism than at any time since the founding of modern psychology in the late 1800s.

Distinctive Christian Worldview Assumptions

Available evidence-based research points to the likelihood that distinctly Christian uses of therapeutic modalities that address the emotions would be helpful in dealing with emotional disorders with Christian clients (Edwards & Davis, 2013). The purpose of this book is to develop a psychotherapy model that is thoroughly based on a Christian worldview. We have already seen that a Christian worldview begins with the assumption of the existence of a triune God and the healing effects of a loving relationship with him, as well as with healthier others. In addition, there will be a special focus on Jesus Christ and the believer's relation to him, to be discussed more at the end of this chapter.

As we noted in the previous chapter, Christian epistemology relies on the Bible as a legitimate source of knowledge, as well as good theory and research. Scripture is essential for our current project, because we cannot know much about the transcendent on our own. Humans need the transcendent Creator to reveal some knowledge to us in human language, in order for us to understand aspects of reality that are inaccessible to purely empirical methods, including God, certain features of human nature (like freedom, values, and ethics), and salvation. Because all knowledge is interrelated, without this revealed knowledge, our knowledge of everything else is deficient. Research in the psychology of religion and Christian psychotherapy has found that orthodox Christian beliefs (emanating from the Bible) are positively correlated with mental and spiritual health (Fullerton & Hunsberger, 1982; Knabb, Pelletier, & Grigorian-Routon, 2014; Watson, Morris, Loy, & Hamrick, 2005), including religious commitment and faith maturity (Knabb & Pelletier, 2012). In fact, a recent study found that orthodox Christian beliefs were negatively correlated with experiential avoidance (a construct often researched in the acceptance and commitment therapy [ACT] literature), meaning that belief in traditional, biblical views (e.g., Jesus is the Son of God, the Bible is God's Word) was linked to the ability to be more accepting and tolerant of psychological pain (Knabb & Pelletier, 2014).

Emotions are complex and often misunderstood and avoided, even within the church, especially in the context of emotional disorders. This provides another reason to allow Scripture to provide guidance into understanding and working with the emotions.

Working with Signs of Meaning

Semiotics is the study of signs. A sign is anything that represents, stands for, or points to something else; for example, smoke is a sign of fire. God has constituted human life through signs. To begin with, humans are embodied souls, and our bodies continuously signify the dynamics of our respective souls, through bodily movements and actions of all kinds, including speech. In addition, humans are endowed with two preeminent sign systems, by which we make sense of reality: a cognitive-linguistic system and an emotion-motivation system. The cognitive-linguistic system employs thoughts and words (that are mysteriously, but closely, linked) to understand, interpret, and describe the nature of reality (signification), whereas the emotional-motivational system employs emotions, desires, and actions to grasp the respective value of reality (significance) and eventually evaluate it (determine its significance) (Johnson, 2007). A well-developed language has a vocabulary of around 50,000 words to describe reality (Stirling & Elliott, 2008). The human emotion-motivation system is much more limited and nuanced (it is hard to tell where one emotion ends and another begins, with psychotherapy clients often struggling to identify emotion because they are feeling multiple emotions at the same time [Orange, 1995]). Depending on how one categorizes them, there are between 8 (basic, biologically hard-wired) and 200 (culturally shaped) emotions that humans use to value and evaluate reality (see, e.g., TenHouten, 2006). However, though limited in "vocabulary," emotions evaluate reality and move us accordingly. Humans have long recognized that emotional experience can be distinguished in terms of *bivalence* (Colembetti, 2005)—some are positive (pleasant) and some are negative (unpleasant)—and *intensity* (from mild to strong). Our positive emotions signify that which we perceive to be our Good and that we are, therefore, moved to pursue; and negative emotions signify that which we perceive to be contrary to our Good and, depending on the emotion, move us to avoid it or overcome it. With these two sign systems (language and emotion), humans come to make sense of their lives; interpret their experiences; and know, love, and act. It is widely recognized that we know through words. However, emotions, too, are a kind of knowing, based on value. Both systems are essential to understand reality and its significance, but we might say language especially helps us discern the True, and emotions are especially helpful to distinguish the Good and the Beautiful and their opposites.

The Meaning of the Emotions

So, the positive emotions signify what we perceive to be our Good, that which enhances our life and enables us to flourish. Positive emotions, therefore, are enjoyable, and the experience of them is associated with a productive and meaningful life (Fredrickson, 2002). Humans, on average, have an emotion set point on the positive side of the ledger, and we generally seek a positive emotion state (Diener & Suh, 1999). Moreover, positive emotions generally lead to curiosity, openness, creativity, supportive relationships, more flexible goals and mindsets, health, wealth, and longitivity (Cohn, Fredrickson, Brown, Mikels, & Conway, 2009). The primary positive emotions include joy and contentment (Turner & Stets, 2005), indicating the experience of a perceived Good.

Negative emotions signify, in somewhat more differentiated ways, that which we perceive to be contrary to our Good, that which harms us, thwarts our prospering, and undermines our flourishing. Accordingly, negative emotions are more or less unpleasant, and humans generally seek to avoid the conditions that produce them (and the negative emotions themselves). Among the most important negative emotions are anger, sadness, fear/anxiety, shame, guilt, and disgust (Turner & Stets, 2005). Anger signifies the perception of injustice, unmet expectations, or the thwarting of reasonable goals; sadness signifies the perception of the loss of something good, whether actually taken away (as in the death of a caregiver) or merely intuited (as in the chronic absence in childhood of adequate caregiving); fear/anxiety signify the perception of harm (either in the moment [fear] or future [anxiety]), physical or psychological; shame signifies separateness, incompleteness, and the perception that there is something wrong with the self; guilt signifies the perception that one has done something wrong; and disgust signifies the perception of something abhorrent (unclean or poisonous).

In a fallen, troubled world, negative emotions are necessary and valuable (Parrott, 2014), for they help us to focus our attention on coping with immediate threats or problems (Cohn et al., 2009) and recognize the aspects of reality that keep us from the Good, aspects that are harmful, bad, and evil. However, chronic exposure to injustice, loss, danger, and mistreatment, especially in childhood, leads to the formation of elaborate and complex negative emotion schemes, as well as defenses to keep such negative emotions out of consciousness, both of which are likely to be activated in the future in similar situations. Tragically, strong, chronic negative emotions in adulthood, especially shame, can lead to distortions in one's perceiving, thinking, evaluating, loving, and acting, and are highly associated with psychopathology (Keltner & Kring, 1998; Tangney & Dearing, 2002). As a result, much of psychotherapy is directed towards addressing negative emotions, whether by alleviating, reducing, or reinterpreting them, enabling people to cope with them in adaptive and productive ways (Parrott, 2014). Furthermore, positive emotions lead to greater ego-resilience, which, in turn, is related to better life adjustment and less depression, and happiness is associated with having more positive emotion experiences than negative (Cohn et al., 2009). Consequently, contemporary psychotherapy is increasingly focused on helping clients cultivate more positive emotion experience (Greenberg, 2011; Seligman & Rashid, & Parks, 2006; Gilbert, 2010).

The Meaning of Persons-in-Communion in Time

According to the theistic religions, humans are images (or signs) of God. We point to, or represent, God on earth. In a Trinitarian theistic scheme, human interrelations of self and others are also intended to signify or image the Trinitarian interrelations of Father, Son, and Holy Spirit, the Archetype of persons-in-communion.

However, finite, temporal creatures like humans must develop in order to realize our inborn image-bearing potential. God has designed humans so that after birth we would mature in relation with adult humans, that is, in relation with signs of God. Furthermore, such relationships provide the primary medium through which meaning is mediated and communicated to children, which they internalize; in this process, they are formed into a relatively mature human being. So, the human form is constituted by other human forms, through language, emotion, love, and action. This, too, is part of the ontology of temporal humans.

According to Christian assumptions, the highest, most noble capacities of human beings are ethical and spiritual: the love of neighbor and God. While humans begin life as biological creatures, we develop psychosocial capacities, for which we have been endowed genetically, as we respond to, and interact with, our social world. As a result, with "good enough" nurturing, humans grow in memory, emotions, language, intelligence, relationality, and the imagination. Sometime in adolescence, capacities develop to make decisions and perform actions, based on reasons and goals, for which the actor is held responsible, in concert with correlated capacities to delight in others, empathize, engage in mutually reciprocal relations, and give of ourselves to promote the wellbeing of others. As a result, new ways of relating to ourselves and others become possible, more so than what could have been experienced in childhood: being an ethical person-in-communion. Around this same time, the ability to relate to God in faith and love emerges, which is central to the image of God (the *imago Dei*). Kierkegaard (1990) argued that the cultivation of such ethical and spiritual capacities was intrinsic to "inward deepening," his term for Christian maturation.

By the time persons reach adulthood, they have also developed a personal narrative, a set of affect-laden episodic memories and associated narrative themes and beliefs about themselves with which they have come to identify. The narrative quality of human life is also a part of its ontology. Today, influenced by relativity theory and quantum mechanics, we realize that time is an intrinsic aspect of human being—perhaps even a fourth dimension in which we live—so it is easier to see how temporality and narrative are fundamental to biblical revelation and a biblical ontology and epistemology.

Favored Modalities of Therapy in a Christian Framework

In principle, all created therapeutic modalities are available to therapists (Johnson, 2007). However, given Christian assumptions and the client's difficulties, the use of some modalities will be especially helpful. In light of the importance of Christian Scripture to understanding God, human nature, ourselves, and the world, cognitive and psychoeducational therapies will involve sharing of relevant Christian truths and information that promote psychospiritual healing of emotional disorders (Johnson, 2017).

Because of Christianity's relational ontology, relational therapy (Knabb, Welsh, & Alexander, 2012; which emphasizes the importance of the therapeutic alliance and transference) and spiritual formation (Coe & Hall, 2007; which addresses our relationship with God) will be particularly fitting. From this perspective, the ability to come to terms with painful emotional experiences (which occur in childhood) involves turning the memories of these events into signals to make sense of the world, utilizing relations with God and others (Krystal, 1988; Stolorow, Brandchaft, & Atwood, 1995). Healthy affect regulation is promoted in the context of a supportive, safe relationship, wherein the "other" is utilized as a source of soothing comfort during instances of environmental uncertainties (Mikulincer, Shaver, & Pereg, 2003).

Based on the importance of emotions in a Christian framework (Edwards, 1959), focusing on emotions will also be an important component of Christian psychotherapy. As Stolorow et al. suggested, "When affects are perceived as signals of a changing self-state rather than as indicators of impending psychological disorganization and fragmentation, the child is able to tolerate his emotional reactions without experiencing them as traumatic" (p. 72). On the other hand, if negative emotional experiences are viewed as shameful, this can lead to recurrent trauma, in which we interpret them as something only to be eradicated (Stolorow et al., 1995), like a malignant tumor. Yet, if negative emotions can be reinterpreted as God-given signs or signals to aid in recovery, then Christian psychotherapy can help Christian clients accept their value in the midst of pain. Furthermore, in the context of an increasingly secure attachment relationship with God, negative emotions can help Christian clients deepen their appreciation of their communion with him and use aspects of their relation with him to modify their negative emotions in healthy ways (e.g., trusting that he will bring good out of bad events). Moreover, whatever experiences of communion they have can serve as "islands" of positive emotion upon which can be built a new self-identity and narrative and hope for further growth.

Finally, Christianity provides a rich metanarrative within which to help Christian clients reinterpret their stories in relation to the story of God's dealing with his people in the Bible, culminating in the story of Jesus Christ. In Christ, we can glory in our sufferings, because we know that suffering produces perseverance; perseverance, character; and character, hope. And hope does not put us to shame, because God's love has been poured out into our hearts through the Holy Spirit, who has been given to us.

(Romans 5:3–5)

Rather than striving to completely resolve emotional disorders, Christian clients can learn to accept their brokenness and embrace their identity as those who are dependent on God, which is consistent with God's original design plan. Instead of striving to be like God in knowing good and evil, erroneously believing they are independent and self-sufficient, Christian clients can obtain greater contentment through giving glory to God by turning to him in the midst of their pain and suffering.

A Christian approach to suffering offers Christian clients a redemptive way to reframe their story. Rather than being victims feeling themselves worthy of mistreatment, their stories are sites of God's glory (2 Corinthians 4:6–10), so that they become signs of God's transforming, redeeming work, as those raised from the dead.

The Unifying, Satisfying Role of Christ

As the eternal Logos (or Word) of God (John 1:1–5, 9–14; see also Proverbs 8; Hebrews 1:1–3), the Son of God is revealed to be the source of all order, natural laws, and good social norms in the universe. He is the "light that gives light to everyone" (John 1:9), "in whom are hidden all the treasures of wisdom and knowledge" (Colossians 2:3), so that everything in the creation finds its nexus in him. Therefore, from a Christian standpoint, ontology and epistemology are based on Christ.

He is *the* image (or sign) of God (Colossians 1:15), the one who reveals God most fully to humanity (Hebrews 1:2–3), providing the transcendent knowledge necessary for the fullest self-knowledge possible; in addition, as the *true* human (Barth, 1960), the *real* human (Bonhoeffer, 1955), he is the one who reveals humanity to us—humanity as it was intended, a flourishing humanity, the epitome and Archetype of a human being (Hebrews 2:5–18). Moreover, the Son of God assumed human nature 2,000 years ago, without ceasing to be divine, and united himself to humanity forever. As a result, he entered time and became a particular human being, with a particular body and unique story, who existed in a certain culture at a moment in history. Given his role as the Logos, the particularity of Christ's human existence and story have universal significance, conveying that every human being's particularity and story are meaningful.

Christ, therefore, brings unity to our knowledge of God and human beings, and unity to our general knowledge of human beings and particular knowledge of ourselves. All of this suggests that a Christian psychology and psychotherapy will be especially distinguished from all other psychologies by the pre-eminent role that Jesus Christ plays (Johnson, 2017).

In addition, Jesus Christ died for the sins of the world to reconcile humanity to its creator. Through faith in him, anyone can become united to Christ and reconciled to God. Through this union with him, we enter into the transcendent communion of the Trinity, which we can access through worship and meditative prayer; we are given by God the attributes of the human, Jesus Christ (holiness, perfect righteousness, beloved, adopted by God); our shame and guilt is taken away; our stories are woven into the narrative of Christ's life, death, resurrection, and ascension; and we are joined to other believers, as the body of Christ, including Christian therapists. As a result, believers are enabled to think and feel differently about reality—so that we see it increasingly from a transcendent perspective, rather than from a perspective embedded in our old ways of perceiving and interpreting. Ultimately, Christians are ontologically different now: we are persons-in-union-with-Christ.

As we saw earlier in this chapter, negative emotions reflect experiences of human fallenness, and chronic exposure to such fallenness in childhood leads to the possibility of emotional disorders in adulthood. Christ's death is especially associated with human fallenness: he experienced anxiety in the Garden of Gethsemane, injustice throughout his trial and slow death, and loss and rejection, taking on the shame and guilt of the world. He became sin for us (2 Corinthians 5:21) and experienced human suffering and temptation, culminating in death and God-forsakenness (Hebrews 2:14–18) and being crucified in weakness (2 Corinthians 13:4).

However, Christ's resurrection was the beginning of the new creation and brought in a new era in human history (Romans 1:4; Colossians 1:18; 2 Corinthians 4:6, 5:17; Galatians 6:15)—the last days (Acts 2:17; Hebrews 1:2). In this new era, Christians have access to the Spirit and the divine glory and blessedness that comes with communion with God, including the fruit of the Spirit: love, joy, peace, patience, kindness, goodness, faithfulness, gentleness, and self-control (John 7:37, 14:26; Galatians 5:22–23)—positive emotions and virtues that Christians now are invited to experience and practice.

Christians, in their entirety, have been united to Christ's death and resurrection (Romans 6:3–6; Ephesians 2:5–6). As a result, our negative emotions, and the experiences they signify, have been joined to Christ's death, which gives such affective states a transcendent ground upon which we can identify them; in turn, our emotional experiences can be taken to the cross and released to God, and our union with Christ's resurrection grants us a share in God's perfect compassion and peace that surpasses human understanding, made available through the Spirit. Christian psychotherapy, then, involves helping Christian clients understand and experience themselves in Christ, including a restored communion with God, so that they work through their negative emotions by means of Christ's death and allow their painful feelings to be modified and resolved by Christ's resurrection, resulting in positive emotions like forgiveness, the love of God, and contentment. Gradually, they are raised from the death of their fallenness and enabled to walk in "newness of life" (Romans 6:4). This process entails the realization of a new self (Ephesians 4:22–24) and the co-authoring (with God) of a new chapter in their story.

Christ, then, is the primary interpersonal means by which Christians are restored to a right relationship with God, self, and others. He is also the archetypal goal towards which Christians aspire and the exemplar of virtuous living and psychospiritual wellbeing (Walker & Frimer, 2007). Most personally, Christians are learning to relate to Christ as their hero, champion, ultimate therapist, and friend.

As Christian clients struggle with emotional disorders, a psychodynamic conceptualization can also help to make sense of their relationship with God in Christ. Consistent with self psychology (Lessem, 2005), need-rupture-repair cycles can help to strengthen their sense of self, repeatedly returning to God when they realize a rift has developed. Worth mentioning, though, in self psychology's conceptualization of rupture, the therapist fails to perfectly meet the needs of the client, contributing to the rupture in the therapeutic relationship. In a Christian psychodynamic model, we suggest that the human tendency to turn away from God (because we struggle to trust in him) to achieve a false sense of autonomy and self-sufficiency is the ultimate reason for the rupture. Nevertheless, Christian clients can now confidently and consistently run into the arms of their always-accepting Father (reminiscent of the parable of the prodigal son in the gospels; Luke 15:11–32) because of the life, death, and resurrection of Jesus Christ. In other words, Christians have a need for connection with God, but tend to disavow this need because of their fallenness. Emotional disorders serve as a signal that a rupture has taken place, with Christian clients having the ability (through the person and work of Christ), in each and every moment, to return to their Father. After all, when Christians reach out to God, God has already reached out to them, evident in his loving pursuit of his children in the work of Jesus, about which he has declared with the definitive words: "It is finished" (John 19:30).

References

Aten, J., O'Grady, K., & Worthington, Jr., E. (2011). *The Psychology of Religion and Spirituality for Clincians: Using Research in Your Practice*. New York: Routledge.

Barth, K. (1960a). *Church Dogmatics: 3.2* (H. Knight, J. K. S. Reid, & R. H. Fuller, Trans.). Edinburgh: T. & T. Clark.

Bonhoeffer, D. (1955). *Ethics*. New York: Macmillan.

Coe, J., & Hall, T. (2007). *Psychology in the Spirit*. Downers Grove, IL: InterVarsity Press.

Cohn, M. A., Fredrickson, B. L., Brown, S. L., Mikels, J. A., & Conway, A. M. (2009). Happiness unpacked: Positive emotions increase life satisfaction by building resilience. *Emotion, 9,* 361–368.

Colembetti, G. (2005). Appraising valence. *Journal of Consciousness Studies, 12,* 103–126.

Diener, E., & Suh, E. M. (1999). National differences in subjective well-being. In D. Kahneman, E. Diener, & N. Schwarz (Eds.), *Well-Being: The Foundations of Hedonic Psychology* (pp. 434–451). New York: Russell Sage Foundation.

Edwards, K. J., & Davis, E. B. (2013). Evidence-based principles from psychodynamic and process-experiential psychotherapies. In E. L. Worthington, Jr., E. L. Johnson, J. N. Hook, & J. D. Aten (Eds.), *Evidence-Based Practices for Christian Counseling and Psychotherapy* (pp. 122–148). Downers Grove, IL: InterVarsity Press.

Fredrickson, B. L. (2002). Positive emotions. In C. R. Snyder & S. J. Lopez (Eds.), *Handbook of Positive Psychology* (pp. 120–134). Oxford and New York: Oxford University Press.

Fullerton, J., & Hunsberger, B. (1982). A unidimensional measure of Christian orthodoxy. *Journal for the Scientific Study of Religion, 21,* 317–326.

Gilbert, P. (2010). *Compassion-Focused Therapy.* New York: Routledge.

Goetz, S., & Taliaferro, C. (2008). *Naturalism.* Grand Rapids, MI: Eerdmans.

Greenberg, L. S. (2011). *Emotion-Focused Therapy.* Washington, DC: American Psychological Association.

Johnson, E. L. (2007). *Foundations for Soul Care.* Downers Grove, IL: InterVarsity Press.

Johnson, E. L. (2017). *God and Soul Care: The Therapeutic Resources of the Christian Faith.* Downers Grove, IL: InterVarsity Press.

Johnson, E. L., & Watson, P. J. (2013). Worldview communities and the science of psychology. In R. L. Piedmont & A. Village (Eds.), *Research in the Social Scientific Study of Religion, 23* (pp. 269–284). Leiden: Brill.

Keltner, D., & Kring, A. M. (1998). Emotion, social function, and psychopathology. *Review of General Psychology, 2,* 320–342.

Kierkegaard, S. (1990). *For Self-Examination: Judge for Yourselves!* (H. V. Hong & E. H. Hong, Trans.). Princeton, NJ: Princeton University Press.

Kitayama, S., & Cohen, D. (Eds.) (2007). *Handbook of Cultural Psychology.* New York: Guilford.

Knabb, J., Pelletier, J., & Grigorian-Routon, A. (2014). Towards a psychological understanding of servanthood: An empirical investigation of the relationship between orthodox beliefs, experiential avoidance, and self-sacrificial behaviors among Christians at a religiously affiliated university. *Journal of Psychology and Theology, 42,* 269–293.

Knabb, J., Welsh, R., & Alexander, P. (2012). Towards an integrated view of the necessity of human interdependence: Perspectives from theology, philosophy, and psychology. *Journal of Spirituality in Mental Health, 14,* 166–180.

Krystal, H. (1988). *Integration and Self-Healing: Affect, Trauma, Alexithymia.* New York: Routledge.

Lessem, P. (2005). *Self Psychology: An Introduction.* New York: Jason Aronson.

Lund, A. (2014). Personality psychology as the integrative study of traits and worldviews. *New Ideas of Psychology, 32,* 18–32.

Magee, R. G. (2014). Worldview beliefs, morality beliefs and decision-making referents: Implications for the psychology of morality and ethics instruction. In A. M. Columbus (Ed.), *Advances in Psychology Research* (Vol. 100, pp. 1–24). Hauppauge, NY: Nova Science.

McGrath, R. E. (2015). Character strengths in 75 nations: An update. *The Journal of Positive Psychology, 10*, 41–52.

Mikulincer, M., Shaver, P., & Pereg, D. (2003). Attachment theory and affect regulation: The dynamics, development, and cognitive consequences of attachment-related strategies. *Motivation and Emotion, 27*, 77–102.

Naugle, D. K. (2002). *Worldview: The History of a Concept*. Grand Rapids, MI: Eerdmans.

Obasi, E., Flores, L., & James-Myers, L. (2009). Construction and initial validation of the worldview analysis scale. *Journal of Black Studies, 39*, 937–961.

Orange, D. (1995). *Emotional Understanding: Studies in Psychoanalytic Epistemology*. New York: Guilford Press.

Pargament, K. I. (2007). *Spiritually Integrated Psychotherapy: Understanding and Addressing the Sacred*. New York: Guilford Press.

Parrott, W. G. (Ed.) (2014). *The Positive Side of Negative Emotions*. New York: Guilford Press.

Piedmont, R., Ciarrochi, J., Dy-Liacco, G., & Williams, J. (2009). The empirical and conceptual value of the spiritual transcendence and religious involvement scales for personality research. *Psychology of Religion and Spirituality, 1*, 162–179.

Sawatzky, R., Ratner, P., & Chiu, L. (2005). A meta-analysis of the relationship between spirituality and quality of life. *Social Indicators Research, 72*, 153–188.

Seligman, M. E. P., Rashid, T., & Parks, A. C. (2006). Positive psychotherapy. *American Psychologist, 61*, 774–788.

Slife, B. D., O'Grady, K. A., & Kosits, R. D. (2017). *The Hidden Worldviews of Psychology's Theory, Research, and Practice*. New York: Routledge.

Smythe, W. E., & McKenzie, S. A. (2010). A vision of dialogical pluralism in psychology. *New Ideas in Psychology, 28*, 227–234.

Spilka, B., Hood, Jr., R. W., Hunsberger, B., & Gorsuch, R. (2003). *The Psychology of Religion: An Empirical Approach* (3rd ed.). New York: Guilford Press.

Stirling, J., & Elliott, R. (2008). *Introducing Neuropsychology* (2nd ed.). New York: Psychology Press.

Stolorow, R., Brandchaft, B., & Atwood, G. (1995). *Psychoanalytic Treatment: An Intersubjective Approach*. New York: Routledge.

Tangney, J. P., & Dearing, R. L. (2002). *Shame and Guilt*. New York: Guilford Press.

TenHouten, W. (2006). *A General Theory of Emotions and Social Life*. New York: Routledge.

Tov, W., & Diener, E. (2007). Culture and subjective well-being. In S. Kitayam & D. Cohen (Eds.), *Handbook of Cultural Psychology* (pp. 691–713). New York: Guilford Press.

Turner, J., & Stets, J. (2005). *The Sociology of Emotions*. New York: Cambridge University Press.

Utsey, S. O., Fischer, N. L., & Belvet, B. (2010). Cutlure and worldview in counseling and psychotherapy: Recommended approaches for working with persons from diverse sociocultural backgrounds. In M. M. Leach & J. D. Aten (Eds.), *Culture and the Therapeutic Process: A Guide for Mental Health Professionals* (pp. 181–200). New York: Routledge.

Walker, L. J., & Frimer, J. A. (2007). Moral personality of brace and caring exemplars. *Journal of Personality and Social Psychology, 934*, 845–860.

Watson, P. J., Morris, R. J., Loy, T., & Hamrick, M. B. (2005). Beliefs in sin: Adaptive implications in relationships with religious orientation, self-esteem, and measures of the narcissistic, depressed, and anxious self. *Edification, 1*, 57–68.

CHAPTER 6

Ontology and Epistemology in Christian Psychotherapy

Introduction

In this chapter, we present a distinctly Christian psychotherapy within the "ontology and epistemology" pillar, exploring the ways in which therapists can effectively address the nature of reality and knowledge when working with Christian clients. Specifically, we offer a central theme in working with Christian clients with emotional disorders, along with goals for treatment and specific interventions from a distinctly Christian worldview. Similar to the third chapter, we draw from a range of Christian resources, building on a theological and empirical understanding of emotional disorders from the previous two chapters in the "ontology and epistemology" section. Above all else, we wish to provide Christian-sensitive interventions for Christians with depressive and anxiety disorders, enhancing a Christian approach with the "common factors" literature (Lambert, 2013) and other relevant theory and research.

Central Theme

Building on the previous two chapters in this section (Chapter 4 and 5), a distinctly Christian psychotherapy employs a biblical understanding of Christian ontology and epistemology so as to guide treatment. Based on this awareness, a uniquely Christian approach suggests that God is the Source of both reality and knowledge, revealing himself to Christians via Scripture (i.e., special revelation). From our perspective, emotional symptoms are God-given signs/signals, capturing Christians' longing to return to God as the Source of life (Bonhoeffer, 1955; Johnson, 2007; 2017; Knabb & Meador, 2016). As Bonhoeffer revealed in his exegesis of the fall of humankind in Genesis, "Shame is man's ineffaceable recollection of his estrangement from the origin; it is grief for this estrangement, and the powerless longing to return to unity with the origin" (p. 24).

For 21st-century Christians, emotional disorders are reverberations from an original estrangement from God, revealing our "incompleteness" without him. Buried beneath a deep sense of loss and uncertainty about the future is an awareness that life is not quite right, illuminating the shame that emanates from an exposed state. In spite of Christians' best efforts to conceal our vulnerable existence, the very actions to cover up are a reminder of the disunion (Bonhoeffer, 1955).

Interestingly, recent research has revealed that shame-proneness is linked to anxiety disorders in a clinical sample (Fergus, Valentiner, & McGrath, 2010), as well as depressive and anxiety-related symptoms in college samples (Tangney, Wagner, & Gramzow, 1992). Rather than erroneously striving to fully get rid of recurrent psychological pain, Christian clients can focus on deepening their relationship with God, cultivating a more spiritual, transcendent understanding of daily living by depending on God for relational support, affect regulation, and effective action. Above all else, Christians' identity is rooted in God, the Source of life, who has revealed himself through the Bible. From a Christian perspective, emotional disorders need to be conceptualized with this understanding in mind.

Reality, Knowledge, and the Secular Psychology Literature

Before offering the goals for treatment within this pillar, we would like to discuss the reasons why ontology and epistemology are so important within a distinctly Christian model of psychotherapy. Although the clinical psychology literature offers an operationalized way to approach reality and knowledge, we believe its contributions are inherently limited due to the assumptions that permeate empirically supported treatments (ESTs). Clinical psychology assumes an ontological materialism and derives knowledge solely from the scientific method and empirical investigation. Although scientific advancements are certainly helpful for Christians enduring an emotional disorder, we argue that clinical psychology possesses some of the "building blocks," but not the "blueprint," for understanding reality, knowledge, and the human condition. Or, to put it differently, clinical psychology may have a limited supply of batteries, but is not plugged in to the power grid. Ultimately, clinical psychology offers many helpful ideas, concepts, and interventions, but is detached from a Godward orientation and the notion that God can help people address their suffering. Because of this, purely secular therapeutic strategies will be—by design— unable to point followers of Jesus towards a more transcendent reality, with God's Word, the Bible, offering Christians a source of knowledge that cannot be "proven to be so" by scientific observation. Nevertheless, because the common factors literature does provide some key building blocks for healing, we suggest that it can aid therapists in working with Christian clients when it is rightly placed against the backdrop of a more transcendent reality.

Goals for Treatment

In applying the "common factors" domains of support, learning, and action (adapted from Lambert, 2013) to the treatment pillar of Christian ontology and epistemology, we offer the following overarching goals (see also Table 6.1):

(a) *Support* involves helping Christian clients to better understand and accept painful emotional states, looking to God's special revelation as a source of knowledge and finding their identity in him. In this identity, Christians realize that they were created for healthy dependency (given that God is personal and relational), which is by no means pathological in any way, and the symptoms of emotional disorders point to a deeper "incompleteness" without God.
(b) *Learning* involves helping Christian clients to understand God's pursuit of humankind (after all, God cares for his creation), reframing emotional disorders as reverberations from the fall. Although painful, emotional disorders are a signal that Christian clients need to return to their Creator—over and over again—when they inevitably wander away. Thus, couching the symptoms of emotional disorders within the grand narrative of Scripture and a Christian worldview is key, given they point us back to our Creator and the author of reality, the ultimate Good.
(c) *Action* involves helping Christian clients to trust in God, facing their deepest fears because God is with them as the Source of reality. In turn, they can look to Scripture to cultivate healthy Christian behaviors, recognizing that the Bible offers a roadmap for Christian living. Ultimately, following Jesus Christ brings unity to both reality and knowledge, helping us to better understand our fallen, broken, and fragmented world.

Christian Resources

In the sixth chapter, several sources are used to develop Christian-sensitive interventions and techniques, including the following (in no particular order):

(a) Jesus' teaching on worry in Matthew, as well as the books of Ecclesiastes and Lamentations, to elucidate the need to depend on God as a spiritual, transcendent source of unwavering support, even when faced with psychological pain.
(b) The psychodynamic literature (Knabb & Newgren 2011; Knabb, Welsh, & Alexander, 2012; Krystal, 1988; Lessem, 2005) to highlight the God-given need for healthy dependence in relationships. In these vital relationships, we experience need-rupture-repair cycles, with affect serving as a signal to help us understand our need for God.

Table 6.1 Christian-sensitive common factors in psychotherapy for the "ontology and epistemology" pillar. Adapted from Lambert (2013)

Support-Related Goals	Learning-Related Goals	Action-Related Goals
Verbalize painful affect, turning to Lamentations as an example of a biblical model of reality and the importance of emotions as "signals" in our relationship with God	Give advice that is rooted in Scripture, helping Christians to reframe their suffering as part of the grand narrative of Scripture	Confront fears and test reality by trusting in God's providential care in the midst of depressive and anxiety-related symptoms (rather than human knowledge of good and evil)
Reduce isolation by turning to a relational ontology, viewing God as the source of life	Process "primary" and "secondary" emotions, viewing painful affective experiences (especially shame) as "signals" that point to a deeper longing for God as the source of life	Master thinking patterns by shifting from the "doing" to "being" mode, sitting at the feet of Jesus in the midst of emotional pain
Provide a scriptural framework for understanding a transcendent, spiritual reality, wherein God is active, present, supportive, and the center of existence, even when struggling with low mood and anxiety	Attain insight into a spiritual reality, recognizing that God understands our pain as the suffering servant, empathizes with our struggles, and is redeeming and restoring us from moment to moment	Practice healthy behaviors that are rooted in Scripture as a source of knowledge
Offer an encouraging, safe, and collaborative working alliance, pointing to the importance of healthy dependence within the human condition, as well as the inevitability of need-rupture-repair cycles and "incompleteness" because of the fall	Offer a corrective relational experience by focusing on need-rupture-repair cycles within both the therapeutic relationship and Christian clients' relationship with God	Take risks by trusting in a more spiritual, transcendent view of reality, wherein God is at the center of existence; healthy Christian behaviors are pursued because of an awareness of God's design, rooted in a relational ontology and grand narrative of Scripture
Explore the inner world, including psychological pain, by turning to Scripture for a spiritual view of reality and knowledge (e.g., Jesus' teaching on worry in Matthew, Ecclesiastes, the Psalms)	Provide feedback on thoughts, feelings, behaviors, and relationships, placing them in the context of the grand narrative of Scripture and the Bible as a source of knowledge	Achieve a sense of efficacy that emanates from God as the source of life, rather than self-generated efficacy

(Continued)

Table 6.1 (Continued)

Support-Related Goals	Learning-Related Goals	Action-Related Goals
Offer Jesus' love, bringing an awareness of God's presence into the therapy room	Attain realistic expectations and accept difficult experiences by surrendering to God's providential care, gaining an awareness of a more transcendent, spiritual reality and the Bible as a source of knowledge (rather than solely focusing on empiricism and reason)	Work through ingrained patterns of thinking, feeling, and behaving by repeatedly returning to a relational view of reality and the Bible as a source of knowledge
Model the "being," rather than "doing," mode in the context of a deeper relationship with God, highlighting the limitations of an empirical, rational approach to reality and knowledge in Christian living	Reframe negative views of the self by recognizing that the true self is found in God alone, who is the source of life and reality	

(c) The Lutheran theologian Dietrich Bonhoeffer's (1955) exegesis of Genesis, focusing on the role that shame plays as a signal, telling us we need to reach for God because of our estrangement from him.

(d) The Puritan author Richard Sibbes' (2011) *The Soul's Conflict and Victory Over Itself by Faith* to better understand the role that sadness and loss play in understanding the ontological reality of God's immanence.

(e) The mindfulness-based cognitive therapy literature (Segal, Williams, & Teasdale, 2012) to gain insight into the need to accept, rather than try to "fix" and "problem solve," low moods and anxiety. Instead of unilaterally striving to know for sure the etiology of emotional disorders, Christians can cultivate the "being mode" (Williams, 2008), learning to sit at Jesus' feet like Mary in Luke's gospel (Knabb, 2016b).

(f) The Trappist monk Thomas Merton's (1961) writings, especially his focus on finding Christians' identity in God alone—recognizing this reality is the key to mental health.

The Support Phase: A Transcendent View of Reality and Knowledge

In terms of support-based interventions and techniques, therapists can help Christians to deepen their awareness of God as the Source of life, even in the midst of emotional disorders. This includes an understanding of a transcendent, spiritual reality, wherein God is active, present, and supportive, contributing to Christians' very sense of self, even when struggling with low mood or anxiety. Along with modeling Jesus' love in the therapeutic relationship and bringing awareness to God's presence in the therapy room, therapists can help Christians to look to special revelation as a source of support to understand spiritual reality (e.g., Jesus' teaching on worry in Matthew, Ecclesiastes, the Psalms).

In the therapeutic encounter, therapists can help Christian clients to ameliorate the shame commonly emanating from the need for connection in Western society (Knabb, Welsh, & Alexander, 2013), normalizing the pain that comes from human relationships and a deeper communion with God (Lessem, 2005). In other words, clients may, at times, believe they must stand on their own because of the individualism promoted in the West, experiencing shame when they need to reach out for others. In this phase of therapy, therapists can highlight the ontological reality that Christians are incomplete outside of relationships (especially with God). As a result, the therapeutic relationship can begin this process of understanding self-in-relationship dynamics in the context of emotional disorders.

Since Christians are inherently relational (that is, created in God's image), emotions are a signal that help to understand relational reality. In other words, emotions should not be automatically disavowed—for example, shame is a helpful reminder of an estranged existence (Bonhoeffer, 1955), the ontological reality of a deep separation and need for finding Christians' identity in Christ. What is more, unilateral attempts to "fix" depression and anxiety fall short when Christian clients struggle to understand their meaning as signs/signals (loss tells Christian clients they are estranged from God, and uncertainty tells them they long for the safety, predictability, and certainty of a relationship with the Creator, who holds Christians in his hands). In the context of emotional disorders, research and reason are important for gaining a deeper knowledge; yet, overly relying on these means can exacerbate pain, given they may lead to futile, unilateral attempts to "fix" emotional pain. Rather than remaining stuck in this "doing mode," the "being mode" is about accepting things as they are in the moment, instead of trying to find reasons and "fix" what cannot be changed (Williams, 2008). Embracing a relational ontology, including an awareness of God as the Source of knowledge, means Christian clients can surrender to him (that is, avoid solely leaning on their own understanding; Proverbs 3:5) during moments of depression and anxiety. In the support-based phase of Christian psychotherapy, we advocate for a return to God as the center of existence, rather than trying to be like God (e.g., self-sufficient, autonomous, all-knowing) in unilaterally understanding good and evil and the "why" of emotional disorders (Bonhoeffer, 1955).

Verbalizing Painful Affect

Support within the "ontology and epistemology" pillar starts with helping Christian clients to verbalize painful affect, turning to Lamentations as an example of a biblical model of reality and the importance of emotions as "signals" in our relationship with God.[1] Within Lamentations, the anonymous writer offered heartfelt, poetic laments about the downfall of Jerusalem and suffering of its people several centuries before the birth of Christ (Wright, 2015). Content-wise, the book moves from offering an account of the destruction of Jerusalem to a variety of characters crying out to God to notice the suffering that has ensued. As Wright revealed: "Lamentations is like a great living canvas in which our eyes are drawn to one character or group after another at every level of society in their voiced or voiceless suffering" (p. 33).

Ultimately, Lamentations offers us a reminder of (a) the suffering Israel has endured, (b) the need for a voice for those who agonize with tremendous pain, (c) the importance of the confession of our brokenness before God in the midst of suffering, (d) the need to question "why" before God when faced with the tragedies and uncertainties of a fallen world, and (e) the importance of a "safe space" for suffering Christians to tearfully cry out to God with themes of loss and abandonment, asking for his compassionate reply (Wright, 2015). Although God did not formally respond to these particular laments in the Old Testament, he does offer a compassionate reply within the grand narrative of Scripture, redeeming a lost, seemingly abandoned world with the offering of his Son (Wright, 2015).

The great paradox of Lamentations is that pain and suffering (e.g., depression, shame) is paired with patience, hope, and trust, as the third chapter presented:

> I am the man who has seen affliction by the rod of the Lord's wrath. He has driven me away and made me walk in darkness rather than light; indeed, he has turned his hand against me again and again, all day long…I remember my affliction and my wandering, the bitterness and the gall. I well remember them, and my soul is downcast within me. Yet this I call to mind and therefore I have hope: Because of the Lord's great love we are not consumed, for his compassions never fail. They are new every morning; great is your faithfulness. I say to myself, "The Lord is my portion; therefore I will wait for him." The Lord is good to those whose hope is in him, to the one who seeks him; it is good to wait quietly for the salvation of the Lord.
>
> (3:1–3, 19–26)

As a result, placing this amalgamation of suffering and hope against the ontological backdrop of the grand narrative of Scripture is vital during the learning phase. As revealed in Lamentations' third chapter, we are helping our Christian clients to cry out to God, but encouraging them to do so with intermingled themes of patience, hope, and trust. This "both/and" reality of the human condition is essential for moving from impaired functioning to steadily walking with Jesus along the treacherous roads of life.

To operationalize this two-step process, we can work with Christian clients to (a) express their pain to God in the form of verbalizing difficult feelings, protests, complaints, and so on, asking God the "why" questions of human suffering, and, simultaneously, (b) placing their hope and trust in him because of the grand narrative of Scripture. Combined, these two steps are like being able to "see the forest for the trees," as the famous saying goes. We are encouraging our clients to focus in on the specifics of suffering, while, at the same time, placing human pain in the context of a bigger picture of redemption and restoration.

Reducing Isolation by Offering a Patient, Silent Presence

Reducing isolation is also an important part of the support phase, helping Christian clients to recognize that God is active and present in the midst of their pain. By turning to a relational ontology, Christian clients are able to view God as the Source of life and knowledge, with the grand narrative of Scripture capturing God's ongoing pursuit of humankind. In his pursuit, God has revealed himself to us via the incarnation, demonstrating his enduring love in his atoning work on the cross. With his perfect timing, he will return again to restore all things, accomplishing his desire to welcome us home.

At times, though, Christian clients may erroneously believe God is distant or absent, especially when they do not seem to hear his voice, and may struggle to patiently endure by waiting upon God's timing for his voice to guide the way. In this perceived silence, to be sure, Christians may experience compounded suffering, given they believe they are utterly alone in their pain. Yet, because God is the Source of reality, and is relating to us in each and every moment, he is also present in what seems to be silent inactivity. As mentioned in 1 Kings 19:11–12, God chose to reveal himself to Elijah in a "gentle whisper," rather than wind, an earthquake, or fire. Different translations of the Bible variously render this famous Hebrew phrase as "a sheer silence," "a low whisper," "a gentle blowing," and "a still, small voice."

According to the 17th-century Puritan Francis Rous (2016), exercising a patient, humble silence before God is an important part of the pursuit of happiness: "The Spirit delights in a meek and quiet spirit. It comes in the still wind, and not in the storm and tempest" (p. 242). To be certain, God sometimes chooses to move in ways we may not expect; thus, we speciously look for his presence in the wrong places, as if God *must* display his love for us with an audible voice and visible theatrics. Yet, reminiscent of a "faint rush we hear when we place a conch shell to our ear" (Mobley, 2009, p. 134), God is active in the silence of the therapy room as Christians struggle with the symptoms of emotional disorders.

Returning to 1 Kings 19, in Elijah's encounter with God, Scripture presented

> a new facet of the diamond-like complexity of the biblical God: wholly
> real, as indispensable as air, yet as elusive and imperceptible and
> modest as the faintest wind that barely stirs the leaves on a tree.
> Rightly, we might consider this quiet, even mystical, approach of the
> Creator a theological advance on those many biblical and extra-biblical
> images of an intimidating deity who revels in tree-splitting, earthshaking
> displays.
>
> (Mobley, 2009, p. 135)

To experience the ontological reality of God in the midst of a variety of
inner and outer distractions, we need to model a patient, comfortable
silence in the therapy room, creating the psychological space for our
clients to slow down enough to attend to what is happening (Nouwen,
2006). To "find God in all things," as the famous Jesuit saying goes, we
must display the ability to be secure with silence. In turn, Christian
clients can begin to notice their overactive, distracting mind, along with
all the environmental noise that may get in the way of God's "gentle
whisper." Rather than assuming silence equates to God's distance and
abandonment, embracing the reality that he is right by our side in the
middle of the quiet is key.

Turning to a Scriptural Framework

Next, providing a scriptural framework is key for understanding a transcendent, spiritual reality wherein God is active, present, supportive, and
the center of existence, even when we struggle with low mood and anxiety. In this framework, the grand narrative of Scripture is presented so
that Christian clients are able to better understand emotional suffering
in the context of God's plan. Although God created us in his image to
be in relationship with him and others, we turned from him, striving to
do it on our own (instead of being dependent on him). Based on this
reality, the world is a fallen place, with humans struggling with brokenness and disordered functioning, which leads to reverberations of the
fall in the form of emotional disorders. Yet, Jesus has redeemed us
through his atoning work on the cross, and God will eventually restore
all things.

In the Genesis (2:9) account of creation, we read that there are two trees—
the "tree of life" and the "tree of the knowledge of good and evil." According
to the Lutheran theologian Dietrich Bonhoeffer (1955), the "tree of life" represents God, who dwells at the center of our existence; on the other hand, the
"tree of the knowledge of good and evil" captures our attempts to falsely be
like God in our knowledge of good and evil, divorced from him. Bonhoeffer
further explained:

Man at his origin knows only one thing: God. It is only in the unity of his knowledge of God that he knows of other men, of things, and of himself. He knows all things only in God, and God in all things. The knowledge of good and evil shows that he is no longer at one with this origin. In the knowledge of good and evil man does not understand himself in the reality of the destiny appointed in his origin, but rather in his own possibilities, his possibility of being good or evil. He knows himself now as something apart from God, outside God, and this means that he now knows only himself and no longer knows God at all; for he can know God only if he knows only God. The knowledge of good and evil is therefore separation from God. Only against God can man know good and evil.

(pp. 21–22)

As a central theme in the metanarrative of Scripture, we can turn towards God at the center or away from him, residing on the periphery of existence and disconnected from our Designer. Yet, God is pursuing us in the midst of our estrangement and suffering, loving us and supporting us as we struggle to gain our footing on the unstable roads of life. Although we chose to place ourselves at the center of the proverbial garden, recognizing that God is actually at the center—offering life—is key to embracing God's design. In other words, we were made to depend on him and are incomplete without his requisite sustenance and support. Instead of trying to make sense of our suffering on our own (drawing from our own distorted knowledge of good and evil), reaching for God (who resides at the center of the proverbial garden) in the midst of daily challenges is paramount for Christian mental health.

In light of the story of Scripture, we can help our Christian clients with emotional disorders to depend on God, rather than their own understanding of human suffering. In the fall of humankind, to be sure, Adam and Eve attempted to be like God, rather than fully dependent on him. Fast-forward to the 21st century, and humans continue to struggle with an inclination to rely on our own knowledge of good and evil, apart from God's infinite wisdom and a more transcendent reality of the grand design.

With Jesus' redemption, though, Christian clients can recognize that God is residing at the center of the proverbial garden, gently moving us to recognize him as the Source of life. Pragmatically, therapists working with Christian clients may wish to help them recognize the ontological reality of God's master plan with a simple phrase, such as "I will not lean on my own understanding" (Knabb, 2016b; Proverbs 3:5–6), when struggling with the symptoms of emotional disorders. In so doing, they are learning to accept painful inner experiences by situating them in a larger context, pivoting from preoccupations with pain to a more transcendent understanding of suffering.

Promoting Healthy Dependence: The Potter and the Clay

Building on this understanding, humans were created in God's image to be in relationship with him and others. Both the psychodynamic and attachment literatures capture this inherently relational dynamic, innate to optimal human functioning (Knabb & Emerson 2013; Knabb, Welsh, & Alexander, 2012). Although these literatures may possess some of the "building blocks," from a Christian perspective, they lack the "blueprint" of God's more transcendent design—healthy dependence on him for sustenance and existential survival.

Helping Christian clients to ameliorate the shame of healthy dependency on God is key, given that humans are necessarily incomplete without him. One way to help Christians deepen this awareness is to point to the biblical metaphor of a potter and clay (e.g., Isaiah 64:8; Jeremiah 18; Romans 9:21). With this biblical image, God is the potter and humans are the clay. God has the power to shape his creation as he sees fit and is concerned about the smallest of details, whereas humankind is vulnerable and fragile, malleable in his hands (Stulman, 2005). What is more, God molds and sculpts the clay for his glory, allowing humans to share in his beauty (Stulman, 2005).

Building on this biblical theme, which captures the ontological reality that God personally relates to his creation, therapists working with Christian clients with emotional disorders may wish to walk them through an imagery exercise:

> Get into a comfortable position, closing your eyes and resting your feet on the floor. Place your hands in your lap, with your palms facing outward towards God to symbolize your willingness to be malleable in his care. Now, imagine that you are clay in God's benevolent hands, being shaped for his good purposes. Although you are not always sure what his plans are for you, just rest in the reality that he is concerned for every detail of your existence and is molding you into the very vessel he designed you to be. Because of this, let go of your own understanding of your inner and outer experiences, surrendering your will to the potter's design. When a distracting thought or feeling comes up, shift your focus back to simply being held in his hands. There is nothing else you need to do and no one else you need to be, other than the pot he is slowly molding you into.

When therapists are finished with this exercise, they may wish to explore their Christian clients' reactions, including the thoughts and feelings that arose, along with any possible barriers to resting safely in the potter's hands.

Exploring the Inner World

As another support-based goal within the "ontology and epistemology" pillar, therapists working with Christian clients with emotional disorders may wish to turn to key teachings in Scripture in order to further explore the inner world. For example, citing Jesus' teaching on worry (Matthew 6:25–34), therapists may wish to highlight the ontological reality that God is caring for his creation. With the book of Ecclesiastes, therapists might highlight that life is meaningless outside of pursuing God's will. Finally, therapists may wish to point to several Psalms of lament to help Christians understand the inevitability of human pain within our short time on this planet, reconciling suffering with hope in, and praise for, God.

Offering Jesus' Love

As another ingredient within the "support" phase, therapists can model Jesus' love so as to capture the ontological reality of God's benevolent care for his creation in general, as well as his loving pursuit of humankind in particular. In other words, love is the guiding force within God's relational ontology, even uniting the Trinity. The Christian term that captures this dynamic is *perichoresis*, which

> denotes that Trinitarian unity which goes out beyond the doctrine of persons and their relations: by virtue of their eternal love, the divine persons exist so intimately with one another, for one another, and in one another that they constitute themselves in their unique, incomparable, and complete unity.
>
> (Moltmann, 1992, p. 86)

What might *perichoresis* mean for Christian clients suffering from emotional disorders?

> The *perichoresis* modeled by the Godhead emerges in the therapeutic relationship because the Christian therapist is fully present for the Christian client and entirely focused on responding to and ameliorating [but sometimes just learning to sit with] his or her psychological pain. This experience is quite unlike the typical responses the Christian client encounters in everyday interpersonal transactions. The Christian therapist, effectively, models a unique and healing intimate relationship via affective attunement that symbolizes—albeit imperfectly—the agape that the Godhead reveals to, and shares with, humankind.
>
> (Knabb, Welsh, & Alexander, 2012, p. 178)

Overall, because God is love (1 John 4:8) and pours out his love to humankind from moment to moment, we can model his love—captured in the ontological reality of God's relationship with humankind—in the therapy room so as to point to his loving presence.

Modeling "Being"

Building on this *perichoretic* understanding of the Trinity's love for human-kind, we can begin to help Christian clients patiently sit at the feet of Jesus, reminiscent of Mary in Luke's gospel (10:38–42; also reviewed in the third chapter). Because Jesus is offering his loving presence from moment to moment, we can help our clients to learn to rest in the ontological reality that God is relating to us in each unfolding second of the day. Thus, frantic, anxious activity—captured in Martha's stance before Jesus—can get in the way of a deeper rest available in God.

Authors within the mindfulness-based clinical literature call this deeper contentment the "being" mode of the mind, in contrast to the "doing" mode (Segal et al., 2012; see also Knabb, 2016b). When "being," which resembles Mary's ability to patiently sit at Jesus' feet, we are firmly planted in the present moment, letting go of the tendency to worry about tomorrow (Matthew 6:25–34), fix, problem solve, and so on (whether applied to our inner or outer world); rather, we are fully accepting of the here-and-now with an attitude of contentment. Ultimately, there is nowhere else we would rather be than resting at Jesus' feet.

Conversely, the "doing" mode is captured in Martha's anxious striving, attempting to fix the perceived challenges in her environment (Segal et al., 2012; see also Knabb, 2016b). Still, in these efforts, she missed the opportunity to sink into true contentment in the presence of her Lord and Savior. Overall, timing is crucial—Christianity certainly advocates "doing" in life; yet, when it comes to relating to the inner world, we argue that an attitude of "being" can help Christian clients connect to the ontological reality of God's *perichoretic* love and peace, unfolding from moment to moment.

To help Christian clients begin the process of resting at Jesus' feet in the midst of the symptoms of depression or anxiety, we might start each session by asking them to sit in silence, repeating the phrase, "Lord, I surrender." When their mind jumps in to evaluate the situation, offering a complaint like Martha in Luke's gospel (Luke 10:40), we can instruct them to gently return to Jesus' feet by repeating the phrase again. Over time, our hope is that Christian clients will learn that, paradoxically, the more they try to directly "fix" themselves, even in a seemingly religious way, "with Jesus' help," the further away they move from the most important position in the room—sitting in front of their Lord and Savior, cultivating an attitude of indirect, trustful surrender as they rest in his love. Stated differently, when we rely on our own understanding and unilateral attempts to somehow fix our suffering, we can end up missing out on actual healing in Jesus' loving presence. (Of course, we also will need to advocate for actively following Jesus with behavioral action, which will be emphasized in the "action" phase in a subsequent section of this chapter.)

As the famous saying goes in acceptance and commitment therapy (ACT), "outcome is the process through which process becomes the outcome" (Hayes et al., 1999, p. 219). For Christians, this means that the preferred outcome of God taking away the pain as we patiently sit at his feet may not be realized in each and every instance; yet, the very process of learning to value sitting at his feet taps into a larger reality—we are yielding to a more transcendent understanding of his unfolding, moment-by-moment love, beyond what we can discover in the material world through empirical investigation or individually discern through human reason.

The Learning Phase: Emotional Pain as a "Sign/Signal"

In moving from support- to learning-based interventions and techniques, a corrective relational experience is the focus, tending to the need-rupture-repair cycles within both the therapeutic relationship and Christian clients' relationship with God (Lessem, 2005). In this process, God's mercy and grace are emphasized and emotional experiences are reframed as important signals that help us to draw closer to God to fortify our relationship with him. With both depression and anxiety, there is a deeper longing to return to God as the Source of life. These painful inner experiences can be verbalized, with Christian clients learning that God is pursuing them in the midst of their suffering. In fact, since Jesus is the suffering servant (Isaiah 53), he empathizes with human pain (Hebrews 4:15). In the metanarrative of the Bible—God's revelation—humankind was created in God's image; although humans are fallen, redemption can take place in the context of a loving, sanctifying relationship with Jesus Christ. Furthermore, God will make everything new, meaning Christians can persevere with the hope that their current pain is by no means permanent (Revelation 21:4). Rather than relying on self-knowledge, trusting in God's providential care is key. Thus, building on the first three chapters of this book, therapists working with Christian clients can help them to let go of their own self-derived attempts to understand suffering. Rather, God is at the center of existence, giving them life. Because of his perfect attributes, he is trustworthy, and his care extends to the symptoms of depressive and anxiety disorders. In this phase of therapy, moreover, Christian clients can learn about the difference between primary and secondary emotions; from a Christian perspective, painful emotional states can be traced back to shame as a reminder of the separation between God and humankind (Bonhoeffer, 1955). Because of this chasm, shame-proneness is at the core of the human experience, with therapists working with Christian clients to understand shame as a primary emotion, which is the original, core feeling. In reaction to shame, secondary emotions (e.g., shame about shame, self-hatred about experiencing depression and anxiety) can exacerbate an already difficult experience.

Processing "Primary" Emotions

To begin the "learning" phase of the "ontology and epistemology" pillar, therapists can help Christian clients to better understand the utility of our God-given emotions (Allender & Longman, 1993). From a relational perspective, our emotions motivate us to take action when interacting with others (Mikulincer & Shaver, 2005). Certainly, emotions can be helpful in a wide variety of ways, allowing us to quickly respond to a threatening situation (i.e., "fight or flight"), recall important situations or salient encounters with others, effectively respond to a range of challenges in life, and deepen our relationships and better understand and share our experiences with others (McKay, Wood, & Brantley, 2007). Among this list of the core functions of emotions, we believe that the relational aspects of affective functioning are especially important, helping us to make sense of our relationship with God and others from moment to moment.

To be more specific, we can help our clients to verbalize their "primary" emotions, drawing a contrast with "secondary" emotions in the process (Greenberg & Safran, 1987). "Primary" emotions are deeper, initial affective experiences (e.g., sadness, fear, shame), often masked by "secondary" reactions (e.g., anger) that attempt to defend against more vulnerable, original feeling states. To be sure, painful affective experiences (e.g., shame) are "signals" that can point to a deeper longing for God as the Source of life (Allender & Longman, 1993; Bonhoeffer, 1955). This reframing of painful emotional experiences is essential, given many Christians struggle with understanding the meaningfulness and utility of emotions.

As a reminder, shame helps us to better understand our separation from God, a deeper loss associated with this rift, powerlessness in our inability (on our own) to restore the rupture, and a yearning to return to God at the center of our existence (Bonhoeffer, 1955). In other words, we were designed to be on the periphery, with God at the center, not the other way around. Yet, because of our banishment from the garden, we continue to experience reverberations from the fall in the form of emotional pain. This pain, from our perspective, points to our incompleteness without God and, thus, serves as a vital signal for understanding our current psychological state and more transcendent need for him.

Sadness, to reiterate, tells us we have lost something important. Throughout the pages of the Bible, sadness is conveyed to indicate a deeper loss, fittingly captured in the writer's response to the fall of Jerusalem in Lamentations (1:1–2):

> How deserted lies the city, once so full of people! How like a widow is she, who once was great among the nations! She who was queen among the provinces has now become a slave. Bitterly she weeps at night, tears are on her cheeks. Among all her lovers there is no one to comfort her. All her friends have betrayed her; they have become her enemies.

Rather than attempting to somehow permanently rid ourselves of this painful feeling state, sadness can help us to better understand our priorities, that is, what is most salient in life. To be certain, whereas sadness signifies loss, the other side of this proverbial coin can point us to what we value (Greco, Barnett, Blomquist, & Gevers, 2008). In our relationship with God, for instance, sadness conveys grief, especially in the context of what we have lost. For the writer of Lamentations, the loss of Jerusalem was a painful event, given the importance of what this city meant to the Jewish people.

Fear and anxiety, to review, alert us to danger, with present-moment fear helping us to better understand current threats and anxiety anticipating potential dangers (real or imagined) in the future. Anxiety, moreover, can point to our struggles with uncertainty, allowing us to recognize what (or whom) we put our faith in during the inevitable ambiguities of life. To offer a biblical example, we can only imagine the anxiety and uncertainty that Adam and Even must have felt as they made the transition from the safety of the Garden to navigating the unreliable paths of a fallen world. When we examine the other side of anxiety's proverbial coin, we can see that we value certainty, safety, and contentment, especially in our relationship with God.

With each of these emotions, we want to help our Christian clients recognize the ontological reality that God is active and present in our pain, generously offering his mercy and grace in every unfolding moment of life. Rather than striving to quickly get rid of depressive or anxiety-related symptoms, God is revealing himself in the midst of human suffering. With his mercy, he is withholding the punishment that is due, along with responding to our suffering with his perfect love; in offering his grace, furthermore, he is extending undue merit and favor to us, despite our fallen nature and estrangement from him. In combination, this means he is compassionately responding to our needs, with his relational pursuit guiding our reality.

Conversely, "secondary" emotions (i.e., reactions to our initial, primary emotional experiences) can actually mask our deeper longings and needs and get in the way of true intimacy with God. For instance, when we are angry with God, we may try to create additional distance by shutting down, withdrawing, and so on, rather than lamenting to him about our fear of abandonment and sadness about a perceived loss in our relationship with him. When this is the case, we want to help our Christian clients to deepen their awareness of core emotional experiences, rather than defending against them through "secondary" reactions.

To repeat once more, life's ubiquitous feeling states, including anxiety, sadness, and shame, can commonly point to reverberations from the fall. Because we were banished from the famous garden, we experience an uncertain future, a deep sense of loss, and the incompleteness of a life estranged from God. However, the good news is that these signals tell us that we need to reach for God, pointing us home to the outstretched arms of the father (Luke 15:11–32).

Attaining Insight into a Spiritual Reality

Since Jesus is the suffering servant (Isaiah 53), he empathizes with human pain (Hebrews 4:15). In the meta-narrative of the Bible, humankind was created in God's image; although humans are fallen, redemption can take place in the context of a loving, sanctifying relationship with Jesus Christ. Furthermore, God will make everything new, meaning Christians can persevere with the hope that our current pain is by no means permanent (Revelation 21:4).

Until this happens, Jesus is with us and can understand the vulnerabilities we face on the roads of life. With this being the case, we have a trustworthy traveling companion who has also suffered in this fallen, broken world. To help Christian clients understand this reality, we can point them to the book of Hebrews (4:14–16):

> Therefore, since we have a great high priest who has ascended into heaven, Jesus the Son of God, let us hold firmly to the faith we profess. For we do not have a high priest who is unable to empathize with our weaknesses, but we have one who has been tempted in every way, just as we are—yet he did not sin. Let us then approach God's throne of grace with confidence, so that we may receive mercy and find grace to help us in our time of need.

Since Jesus was "tempted in every way," he understands our psychological distress, even in the context of 21st-century emotional disorders. Within this section of Scripture, "empathize" is translated from the Greek word, *synpatheo*, which conveys to "suffer along with," and "weaknessses" comes from *astheneia*, meaning "any form of felt need" (Guthrie, 1983, p. 122). Overall, articulating that Jesus suffers with us and understands our psychological needs is key so that Chritsian clients can balance the ontological reality of God's transcendence and immanence.

To do this, we can ask Christian clients to write a letter to God to convey their pain; in turn, they can write a fictional response from Jesus, grounded in a scriptural understanding of his loving, empathic responsiveness to their needs. Included in the letter can be God's promises in the Bible, reflected in clients' carefully chosen passages in Scripture so as to rely on special revelation (rather than their own undertanding; see Proverbs 3:5) as a key source of knowledge. In this process, learning involves recognizing that God is with us in our pain, even when we may not *feel* his presence during instances of perceived silence. This ontological reality is especially salient during this phase of therapy, cultivating an unwavering confidence in God's imminence.

Offering a Corrective Experience: Embracing Need-Rupture-Repair Cycles

In the psychodynamic literature, need-rupture-repair cycles are emphasized as a part of the healing process (Lessem, 2005). To begin, clients come in to therapy with a relational need, which is sometimes unrealistic and based on faulty family of origin experiences. Inevitably, therapists will be unable to perfectly meet the needs of their clients, leading to a rupture in the therapeutic relationship. This rupture can be especially painful, resulting in echoes of the distress clients originally experienced in their family of origin. Yet, this relational rift is not the end of the story. Rather, therapists actively work towards repairing the rupture, which can serve as a source of healing. Because clients are replacing a prior expectation (i.e., ruptures inevitably lead to the permanent dissolution of relationships) with a new reality (i.e., conflict can lead to added support and responsiveness), change can slowly take place—a "working through" experience. In other words, repairing recurrent ruptures fortifies the relationship, with clients learning that interpersonal disruptions can be repaired. This new reality leads to a deeper trust in the unavoidable ups and downs of healthy relational functioning. Overall, the regular repairing of ruptures cultivates interpersonal effectiveness and a sense that the other person offers sensitivity and responsiveness (Tronick, 2007).

With God, we can certainly experience need-rupture-repair cycles, too. In this dynamic, though, a perfect God does not actually let us down. In other words, the problem is not on *his* end. Rather, we approach God with a need, experiencing a perceived rupture because of our fallen nature and struggle with prioritizing our own desires above God's will. Still, in this perceived rupture (which, again, occurs on our "side of the aisle"), we have the opportunity to repair the experienced chasm, given God is patiently waiting for our return (Luke 15:11–32). In repairing this rupture, we begin to see God as sensitive and responsive, like a child views a caring parent (Tronick, 2007).

To begin the process of moving through these three steps, we can encourage our clients to read the Parable of the Lost Son (Luke 15:11–32), highlighting the son's need, the rupture on the part of the son, and the son's willingness to humbly return to the outstretched arms of the father. In this dynamic, the son's willingness to return home results in his ability to fall into the outstretched arms of the father, consistent with our relationship with God. Because God is infinitely benevolent, he has our best intentions in mind and celebrates each and every time we return home.

Once Christian clients have read this story, they can explore their own "lost son [or daughter] narrative," reflecting on the following in the context of depression and anxiety:

(a) Their thoughts, feelings, and behaviors surrounding their original need in their relationship with God.

(b) Their perceived rupture in their relationship with God, including the "who, what, when, where, and how" questions that reveal the precise details of the experience.

(c) The concrete steps they can take to return home to the outstretched arms of their loving Father. This third and final step may involve prayer, journaling to God, writing God a letter, meditation, and so on. The most important part, of course, is to recognize that God has always been present, patiently waiting for the Christian client to make the trek home.

To be sure, relational disappointments can often be central to emotional disorders, with themes of low self-worth in the eyes of others, interpersonal guilt, ruminations about past conversations and events, and worries about future catastrophes in important relational encounters. For Christian clients, these themes can also emerge in their relationship with God. With this being the case, normalizing the relational hurts that come with living in a broken world is essential during this phase of the "ontology and epistemology" pillar, helping Christians turn to God's Word, the Bible, to gain a deeper knowledge of God's patient, benevolent sensitivity and responsiveness.

Pursuing Realistic Expectations Because of the Fall

After highlighting the inevitability of need-rupture-repair encounters with God, we can work with Christian clients to develop realistic expectations about psychological pain, emphasizing the grand narrative of Scripture as a way to understand the human condition. In *The Soul's Conflict and Victory Over Itself by Faith*, 17th-century Puritan Richard Sibbes (2013) explored the human reality of "a broken and troubled spirit," pointing to Psalm 42:5: "Why, my soul, are you downcast? Why so disturbed within me?" In this important writing, far ahead of its time in promoting theocentric self-awareness, self-talk, and remediation, Sibbes noted that discouragements, sorrow, and grief can come from a variety of inner and outer experiences, such as overly relying on worldly comforts, being preoccupied with the perspectives of other people, and looking too closely at our own shortcomings.

As a remedy, Sibbes (2013) suggested, "Those that love too much will always grieve too much. It is the greatest of our affections which causeth the sharpness of our afflictions" (p. 86). As revealed in previous sections of this chapter, our emotions serve as signals, with sadness telling us that we have lost something important. Sibbes went on to argue, "The life of a Christian should be a meditation [on] how to unloose his affections from inferior things" (p. 86). Here, we see that sadness helps us to better understand, then let go of, the "inferior things" that get in the way of our relationship with God. As another ubiquitous example, anxiety tells us when we are preoccupied with future danger, allowing us to return to God as our true Source of comfort and contentment. Inspired by this work of Sibbes' (2011), we can help Christian clients allow their sadness and anxiety to lead them closer to God.

Inspired by Sibbes' (2011) *The Soul's Conflict and Victory Over Itself by Faith*, we can help Christian clients to recognize their sadness and anxiety, which serve as important signals in our relationship with God (Mikulincer & Shaver, 2005). As noted previously, sadness helps us to better understand what we value, what we have lost, and the central role that God plays in meeting our deepest needs; in addition, anxiety helps us to realize when we are preoccupied with future danger and struggling to rely on God as the ultimately Source of safety and contentment.

For Sibbes (2011), meditating on (a) God's goodness and power, (b) the joyful reality of heaven, (c) the inherent limitations of earthly things for satisfying the soul, and (d) the uncertainty of the human condition is key. In doing so, we are cultivating a deeper, loving faith in reality, including the fact that God is relating to his creation from moment to moment with his perfect providential care. Because our imagination has a tendency to wander away from God's plan, getting stuck in repetitive negative thinking in the process, and because our senses can be inaccurate and deceiving in a fallen world, Christians are called to turn to God for comfort: "[The way to comfort] is to yield unto [a man] that there is cause of grieving, though not of overgrieving, and to shew him grounds of comfort stronger than the grief he suffers" (Sibbes, 2011, p. 136).

To pursue realistic expectations in the midst of emotional disorders, we can help our Christian clients to spend time with God in solitude, practicing turning to him for comfort in the midst of inner distress. To begin with, we can ask our clients to think about the uncertainty of the world and inherent limitations of earthly comforts. Following this period of reflection, we can ask our Christian clients to meditate on God's goodness and the reality of heaven. With this second step, we can ask them to select short passages in Scripture to meditate on, thinking deeply about the ontological reality of God's loving responsiveness. Whenever they get stuck in repetitive, perseverative thinking, they can shift their focus to God's attributions, actions, and promises—especially his providential care—so as to ameliorate the tendency to overly rely on the senses to discern reality. Instead, they are drawing from Scripture—with God at the center—as the source of reality, over and over again.

Reframing the Self as Dependent on God

In contemporary Western society, individualism is highly prized, with many Christians struggling to fully embrace our utter dependence on God. Thus, Christian clients may begin to develop shame surrounding the need for God, especially given the common message emanating from the West that says we should be able to think, feel, and act independent of the micro- and macro-systems that surround us. Yet, this notion of independence and autonomy is inconsistent with a biblical view of reality, which includes our identity development, rooted in God's loving presence.

Writing on the relationship between identity and reality, Merton (1961) said the following:

> The secret of my identity is hidden in the love and mercy of God. But whatever is in God is really identical with Him...Ultimately the only way that I can be myself is to become identified with Him in Whom is hidden the reason and fulfillment of my existence. Therefore there is only one problem on which all my existence, my peace and my happiness depend: to discover myself in discovering God. If I find Him I find myself and if I find my true self I will find Him. But although this looks simple, it is in reality immensely difficult. In fact, if I am left to myself it will be utterly impossible. For although I can know something of God's existence and nature by my own reason, there is no human and rational way in which I can arrive at that contact, that possession of Him, which will be the discovery of Who He really is and of Who I am in Him. That is something that no man can ever do alone. Nor can all the men and all the created things in the universe help him in this work. The only One Who can teach me to find God is God, Himself, Alone.
>
> (p. 34)

As Merton revealed, Christians' true identity is found in God alone, rather than in broken human relationships and fallible societal systems. With this being the case, we can help our Christian clients to explore the ways in which they are potentially relying on a pseudo-sense of self, which can exacerbate the symptoms of emotional disorders. For example, with depression, our clients may be overly relying on a socially constructed sense of self that is deeply flawed, unlovable, and defined by others. In consideration of anxiety, our clients may be preoccupied with a powerless, isolated self that is unable to navigate the perceived dangers ahead, built upon prior instances of catastrophe and relational letdowns. In either case, overly relying on a pseudo-autonomous self can undermine Christians' ability to radically follow Jesus on the roads of life; this ubiquitous struggle can be traced back to the fall of humankind—originally, we chose to be like God, rather than dependent on God (Bonhoeffer, 1955).

Building on the support phase, we can work with our clients to recognize the distinction between Martha's "doing" and Mary's "being" in Luke's gospel (Luke 10:38–42; Knabb, 2016b). As we noted earlier, Martha missed out on the opportunity to sit at Jesus' feet to listen to him and find rest in his presence. By contrast, Mary was focused exclusively on Jesus; she did not engage in unnecessary activity that pulled her away from the most important person in the room. Whereas Martha was seemingly focused on herself, including accomplishing the tasks she believed were most important, Mary was able to keep her attention on her Lord. This shift in awareness is especially important when Christians are struggling with emotional disorders—although by no means easy, turning from the self to God is central. Of course, learning to sit at Jesus' feet so as to find our identity in him requires consistent practice, revealed within the action phase of treatment. For now, though, we can at least help our clients to learn about this distinction, pointing Christians to the famous contrast in Luke's gospel.

As one more example, we can help our Christian clients to contrast the "tree of life" and "tree of the knowledge of good and evil" in Genesis (2:9). The former represents God's place at the center of the garden, whereas the latter captures our erroneous desire to be at the center of our own garden—like God, rather than dependent on him (Bonhoeffer, 1955). Due to the fall, we struggle with the tendency to unilaterally construct our own ideas, placing ourselves at the center of our proverbial garden. Yet, from a Christian perspective, God resides at the center of reality. As a result, we can explore this contrast—"like God" versus "dependent on God" (Bonhoeffer, 1955)—in the context of emotional disorders, preparing our clients to take action by practicing this intentional pivot. With this shift, we are helping Christians let go of their own attempts to define themselves and independently interpret their suffering, moving towards a deeper awareness that God is the author of their unfolding story.

The Action Phase: Trusting God and Following His Will

With action-based interventions and techniques, Christian clients can practice trusting God in the midst of depressive and anxiety disorders (rather than an independent knowledge of good and evil), cultivating healthy behaviors that are rooted in Scripture as a source of knowledge (instead of a unilaterally derived understanding of the best course of action). Jesus' Sermon on the Mount is a fitting starting point, with Christians learning to apply Jesus' teachings to daily living. Although Christians may continue to notice rumination, worry, and uncertainty, they can work towards trusting in him because of his providential care (Matthew 6:25–34). Of course, one of the major interventions during this phase of therapy is to help Christians test their assumptions of reality—a distinctly Christian epistemology can help Christians gain this deeper knowledge in order to attain a skillful grip on the world by getting outside their own head and grasping what is real. With emotional disorders, there may be themes of God's absence, given that depression often involves low self-esteem, guilt, and pessimistic thinking, and anxiety can involve catastrophic, doomsday predictions about the future. In that a Christian ontology involves the reality that God is infinitely wise, good, powerful, and present (as revealed in God's revelation, the Bible), action must include a recognition of this spiritual reality so as to cultivate a hopeful endurance in the midst of pain.

Trusting in God, Rather than Human Knowledge

Because of the fall of humankind, Christians struggle with falsely trying to be "like God," rather than "dependent on him" (Bonhoeffer, 1955). In other words, we tend to place ourselves at the center of the proverbial garden, rather than relying on God at the center. Because of this, we can work with our Christian clients to ameliorate the tendency to take a bite out of the forbidden fruit, shifting from relying on our own arbitrarily constructed knowledge to total reliance on God as the Source.

To do so, we can help our clients notice their perseverative thoughts (e.g., ruminations, worries, self-judgments), which are self-generated, before shifting to a biblical understanding of God's active, loving presence (Knabb, 2016a). Instructions for a guided meditation exercise, inspired by the Genesis account of the fall, can be presented to Christian clients as follows:

> With this guided meditation, you will simply notice your mind's tendency to eat from this outlawed tree, labeling your thoughts (e.g., "judging") when they arise. In turn, you will gently allow these lingering thoughts to run their natural course, without "biting into" them and tasting them, reminiscent of just noticing the forbidden tree in the garden without actually eating the fruit. If possible, with your eyes closed, try to do this exercise for about twenty minutes in a quiet environment, sitting upright in a comfortable position.
>
> (Knabb, 2016a, p. 57)

This exercise can be practiced over an extended period of time in order to help our clients simply notice the inner workings of the mind, recognizing they do not need to automatically believe the thoughts that pop into their head. Rather, they can pivot towards an awareness of a more transcendent reality, wherein God is active, present, and loving them from moment to moment. To be dependent on God, to be sure, means we are reliant upon Scripture as a source of knowledge, which unveils the "good news" of God's love for humankind (John 3:16).

Shifting from the "Doing" to "Being" Mode

In turn, we can help our Christian clients to shift from the "Martha/doing" mode to the "Mary/being" mode, cultivating a deeper awareness of the ability to simply rest in Jesus' presence. Characteristics of the "Mary/being" mode include the following (adapted from Frenette, 2012; Gilbert, 2010; Knabb, 2016b; Knabb, 2018; Segal, Williams, & Teasdale, 2002):

- Surrendering the inner world (e.g., thoughts, feelings, sensations) to God (rather than striving to get rid of unpleasant intrapsychic experiences).

- Being content and at peace with both inner and outer experiences because God is present (rather than trying to unilaterally change things by making demands of God).
- Staying anchored to the here-and-now, where God is active and present (rather than ruminating about the past or worrying about the future).
- Focusing on Jesus for an extended period of time, given we are sitting at his feet (rather than being distracted in pursuing our own wants and needs).
- Listening to Jesus, given he is the most important person in the room (rather than doing all the talking in our relationship with him).

To cultivate the "Mary/being" mode, we can help our Christian clients to sit in silence with Jesus, imagining they are resting at his feet. Whenever a thought, feeling, or sensation arises, we can instruct them to use a simple, single-syllable word to anchor them to Jesus in the here-and-now. As an example, "Lord" can be repeated to capture the reality that Jesus is the Lord of our life; in fact, we are called to surrender to him as our Lord in this very moment. In practicing the ability to rest at Jesus' feet, our clients will be learning to ameliorate the tendency to get caught up in perseverative think-ing patterns, reminiscent of Martha's compulsive activity in Luke's gospel.

Practicing Following Jesus

In Matthew's gospel, Jesus provided a wide variety of teachings on Chris-tian living. For example, he taught us to quickly repair ruptures when we have conflict with others (5:23–24), love our enemies (5:44), give to those in need (6:2), avoid placing our trust in earthly things (6:19–21), and have faith in God's providential care (6:25–34). Unfortunately, Christian clients may struggle to live out these teachings in a concrete manner, given they are waiting for the wrong proverbial train to safely transport them along the tracks of life (Stoddard & Afari, 2014).

To help Christian clients authentically follow Jesus, applying his teach-ings to daily life, we can ask them to imagine they are at a train station, waiting for a train to take them where they would like to go (Stoddard & Afari, 2014). Unfortunately, though, they are waiting for a fictional train that may never leave the station. This imaginary train offers perfect comfort and protection and seemingly guarantees they will safely get to their destin-ation. Day after day, they wait for this safe, comfortable, perfect train, only to eventually realize that it will never come. As they watch all the other trains pull away from the station, they start to notice that other people are living their lives, traveling on the tracks of life on a daily basis in spite of the uncertainties that lie ahead.

We might also offer a Christian parallel to the above therapeutic meta-phor by noting that Christians can often wait for Jesus to take them on a safe, predictable journey, traveling down a fictional path that somehow guarantees they will be free from pain. Yet, they may spend their whole life waiting, given Jesus literally calls us to follow him by carrying a cross of suffering and hardship (Matthew 16:24–26), a reference to the inevitability of self-sacrifice and pain that lies ahead on the roads of life. Overall, following Jesus requires a willingness to bring the pain along for the arduous hikes of life, staying connected to the more transcendent realities that (a) we live in a fallen world, (b) Jesus has redeemed us (although we still experience psychological and physical pain), and (c) Jesus will eventually return to restore all things. As we press forward, Jesus' teachings offer a trustworthy map, given he has revealed himself to us in the pages of the New Testament.

Achieving Efficacy from God

Christians almost universally will state that they desire to follow Christ and that his teachings are the way to live life in this world. This is similar to the position of many who come for psychotherapy—they desire change, but may feel ambivalence about it. The therapist then seeks to help move the client to articulate motivation to change and act accordingly. This issue led to the development of the popular secular therapeutic model of motivational interviewing (Miller & Arkowitz, 2015). Often, problems stem in part from feeling ineffective and, thus, being hesitant to change in ways that produce growth and improvement of emotional problems. Secular therapy might at this point work to promote a sense of self-efficacy in clients. Yet, the ontological model of Christianity tells us our efficacy is rooted in God, not ourselves, particularly in the pursuit of *his* goals (Johnson, 2017, ch. 4).

Scripture teaches that there is a source of actual power to act and change to live more in accordance with Jesus' teachings. Greater appreciation of the hope we have in Christ and the power God provides are additional tools for the Christian's therapist to move past ambivalence in anticipation of the work of the Holy Spirit in promoting change. Several core texts may be helpful here. Colossians 1:27 informs us that it is Christ within us that is the hope of glory. Even when emotional problems render us discouraged and avoidant, our pivoting to Christ puts our eyes on hope for change and for the glory that awaits Christ's followers. Add to this Philippians 4:13, which teaches that we can do "all [things] through [Christ] who gives [us] strength." Herein is the hope to change, but there is more than this. It is actual power to change—to be efficacious in living the Christian life. Finally, Philippians 2:13 informs us that, ultimately, it is "God who works in you to will and to act in order to fulfill his good purpose." Here is hope that God himself plays a role in our motivation and action.

Christians in therapy can be encouraged that they have access to the power of Almighty God to promote willingness and action. One can put a car in neutral and push it from point A to point B, but this strategy undermines the whole purpose of a car: to be an instrument of power to reach destinations. We turn on the engine and activate the power it has to take us where we are going. Though this metaphor is a bit rough, it points us to how we can support clients to seek and utilize the power of God to change and become spiritually efficacious by connecting to God as the center of all.

Relating Differently to Thoughts and Feelings

One struggle faced by many (if not most) clients is being tangled in their thoughts and feelings. We get so wrapped up in these, trying to make sense of them or force control on them, that we are consumed and lose perspective. It is important to understand that as God's children, we have thoughts and feelings, but we are not these thoughts and feelings. If we are to develop the mind of Christ (1 Corinthians 2:16), we may need to get perspective on our own thoughts and feelings so we can pivot toward seeing things from a deeper ontological reality through our Christian "eyes."

A popular exercise to promote awareness of thoughts and feelings with some sense of perspective on them is called the "leaves on a stream" metaphor (Hayes et al., 2012). In this exercise, the client is asked to close his or her eyes and imagine sitting under a tree by a stream. As the person sits, he or she is asked to imagine a leaf falling on his or her body. The person imagines picking up the leaf, briefly observing it, then laying it on the stream and watching it float away. After doing this with several leaves, the client is invited to consider his or her thoughts or feelings as leaves: notice them without getting into evaluating them or wrestling with them. Then the person releases the thought or feeling by laying it on the stream. In practicing this skill, we learn that the thoughts and feelings may come from our mind, but they are not our mind.

A Christian adaptation of this might have the person imagining Jesus sitting next to us (Knabb, 2016b); as we hold each "leaf," we present it to him and ask him his perspective on it. Then, we look at it through Jesus' eyes and what he has taught us, gaining flexibility in our responses to thoughts and feelings as they come to us. The therapist may need to model this a few times for the individual to catch on.

A Case Example

Aaron is a 39-year-old male who has a history of being a successful attorney, though with a rather anxious temperament. Things changed dramatically for him when his wife was killed in a car explosion (likely a murder). Since then, he has been extremely anxious and fearful about many things. He is highly fearful of germs and intolerant of uncertainty, ambiguity, or irregularity. Almost any situation cues him to think "what if" about bad things that might happen. Because of these, he avoids any places or situations that might trigger anxiety. He lost his job because his fears incapacitated him, though he still consults to some extent, as he can function to a degree with his assistant at his side who accommodates his anxieties by comforting, reassuring, and supplying the occasional antibacterial wipe.

Aaron became a Christian three years ago and has pursued his faith rather "religiously." He prays regularly for his fears to go away and for God's peace in his life, but feels like a failure because he is still anxious. He genuinely loves God, but still struggles with why his wife died, and he desperately wants to get his old job back. He agrees to see a therapist to help him become more functional and regain his job.

The Support Phase

Here, Aaron may struggle with relationships. He depends excessively on others for reassurance and has had the tragic death of his wife to deal with. One might expect that he would either try to avoid the relationship with the therapist or move toward being dependent. While offering support, the therapist will want to help Aaron see the unfailing friend he has in Jesus and to develop a secure attachment to God. The therapist will want to develop the alliance carefully with generous support, while not becoming a "compulsion" used to reassure the client of irrational fears. Rather, the relationship should grow to be a context to point to the realities that his feelings of fear are not revealing actual dangers and to the realities of God's care for him. Work may focus on helping Aaron see how his situation ruptures his relationship with God and how to repair this perceived chasm, as discussed earlier in the chapter.

The Learning Phase

As a relatively new Christian facing multiple emotional and relational challenges, there will be much for Aaron to learn. Foremost will be to develop a clear understanding of God's nature. Bibliotherapy might include the classic work of J. I. Packer (1973), *Knowing God*. The therapist might assign one chapter per week, and ask Aaron to journal on what each aspect of God means in his situation. The client might also want to grieve his wife more "Christianly" now that he is saved. Reflection on death from this tradition may prove helpful, and resources such as Sisemore (2017) may be useful. The Christian version of the "leaves on a stream" exercise (described above) could also support Aaron learning to see his life though God's eyes and gain some perspective from his fearful thoughts and feelings.

The Action Phase

Following Jesus through behavioral action despite his overwhelming fears will be a challenge to him. His faith can give motivation and power to do as he seeks the power of the Holy Spirit to endure difficult things and exposes himself to his obsessions and fears. One way to promote this is to help Aaron visualize how he would want his life to go. Here is an exercise that may help (adapted from Harris, 2009):

Close your eyes and try to imagine being at your 90th birthday party. This is imagination, so make this what you want. Where will it be? Visualize the room, decorations, etc. What would the theme be? Now, make your guest list. Who would you want to be there with you? Spouse? Children? Grandchildren? Former co-workers? Friends? Neighbors? Fellow church members? Why? Now, each attendee will be given an opportunity to say one quality about you that impacted their lives and for which they thank God. Consider what each will say as they take turns speaking. What is it that you would be gratified to hear as affirmation that your life had manifested the glory of God along the way? Finally, you give a brief speech on what you hope your life has meant to others and what God has meant to you along the way. Close the party with a prayer of thanksgiving.

The material in this chapter on accessing God's power and hope to change behavior would also be useful for Aaron. The courage to change will require a strong dependence on God and the support of a therapist who cares for him while pointing toward acting in faith, not fear in the world, as he pursues his most important life goals. Further resources for helping believing clients who have obsessive-compulsive disorder (which has been moved from the "Anxiety Disorders" to the "Obsessive-Compulsive and Related Disorders" section in the DSM-5) may be found in Sisemore (2018).

Conclusion

In this chapter, we reviewed the "ontology and epistemology" pillar, focusing on the ways in which Christian clients can benefit from a deeper understanding of reality and a scriptural emphasis on virtuous living. Because our emotions are a signal, we can work with our clients to slow down enough to notice the inner world, recognizing the role that their feelings play in better understanding their relationship with God. Over time, helping Christians to recognize the utility of emotions can allow them to participate in life again, rather than avoid daily living because their emotional pain will not go away. As they learn to follow Jesus by bringing the pain along for the journey (Knabb, 2016), they are in a better position to experience the joys of walking with their Lord and Savior moment by moment and step to step.

Note

1 Worth mentioning, by turning to Lamentations, we are in no way suggesting that God is somehow punishing Christians with emotional disorders because of a lack of faithfulness. Instead, the point is to highlight the salient role of emotions in the Christian life, especially sadness and loss, and emphasize the importance of lamenting to God when in pain in order to patiently wait for his compassionate reply.

References

Allender, D., & Longman, T. (1993). *The Cry of the Soul: How Our Emotions Reveal Our Deepest Questions about God*. Colorado Springs, CO: NavPress.

Bonhoeffer, D. (1955). *Ethics*. New York: Touchstone.

Fergus, T., Valentiner, D., & McGrath, P. (2010). Shame- and guilt-proneness: Relationships with anxiety disorder symptoms in a clinical sample. *Journal of Anxiety Disorders, 24*, 811–815.

Frame, J. (2002). *The Doctrine of God*. Phillipsburg, NJ: P & R.

Frenette, D. (2012). *The Path of Centering Prayer: Deepening Your Experience of God*. Boulder, CO: Sounds True.

Gilbert, P. (2010). *Compassion-Focused Therapy: Distinctive Features*. New York: Routledge.

Greco, L., Barnett, E., Blomquist, K., & Gevers, A. (2008). Acceptance, body image, and health in adolescence. In L. Greco & S. Hayes (Eds.), *Acceptance and Mindfulness for Children and Adolescents: A Practitioner's Guide* (pp. 187–216). Oakland, CA: New Harbinger Publications.

Greenberg, L., & Safran, J. (1987). *Emotion in Psychotherapy: Affect, Cognition, and the Process of Change*. New York: The Guilford Press.

Harris, R. (2009). *ACT Made Simple: An Easy-to-Read Primer on Acceptance and Commitment Therapy*. Oakland, CA: New Harbinger Publications.

Hayes, S., Strosahl, K., & Wilson, K. (1999). *Acceptance and Commitment Therapy: An Experiential Approach to Behavior Change*. New York: The Guilford Press.

Johnson, E. L. (2007). *Foundations for Soul Care: A Christian Psychology Proposal*. Downers Grove, IL: InterVarsity Press.

Johnson, E. L. (2017). *God and Soul Care: The Therapeutic Resources of the Christian Faith*. Downers Grove, IL: InterVarsity Press.

Knabb, J. (2016a). *Acceptance and Commitment Therapy for Christian Clients: A Faith-Based Workbook*. New York: Routledge.

Knabb, J. (2016b). *Faith-Based ACT for Christian Clients: An Integrative Treatment Approach*. New York: Routledge.

Knabb, J. (2018). *The Compassion-Based Workbook for Christian Clients: Finding Freedom from Shame and Negative Self-Judgments*. New York: Routledge.

Knabb, J., & Emerson, M. (2013). "I will be your God and you will be my people": Attachment theory and the grand narrative of scripture. *Pastoral Psychology, 62*, 827–841.

Knabb, J., & Meador, K. (2016). A theological lens for integrating ACT with conceptions of health, healing, and human flourishing. In J. Nieuwsma, R. Walser, & S. Hayes (Eds.), *ACT for Clergy and Pastoral Counselors: Using Acceptance and Commitment Therapy to Bridge Psychological and Spiritual Care*. Oakland, CA: New Harbinger Publications.

Knabb, J., & Newgren, K. (2011). The craftsman and his apprentice: A Kohutian interpretation of the gospel narratives of Jesus Christ. *Pastoral Psychology, 60*, 245–262.

Knabb, J., Welsh, R., & Alexander, P. (2012). Towards an integrated view of the necessity of human interdependence: Perspectives from theology, philosophy, and psychology. *Journal of Spirituality in Mental Health, 14*, 166–180.

Krystal, H. (1988). *Integration and Self-Healing: Affect, Trauma, Alexithymia*. New York: Routledge.

Lambert, M. (2013). The efficacy and effectiveness of psychotherapy. In M. Lambert (Ed.), *Bergin and Garfield's Handbook of Psychotherapy and Behavior Change* (pp. 169–218). New York: John Wiley & Sons.

Lessem, P. (2005). *Self Psychology: An Introduction.* New York: Jason Aronson.

McKay, M., Wood, J., & Brantley, J. (2007). *The Dialectical Behavior Therapy Skills Workbook: Practical DBT Exercises for Learning Mindfulness, Interpersonal Effectiveness, Emotion Regulation and Distress Tolerance.* Oakland, CA: New Harbinger Publications.

Merton, T. (1961). *New Seeds of Contemplation.* New York: New Directions Books.

Mikulincer, M., & Shaver, P. (2005). Attachment theory and emotions in close relationships: Exploring the attachment-related dynamics of emotional reactions to relational events. *Personal Relationships, 12,* 149–168.

Miller, W. R., & Arkowitz, H. (2015). Learning, applying, and extending motivational interviewing. In H. Arkowitz, W. R. Miller, & S. Rollnick (Eds.), *Motivational Interviewing in the Treatment of Psychological Problems* (2nd ed., pp. 1–32). New York: Guilford Press.

Mobley, G. (2009). 1 and 2 Kings. In G. O'Day & D. Petersen (Eds.), *The Theological Bible Commentary* (pp. 119–144). Louisville, KY: Westminster John Knox Press.

Nouwen, H. (2006). *Spiritual Direction: Wisdom for the Long Walk of Faith.* New York: HarperCollins Publishers.

Packer, J. I. (1993). *Knowing God.* Downers Grove, IL: InterVarsity Press.

Rous, F. (2016). *The Art of Happiness.* Crossville, TN: Puritan Publications.

Segal, Z., Williams, J., & Teasdale, J. (2002). *Mindfulness-Based Cognitive Therapy for Depression: A New Approach to Preventing Relapse.* New York: The Guilford Press.

Segal, Z., Williams, J., & Teasdale, J. (2012). *Mindfulness-Based Cognitive Therapy for Depression* (2nd ed.). New York: The Guilford Press.

Sibbes, R. (2011). *The Soul's Conflict and Victory over Itself by Faith.* Coconut Creek, FL: Puritan Publications.

Sisemore, T. A. (2017). *Finding God while Facing Death.* Ross-shire, Scotland: Christian Focus Publications.

Sisemore, T. A. (2018). Religious and spiritual interventions for obsessive compulsive disorder. In T. Plante (Ed.), *Healing with Spiritual Practices* (pp. 196-207). Santa Barbara, CA: ABC-Clio.

Stoddard, J., & Afari, N. (2013). *The Big Book of ACT Metaphors: A Practitioner's Guide to Experiential Exercises and Metaphors in Acceptance and Commitment Therapy.* Oakland, CA: New Harbinger Publications.

Stulman, L. (2005). *Jeremiah.* Nashville, TN: Abingdon Press.

Tangney, J., Wagner, P., & Gramzow, R. (1992). Proneness to shame, proneness to guilt, and psychopathology. *Journal of Abnormal Psychology, 101,* 469–478.

Tronick, E. (2007). *The Neurobehavioral and Social-Emotional Development of Infants and Children.* New York: W. W. Norton.

Williams, M. (2008). Mindfulness, depression and modes of mind. *Cognitive Therapy Research, 32,* 721–733.

Wright, C. (2015). *The Message of Lamentations.* Downers Grove, IL: InterVarsity Press.

CHAPTER 7

Biblical Anthropology and Axiology in the Christian Tradition

Introduction

Humankind exists, like all other created things, interweaved in a *relational ontology*. Indeed, within the Christian tradition, relationship with God is constitutive of human identity. Biblically, the defining characteristic of human identity is having been created in God's image—or, rather, humanity reflects the image of God in their living. Human identity, then, is only truly understood in and from this relationship, and it is by this relationship with God that all other relations are meaningfully ordered.

As created, humankind also shares creaturely finitude. Human completeness, like identity, is found only in communion with God. Thus, all human activity is naturally oriented to God. In actively tending to develop the potential in creation, humankind experiences the power of God in our activity; in turn, in our activity, humans find our own potential being developed. Righteousness in humanity, then, becomes "rightly" ordering activity and life toward God.

Understood together, we see the mutually supportive nature of humanity and morality. This chapter will focus on the implications of a biblical view of humankind (anthropology) and virtue (axiology) for the clinical context and demonstrate how a deeper understanding of our communion with God displays the remarkable nature of humankind. Further, we will see how the fullness of life produced by faithful activity within our communion with God includes rightly understanding our experiences in light of communion in our inter-cohering relational world.

Life as the Practice of Communion

As we have seen in previous chapters, communion is a framing concept. Here as well, communion shapes how the Christian tradition understands human life. From the start, the "being" and "knowing" of humankind were grounded in relationality, which included the whole of creation such that daily life was a practice in communion—everything received as a gift and enjoyed in deep gratitude with faithful response. Another name for this faithful response in communion is obedience. While this term carries so many negative connotations, it is quite extraordinary in the creational context. Far from sacrificing personal autonomy, it establishes our creaturely integrity. In a relational world, efforts toward autonomy always turn us away from completion and undo us by attempting to be something we are not, namely, God. In attempting to be what we are not, we lose what we are. Indeed, we are *what* and *who* we are only in relationship with God, and we live the life for which we were created when we live into the dynamic exchange of communion.

God created a relational world intentionally designed for, and to be developed by, creatures bearing his image. In this interconnected world, humans worked to cultivate the earth in active and loving reply to God's good gifts; in such work—to "work" and "keep/tend" creation—humans developed skills and virtues, which, in turn, cultivated their humanness.[1] Communion characterized the interconnected relationality between humankind and the world, and both were sustained and enlivened by loving communion with God. To put it another way, "There is an integral connection between the Christian doctrines of God the Trinity, of creation, and of the human person" (Ware, 2010, p. 128).

Because of God's intentionality, he knows the world and guides human activity in his caring providence. Thus, God's guidance was to lead humankind to *both* the fullest development of his bountiful creation *and* our deepest satisfaction. Obedience was as natural as breathing, and every act of obedience confirmed the goodness of God's guidance. To faithfully obey the Creator was for humans to seek their good and find their deepest satisfaction in God. Indeed, the common term for communion in Scripture is *koinonia*, which carries the sense of sharing, specifically, to share with someone in something which he has (Canlis, 2010). Further, the term expresses "a two-sided relation" whose "emphasis may be on either the giving or the receiving" (Hauck, as cited in Canlis, 2010, p. 9). It is a blessing for humankind to "share with" God in his very life; it is an incomparably greater blessing to do so intentionally through God's redeeming work in Christ. Recognizing the relational and communal nature of creation, and the principles at work in such a communion, can guide the clinical practitioner in understanding the deep longing for human connectedness, the need for purposeful activity, and the healing value of right relationships, along with why our human efforts toward such good things are perpetually frustrated as we experience existential bewilderment because of broken communion. But first, we need to consider the extraordinary part of creation we call humankind.

Communion and the *Imago Dei*

The Bible depicts the creation of humans in a rather intriguing way. It is the first part of creation over which God reflects. All elements of creation follow the "And God said, 'Let there be...,' and there was" pattern. Yet, when we come to the creation of humankind, there is a break in the pattern, "Then God said, 'Let us make mankind in our image... God blessed them" (see Genesis 1:26–28). Also, while the rest of creation is said to have been created "according to their kinds," it is uniquely the human that is said to be created in God's image. Further, we see a level of personal investment of God in creating humankind. In Genesis 2:7, God forms man from dust and "breathed into his nostrils the breath of life." Old Testament scholar Derek Kidner (2008) stated that humankind receives life from the breath of the Creator himself, who was hovering over him and suggests, "*Breathed* is warmly personal, with the face-to-face intimacy of a kiss and the significance that this was giving as well as making; and self-giving at that" (p. 65). Keil and Delitzsch (1996), also Old Testament scholars, add an important note worth considering, "what God breathed into man could not be the air which man breathes" (p. 79). What God breathes into us is the very life by which we live—respiration is simply a sign of the in-spiration of life. Humankind, from the beginning, was defined by intimate communion; the image not being something simply *in* us, but something *between* God and humans (Horton, 2012).

Biblically, the core idea of the image of God is that of an inherent and unique relationship humans have with God. While all reality stands in relationship with God, it is humankind that shares God's personhood-in-relationship, and further, what it means to be a human *person* is inconceivable outside of relationship to him. To be human, then, is to be related to God, which inevitably returns us to the concept of communion. Timothy Ware, an Oxford theologian, shows the deep connection between these ideas:

> The being of God is relational: so also is our being as human persons. Without the concept of communion it is not possible to speak about the being of God: so also without the concept of communion it is not possible to speak about human beings.
>
> (Ware, 2010, p. 126)

Indeed, this seems to be what John Calvin had in mind when he talked about the integrated nature of our knowledge of God and our knowledge of self. Because humans were created in God's image, knowledge of self requires knowledge of God. Calvin states, "Again, it is certain that man never achieves a clear knowledge of himself unless he has first looked upon God's face" (Calvin, 1960, p. 37). In the creational communion, this was natural and every activity, every breath, was to be practiced in communion. Interestingly, the translator of Calvin's *Institutes of the Christian Religion* notes in reference to "knowledge of self" that "Our knowledge of ourselves may be construed to include both all mankind and all creation (of which man is a microcosm)" (Calvin, 1960, p. 37). Thus, all knowledge, but knowledge of self in particular, requires knowledge of God, and in proper knowledge of self, humans are properly disposed to know and understand creation more effectively—this is what we would expect, given the nature of relational ontology.

When the natural communion with God is broken, however, we are alienated from God and, therefore, experience self-alienation. Self-alienation has made humans a riddle to themselves, and this dismay is their current (un)natural experience. Such perplexity is captured well in the ancient Greek entreaty to "know yourself." It is easy to miss the profundity of this statement if we simply focus on the Socratic truism, "the unexamined life is not worth living." While certainly true, the significance of both statements is that we do not currently have adequate self-knowledge, that such knowledge is not reflexive and obvious, but a difficult task that, from the results of things, seems as confused today as it was to the Greeks. Scripture gives us a sense of why such confusion surrounds our self-understanding and how humans have become a riddle to ourselves.

Human nature is constituted by the image of God. Yet, this image should not be considered as simply the "hardware" of our nature, abstracted from our relationship with God. While human nature may be studied in the abstract—considering the structural or functional aspects of humanity—understanding the image of God requires viewing humans as whole and wholly related to God (whether this relationship is recognized or not). When we consider in Chapter 8 the structural and functional dynamics of the *imago Dei*, it should be understood in light of communion—structural (e.g., intellectual, moral, decision-making) and functional (e.g., loving God and others, living out God's will) qualities (Hoekema, 1986) all make sense in light of God's calling on humans to be his image bearers. In Chapter 10, the *imago Dei* will be discussed as a shattered mirror—the wholeness and completeness of humanity in proper communion with God gets shattered and fragmented in the fall. Such fragmentation is our current (un)natural state and engenders the possibility of studying and understanding human nature independently of divine communion. As will be mentioned below, such fragmentation also engenders the current bewilderment humankind faces, which manifests itself in persistent emotional and psychological difficulties.

To understand the *imago Dei* in its wholeness, the words of theologian Kevin Vanhoozer (2010) should be kept in mind:

> one can also appeal to the *imago Dei* in the opposite direction to argue not that we are projecting our image upon God but that God is projecting his image onto us. Relationality would be in this case not a human projection onto God but a *theomorphic* projection onto humanity.
>
> (p. 161, italics added)

Scripture and the core understanding of human nature in the Christian tradition never focuses on humans by themselves, "but demands our fullest attention for man in his relation to God" (Berkouwer, 1962, p. 195). So, what constitutes us in our particular humanity—including the structural and functional qualities—our very identity, is God's self-relation to humans. This, again, makes the image not something we "have," but something we "are" in relation to via our communion with God (Berkouwer, 1962; Bavinck, 2008). In this case, human nature is not something that can be abstracted from our relationship with God, such that human nature somehow exists independently of God and our relationship to him is something "added" or "optional" to human nature. Literally, in having abstracted ourselves from our relationship with God—the declared autonomy mentioned above—we have lost all sense of self; in turn, in living life independently from God, we undo ourselves. In losing our orientation toward God in whose image we are made, we end up defining ourselves by other "images," either self- or socially constructed "identities," which are inherently transient. Further, the transience is simply a display of the perpetual confusion and ever-shifting sense of our identity.

The disorientation that occurs from broken communion "problematizes" human incompleteness, and we are confronted with our limits, the limits of human finitude. From a Christian perspective, this holds for *all* humankind. It is precisely when we move to find completion in ourselves, or orient and autonomously direct our lives on our own, that we move beyond our natural limits—we "over-reach." The great Reformation scholar Heiko Oberman (1993) described this move by saying of Calvin that he

> is intent to follow the biblical story and vocabulary portraying created man as "in communion with God" and fallen man as "alienated from God.".... When the imago Dei is lost, then this is not a loss in "substance" or "essence," but in *orientation*: since the fall man is bewildered.
>
> (p. 266)

It is a great irony that in the move to overcome human limits and autonomously define life ourselves, that humankind loses its identity and now lives in alienation of self and God. That is, we live in bewilderment. In such a move, however, humankind did not lose its limits, its finitude, or its incompleteness, just its Godward orientation. But how does communion get broken in the idyllic setting of Eden where communion naturally overflows in obedience? The answer is, in a word, "over-reaching."

Projecting versus Possessing

As noted previously, the Christian tradition has often held that the image of God in humankind is not something we have, but something we are in God's self-relation to us. St. Augustine (1991) stated it this way, "For man's true honor is God's image and likeness in him, but it can only be preserved when facing him from whom its impression is received" (p. 331). When what is a *projection* onto or into humankind becomes desired as a *possession*, we turn away from "facing him" and we lose our true honor. The move of Adam that all humankind follows is a move from loving and trusting God to loving and trusting the self. In trying to be something we are not, we lose what we are, turning away from God and destroying our very creatureliness (Berkouwer, 1962). The over-reach of attempting to be God, according to theologian Wolf-hart Pannenberg (1985), "represents a perverse form of love or volition. This 'perverse will' distorts the order of the universe by turning to inferior goods and for their sake abandoning better and higher goods—namely, God, his truth and his law" (pp. 87–88). In turning to ourselves, we are pursuing something that is genuinely good, but not the greatest good—we try to make the "lesser good" into the "greater good." In doing so, we disrupt our proper relationship to the Creator and created things. We experience existential bewilderment because we do not cease desiring, but redirect it—or "self-direct" it—in our effort to be God. In short, we trust ourselves more than God.

Pannenberg (1985) cuts to the heart of the matter when he explained that prideful humans attempt to

> claim an ungrounded superiority that they do not possess; they are excessively pleased with themselves as they make themselves the origin of things instead of attaching themselves to the real origin of things... This attitude lies behind the distorted desire for transitory things, since the latter are no longer desired as a means of serving God but are desired instead as means of obtaining the enjoyment of the one desiring them... When the ego which is proud in the sense described wills itself to be the center and ultimate end, it usurps the place in the order of the universe that belongs to God, its creator and supreme good.
>
> (p. 88)

There are a number of ways to discuss the act of over-reaching—covetousness, unfaithfulness, pride—each drawing out an aspect of the action, but none, alone, explaining the over-reach. An aspect that is somewhat under-discussed is a lack of trust, or disbelief. This relates to pride in that humankind thinks we know better than God, covetousness in that we desire more or better than God provides, and unfaithfulness in that we turn away from God, who is steadfast in his loving provision for us.

In the fifth chapter, it was established that emotions are signs/signals. They point to what is important to us, what we count as our good. We can begin to see the importance of the image of God for the clinical setting when we join these two ideas. Humankind's over-reach reveals in what, where, and whom our true trust resides. Consider the negative emotions discussed in the fifth chapter: anger, sadness, fear/anxiety, shame, guilt, and disgust. These emotions are valuable to identify possible problems and make us attentive to important things in ourselves and our world, but, for Christians, they can also reveal our level of trust in God.

Take anxiety as an example. This is an uneasiness about the future and expectation of pain, failure, or harm that seems imminent. There may be difficulties on the horizon that are rightly perceived—thus, the importance of negative emotions—but this does not mean that Christians should turn in anxiety away from the God who made us, stands with us, holds us in relationship with him, and providentially guides all things for good. Indeed, as has just been explicated with the image of God discussion, humans are undone and experience dismay when we turn from God and trust in our own devises.

As Augustine (1991) and Pannenberg (1985) suggested, we turn to lesser goods—namely, ourselves and our abilities—instead of our greater good, God. Though it sounds counterintuitive, far from being destructive, it is precisely these situations that God uses to teach us about ourselves and who he is. Recall the Greek philosophical quest to "know yourself." This can only be done in relationship with God, and God uses many different ways to help us know ourselves—struggles and difficulties, though painful, are clear lenses through which we can learn to accurately see. In these times, when we turn toward God, entrusting our safety, security, and lives to him, we find him utterly faithful; in turning to him, moreover, humankind finds its deepest strength and honor.

Lest this sound like pious, empty words, it might be good to follow the advice found in Hebrews 12:2 and "[fix] our eyes on Jesus, the pioneer and perfecter of faith. For the joy set before him he endured the cross, scorning its shame, and sat down at the right hand of the throne of God." The book of Hebrews gives insight into the struggles of Jesus and how he serves as a model for us as we face our struggles and learn to skillfully cope with daily difficulties in a way that deepens our communion with the "pioneer and perfecter of our faith."

The immediately preceding verse in Hebrews 12 properly frames the human life with an athletic metaphor, a race that we are to run with endurance. This beloved symbol is powerful, conjuring up images of a marathon, or perhaps the hurdles in a track and field event; each, at times, aptly describing aspects of life. But looking to Jesus serves as both an example and source of encouragement, which we examine next.

Earlier in Hebrews (2:10–18), the reader is told that Jesus is nothing less that the Son of God, the second person of the Trinity, who took on humanity in order to become humanity's savior:

> it was fitting that God, for whom and through whom everything exists, should make the pioneer of their salvation perfect through what he suffered... Since the children have flesh and blood, he too shared in their humanity... For this reason he had to be made like them, fully human in every way... Because he himself suffered when he was tempted, he is able to help those who are being tempted.

It is important to understand that the life of Jesus was a fully human life, complete with all the struggles and temptations that every human faces, yet without sin.

Indeed, in Hebrews 4:14–16, we read the following:

> Therefore, since we have a great high priest who has ascended into heaven, Jesus the Son of God, let us hold firmly to the faith we profess. For we do not have a high priest who is unable to empathize with our weaknesses, but we have one who has been tempted in every way, just as we are—yet he did not sin. Let us then approach God's throne of grace with confidence, so that we may receive mercy and find grace to help us in our time of need.

Notice the terms used to describe Jesus' experiences: he was made perfect through suffering, he suffered when tempted, so he is now able to empathize with our weakness. It is important to realize the full humanity of Jesus, because it is easy to misperceive what Christianity believes about Jesus. Such misunderstanding can lead some to say that, because he was the Son of God, he did not really struggle like we do. Yet, Hebrews makes his struggles clear. Hebrews 5:9–10, in particular, underscores this, as well as the practical results of the struggle, "Son though he was, he learned obedience from what he suffered and, once made perfect, he became the source of eternal salvation for all who obey him."[2] Obedience is an act of trust, and notice how Jesus learned obedience—it was through what he *suffered*. But if Jesus is God and God knows all things, how does Jesus "learn obedience?" It is important to recall, here, the full humanity of Jesus. As a man, he learned obedience through constantly making the Father's will his own in active obedience (Luke 2:52). In the garden of Gethsemane and on the cross, we see the culmination of Jesus's obedience as he, though experiencing incredible pain and suffering, entrusted himself to the Father. John Calvin (1960) offered a profound consideration of the Gethsemane prayer of Jesus and his cry to the Father from the cross. There, he said, we see Jesus in his full humanity, including its frailties, and the distress "arising from the feeling of pain and fear," which, he reminded us, "is *not* contrary to faith" (p. 519, italics added). In relation to Jesus' words on the cross, Calvin beautifully stated:

> For feeling himself, as it were, forsaken by God, he did not waver in the least from trust in his goodness. This is proved by that remarkable prayer to God in which he cried out in acute agony: "My God, My God, why hast thou forsaken me?" [Matt. 27:46]. For even though he suffered beyond measure, he did not cease to call him his God, by whom he cried out that he had been forsaken.
>
> (pp. 519–520)

Calvin's point has remarkable implications for the clinical setting and for Christians who are suffering and struggling to trust in God's providential care. Note that Jesus understood that his current suffering was according to the will of God, "My Father, if it be possible, may this cup be taken from me. Yet not as I will, but as you will" (Matthew 26:39). In the midst of a brokenness we can never truly understand, Jesus felt utterly forsaken; yet, he did not cease to trust in God the Father, whom he knew to be faithful. Jesus did not turn away from the Father, but toward him. In his humanity, Jesus, like us all, would prefer not to suffer at such a deep level. But Jesus bent his will to the Father's will in costly obedience, trusting that good would be the result.

Only after understanding this can we make sense of such verses in the Bible that call Christians to rejoice in suffering, trials, and difficulties. While they are many, two will suffice. James 1:2–4 exhorts Christians to

> Consider it pure joy, my brothers and sisters, whenever you face trials of many kinds, because you know that the testing of your faith produces perseverance. Let perseverance finish its work so that you may be mature and complete, not lacking anything.

Romans 5:3–5 states:

> we also glory in our sufferings, because we know that suffering produces perseverance; perseverance, character; and character, hope. And hope does not put us to shame, because God's love has been poured out into our hearts through the Holy Spirit, who has been given to us.[3]

It is important to understand what these verses are calling the Christian to do.

Christians are not called to either relish or pursue suffering. Like Jesus, pain and suffering are experiences, all things being equal, most humans would rather avoid. These verses reframe how Christians perceive their suffering. In light of the suffering of Jesus, his death, burial, and, more importantly, his resurrection, Christians can see that suffering is not final. In light of Jesus, the Christian tradition has viewed all suffering as redemptive. Not painless, of course, but meaningful. As the verses above note, through the loving, caring hand of our transcendent, personal God, suffering and trials can produce more complete persons, people with character more like Jesus. In short, we are made more ethical.

Ethics as Proper Communion

The large conceptual category of axiology, or value, is broad and complex. The particular focus of this chapter is ethical values and character or virtue. While the Christian tradition wrestles with larger axiological and moral issues, our particular focus on character is typically described as sanctification; that is, becoming more and more like Jesus through union with Christ, in his life, death, resurrection, and the communion we now have with God.[4]

Though redemption will be discussed in more detail in the final section of this book (i.e., the last three chapters), minimally, our union with Christ and restored communion through him enables us now to reorder our lives in relation to God, so that we can live more rightly or righteously. In short, Christianity believes that in Jesus Christ, empowered and enabled by the Holy Spirit, Christians can live a life that more closely corresponds to the will of the Father. This is what Christianity means by sanctification. In Christ we can now obey God in greater degree, entrusting ourselves to him and his care because God demonstrates his love to us in that, while we were still sinners, Christ died for us (Romans 5:8). One outcome goal of our union with Christ is greater obedience.

Earlier in the chapter, we stated that obedience to God involves trusting in God; that is, choosing the greater good, instead of trusting ourselves, the lesser good. (The lesser good is trusting in our *own* control, perception of events, and experiences.) Because we are not God, we cannot see or fully understand our experiences, including what they are producing in us. So, when we begin to encounter the trials and suffering mentioned above, we only see vaguely and understand partially, which can lead to unhealthy emotions. Reframing our experiences in light of Christ and our union with him allows the Christian to more adequately cope with the difficulties of daily life. As we begin to know ourselves in Christ and see God working in and through our suffering, our trust in God's goodness can deepen. The image of an upward spiral may help to more fully capture this reality—the more we trust God with our experiences, the more we find him faithful and are enabled to trust him more fully, which allows us to experience his faithfulness more fully. This upward spiral is, again, what Christians mean by sanctification.

Another aspect of sanctification is that we begin to see things more like God sees things. As God transforms us more into the image of Christ, the more we see ourselves and our lives like Jesus does. We develop the "mind of Christ" (1 Corinthians 2:16; Philippians 2:5). This process is seen in Ephesians 4:22–24, where Christians are told to "put off" their "old self," that is, choosing themselves instead of God—that which caused their minds to be "futile," which, recall from the fourth chapter, means vain, not simply unproductive. Christians are, however, to "put on the new self." This means "to be made new in the attitude of your minds," which is, in Christ, "created to be like God in true righteousness and holiness" (Ephesians 4:23–24).

The mind that is *re*-newed in Christ progressively *re*-orders actions, attitudes, and emotions. The latter may surprise some, but emotions have traditionally been seen as a fundamental part of moral character. The virtuous person loves the right sorts of things and passionately pursues the right sorts of actions. The reordering of life reverses the "over-reach" that causes disorder. Consider, again, Pannenberg's (1985) words describing the attitude lying behind the over-reach. He says it is

> the distorted desire for transitory things, since the latter are no longer desired as a means of serving God but are desired instead as means of obtaining the enjoyment of the one desiring them... When the ego which is proud in the sense described wills itself to be the center and ultimate end, it usurps the place in the order of the universe that belongs to God, its creator and supreme good.
>
> (p. 88)

When our desires are oriented toward God, we tend to desire more what God desires and desire all other things with God in mind; that is, we are more inclined to rightly order our desires and act righteously in our daily life.

Now, to return to reframing our struggles in light of the renewed Christian mind and heart, we can see many practical results for the clinical setting. To encounter difficult experiences and psychological pain in light of Jesus is to perceive them not as potentially destructive, but as potentially constructive. If God loved us so much that he sent his son, Jesus, to die for us so that communion could be restored and we could experience an abundant life, then why would he now harm us? This is the whole point of the magisterial words of Romans 8, which begins with "Therefore, there is now no condemnation for those who are in Christ Jesus," and ends with the declaration that "[nothing] will be able to separate us from the love of God in Christ Jesus our Lord" (vv. 1, 39). With this, we can now return to where this section began, Hebrews 12.

The reason Christians are told to "[fix] our eyes on Jesus, the pioneer and perfecter of faith" (Hebrews 12:2) is that he is our model for handling suffering—in any and all of its variations—and our motive precisely because he is the *perfecter* of *our* faith. As the perfecter, Jesus is the *telos*, or "end," toward which we strive, that is, we aim to be like him. Yet, our being like him does not sacrifice our uniqueness, for he is the perfecter of *our* faith, that is, in our own unique way—a way only we can be as unique persons with our own story—we are made like him. This is why the difficulties we face, while they may be common to many—fear and anxiety are ubiquitous emotional experiences within the human condition—they are uniquely our own. Our Father knows us and only allows what has the potential to form us into a Christ-like character. Indeed, the whole reason the Hebrews passage tells us to "[fix] our eyes on Jesus" is because we each face struggles. Yet, these struggles are framed as "discipline," a word specifically related to God intervening with his children "for our good, in order that we may share in his holiness." In turn, Hebrews goes on to say, "No discipline seems pleasant at the time, but painful. Later on, however, it produces a harvest of righteousness and peace for those who have been trained by it" (12:7–12).

In light of what we have seen, a Christian context is essential in our work with Christians who have faced, or are facing, painful experiences. Psychological pain is difficult, unpleasant, trying, and often ongoing. But the pain and difficulty is not the final word, and the life of Jesus is our glaring proof. Though the pain of the cross is profound, the joy of the resurrection and redemption—"the joy set before him" (Hebrews 12:2)—is the hope for all who are in Christ. St. Augustine's (1991) words can now be more deeply appreciated, for in Christ our "true honor," that is "God's image and likeness," can be preserved because we can live toward him, "facing him from whom its impression is received" (p. 331). In this trust, we live in restored communion; though we walk through difficulties now, we do not walk through them alone or without hope.

Notes

1 This is sometimes called the "cultural mandate." God's instruction for Adam and Eve to "be fruitful and multiply" and to "tend and keep," thus cultivating God's good creation. Terry Eagleton thoughtfully expresses the dialect between "cultivating the land" and humans "cultivating themselves" in the very term "culture." He says, "If culture means the active tending of natural growth, then it suggests a dialectic... what we do to the world and what the world does to us" (Eagleton, 2000, p. 2).
2 The phrase "once made perfect" should not be understood as there being a time when Jesus was not perfect. The language and emphasis of this verse is on the ever-present reality of his perfection (Guthrie, 1983).
3 The Romans passage, particularly, frames the Christian approach in clear Trinitarian language—it is in Christ that we experience the Father's love, which is poured into our hearts by the Spirit. Though it is beyond our ability to fully comprehend, we are invited into the very triune life of God. Recall the *perichoretic* life of God. The Christian tradition holds that it is into this very life that we participate when we are "in Christ." It is often through suffering and trials that we come to realize this life as we walk the path of Jesus and find the very strength of God supporting and sustaining us.
4 The death of Christ is often called the atonement. This complex topic cannot be fully presented in this brief discussion, but there are many fuller treatments that have been written in the Christian tradition. For an accessible introduction to this topic, see the edited book *Atonement* (Fluhrer, 2010), with contributions by a range of contemporary pastor-theologians. As another example, see *Salvation Accomplished by the Son: The Work of Christ* (Peterson, 2012).

References

Augustine (1991). *The Trinity* (Edmund Hill, Trans.). New York: New City Press.
Bavinck, H. (2008). *Reformed Dogmatics*. Grand Rapids, MI: Baker Academic.
Berkouwer, G. (1962). *Man: The Image of God*. Grand Rapids, MI: William B. Eerdmans Publishing.
Calvin, J. (1960). *Institutes of the Religion* (F. Battles, Trans.). Louisville, KY: Westminster John Knox Press.

Canlis, J. (2010). *Calvin's Ladder*. Grand Rapids, MI: William B. Eerdmans Publishing.

Eagleton, T. (2000). *The Idea of Culture*. Malden, MA: Blackwell Publishing.

Fluhrer, G. (Ed.) (2010). *Atonement*. Phillipsburg, NJ: P&R Publishing Company.

Guthrie, D. (1983). *Hebrews*. Downers Grove, IL: InterVarsity Press.

Hoekema, A. (1986). *Created in God's Image*. Grand Rapids, MI: William B. Eerdmans Publishing.

Horton, M. (2012). *Pilgrim Theology*. Grand Rapids, MI: Zondervan.

Keil, C., & Delitzsch, F. (1996). *Biblical Commentary on the Old Testament, Vol. 1*. New York: C. Scribner.

Kidner, D. (2008). *Genesis*. Downers Grove, IL: InterVarsity Press.

Oberman, H. (1993). The pursuit of happiness. In J. O'Malley (Ed.), *Humanity and Divinity in Renaissance and Reformation* (pp. 251–283). New York: Brill.

Pannenberg, W. (1985). *Anthropology in Theological Perspective*. Edinburgh: T. & T. Clark Publishing.

Peterson, R. (2011). *Salvation Accomplished by the Son: The Work of Christ*. Wheaton, IL: Crossway.

Vanhoozer, K. (2010). *Remythologizing Theology*. Cambridge: Cambridge University Press.

Ware, T. (2010). The holy Trinity: Model for personhood-in-relation. In J. Polkinghorne (Ed.), *The Trinity and an Entangled World* (pp. 107–129). Grand Rapids, MI: Eerdmans.

CHAPTER 8

Biblical Anthropology and Axiology in Christian Mental Health
A Theoretical and Empirical Exploration

Introduction

The teaching that humans exist in the *imago Dei* results in a "high" anthropology, a view of human beings as unique and especially dignified among all the creatures in the visible universe and, therefore, of greater significance than merely being a highly evolved organism, as is assumed by the worldview of naturalism. It is well documented now that humans flourish best when they live meaningful lives. The robust finding that mental health in the West is associated with religion is likely due, in some part, to the perceived meaningfulness of human beings according to a theistic worldview.

As we have seen, the *imago Dei* teaching means that humans exist in a singular relationship with God, one of dependence and fulfillment. Humans are not self-sufficient beings, but are kept in existence by God, and they find their greatest fulfillment in devotion to God (Adams, 1999)—also known as the love of God (Matthew 22:37)—which gives human life a sense of unity and coherence. Assuming that is true, at least some human misery, for many, may be due to the lack of having a transcendent, orienting person or principle in one's life.

To believe in and be devoted to God implicitly posits a hierarchy of goods for humans, since God is typically understood to be the highest good, and his creation includes a set of goods that are necessarily secondary. Moreover, theism typically assumes that the Creator God has a design plan for human beings that entails a proper ordering of all goods, along with a corollary assumption that a significant proportion of human problems results from an inappropriate ordering of one's goods (Adams, 1999).

According to the Christian tradition, humans are now alienated from their Creator and, while most are aware of God, they have all lost communion with him. Evidence of this alienation from God is seen in the common experience today of a sense of autonomy and self-sufficient completeness, without God having a preeminent role in one's life. However, in the absence of a satisfying relation with our Creator, humans have "worshiped and served created things rather than the Creator" (Romans 1:25), indicating that their loves have become disordered. Christians have called this state of alienation and disordered loves "sin."

The Nature and Values of Human Beings According to Christianity

Humans beings are arguably the most complex creatures in the universe. Neuroscientists are still far from understanding how a biological organ like the human brain can provide the material ground for the complex activities of which humans are capable. A basic division of human nature into matter and mind (or "soul") has been widely recognized in most cultures at most times, even if understanding how they relate has been sharply disputed. Contemporary psychiatry and psychology recognize that the human body is the material substrate of human life. Of particular interest to psychotherapy is the nervous system, especially the brain, as well as the endocrine system. Distinctions can also be made regarding the wide range of phenomena that characterize the mind or "soul"—what most Westerners, including Christians, have historically considered to be the *immaterial* aspect of human beings—including sensation and perception; memory; multiple intelligences (logico-mathematical, linguistic, visuo-spatial, musical, and so forth); motives, emotions, and desires; the initiation of behaviors and actions; as well as more global dynamic structures like the self and personality. As these phenomena become increasingly elaborate through development, new functions emerge in adolescence and early adulthood, qualitatively different from what the most advanced primates are capable of: moral agency and character, as well as spirituality, and the possibility of a mature relationship with God.

Human life, however, is far from ideal. Many things can go wrong with the body in its genetic activity, the release of hormones, or the proliferation of neurons and their eventual organization in neural networks. Suffering in childhood through maladaptive parenting, abuse, and neglect can further lead to various kinds of biopsychosocial damage, evidenced in poor psychosocial functioning, including traumatic memories, distorted thoughts, a preponderance of negative emotion schemes, and anxious or malevolent expectations of oneself and others. As personal or moral agency emerges, humans make plans and decisions, act in ways for which they are held more or less responsible, and begin to contribute to the formation of their character and a particular configuration of vices and virtues. Sin is the biblical term that labels actions that are contrary to God's law (his design plan) for human life (which are called "personal sins"), as well as the disposition to live autonomously from God (which is called "original sin").[1]

Normal maturation and the variance between God's design plan for human life and actual human functioning lead to the conclusion that humans are necessarily teleological creatures, who are designed to pursue and realize a harmonious state of wellbeing in body and soul. Put a little more briefly, yet comprehensively, humans naturally seek biopsychosocial wholeness and ethicospiritual holiness (Johnson, 2007; 2017).

Humans Are Communal

We have noted repeatedly that humanity's fundamental relation to God leads naturally to a relational model of human beings, since humans are made for relationship with God and the mutual relations of humans reflect the relational nature of the triune God. Slife and Wiggins (2009) distinguished between psychologies characterized by strong and weak relationality. Strong relationality views humans as fundamentally embedded in a network of relations, such that our essence and identity are realized within our context and history and whose individuality emerges out of our relations with others; on the other hand, weak relationality approaches humans as fundamentally self-contained individuals whose identity is independent of our context and history and whose relationships with others are, therefore, additive, rather than constitutive. Given the prominence of the two-fold command of the love of God and neighbor in the Christian faith (Matthew 22:37–40), a Christian psychology will be characterized by strong relationality.

This theoretical stance accords well with research on human development and the impact of one's early attachments on subsequent maturation. By means of one's earliest relational experiences, beliefs and values about oneself and others are formed, so that, in effect, the semantic and axiological perspectives of significant others get internalized and come to shape the form of one's personhood accordingly. Strong relationality also helps to explain the most widely confirmed finding of evidence-based psychotherapy research that the best predictors of the success of therapy are relational factors that characterize the client-therapist relationship (e.g., the therapeutic alliance, empathy, collaboration) (Laska, Gurman, & Wampold, 2014).

Humans Are Developing Individuals

A variety of theologians in the 20th century have recognized the relational aspect of the *imago Dei* (Barth, 1960; Bonhoeffer, 1959). Historically, though, some Christian thinkers have linked the *imago Dei* to certain features that humans were believed to have in common with God, especially rationality. This has been called the structural approach to the *imago Dei* (Johnson, 2017). If human relationality images the communal nature of the triune God, individual humans might be supposed to image the persons of the Trinity. However, because humans are finite, temporal creatures, both capacities are grown into and lived over time. Below, we will trace some of the most important features of human individuation relevant for psychotherapy that emerge in human development out of one's early relationships with others.

Becoming a Thinking and Evaluating Person

Among the many ways that humans bear a structural resemblance to God is we are knowers and evaluators of meaning. Human perception, attention, memory, reasoning, and language form a *cognitive* system that enables our understanding of the nature of reality. Humans can think before they can use language. However, language quickly comes to structure thought, allowing humans great ability to describe, represent, store, and communicate to one another the nature of the universe, including ourselves.

Motives, emotions, and desires compose a system of evaluation. They reflect our perception of value—the goodness and badness of reality, including ourselves—and indicate that humans are constantly assessing reality in terms of whether it promotes or thwarts their wellbeing and the wellbeing of those they care about. This *experiential* system operates automatically, rapidly, nonverbally, unconsciously (implicitly), and holistically; the cognitive system, by contrast, operates intentionally and with effort, slowly, verbally, consciously (explicitly), and linearly and analytically (Epstein, 2014). Therapy orientations have arisen that work primarily with each system (cognitive and insight therapy, on the one hand, and experiential, emotion-focused, relational, and behavioral therapy, on the other), but most therapy inevitably utilizes both.

Both systems store their respective information and developing capacities in memory, but experiential memory is especially implicit, embodied, and relational, beginning before birth and demonstrated in the attachment bond, which tends to influence subsequent human relationships profoundly throughout life. Conceptual-linguistic knowledge is stored in semantic memory, which emerges in the second year of life, and is considered more explicit, because it is easily put in words. Episodic memory—memory for events that emerges around the third year—is also categorized as explicit, because it can also be articulated, but it uniquely has access to both cognitive and experiential systems and eventually allows humans to form a narrative. The elements of the cognitive system include describable beliefs about reality, including oneself, and are the primary focus of cognitive and rational-emotive therapy. Emotion schemes (emotions stored in memory) are affect-laden, implicit or episodic memories that are a record of previous perceptions of value, and emotion-focused therapy especially works with them. As we saw in Chapter 5, negative emotions are unpleasant, but such experiences are necessary to evaluate reality in a fallen world in which things are not the way they are supposed to be.

So, emotions are "signs" that represent the value/significance of the universe, including ourselves (Johnson, 2007). Positive emotion schemes signify one's previous exposure to aspects of life that were perceived to promote one's wellbeing, stored in memory. Negative emotion schemes, by contrast, signify one's previous exposure to aspects of life that were perceived to hinder one's wellbeing, evidence of what Christianity considers to be the fallen condition of human beings: suffering and sin, some of which can lead to biopsychosocial damage. Chronic exposure to bad experiences result in well-elaborated negative emotion schemes, which tend to manifest as symptoms of psychopathology, such as chronic anxiety or depression, relational conflict, or vocational difficulties.

We noted previously that children are formed in relation to others, who communicate meaning to them through affect-laden words and actions. The more caregivers resemble the communal love of the Trinity in the course of their interactions, the healthier the children will be. However, the more children suffer, exposed to human fallenness, particularly the sinfulness of others, the more *these* maladaptive experiences will get stored in negative emotion schemes and come to shape the form of developing persons and their stories.

As discussed in Chapter 5, each of the negative emotions has a unique core meaning. Because all humans are born in sin, all possess a sense of true shame, signified by Adam and Eve hiding from God in the garden (Genesis 3:8), which all religious and philosophical worldviews try to address one way or another, including secular psychotherapy. Besides for this universal experience, everyone's story is different, resulting in a different configuration of positive and negative emotion schemes of varying permutations and elaborations. People whose experiences generally promoted their wellbeing may go on to have relatively well-developed positive emotion schemes and comparatively undeveloped negative emotion schemes. By contrast, those who have been exposed to chronic loss (including parental neglect) might grow up with a set of well-elaborated sadness emotion schemes; those who were exposed to dangerous situations (e.g., a potentially aggressive parent) may develop well-elaborated fear/anxiety schemes, and perhaps some anger schemes, both from the model they were exposed to, as well as a deep sense of injustice; those whose parents chronically criticized them may develop an excessively shame-prone personality, and they will likely have difficulty with criticism in adulthood, because the pain of excessive shame is so intense and will never be far from their subconscious awareness.

In addition, children usually come to learn that their negative emotions are not wanted. In a thousand ways, parents can discourage the experience and processing of negative emotions—"Stop that crying!" "Don't be angry." "Other people have it worse than you do." They usually mean well. Humans were, after all, part of a very good creation (Genesis 1:31) and were designed to avoid bad (pain, suffering) and pursue good (joy, flourishing). However, skilled parenting (like skilled psychotherapy) helps children process their negative emotions and transition to a place of recovery and resolution. Poor parenting—where love is contingent upon meeting unrealistic parental standards—squelches the expression of children's negative emotions and communicates to them that their very real emotional experience—their *true self*—is not desired, wanted, or cared for, and this leads them to adapt, as best as they can, to the demands of their caregivers in order to obtain their approval (Harter, 2012). Unfortunately, in the process, children develop inauthentic core beliefs about themselves and patterns of automatic behavior that are dissociated from their actual, core experiences.

Winnicott (1965) was the first to call these global patterns *false selves*. Around the same time, Merton (1962) independently used the term to label the selves that humans pretend to be to fill the vacuum left by their alienation from God. In the absence of communion with God, Merton argued, we create an illusory self, the person we want to be, but currently are not, in order to garner the favor of others (and themselves), but as a result, we live in pretense (hiding) and are continuously unconsciously worried that we will be found out. These theological and developmental explanations are complementary and the dynamics are mutually reinforcing. Such subterfuge—maintained before God, others, and oneself—leads to increased shame about the duplicity, anxiety about possible discovery, and sadness about the resultant poverty.

As is well known, Freud (1894/1962) termed smaller-scale patterns of avoiding negative beliefs and emotions "defense mechanisms." However, such dynamic structures are also evident in the Bible (consider the Pharisees' condemnation of Christ), and many of Kierkegaard's writings were written to expose such defenses before Freud was born.

As children interact with persons over time who are consistently characterized by strong emotions, their well-elaborated responses take on a relatively holistic pattern, which some have referred to as a "part" (Schwartz, 1995), as it is experienced as a discrete brain/mind-state with somewhat distorted perceptions, thinking, and affect. These parts get activated in people in relational contexts that are similar to their earlier relational experiences. (Such experiences are especially common in those with personality disorders.)

The challenge for therapy is these "parts" are not completely false, since they are the cumulative record of actual experiences, and they are usually composed of strengths and resources that can be redeemed and utilized in healthy ways. However, their sinful, unresourceful dynamics need to be recognized and relinquished in order to be reincorporated into healthier functioning. Consequently, therapists help clients distinguish between their healthy and unhealthy aspects by affirming the former and helping clients identify the latter in session and through homework.

From a Christian perspective, nothing is better suited to enable people to identify their false self and other deceptive dynamic structures than the gospel of Jesus Christ. Knowing that one is beloved, reconciled to God, united to Christ, and, therefore, identified by God with all of Christ's human goodness through faith in him creates a safe, secure context within which to recognize one's patterns of defenses and false selves and risk relinquishing them more and more to Christ on the cross and be raised from the dead of such deception to live more authentically.

Becoming a Personal Agent-in-Communion

Throughout childhood, children are developing the mental, emotional, and volitional capacities that together make the emergence of personal agency possible, sometime between mid-adolescence and early adulthood. Personal agents are characterized by substantial self-awareness, rationality, and the abilities to form intentions, make plans and decisions, and act, such that personal agents have reasons for their actions and are, therefore, responsible and accountable for them. Personal agency also entails some degree of communion (or love) with other persons, the imaginative projection of oneself into the future, and the creation of uniquely human kinds of things (like works of art) (Johnson, 2007; 2017). Communion is particularly important in a Christian worldview, since, as we have seen, the triune God's communion is the source of reality and redemption, and the love of God and neighbor are humanity's chief, two-fold virtue. The Christian tradition has developed an understanding of love as delight in the beloved, a desire for the beloved's good, and a desire for a fitting union with the beloved, which entails sharing of thoughts, feelings, and story, and a relatively integrated soul (Edwards, 1765/1960; Eleonore Stump, 2012; Thomas Aquinas, 1945). We might consider the emergence of personal agency to be a sort of paradigm shift into a new stage of human life. The image of God in which we were conceived is now starting to be concretely realized as we become mature personal agents responsible for ourselves, our decisions, and our objects of devotion before God.

Most complex cultures have some rules for establishing the capacity of personal agency, when they start holding individuals fully accountable for their actions. In the West, this state is signified by an age standard, when one can be tried as an adult for crimes, usually around 18 years old. This state is also usually crowned with additional privileges, like the possibility of full-time employment and the right to drive a car, vote for political office, and drink alcohol. The major psychological sign of reaching this stage is the emergence of a mature conscience, indicated by guilt feelings for actions that violate one's ethical code, even when no one else knows about such actions (Johnson, 2007). However, the greater the suffering in one's childhood, the more one's developing biopsychosocial capacities may get damaged, which usually compromises (to at least some degree) the formation of personal agency. The emergence of personal agency is important to a Christian understanding of human beings, since the Bible teaches God holds adults accountable for their actions, and actions that violate God's will are called "sins" that require God's forgiveness. Often, the fostering of greater personal agency is part of the focus of Christian psychotherapy.

So human nature changes in certain important respects during development. As temporal images of God, adult humans are not just *beings*; we are also *becomings*. Moreover, our nature as personal agents-in-communion is such that we have the capacity to transcend our past and avoid simply reenacting our previous narrative, by acting in new ways, with the result that the plot of our narrative can take surprising, creative turns.

Becoming an Author of One's Story

During the preschool years, as a result of the capacity to form episodic memories, children begin to construct a personal narrative, within which they make temporal sense of themselves. Coinciding with these developing capacities, on account of one's experiences, relatively consistent patterns of emotion activation develop. For those exposed to a significant degree of suffering, negative emotion dispositions can be formed that can eventually cause respective negative emotions to intrude into one's awareness, beginning for some people in childhood, becoming more common in early adulthood, leading to anxiety or depressive disorders that call for clinical attention. Such brain/soul states should also be considered signs, in that they signify the person's story, including his or her stored experiences and relations with others, which comes to shape his or her future perceptions and experiences, and relations with others, including God.

In early adulthood, we understand ourselves in light of our previous stories, given our socialized, conceptual-linguistic and emotional understanding of ourselves, others, and God, which is the legacy of our pre-adulthood experience. However, as personal agency forms, humans start to act for reasons, and our personal actions come to shape our narratives and ourselves, with increasingly moral and spiritual consequences. As a result, individuals are enabled to become, to some degree, the authors of their own story. Moreover, new themes can be incorporated in adulthood. McAdams (2006) has identified a common narrative identity in America, which he terms the "redemptive self," borrowing from the Christian tradition. The redemptive self is marked by the overcoming of struggles to arrive at a place of greater wellbeing, an identity very helpful for those in psychotherapy.

Research on adult attachment has found that the development of a coherent narrative is a consequence of early secure attachment and fundamental building block for healthy psychological functioning (Siegel, 2012). Healing in adulthood, therefore, may be facilitated by efforts to construct one's life-narrative.

The foregoing helps us to see why therapy that uses conceptual-linguistic, emotion, relational, and narrative modalities can help clients transform their understanding of themselves, others, and God; promote emotion regulation; and take greater responsibility for themselves and their future. Christian clients will typically desire that that transformation occur in relation to Christ and his story (as well as the entire biblical meta-narrative), using Christian spiritual disciplines and virtuous practices, in addition to mentoring by a skilled therapist.

Maturation and Human Fallenness

As Christians mature in their faith and their identity becomes increasingly grounded in their union with Christ (which we will discuss more in Chapters 10, 11, and 12, the "redemption" pillar), they are enabled to become increasingly honest with God, themselves, and others and take responsibility for their lives and hearts. As adults, we are not responsible for the abuse, neglect, and trauma that we may have suffered in childhood, but we are responsible for what we do about its consequences in adulthood, including inner conflict, false selves, anxiety, and depression. We have already seen in the "theology" pillar (Chapters 1, 2, and 3) that God is omniscient and knows everything, so he knows all our shortcomings and cannot be surprised by anything about us. But because of our sinfulness, humans are more or less deceived about themselves, as we seek to avoid pain and live in the illusions of our false self (Jeremiah 17:9; James 1:22–26). So, we need God's help in illuminating our tendencies to hide from God, ourselves, and others and bring it into the light (1 John 1:5–10).

As we have seen, negative emotions like shame, guilt, sadness, and anxiety/fear are signs/signals of human fallenness. Rather than avoid these meaningful indicators of our stories and experiences, we grow as we are able to open up our hearts to God and ourselves (and possibly others) and share these emotions with our heavenly Father, who loves us and wants to heal us, as it says in 1 Peter 5:7: "Cast all your anxiety on [God] because he cares for you." God loves us and love involves sharing our hearts and our stories with one another (Stump, 2012). Consequently, Christians are learning how to "Pour out your heart like water in the presence of the Lord" (Lamentations 2:19) and follow the example of the Psalmists, who continually shared life's joys and sorrows with God. Opening up to oneself and other humans has been shown to be psychologically beneficial (Pennebaker, 1997). We have good reason to believe that opening up to God has similar benefits.

Maturation and Redemption

In light of humanity's alienation from its Maker and one another, God devised a plan to redeem those made in his image, by sending God's Son to die for humanity's sin and giving those who believe in Christ new capacities to love God supremely and other humans as themselves. God's redemption in Christ was given to promote the fullest psychospiritual healing and restoration, so that humans might flourish as much as possible, in spite of, and perhaps in the light of, human sin, suffering, and biopsychosocial damage.

Jesus Christ, therefore, plays a special role in a Christian psychotherapy, as the primary mediator of divine redemption (1 Timothy 2:5) through faith in him. Moreover, as the true human (Barth, 1960), Jesus Christ reveals to us the ideal form of human life, living in love with the Father and in responsive dependence and active receptivity towards him and having compassion towards his fellow humans. Research on moral exemplars has identified individuals whose notable moral activities distinguish them from their peers (Dunlop, Walker, & Matsuba, 2012). According to Christianity, Jesus Christ is the moral exemplar *par excellence* for Christians. Though relatively rare, moral exemplars can be found in everyday life, as well as in written accounts. Significantly, the Bible contains four books containing stories of Christ's ministry on earth and teaches that he is alive in heaven today, interceding and caring for his people, suggesting that Christians can experience him now, as well as through the gospel narratives, to promote his influence in our lives. This helps explain why prayer, meditation, and Bible reading are foundational therapeutic practices in Christian psychotherapy.

Becoming a Virtuous Character

Western philosophy, and more recently positive psychology, has used the term "character" to label the ethical form and goal of the individual human being, composed of certain virtues. While communities overlap considerably in what they consider a virtuous character, they also typically differ in the virtues they prize, and how they are understood and realized. Christian psychotherapy can, therefore, benefit from recent research in contemporary positive psychology, which seeks to describe virtues in general, as it seeks to understand and promote its own unique vision of virtuous human beings. A few virtues will be discussed, which are of special importance to Christianity, in light of redemption in Christ.

Faith maturity builds on the notion that humans are relational beings. Composed of both *vertical* (relating to God) and *horizontal* (relating to others) dimensions, this Christian construct is defined as "the degree to which a person embodies the priorities, commitments, and perspectives characteristic of vibrant and life-transforming faith" (Benson, Donahue, & Erickson, as cited in Dowling & Scarlett, 2005, p. 162). Faith maturity involves a trusting relationship with God, peace that emanates from a strong religious commitment, an authentic emphasis on living out the Christian faith in day-to-day occurrences, motivation for continued spiritual growth, connection to a faith community, adherence to Christian values, and commitment to loving others and pursuing justice (Dowling & Scarlett, 2005). Moreover, faith maturity is associated with lower psychological distress, including depression and anxiety (Salsman & Carlson, 2005).

Religious commitment has been defined as "the degree to which a person adheres to his or her religious values, beliefs, and practices and uses them in daily living" (Worthington et al., 2003, p. 85), and recent research has revealed a negative relationship between religious commitment and mental health-related variables, like depression and anxiety (Abu-Raiya, Pargament, Krause, & Ironson, 2015).

Paramount in a Christian account of faith maturity and religious commitment is the Christian's communion with, and love of, the triune God, accessible in Jesus Christ. Additional research is needed to document how these distinctive features contribute specifically to the wellbeing of Christians.

Humility has been defined intrapersonally as having a realistic view of oneself and interpersonally as being more other-oriented than self-focused, manifesting in behaviors that signify a lack of superiority in relation to others (Davis, Hook, McAnnally-Linz, Choe, & Placeres, 2017). Humility has been found to be negatively correlated to avoidant attachment defenses (Dwiwardani et al., 2014) and insecure attachment to God (Sandage, Paine, & Hill, 2015), whereas emotional maturity and self-regulation were positively related to it (Jankowski & Sandage, 2014). Humility also has been found to be negatively correlated with depression and anxiety (Davis, McElroy, Choe, Westbrook, & DeBlaere, 2017). Emerging research suggests that humility may serve as a protective factor in the context of depressive and anxiety-related symptoms (Krause, Pargament, Hill, & Ironson, 2016).

Christianity has some special themes that would seem likely to promote humility, including the teaching that all humans are sinners and, therefore, have significant ethical and spiritual limitations. Watson, Morris, Loy, and Hamrick (2007) found that certain beliefs about sin relating to self-improvement, humility, avoidance of perfectionism, and self-reflective functioning were associated with higher self-esteem and lower narcissism, depression, and anxiety. Healthy beliefs in sin can promote a realistic view of oneself that can help one cope with one's limitations, particularly in relationship with the loving, forgiving God revealed especially in Christ.

Gratitude "is a felt sense of wonder, thankfulness, and appreciation for life" (Emmons & Shelton, 2002, p. 460), and it has been found to be positively associated with measures of positive affect, wellbeing, prosocial behaviors and traits, and religiosity (McCullough, Emmons, & Tsang, 2002). In a meta-analysis of gratitude interventions, gratitude was found to be related to higher levels of psychological wellbeing (Davis et al., 2016). Unsurprisingly to Christians, religious commitment is strongly related to gratitude, and most of the relation is due to specifically religious gratitude (Rosmarin, Pirutinsky, Cohen, Galler, & Krumrei, 2011). Gratitude obviously makes good sense within a theistic framework, arguably better than within a naturalistic one, since, from a cosmic standpoint, there is no ultimate object of gratitude in naturalism.

Finally, we will mention the virtue of *grace*. Though only recently investigated, it has been a major theme of the Christian religion since its beginnings. Grace has been defined psychologically as "the gift of acceptance given unconditionally and voluntarily to an undeserving person by an unobliged giver" (Emmons, Hill, Barrett, & Kapic, 2017, p. 277). Christianity teaches that humans owe our Creator absolute respect, love, and obedience, but have fallen radically short of our obligations, because of sin. Nevertheless, God has revealed himself as gracious by inviting all humans to be reconciled to him freely through faith in Christ. Christians, therefore, believe ourselves to have become beneficiaries of God's grace. Bufford, Sisemore, and Blackburn (2017) found that the experience of divine grace is related to being able to extend grace to self and others. Moreover, grace is positively related to gratitude, forgivingness, humility, and empathy (Bufford et al., 2017), positive self-esteem, mental health, and spiritual growth, and negatively related to depression and hopelessness (Watson, Morris, & Hood, 1988).

Although we certainly could have discussed additional virtues, in its current form, this selection shows the tremendous value of promoting virtuous character in Christian psychotherapy for anxiety and depression. Research has just begun to document the wellbeing that is associated with Christian values and virtues. As a result, psychotherapists working with Christian clients have good reasons—theoretical and empirical—to seek to address depression and anxiety symptoms by cultivating Christian values and the practice of the Christian virtues with Christian clients.

To conclude the chapter, most complex religions and life-philosophies have some notion of the goal of human development and maturation, what we might call their "maturity-telos," based on its own unique values. Christianity has a long history of reflecting on, as well as promoting, its maturity-telos. Today, the Christian psychotherapy community has the opportunity to synthesize its own long tradition with the best of relevant contemporary research in order to develop an empirically based model of therapy that corresponds to Christian values and its own unique maturity-telos.

Note

1 For a more thorough discussion of how these aspects relate to psychopathology, see Johnson (2017).

References

Abu-Raiya, H., Pargament, K., Krause, N., & Ironson, G. (2015). Robust links between religious/spiritual struggles, psychological distress, and well-being in a national sample of American adults. *American Journal of Orthopsychiatry, 85*, 565–575.

Aquinas, T. (1945). *Basic Writings of Saint Thomas Aquinas* (A. C. Pegis, Ed.). New York, NY: Random House.

Barth, K. (1960). *Church Dogmatics: 3.2* (H. Knight, J. K. S. Reid, & R. H. Fuller, Trans.). Edinburgh: T. & T. Clark.

Bonhoeffer, D. (1959). *Creation and Fall. Temptation: Two Biblical Studies*. New York: Macmillan.

Bufford, R., Sisemore, T. A., & Blackburn, A. M. (2017). Dimensions of grace: Factor analysis of three grace scales. *Psychology of Religion and Spirituality, 9*, 56–69.

Davis, D. E., Choe, E., Meyers, J., Wade, N., Varjas, K., … Worthington, Jr., E. L. (2016). Thankful for the little things: A meta-analysis of gratitude interventions. *Journal of Counseling Psychology, 63*, 20–31.

Davis, D. E., Hook, J. N., McAnnally-Linz, R., Choe, E., & Placeres, V. (2017). Humility, religion, and spirituality: A review of the literature. *Psychology of Religion & Spirituality*, 9, 242–253.

Davis, D., McElroy, S., Choe, E., Westbrook, C., & DeBlaere, C. (2017). Development of the experiences of humility scale. *Journal of Psychology and Theology*, 45, 3–16.

Dowling, E., & Scarlett, G. (Eds.) (2005). *Encyclopedia of Religious and Spiritual Development*. Thousand Oaks, CA: Sage Publications.

Dunlop, W. L., Walker, L. J., & Matsuba, M. K. (2012). The distinctive moral personality of care exemplars. *The Journal of Positive Psychology*, 7, 131–143.

Dwiwardani, C., Hill, P., Bollinger, R., Marks, L., Steele, J., ... Davis, D. (2014). Virtues develop from a secure base: Attachment and resilience as predictors of humility, gratitude and forgiveness. *Journal of Psychology and Theology*, 42, 83–90.

Edwards, J. (1960). *The Nature of True Virtue*. Ann Arbor, MI: University of Michigan Press.

Emmons, R. A., Hill, P. C., Barrett, J. L., & Kapic, K. M. (2017). Psychological and theological reflections on grace and its relevance for science and practice. *Psychology of Religion and Spirituality*, 9, 276–284.

Emmons, R. A., & Shelton, C. M. (2002). Gratitude and the science of positive psychology. In C. R. Snyder & S. J. Lopez (Eds.), *Handbook of Positive Psychology* (pp. 459–471). New York: Oxford University Press.

Epstein, S. (2014). *Cognitive-Experiential Theory: An Integrative Theory of Personality*. New York: Oxford University Press.

Freud, S. (1962). The neuro-psychoses of defense. *Standard Edition of the Complete Psychological Works of Sigmund Freud* (Vol. 3, pp. 45–61). London: Hogarth Press.

Harter, S. (2012). *The Construction of the Self: Developmental and Sociocultural Foundations*. New York: Guilford.

Jankowski, P. J., & Sandage, S. J. (2014). Attachment to God and humility: Indirect effect and conditional effects models. *Journal of Psychology and Theology*, 42, 70–82.

Johnson, E. L. (2007). *Foundations for Soul Care*. Downers Grove, IL: InterVarsity Press.

Johnson, E. L. (2017). *God and Soul Care: The Therapeutic Resources of the Christian Faith*. Downers Grove, IL: InterVarsity Press.

Krause, N., Pargament, K., Hill, P., & Ironson, G. (2016). Humility, stressful life events, and psychological well-being: Findings from the Landmark Spirituality and Health Survey. *The Journal of Positive Psychology*, 11, 499–510.

Laska, K., Gurman, A., & Wampold, B. (2014). Expanding the lens of evidence-based practice in psychotherapy: A common factors perspective. *Psychotherapy*, 51, 467–481.

McAdams, D. P. (2006). *The Redemptive Self: Stories Americans Live By*. New York: Oxford University Press.

McCullough, M. E., Emmons, R. A., & Tsang, J. (2002). The grateful disposition: A conceptual and empirical topograph. *Journal of Personality and Social Psychology*, 82, 112–127.

Merton, T. (1962). *New Seeds of Contemplation*. New York: New Directions.

Pennebaker, J. W. (1997). *Opening Up: The Healing Power of Expressing Emotions* (rev. ed.). New York: Guilford.

Rosmarin, D. H., Pirutinsky, S., Cohen, A. B., Galler, Y., & Krumrei, E. J. (2011). Grateful to God or just plain grateful? A comparison of religious and general gratitude. *The Journal of Positive Psychology, 6,* 389–396.

Salsman, J. M., & Carlson, C. R. (2005). Religious orientation, mature faith, and psychological distress: Elements of positive and negative associations. *Journal for the Scientific Study of Religion, 44,* 201–209.

Sandage, S. J., Paine, D., & Hill, P. (2015). Spiritual barriers to humility: A multidimensional study. *Mental Health, Religion & Culture, 18,* 207–217.

Schwartz, R. C. (1995). *Internal Family Systems Therapy.* New York: Guilford.

Siegel, D. (2012). *The Developing Mind* (2nd ed.). New York: Guilford.

Slife, B. D., & Wiggins, B. (2009). Taking relationship seriously in psychotherapy: Radical relationality. *Journal of Contemporary Psychotherapy, 39,* 17–24.

Stump, E. (2012). *Wandering in Darkness: Narrative and the Problem of Suffering.* New York: Oxford University Press.

Watson, P. J., Morris, R. J., & Hood, R. W., Jr. (1988). Sin and self-functioning, Pt. 2: Grace, guilt, and psychological adjustment. *Journal of Psychology and Theology, 16,* 270–281.

Watson, P. J., Morris, R. J., Loy, T., Hamrick, M. B., & Grizzle, S. (2007). Beliefs about sin: Adaptive implications in relationships with religious orientation, self-esteem, and measures of the narcissistic, depressed, and anxious self. *Edification: The Journal of the Society for Christian Psychology, 1,* 57–67.

Winnicott, D. W. (1965). Ego distortion in terms of true and false self. In *The Maturational Processes and the Facilitating Environment: Studies in the Theory of Emotional Development* (pp. 140–152). Madison, CT: International Universities Press.

Worthington, E., Wade, N., Hight, T., Ripley, J., McCullough, J., & Berry, J. W. (2003). The Religious Commitment Inventory-10: Development, refinement, and validation of a brief scale for research and counseling. *Journal of Counseling Psychology, 50,* 84–96.

CHAPTER 9

Biblical Anthropology and Axiology in Christian Psychotherapy

Introduction

In this chapter, we present a distinctly Christian psychotherapy within the "biblical anthropology and axiology" pillar, exploring ways in which therapists can effectively practice according to a Christian view of the nature of humanity and values when working with Christian clients. In particular, we provide a central theme in working with Christian clients with emotional disorders, along with goals for treatment and specific interventions from a distinctly Christian worldview. Similar to the first and second sections, we rely upon a range of Christian resources, enhanced by a theological and empirical understanding of emotional disorders from the previous two chapters in the "biblical anthropology and axiology" section. Ultimately, we aim to offer Christian-sensitive interventions for Christians with depressive and anxiety disorders, strengthening a Christian approach with the "common factors" literature (Lambert, 2013) and other relevant theory and research.

Central Theme

Expanding on the previous two chapters in this section, a distinctly Christian psychotherapy employs a biblical understanding of anthropology and axiology so as to guide treatment in a Christian-sensitive manner. Grounded in this viewpoint, a Christian conceptualization of human development suggests that selfhood is found exclusively in God. Yet, because of the fall of humankind, a false self begins to develop, resulting in "disordered loves." In a manner similar to those described in relational and cognitive behavioral models of self-development, Christians start to develop a distorted self, which can lead to an emphasis on the pursuit of self-derived values that exacerbate the symptoms of emotional disorders.

The Pharisees would seem to exemplify this development in the New Testament, wanting to achieve prestige through others' perceiving them as highly spiritual (e.g., Luke 20:47, where they make long prayers, yet exploit widows). This is more dramatically seen in the story of the publican and Pharisee (Luke 18:9–14), where the humble penitence of the publican is presented as a positive model in contrast to the false piety of the Pharisee. The problem is also identified in the epistles, where Paul noted that there are varying motives among those who preach the Gospel (Philippians 1:15–18), with poor motives including envy, rivalry, and selfish ambition, contrasted with the pure motive of love. The theme continues in Revelation 2–3, where Christ calls out churches that appear afire for the Gospel, but are not really (particularly Sardis, which is dead, and Laodicea, which is lukewarm). In all, there is a tendency to want to falsely project oneself against the humbler reality of who one really is.

But the false self also has a more strictly internal dimension, which Merton (1961) explained as follows:

> Every one of us is shadowed by an illusory person: a false self. This is the man that I want myself to be but who cannot exist, because God does not know anything about him. And to be unknown by God is altogether too much privacy. My false and private self is the one who wants to exist outside the reach of God's will and God's love—outside of reality and outside of life.
>
> (pp. 34–35)

Merton went on to state that the false self can be organized around relying on knowledge, power, and honor, rather than God's enduring, perfect love. In other words, the false self is isolated from God, whereas the true self is dependent on him, given we are made in the image of God.

Interestingly, in relational and cognitive behavioral models of psychotherapy, these kinds of distortions have been given many names, including Winnicott's (1965) "false self" (noted in the previous chapter; Welsh & Knabb, 2009), a faulty internal working model of relationships (Mikulincer et al., 2003), a negative core schema (Leahy, 2017), and being fused with a verbal, storied self that can distract from value-based living (Hayes, Strosahl, & Wilson, 2012; Knabb, 2016).[1] Although these conceptualizations have some distinctions, a central feature involves a deeply embedded representation of a self that is incomplete, whether this self (a) is hidden from others due to shame; (b) is preoccupied with abandonment; (c) strives for self-sufficiency based on prior relational wounds; (d) is convinced it is flawed and unlovable; or (e) is overly reliant on self-generated stories that get in the way of living out a set of values. And, of course, there is the longstanding problem of false pride.

In the Christian tradition, Pennington (2000) argued that the "false self" is preoccupied with accomplishments, a reputation, and possessions. Linking his understanding of the false self to Jesus' temptation in the wilderness (Matthew 4:1–11), Pennington suggested that the true self is found in God, rather than these pseudo-building blocks of selfhood. When the true self is increasingly located in God, Christians are able to more effectively follow

Jesus, living out a set of Christian virtues (e.g., kindness, patience, hard work, self-control, love, humility) as a by-product of this right relationship of "reordered loves."

As another example of a distinctly Christian teaching on the development of the self, the Jesus Prayer (also utilized in the third chapter) is an *apophatic* form of meditation used within the Orthodox tradition to ameliorate the fallen self by seeking God's compassionate response. With this meditation, the focus is on healing the darkened *nous*, or "eye of the soul/ heart." From this perspective, humans struggle with a deeper, existential sickness due to the fall of humankind and need a strategy to help them (a) protect the inner self, or "guard the heart" (the Greek phrase, *phylaki kardia*), from compulsive, tempting thoughts (the Greek word, *logismoi*), and (b) constantly remember God (the Greek phrase, *mneme theou*) (Johnson, 2010). Johnson described this process in detail:

> The heart is purified when attention and watchfulness prevent the disturbance of the continuous memory of God by guarding against the entrance of outer thoughts. The memory of God is often accomplished with the help of the repeated use of a prayer, typically the Jesus Prayer.
> (p. 16)

Above all else, when considering the relationship between self-development and virtuous living, Christian psychotherapy involves helping Christian clients to find their true self in Christ, which can allow them to live out a set of virtues that are rooted in God's Word. Although the fall has led to humankind's ongoing struggle with "disordered loves," returning to God at the center of existence—that is, finding the true self in him—can help Christians to reorient themselves to a life devoted to Christ-likeness. Cognitive, affective, behavioral, and relational strategies for doing so are discussed in this chapter, drawing from the Christian tradition, "common factors" literature, and relational and cognitive behavioral models.

Sin, Values, and the Secular Clinical Psychology Literature

Although the field of clinical psychology has historically striven to remain neutral when it comes to morality, more recent efforts are underway to bring attention to the moral dimension in the therapy room, illuminating the importance of commitment, justice, truthfulness, community, courage, and prudence, among other virtues (Doherty, 1995). What is more, the positive psychology movement has re-emphasized the role that virtues play in psychological functioning, as revealed in *Character Strength and Virtues: A Handbook and Classification* (Peterson & Seligman, 2004). To offer one more example, acceptance and commitment therapy (ACT) advocates helping clients to be more accepting of difficult thoughts and feelings so as to live out a set of values—that is, principles for living (Harris, 2009)—on the roads of life. While we applaud these developments, the focus tends to be on subjective, client-derived, arbitrarily constructed values, rather than biblically derived virtues that capture the moral behaviors Jesus modeled in the New Testament, which is at the heart of Christian psychotherapy.

With each of the previous models, Christian clients can, of course, draw from a Christian worldview (substituting client-derived values with Christian teachings), wherein biblical virtues are cultivated as Christians follow Jesus along the rugged trails of this fallen world. Yet, in order to work effectively with Christian clients in psychotherapy, therapists should strive to better understand the Christian notions of sin and virtue, which emanate from the Bible, rather than promote an ontological materialism that is all too common in secular clinical circles. To be sure, by only focusing on the material world, therapists can unknowingly (or sometimes knowingly) prioritize clients' self-interest (Doherty, 1995) above a more transcendent, Christian-sensitive understanding of the proverbial map for daily living.

Regrettably, a Christian understanding of "sin" is seldom discussed in the clinical literature or in therapists' work with Christian clients, although "sin" is a central concept within the Christian tradition. Defined in its simplest form as turning away from God (e.g., "idolatry"; see Exodus 20:3), the Christian tradition suggests that Jesus' work on the cross is sufficient (i.e., whereby we can be justified; Romans 3:23–26) for reconciling us to God; yet, when we turn to some other form of salvation, we are reaching for an idol (Keller, 2010).

This struggle, from a Christian perspective, can exacerbate emotional disorders. To offer a basic trajectory, Christian clients begin to develop the symptoms of emotional disorders, which are reverberations from the fall of humankind. These salient emotional experiences, though, are a sign/signal that reveals a deeper incompleteness without God. In an effort to ameliorate the pain, unfortunately, Christian clients may unilaterally strive to deny the pain. In these understandable, yet misguided, attempts to eradicate the pain, Christian clients may end up experiencing suffering on top of suffering (a tendency recognized by Hayes et al., 2012), given they are looking to a source other than God as the antidote for a fallen, estranged existence.

More recently, some Christian authors have highlighted the importance of discussing sin's role in Christian psychotherapy (e.g., McMinn, 2008; Johnson, 2007, 2017), since sin is both a state (original sin), deeply impacting biological, psychosocial, ethical, and spiritual functioning, and actions that involve turning away from God. In the realm of psychotherapy, working effectively with Christian clients means we are avoiding the tendency to offer an overly simplistic view of sin as a list of behaviors to avoid in daily living (McMinn & Campbell, 2007). Rather, sin is pervasive, impacting every aspect of the human condition because of the human tendency to wander away from God (McMinn & Campbell, 2007; Johnson, 2007, 2017).

In this chapter, we argue that the notion of the "false self" is based on this habitual, automatic tendency (commencing with the fall of humankind) to turn away from God, with the "true self" found in Christ as we return to him at the center of existence. With this intentional pivot towards Jesus, we are striving to emulate him by living out his teachings in the form of biblical virtues. As a result, this chapter will explore a Christian understanding of the self, including the role that moral behaviors play in authentic Christian living. Ultimately, because of the fall of humankind, we strive to be a God unto ourselves, rather than be "dependent on God," the real God (Bonhoeffer, 1959). In doing so, we develop a false self that exists apart from God, so it cannot be known by him; and we must reorient our attention to God in order to overcome a separate, isolated existence (Merton, 1961). With emotional disorders, our sinful state of existence means we are vulnerable to depression and anxiety, reverberations from the fall that capture our incompleteness without God at the center. In turn, we may end up struggling with compounded suffering in our unilateral efforts to remedy the situation. Whereas the true self is found in God, living in the false self produces a pseudo-sense of autonomy and independence, forsaking the ontological reality that God created us for him (Finley, 1978).

Goals for Treatment

In applying the "common factors" domains of support, learning, and action (adapted from Lambert, 2013) to biblical anthropology and axiology, we offer the following overarching goals within this pillar of treatment:

(a) *Support* involves helping Christians turn to God to find the true self, letting go of the false self along the way. In this process, therapists working with Christian clients can model love, kindness, and humility—Christian virtues that are grounded in Scripture. In this initial phase, therapists working with Christian clients promote the development of a biblical view of the self, contrasting the false self (originating from the fall) with the true self (found in Christ, based on his death and resurrection). Ultimately, turning to the greater good, God, helps our Christian clients to embrace their true self and abandon their false self.

(b) *Learning* involves working with Christian clients to explore painful emotions associated with the false self, gaining skill in distinguishing between the true self and false self. The true self emerges, to be sure, when humans depend on God in Christ, our greatest source of fulfillment. Therapists can also offer a corrective relational experience, exploring clients' inner world, reframing their view of self and others, and helping them to accept difficult experiences. As the true self emerges, Christians learn about the form of the Christian life—the Christian virtues—described in the Bible as God's revelation to humankind. By focusing on Jesus' model of servanthood and self-sacrifice,

Christians can develop a proverbial road map for life, following Jesus along the twists and turns of life's treacherous paths.

(c) *Action* involves working with Christian clients to face their fears about letting go of the false self. Although this self actually exacerbates psychological pain, including the symptoms of emotional disorders, the false self can seem ego-syntonic, since clients may have been relying on a pseudo-sense of self-sufficiency and autonomy for some time. As Christians learn to pivot from the false self, which is self-generated, to the true self, which is found in Christ, a wide variety of painful reactions might emerge, reminiscent of St. John of the Cross' famous "dark night of the soul." In this two-step process of turning away from (via detachment) and turning towards (via union with Christ), the false self will likely protest, kicking and screaming along the way. Yet, therapists can help Christians to recognize the false self's familiar voice, acknowledge its presence, and find refuge in God. As a next step, Christians can get back on the roads of life, walking faithfully with Jesus from moment to moment and town to town. In this process, virtues are developed as habits of daily living, with Christian clients cultivating faith maturity, religious commitment, humility, gratitude, grace, and a host of other moral behaviors for optimal living.

Christian Resources

In the ninth chapter, several Christian sources are used to develop Christian-sensitive interventions and techniques, including the following (in no particular order):

(a) Merton's *New Seeds of Contemplation* (1961) to help operationalize the distinction between the true self and false self. This understanding is also viewed through the lens of Jesus' temptations in the desert in the New Testament, with Jesus fully exemplifying the true self and clearly rejecting the temptation of a false self (Matthew 4:1–11; Pennington, 2000). To help operationalize this distinction, the psychodynamic, attachment, and traditional and acceptance-based cognitive behavioral literatures are drawn from, reviewing the following concepts: internal working models (Bartholomew & Horowitz, 1991), core schemas (Leahy, 2017), and the verbal, storied self (Hayes, Strosahl, & Wilson, 2012).

(b) The *Philokalia* (Pyrne, 2015) to explore a Christian view of inner healing, utilizing the Jesus Prayer as a way to remember God, focus on God, pivot away from distracting thoughts, and guard the heart (Johnson, 2010).

(c) Writings from the early desert Christians (e.g., the *Sayings of the Desert Fathers*; Burton-Christie, 1993) are drawn from to explore detachment, helping Christians to surrender the false self in order to find the true self in Christ.

Table 9.1 Christian-sensitive common factors in psychotherapy for the "biblical anthropology and axiology" pillar. Adapted from Lambert (2013)

Support-Related Goals	Learning-Related Goals	Action-Related Goals
Verbalize painful affect surrounding clients' false self	Give advice that is rooted in Scripture, helping Christian clients to find their true self in God and live an authentic life that is rooted in biblical teachings	Confront fears and test reality surrounding the false self, gaining an awareness of the true self by living out Jesus' teachings; this can be accomplished, in part, with the Jesus Prayer: "Lord Jesus Christ, Son of God, have mercy on me"
Reduce isolation by highlighting that Christians' true self is created in God's image to be in relationship with him and others	Help Christian clients to express painful emotions surrounding their false sense of self, gaining insight into the distinction between the true self and false self	Master thinking patterns by recognizing the false self, shifting to the true self, and following Jesus' teachings
Continuously point Christian clients to a biblical view of the self, suggesting self-healing involves a recognition of Christians' dependence on God as the author of selfhood	Attain insight into the notion that Christian clients become fused with arbitrarily generated stories about the self, which leads to getting stuck in life and struggling to live out the values that are most meaningful to them	Help Christian clients to live out Christian virtues in response to tempting, compulsive thoughts (*logismoi*), consistent with the early desert Christians (e.g., Evagrius of Ponticus)
Offer an encouraging, safe, and collaborative relationship to remind clients they are created in God's image	Offer a corrective relational experience by helping Christian clients to see that trusting in Jesus' redemptive work means they can let go of their own knowledge of who they are, prioritizing Jesus' view of them (i.e., the true self) as the starting and ending point of daily living	Take risks by living out Jesus' teachings, which are connected to a set of biblical virtues from Scripture; utilize a worksheet to serve as a proverbial map for living out virtues in daily life
Model Christian virtues, such as kindness, love, and humility, to Christian clients struggling with emotional disorders,	Help Christian clients to begin to shift towards radically following Jesus, remaining anchored to his	Achieve a sense of efficacy that emanates from the true self, which is found in God as the source of life; this can be accomplished

(*Continued*)

Table 9.1 (Continued)

Support-Related Goals	Learning-Related Goals	Action-Related Goals
especially since they may exhibit shame-proneness, rumination, worry, doubt, uncertainty, and other cognitive and affective processes that are linked to a "flawed" sense of self	teachings as they pursue virtuous living	by balancing Mary's contemplation and Martha's action

(d) The writings of several theologians are explored in the context of contemplation and action, including Augustine, Bernard, and Gregory the Great (Cutler, 2003). From our perspective, blending contemplation and action is ideal for Christians with emotional disorders, helping them to surrender the false self to God and discover the true self via contemplative practice (sitting at Jesus' feet, like Mary in Luke's gospel) and follow Jesus by way of a set of Christian virtues (reminiscent of Martha's activity in Luke's gospel).

The Support Phase: Turning to God for Help

In the support phase of treatment, therapists can help Christian clients to verbalize painful affect surrounding the self. In addition, since a Christian view of the self requires a self-in-relationship perspective (especially with God), exploring their view of others (including God) is important. Thus, a healthy view of the self, from a Christian viewpoint, involves recognizing the true self emanates from God. In the therapeutic relationship, therapists working with Christian clients can offer an encouraging, safe, and collaborative relationship, by which they remind them they were created in his image. In this process, therapists are modeling Christian virtues, such as kindness, love, and humility, to Christian clients struggling with emotional disorders, especially since they may exhibit shame-proneness, rumination, worry, doubt, uncertainty, and other cognitive and affective processes that are linked to a "flawed" sense of self. In the support phase, therapists are continuously pointing Christian clients to a biblical view of the self, suggesting their healing involves a recognition of Christians' dependence on God as the ultimate author of their selfhood. In turn, a God-centered view of the self can help Christians to more effectively follow Jesus, who has already "finished" his redeeming work on the cross (John 19:30) and given his Spirit to them (Romans 8:15). In other words, Christians are a "new creation" in Christ (2 Corinthians 5:17), meaning they can let go of the false self in the here and now.

Exploring the False Self

To begin the support phase, we can help our Christian clients to better understand the pain that emanates from the false self. This pseudo self, traced back to the fall of humankind, strives to be independent of God, rather than reliant upon him. To do so, we may wish to explore the conflict between wanting to be dependent on God and live autonomously from God, with Christian clients struggling to ameliorate the tendency to define themselves in isolation.

As discussed in the sixth chapter, humans can struggle to accept their God-given design, which involves relying on God, who is at the center of life. Instead, we tend to place ourselves at the center, becoming our own moral authority in our knowledge of good and evil (Bonhoeffer, 1959). Fast-forward thousands of years, and Jesus was tempted in the desert in a similar fashion. In the fourth chapter of Matthew's gospel, we read that the Devil attempted to convince Jesus to turn stones into bread, throw himself off the temple to be rescued by angels, and worship the Devil in order to attain the world. In each of these instances, the Devil strived to get Jesus to act on his own, rather than depend on God for sustenance and survival.

For the late Trappist monk Basil Pennington (2000), Jesus' three temptations illustrate our struggles with the false self, which is intimately connected to our accomplishments, reputation, and possessions. In resisting the temptation to turn stones into bread, Jesus rejected unilateral efforts to accomplish goals outside of God's plan; by avoiding the temptation to be rescued by angels in front of others, Jesus focused on God's views of him, not how onlookers might see him; and by saying no to worshiping the Devil, Jesus would not accept owning the world apart from his Father. With each intentional decision, Jesus turned from an autonomous definition of who he was in order to rely, instead, on Scripture to define him. He first pointed to the need to rely on God (Deuteronomy 8:3); next, he emphasized the biblical command to not put God to the test (Deuteronomy 6:13); finally, he illuminated the importance of worshiping and serving God (6:13).

Exercise-wise, we can help Christian clients to explore their deeply ingrained thoughts, feelings, and behaviors surrounding the false self by turning to this famous biblical story. In turn, we can ask them to explore their thoughts and feelings connected to their accomplishments, reputation, and possessions (Pennington, 2000). Finally, we can help them to imagine what it might be like to let go of their self-reliance, turning to God as their ultimate source of value when it comes to what they do, how others view them, and what they possess.

A Biblical View of the Self: What It Means to Be Human

As noted in Chapters 7 and 8, when it comes to a biblical view of the self, a Christian-distinctive psychotherapy must involve a Christian understanding of the *imago Dei*. Although there are several views on what exactly the *imago Dei* consists of (e.g., the substantival perspective, the functional perspective, the relational perspective), a central element involves our relationality as human beings (Boyd & Eddy, 2009). In creating us in his image (Genesis 1:27), God designed us to optimally function in the context of loving relationships, in a fashion somewhat modeled after the Trinity. To be sure, God exists in perfect relationship as the Father, Son, and Holy Spirit. God made Eve for Adam so that the image of God, in this view, is perfected in relationship. Unfortunately, due to the fall of humankind, our relationships are marred by sin, and we struggle to love like Jesus loved while on earth. As Anderson would say, we turn to Jesus as our notion of humanity now, but to each other for co-humanity (drawing this from Karl Barth; Anderson, 2001).

If we return to our general definition of sin in the second chapter, we end up turning from God towards something or someone else—an "idol"—which is often captured in our pursuit of self-sufficiency and autonomy (Bonhoeffer, 1959). Overall, being image-bearers means we must repeatedly return to God at the center, finding our "true self" in him (Bonhoeffer, 1959; Merton, 1961).

In the support phase, we can begin to help our Christian clients return to God—rather than the autonomous self—at the center by emphasizing a biblical view of the self as dependent on God. There are a variety of biblical passages that capture our need to depend on, be guided by, and submit to God. To be sure, these verses reveal that Christian mental health involves maintaining an awareness that God is at the center of our psychological and spiritual existence (rather than turning from him by placing something or someone else in his place at the center).

Christian clients facing emotional struggles may end up being preoccupied with themes of low self-worth, a lack of safety, uncertainty, and so on, with depression leading to the tendency to criticize and shame the self and anxiety resulting in a struggle with self-preservation and self-sufficiency to ameliorate the perceived dangers that lie ahead. Unfortunately, when Christians strive to unilaterally "fix" their symptoms, they may end up wandering from God, placing themselves (rather than God) at the center of existence. In doing so, they may be erecting barriers that distract them from God's loving comfort.

As a simple exercise, we can have Christian clients with emotional disorders briefly review some Bible passages to better understand their responsibility before God as one made in his image, which we struggle with due to the fall. In other words, God designed us to depend on him, love him, trust in him, and reach for him at the center of our existence, but we continually fall short of his goodness and love, regularly wandering away and striving for unilateral comfort and self-sufficiency (Romans 3:23; Ephesians 2:1–3). Christian maturation and healing involve learning how to take responsibility for our actions and no longer blame others for our shortcomings:

(a) Read 1 John 1:5–9. What does it teach us about walking in the light? What are we to do when we discover we fall short of God's goodness and love?

(b) Make a list of some areas of your life where you know you are falling short of God's goodness and love.

(c) One by one, share each of these areas with your loving Father, knowing you are accepted in his beloved Son (Ephesians 1:7).

(d) Trust that the blood of Jesus Christ cleanses you from all your sins and shortcomings and that you are completely forgiven by God (1 John 1:9). Imagine that holy water is being poured out upon you by God, cleansing away all your shame and guilt and washing it down the drain. Feel the badness being washed away.

(e) Tell God how you feel about what he has done for you.

(f) If your actions led to alienation from any others, give some consideration to how you might repair the relationship and reach out to that person.

(g) Thank God for helping you through this exercise.

Modeling the Imago Dei

In the support phase, therapists can model the image of God as image bearers, focusing on showing supportive care to our Christian clients as neighbors and fellow human beings. In that they are suffering with the symptoms of emotional disorders, we can work to deepen our relationship with them to mirror and reflect God's image, caring for them, serving them, and praying for them (Hoekema, 1986). In other words, based on our union with Christ (Wilbourne, 2016), we can participate in and reflect Jesus' servanthood and love of others in our ability to walk alongside our suffering clients in their moment of need.

The Christian Virtue of Love

As image-bearers, we are called to resemble God. The Trinitarian God is love (1 John 4:8), so love is our foundational virtue, with all other biblical virtues emanating from it (Harrington & Keenan, 2002). In other words, because Father, Son, and Holy Spirit love one another supremely, we are called to love both God and each other (echoing Jesus's Greatest Commandment in Matthew 22:36–40; Harrington & Keenan, 2002). When we (as fallen creatures) engage in sinful behavior, we end up turning away from God and "failing to love," whereas true repentance reflects a return to God as the center of our existence (Bonhoeffer, 1959; Harrington & Keenan, 2002). At the same time, we recognize that Christian clients with emotional disorders may struggle to give and receive love, given their relational history and consequent low self-worth, shame, guilt, hopelessness, a lack of safety, uncertainty, and so forth. As a result, Christian psychotherapy requires great patience and continual acceptance of clients wherever they are at.

We can begin to explore the centrality of love in Christian clients' lives by inquiring about their beliefs about the link between God's love as the foundation and source for their love for God, others, and themselves (Harrington & Keenan, 2002). In this preliminary exploration, the therapist models Jesus' love being with them in their suffering and responding to their needs. In other words, we are promoting experiences of "communion," rather than "alienation," helping our clients to ameliorate the tendency to rely on the false self, who turns inward and pursues its own desires and ambitions, and encouraging the realization of the true self, who turns towards God and others, trusting that God's love is now being expressed everywhere in life, including in the therapeutic relationship (Merton, 1961). By focusing all our attention on our clients, we are also modeling the ability to practice Christian "communion," instead of the "alienation" that naturally flows from our fallen state (Merton, 1961), helping our clients begin to participate in God's love in their relationships with God and others.

As the Trappist monk Thomas Merton (1961) suggested, "souls are like wax waiting for a seal" (p. 161). On our own, we are all disconnected from God, hardened and unable to receive God's loving seal to authenticate us as belonging to him (Merton, 1961). Yet, we can love our clients as a means to "soften" them, so they can become malleable enough to receive God's seal of love; in turn, they can learn how to extend this love to themselves and others on a daily basis. A simple exercise (inspired by Merton, 1961) at the beginning of each session can help to prepare our clients to receive God's love as the proverbial glue that holds together their identity in him:

> We are able to love God and others because God first loved us (1 John 4:7–21). Resting in God's love to us in Christ, and with our true identity rooted in our union with Christ, when you are ready, close your eyes and get into a comfortable position. Rest your hands on your knees, with your palms facing upward to God to signify your openness to his enduring love. Now, begin to imagine your entire being is like warm, malleable wax, ready to be shaped by God in whatever way he pleases. In this very moment, you are relinquishing your own effort to unilaterally define who you are with your own seal. Instead, you are ready to receive God's seal of love, stamped firmly into the middle of your very self, symbolized by a warm wax center. In this process of faithfully waiting for God's seal, try to really feel God's love for you as you gratefully await his definition of who you are. Because he loves you and cares for you, you can confidently let go of your own self-derived seal and, instead, receive his stamp to authenticate you and call you his own. Above all else, his seal signifies that you were created in his image and are his beloved. He died for you, personally, so that you will be with him forever.
>
> (John 3:16)

When finished with this exercise, you may want to slowly explore this experience with your Christian clients, including the thoughts and feelings that come up as they envision receiving God's seal of love. Next, you may want to explore how they can extend this love to themselves and others throughout the day, especially in the context of emotional disorders and their struggles to deepen their relationships.

The Learning Phase: Differentiating the True Self and False Self

Turning to the learning phase, therapists working with Christian clients can help them to process painful emotions surrounding their false sense of self, as well as gain insight into the distinction between the true self and false self. Using relational and cognitive behavioral models, therapists can explore clients' internal working model of relationships, including a view of self and others (Bartholomew & Horowitz, 1991). A common way this is done within a relational model is to explore the client's transference experiences with the therapist. According to a cognitive model, therapists can help Christians to identify their core beliefs, often involving themes of powerlessness and unlovability (Beck, 2011). For Christians, of course, a recognition of powerlessness can be healthy, especially since God displays his power in the midst of human frailty (2 Corinthians 12:8–10), and Christians are being recreated according to his image (Ephesians 4:24), enabling them to perceive themselves as weak in themselves, but strong in Christ (2 Corinthians 12:9–10). To offer one more example, acceptance and commitment therapy (ACT) suggests that humans have a verbal self, which, while sometimes helpful, can get in the way of value-based living (Hayes et al., 2012; Knabb, 2016). When humans become fused with the false, idealized stories they tell themselves, they can get stuck, struggling to live out the values that are most meaningful to them. From a Christian perspective, this storied self (when it develops outside of God's definition of who we are) can be traced back to the fall of humankind, with humans wanting to become their own God, rather than be dependent on God (*imago Dei*) (Bonhoeffer, 1959). To trust in Jesus' redemptive work means Christians can let go of our own knowledge of who we are, prioritizing God's view of us in Christ (the true self) as the starting and ending point of daily living. As this happens, Christians can shift towards radically following Jesus, remaining anchored to his teachings as we pursue virtuous living. Turning to the Bible is an important part of this process, given the Word of God reveals God's plan for optimal human functioning.

The True Self: Jesus in the Desert

Returning to Jesus' temptations in the desert (Matthew 4:1–11), he was able to combat the Devil's false statements by basing his identity on Scripture. Building on the support phase, you can begin by helping your Christian clients respond to the voice of the false self with Scripture. First, you can help your clients to identify the false self, wrapped up in what they do (e.g., behaviors, accomplishments), what other people think of them (e.g., reputation, popularity), and what they have (e.g., wealth, possessions) with the following questions (see Matthew 4; adapted from Pennington, 2000):

(a) What are some examples of accomplishments you may be relying on to define who you are (e.g., a job, education, awards)? How has this identity gotten in the way of your true identity, found in Christ? How might this false self—reliant upon your possessions or desired image before others—be contributing to symptoms of depression and anxiety? Are you experiencing a deep sense of loss that is wrapped up in a sense of a lack of accomplishments? Are you anxiously anticipating that your accomplishments will be taken away or somehow diminished?

(b) What are some examples of relying on what other people think of you and your reputation to define who you are (e.g., popularity, status)? How has this reliance gotten in the way of your true identity, found in Christ? How does this false self—reliant upon your reputation—relate to your symptoms of depression and anxiety? Are you experiencing a sense of loss that is due to a sense of disappointing others or a lack of appreciation from them? Are you anxiously anticipating that your reputation will be taken away or somehow diminished?

(c) What are some examples of relying on your possessions to define who you are (e.g., finances, wealth, a house, a car)? How might this orientation have gotten in the way of your true identity, found in Christ? How might this false self—reliant upon possessions and material worth—contribute to your symptoms of depression and anxiety? Are you experiencing a sense of loss that is due to possessions, such as your wealth being taken from you or a lack of material worth? Are you anxiously anticipating that your possessions or material worth will be taken away or somehow diminished?

In this exercise, the goal is to help our clients identify the false self—recognizing that sadness and anxiety can serve as signals—and then shift towards Scripture, reminiscent of Jesus in Matthew's gospel, in order to find our true self in Christ:

(a) "Man shall not live on bread alone, but on every word that comes from the mouth of God" (Matthew 4:4).
(b) "Do not put the Lord your God to the test" (Matthew 4:7).
(c) "Worship the Lord your God, and serve him only" (Matthew 4:10).

You may want to have your clients identify several passages in Scripture to help them effectively respond to the false self, ameliorating the tendency to unilaterally rely on what they do, what other people think of them, and what they possess.

Overall, working with our Christian clients to shift from the false self to the true self involves four major steps (adapted from Matthew 4:1–11; Pennington, 2000):

(a) Identifying the familiar voice of the false self. In this process, clients can notice their thoughts about what they do, how others view them, and what they possess, as well as the affective signals of sadness and anxiety. Sadness may convey a deep sense of loss, identifying what clients hold on to as important, and anxiety might reveal anticipated catastrophes or danger. Both emotional experiences can serve as signs/ signals that reveal themes of being preoccupied with accomplishments, a reputation before others, and possessions and wealth.
(b) Rejecting the false self. Once the false self is identified, our Christian clients can choose to reject the false self, like Jesus, by pivoting towards God's revelation—the Bible.
(c) Shifting to the true self found in God's Word. Christian clients can choose to rely on God to define who they are, according to his revelation in Scripture, rather than their accomplishments, reputation, or possessions.
(d) Replacing the false self with the true self. Christian clients can repeatedly shift from a reliance on what they do, how others view them, and what they possess to a deeper reliance on God to define who they are.

The False Self and Christian Detachment

Among the early desert Christians who moved to the deserts of Egypt, Palestine, and Syria in the first half of the first millennium, a central aim was freedom from the preoccupations of the past, worries about the future, and an overemphasis on the self (Burton-Christie, 1993). In other words, they strived for detachment, or the amelioration of "anxious grasping" (Miles, 1983, p. 111). As one of the Desert Fathers, Abba Agathon, taught, "Go, cast your powerlessness before God and you shall find rest" (as cited in Burton-Christie, 1993, p. 223). Here, we see that total dependence on God is key, rather than unilaterally striving for self-sufficiency. In other words, instead of erroneously aiming for autonomy, freedom naturally (and paradoxically) emanates from depending on God: "Our freedom is proportionate to the love and childlike trust we have for our heavenly Father" (Philippe, 2002, p. 15).

To help Christian clients hand over the false self to God, we can help them imagine they are relinquishing the grip they have on the false self, wrapped up in their accomplishments, reputation, and possessions (Pennington, 2000), reminiscent of the early desert Christians' efforts to shed their material possessions in a harsh, barren desert landscape. Since the desert can symbolize the inner world, we can help Christians to imagine that the interior life represents the desert, with total dependence on God as the central aim. In the desert, our societal comforts are stripped away as we learn to depend on God's providential care from minute to minute. Instructions for doing so may resemble the following:

> Imagine that your inner world is like a spacious, arid desert landscape. In the desert, you have nothing to rely on, such as a stockpile of food and water for survival, entertainment for distraction, human relationships for comfort, and so on. Instead, your entire being is dependent on God for getting through each day. In this hot, scorching environment, you must totally surrender to God for comfort, sustenance, and, ultimately, life itself. As a parallel, see if you can let go of your reliance on your accomplishments, reputation, and possessions, leaving them in the city you traveled from. Rather, in your new home, the desert, your job is to just be with God in solitude and silence, learning to trust him and "cast your powerlessness before God," as Abba Agathon suggested. In other words, total dependence on God is key to your freedom, even in the harsh terrain of a dry, hot desert landscape.

Internal Working Models, Core Schemas, and Storied Selves

In the clinical psychology literature, there are a wide variety of ways to conceptualize the development and maintenance of the self. Attachment theory points to an internal working model of relationships, with a view of self and view of others forming a template of relationships, which leads to an attachment style (Bartholomew & Horowitz, 1991). More specifically, a negative view of self and positive view of others can lead to an anxious attachment style, whereas a negative view of self and negative view of others can result in an avoidant attachment style. Of course, secure attachments involve a positive view of both self and others, leading to the ability to form and maintain close, safe connections with others.

Traditional cognitive behavioral therapy suggests there are several layers of cognition, with automatic thoughts, intermediate beliefs, and core beliefs (Beck, 2011; Leahy, 2017). Foundationally, core beliefs—or core schemas—fuel intermediate beliefs (e.g., ingrained rules, unquestioned assumptions), which give rise to automatic thoughts. Common negative core schemas include themes of abject powerlessness and unlovability (Beck, 2011).

As one more example, acceptance and commitment therapy (ACT)—a "third-wave" cognitive behavioral approach—suggests that we can overly rely on a distorted, storied, verbal self, which gets in the way of living out our values (Hayes et al., 2012). For example, we may become entangled with a story that suggests we are deeply flawed and unlovable because of experiences of verbal abuse in our family of origin. Rather than simply noticing this verbal content with openness and curiosity, we may automatically assume our negative thoughts (e.g., "No one will love me because I am ugly") are true, accurate, and best represent reality.

In each of these instances, our life experiences can shape our view of ourselves in the context of our most important relationships. In fact, we may struggle to question the accuracy of our deeply held views of ourselves, leading to the far-reaching struggle to follow Jesus on the roads of life. In the learning phase, we can work with Christian clients to identify the ways in which they rely on an arbitrarily generated view of the self, divorced from God's view of them. As we do so, we are helping them to shift from their own understanding (that is, their own self-knowledge, which originally emanates from the fall and is reinforced in their family of origin) to a scriptural definition of who they are. In this process, they are returning to God at the center, rather than relying on their flawed notion of the self, inaccurately fashioned according to self-sufficiency and autonomy.

Questions to consider (adapted from Bartholomew & Horowitz, 1991; Beck, 2011; Hayes et al., 2012; Leahy, 2017), which come from attachment and cognitive-behavioral conceptualizations of the self (e.g., an internal working model, a core schema, the verbal self):

(a) Do you believe you are worthy of love from others (including God)? Why or why not? Where did this belief about yourself come from? How might God answer this question? What does the Bible say about this?

(b) Do you believe others (including God) are willing to love you and respond to your needs? Why or why not? Where did this belief about others come from? How might God answer this question? What does the Bible say about this?

(c) Do you believe you are able to exercise some personal agency in daily living? In other words, do you have at least some God-given control over your own life? Do you have the will-power and self-control to choose what is best for you? Why or why not? Where did this belief about yourself come from? How might God answer this question through your salvation in Christ? What does the Bible say about this?

Once you have explored these questions with your Christian clients, you can have them identify a possibly faulty, distorted view about themselves, then pivot towards a biblical understanding by having them meditate on God's Word, the Bible. For example, a Christian client may originally state, "I'm unworthy of God's love," leading to symptoms of depression and anxiety. In turn, he or she can simply notice this thought, then gently pivot towards the central theme of John 3:16:

> Although I'm having the thought that "I'm unworthy of God's love," which comes from my false self and tendency, due to the fall, to

define myself on my own, I know that God loves me so much that he sent his Son for me.

In placing "I'm having the thought that" before the thought, Christian clients are creating some space between their true self and their false self-generated thoughts, learning to turn to God, rather than their own understanding (Harris, 2009; Knabb, 2016; Proverbs 3:5).

"It Is Finished": Jesus' Experience on the Cross

On the cross, Jesus famously declared, "It is finished" (John 19:30). With this powerful expression, Jesus' work was done—he offered himself as the perfect Lamb in response to humanity's estrangement from God, displaying God's enduring love (Kostenberger, 2009). In Jesus' atoning work on the cross, those who believe in him are reconciled to God and are a new creation in Christ (2 Corinthians 5:17–18). As a new creation, "those alive in Christ live for Christ by Christ's principles and mandates," reflecting Jesus' infinite love (Guthrie, 2015, p. 308). In other words, "The individual's whole being, value system, and behavior are changed... God has now delivered us from the bondage of sin and led us back from the exile of our estrangement from God to a new reconciled relationship" (Garland, 1999, p. 287).

To capture the contrast between the old, false self and new, true self, we can help Christian clients to imagine that they are literally walking with Christ, relying on him from moment to moment and step to step on the roads of life, just like a 1st-century disciple would follow a rabbi (Knabb, 2016). If this is the case, how might they think, feel, and act differently? If Jesus is their Source, what does a changed life look like? A visualization exercise can be helpful in this regard, allowing Christian clients to vividly imagine what daily life might be like in their town, work, home, and so on if Jesus was leading the way. How might their relationships be different? How about work life? What about family life? Finally, how might they relate differently to depression and anxiety if Jesus was their traveling companion?

> Imagine that you have just gotten up in the morning. You begin your morning routine and notice that the doorbell rings. Answering the door, you notice that Jesus is patiently waiting for you to invite him in. He tells you that he is with you and will be empowering you today as you venture out into the world to accomplish your daily tasks. After getting ready, you head for the door with Jesus by your side, driving to your job, walking in to your office, and interacting with your co-work-ers. As you do so, you notice that you are thinking, feeling, and behav-ing differently because Jesus is with you, giving you all you need in your relationship with him from moment to moment. What, specific-ally, do you notice? How are your interactions different in considering

your thinking, feeling, and behaving? How are you a "new creation" in Christ as you go about the rest of your day? In what ways are you leaving behind the old, false self in order to make room for the new, true self found in Jesus as your traveling companion? How does his loving you and empowering you from moment to moment affect the way you live?

Thoughts and Feelings versus Virtues: Who's the Captain of My Ship?

As a final example of an intervention in the learning phase, you can work with your Christian clients to better understand "who is the captain of the ship" when it comes to making life decisions and daily functioning. In acceptance and commitment therapy (ACT), authors often point out that our default thoughts and feelings, derived from our earlier development, are notoriously unreliable as a guide for life, commonly leading us in the opposite direction of our values (Hayes et al., 2012). On the other hand, our God-given values—that is, principles for living that are expressed as behaviors, rather than mere abstract thoughts (Harris, 2009)—are more consistent and stable, helping us to press forward in spite of psychological pain. For example, to be a loving spouse and parent means we need to determine what being "loving" actually looks like (behaviorally speaking) in daily living and make a determination to continue to be loving in spite of fallen thoughts and feelings that tell us otherwise.

As a quick exercise, you can help your clients to identify who is steering their proverbial ship on the oceans of life. In other words, how are they determining the direction they should take? Are their fallen thoughts and feelings steering them on the stormy seas? Or, do they have a more stable, trustworthy navigation system to get them to shore? If the latter, *who* is guiding them? Is it themselves, reminiscent of placing themselves at the center of the proverbial garden? Or is Jesus the captain, helping them to live out a set of biblical virtues on the seas of life based on their union with him? Ultimately, to hand over the helm to Jesus means they must make room for some psychological pain, given he will be taking them into uncharted territory, asking them to go to places they have never been before (Matthew 4:19).

The Action Phase: Noticing the False Self, Shifting to the True Self, and Following Jesus

Building on a supportive relationship and cognitive, affective, behavioral, and relational learning, Christians can take action in the next phase of therapy. One way to help Christians let go of the false self is through the Jesus Prayer—repeated again in this chapter with a special emphasis on the last phrase in the prayer, "have mercy on me." In this famous prayer from the Orthodox tradition, Christians are working to gently pivot from ruminations, worries, uncertainties, and self-doubts (which often feed the false self) and towards Jesus as the master physician, asking him to heal the self with his perfect empathy and compassion (Talbot, 2013). This famous prayer can help Christians to remember God throughout the day, including his loving mercy, applied to the self. Finally, as Christians practice sitting at the feet of Jesus so as to surrender the false self to God (reminiscent of Mary's yielding posture in Luke's gospel; Luke 10:38–42), they are preparing themselves to serve both God and others (consistent with Martha's activity in Luke's account; Luke 10:38–42). However, rather than anxiously striving, like Martha, Christian clients can humbly work towards serving both God and others with a well-developed set of Christian virtues in mind, asking Jesus for strength to follow him wherever he wants them to go.

Over 1,500 years ago, one of the early desert Christians—Evagrius of Ponticus—taught that Christian virtues can be used to respond to tempting, compulsive thoughts (*logismoi*) (Harmless, 2008). In this process, Christians are cultivating detachment (*apatheia*) from earthy preoccupations (e.g., ruminating about the past or worrying about the future) in order to contemplate God's love (Casey, 2005; Harmless, 2008). Although by no means synonymous with a contemporary understanding of major depressive disorder, Evagrius mentioned sadness (*accidie*) as one of the thoughts that can be distracting, getting in the way of monks' daily duties and pulling them away from God (Keller, 2005). From our viewpoint, his account of tempting, compulsive thoughts, as well as the use of virtues to combat inner struggles, anticipated some insights of contemporary psychotherapy, especially in terms of offering a psychospiritual understanding of the inner world. This conceptualization is consistent with acceptance and commitment therapy (ACT), which advocates noticing the inner world with flexibility so as to pivot towards value-based living (Knabb, 2016).

The Jesus Prayer: Getting to Know the Inner World

In the *Philokalia*, a manual of spiritual writings within the Orthodox Church that are dated between the 4th to 15th centuries, several stages are mentioned that capture the Christian struggle with negative thoughts, which can quickly lead to problematic behaviors (Pyrne, 2015). St. Hesychios the Priest, for example, offered four phases (adapted from Pyrne, 2015) to conceptualize the link between thoughts and behaviors:

(a) Provocation: we experience an initial thought, possibly in the form of a suggestion (e.g., "Maybe I don't need to go to work today because I'm depressed").

(b) Coupling: we begin to focus on the thought, perseverating on it in an intentional way (e.g., "I really am depressed. I can't go to work").

(c) Assent: we start to plan how to carry out the thought (e.g., "I can call in sick. I'll leave a voicemail for the secretary in my office to notify my manager").

(d) Action: we act out the thought via problematic behaviors (e.g., we leave the message, then isolate and withdraw for the rest of the day).

St. Hesychios advocated the use of "watchfulness" in order to guard the mind against tempting thoughts, with the steady invocation of Jesus' name leading to "great attentiveness with joy and tranquility" (Pyrne, 2015). When we ask Jesus to have mercy on us, we are asking for his compassion and empathy (Talbot, 2013). In other words, "we are asking for him to be inside of us...He is merciful from within us, more internal to us than we are to ourselves. He reveals a mercy that is the very best of the best for us" (Talbot, 2013, p. 104). Ultimately, with the Jesus Prayer,

> We beg God to be with us, inside of us. We beg God, who knows who we truly are, to reveal our true selves to ourselves. We beg the one who is closer to us than we are to ourselves to bring us back into union with ourselves through communion with all in Christ.
>
> (Talbot, 2013, p. 106)

The Jesus Prayer, then, is a way to shift from unhelpful inner dialogue (which frequently contributes to a false sense of self, outside of our relationship with Christ) to a focus on Jesus' empathic, compassionate reply.

The below transcript (adapted from Talbot, 2013) can be used to guide Christian clients through a Jesus Prayer meditative exercise:

> When you are ready, get into a comfortable position, closing your eyes and resting your feet on the floor. Sit up straight, with your hands on your lap and palms facing outward to symbolize your openness to Jesus' active, loving presence.
>
> Now, begin to notice that you are thinking, recognizing the content of your thoughts in this very moment. As you observe your thinking with a calm vigilance, pay particular attention to the thoughts that are emanating from your false self. These may be thoughts about your accomplishments, reputation, or possessions (Pennington, 2000). Regardless of the content, just notice your thoughts without judging them in any way; rather, simply label them as thoughts that originate from your false self (e.g., "There's the 'false self' talking again").
>
> After doing this for a few minutes, begin to recite the Jesus Prayer in your mind: "Lord Jesus Christ, Son of God, have mercy on me," emphasizing Jesus' mercy. Inhale the first part, "Lord Jesus Christ, Son of God," and exhale the second part, "have mercy on me." In doing so,

you are symbolically breathing in Jesus' loving presence, recognizing that his empathy and compassion are exactly what you need. "Lord Jesus Christ, Son of God" with the in-breath and "have mercy on me" with the out-breath. Over and over again, you are requesting Jesus' merciful, compassionate reply, asking that he dwell in you from moment to moment.

As this time comes to an end, thank Jesus for his mercy, compassion, and empathy, applied to your very self. Because he is the master physician, he offers you exactly what you need in this very moment. Ask him to be with you throughout your day, helping you to pivot from your false self to him over and over again.

Many Christians use a more recent form of the Jesus Prayer that concludes with the phrase, "a sinner," after "have mercy on me," echoing the tax collector in Jesus' parable in Luke 18:9–14. Some clients may benefit from this more recent form, particularly if they have a sufficient grasp of the gospel and are able to acknowledge their sinfulness without being severe towards themselves. In the third section (the "biblical anthropology and axiology" pillar), where we are considering how a Christian view of human nature and values might reshape psychotherapy with Christian clients, we recognize that acknowledging that one is still a sinner can be an important step in developing a mature, holistic Christian self-understanding that is able to undermine the false, "perfect" religious self that keeps Christians in denial about their remaining sins and psychopathology.

Therapists should also periodically remind their clients that the Jesus Prayer is not a magical incantation that heals automatically. Jesus taught us to avoid mindless repetition in our prayers (Matthew 6:7); so, the goal here is to cultivate a calm, but focused, meditative state of mind on our Savior. Its transforming power is realized through its practice in the Spirit, slowly savoring the words because of the power of Jesus' name and the reality that his perfect mercy is available to us from moment to moment in the Christian life, not as a rote exercise or mantra.

A Condensed, Three-Step Process: Noticing, Shifting, and Following

As was revealed in the last exercise, you are working with Christian clients to take several steps. A more condensed, Christocentric version of the four steps outlined in the learning phase of this chapter is as follows, adding the importance of walking with Jesus after the false self has been rejected and the true self in Christ has been embraced:

(a) Notice the thoughts associated with the false self.
(b) Shift towards the true self, found exclusively in Jesus.
(c) Follow Jesus by living out his teachings in the form of biblical virtues.

With the third step, the early desert Christians advocated for living out a set of virtues as a way to effectively respond to the cognitive distractions that pulled them away from their focus on God (Harmless, 2008). Evagrius of Ponticus offered the following list of Christian virtues to respond to tempting, compulsive thoughts (adapted from Harmless, 2008):

(a) The virtue of moderation in response to tempting thoughts about gluttony.
(b) The virtue of love in response to tempting thoughts about sex.
(c) The virtue of self-control in response to tempting thoughts about greed.
(d) The virtues of patience and courage in response to tempting thoughts about sadness, anger, and boredom.
(e) The virtues of wisdom, understanding, and prudence in response to tempting thoughts about vanity and pride.

Consistent with acceptance and commitment therapy's (ACT) emphasis on accepting the inner world so as to live out a set of well-defined values in the outer world (Hayes et al., 2012), these biblical virtues can help Christian clients shift from perseverative thinking and overly relying on the verbal content of the false self to radically following Jesus on the roads of life. Of course, a plan of action is needed so that a set of biblical virtues are lived out in a concrete manner.

Putting Together a Plan: Biblical Virtues in Daily Life

To help Christians live out a set of virtues, Table 9.2 can be utilized. As the table reveals, Christians can begin to identify a set of biblical virtues, including the behaviors to live them out. In addition, in order to effectively follow Jesus on the roads of life, a wide variety of inner experiences will need to be surrendered to God, such as difficult thoughts, feelings, and sensations. In doing so, Christian clients are prioritizing following Jesus above the complete, permanent eradication of suffering, recognizing that waiting for the symptoms to go away is not a realistic goal (Hayes et al., 2012). Rather, as revealed in the above three-step process, our clients are learning to notice the inner world, then indirectly address their psychological pain by intentionally pivoting to Jesus (rather than erroneously striving to make the pain go away; Ware, 2000). As our clients are striving to live out a set of biblical virtues, they can recite the Jesus Prayer, as well as meditate on Jesus' teachings and other verses in the Bible to keep their mind focused on God. Ultimately, following Jesus involves learning when to sit at his feet and when to serve him, with both sides making up the proverbial coin of the Christian faith.

Table 9.2 Living out Christian virtues. Adapted from Harris (2009) and Knabb (2016)

Christian Virtues I Will Live Out		
	Christian Virtues	
	Specific Behaviors to Live Out Virtues	
Inner Experiences I Will Surrender to God		
	Thoughts	
	Feelings	
	Sensations	
	Memories	
Bible Verses I Will Meditate On When Living Out Christian Virtues		
	Jesus' Teachings	
	Other Verses in the Bible	

Mary's Contemplation and Martha's Action: Two Sides of the Same Coin

In daily living, human beings are commonly tasked with deciding whether to work towards change or accept unalterable situations. In acceptance and commitment therapy (ACT), the idea is to be more accepting of the inner world so that we can live out our values in the outer world (Harris, 2009). Instead of trying to fully eradicate psychological pain—which does not typically work and leads to being sidelined on the roads of life as we futilely wait for the pain to go away—being more accepting of difficult thoughts, feelings, and sensations frees us up to focus on the task at hand, which is to pursue our deeply held values (Hayes et al., 2012).

We revisit the story of Mary and Martha to underscore the insights it contains for Christian psychotherapy (Luke 10:38–42). As we recall, Mary was sitting at Jesus' feet and Martha was attempting to serve Jesus. Historically, Christian writers have employed the story of Mary and Martha to capture the contemplative and active life, respectively. Throughout the ages, a variety of Christian authors have explored this contrast, including Augustine, Gregory, and Bernard (Cutler, 2003). Gregory the Great, a 6th-century theologian, suggested that the two differ in the following ways (adapted from Cutler, 2003; Knabb, 2016):

(a) Mary reflects a life dedicated to contemplation, embodying rest, behavioral non-action, God's love, and a state of surrender. In the context of emotional disorders, Mary can help us learn to sit patiently at Jesus' feet, trusting in him, rather than the symptoms of emotional disorders.

(b) Martha reflects a life of action, embodying service, behavioral action, and a servant's heart. In the context of emotional disorders, Martha can help us learn to engage in behavioral action—connected to biblical virtues— rather than merely waiting around for the symptoms to go away.

ACT authors frequently point to the first sentence of Reinhold Niebuhr's *Serenity Prayer* as a way to balance acceptance and change (Hayes et al., 2012), although they often leave out several of the most salient sentences:

> God grant me the serenity to accept the things I cannot change; courage to change the things I can; and wisdom to know the difference. Living one day at a time; enjoying one moment at a time; accepting hardships as the path to peace; taking, as He did, this sinful world as it is, not as I would have it; trusting that He will make all things right if I surrender to His Will; that I may be reasonably happy in this life and supremely happy with Him forever in the next. Amen.

Returning to the story of Mary and Martha, Mary can help us recognize the importance of sitting at Jesus' feet so as to accept what we cannot change, living in the moment by making peace with the symptoms of emotional disorders that may never fully go away and trusting in God's providential care with an attitude of surrender. On the other hand, Martha captures the decision to change what we can by following Jesus as we live out a set of biblical virtues in spite of the symptoms of emotional disorders. Although we are accepting that we live in a fallen world, following Jesus by taking behavioral action is key.

As the last exercise in this chapter, we can work with Christians to balance acceptance and action by encouraging them to spend time in silence with Jesus, reciting the Jesus Prayer so as to focus on him and surrender to his loving care. In turn, we can work with our clients to take the next step towards behavioral action by living out the virtues documented in Table 9.2. Finally, to bind acceptance and action together, we can encourage them to start each day by reciting the *Serenity Prayer*, asking God for the "wisdom to know the difference" between acceptance and action as they faithfully look to Jesus to guide the meandering paths of life.

A Case Example

Maria is a 38-year-old woman who is married and has three children. She is a pillar in her church, having been a Christian since she was a child. She has a good job as a nurse and is admired by her co-workers, her fellow church members, and her friends. Yet, Maria is rarely happy. Throughout her life, she has felt sad much of the time. Some days it takes all she has to get out of bed to face the day. She is well aware of the fact that she has no real reason to feel depressed, as she has a good life. And this fact makes it all worse: she feels guilty for feeling sad. She largely blames her poor relationship with God, though to others she does all the things that should work. She has quiet times, is active in church, prays frequently, and lives a life that is exemplary. She is convinced, nonetheless, that her sad feelings are due to God's displeasure and speaks very negatively of herself in the therapist's office, seeing herself as ungrateful, unfaithful, and a burden to others because of her depressed and irritable moods. She has tried medication for years and, while it may help to some extent, it has not solved the problem. At her husband's insistence, Maria comes to see you, but still feels the real problem is her shallow (as she sees it) walk with God.

The Support Phase

Maria clearly shows signs of struggling with a false self, but in a strange way. For all of her Christian faith, she seems intent on earning God's pleasure by being a good Christian and has apparently convinced herself "good Christians" don't feel sad very often. This is not uncommon and likely is facilitated by Christian media, in which leaders are portrayed with constant smiles and unceasingly joyful dispositions. In this phase, the therapist will want to be careful not to pressure Maria too quickly for change, for this pattern is longstanding.

Maria seems to see God as frowning on her as she strives to please him so she can feel better. A good place to start with her might be to help her know how other Christians have struggled with emotional problems, even as they were used greatly by God. Three examples suffice for now: John Bunyan struggled with what was likely a form of obsessive-compulsive disorder (OCD) and his walk through this valley is detailed in *Grace Abounding to the Chief of Sinners*, originally published in 1666. The famous preacher Charles Spurgeon wrestled with depression all of his life, and his story and its implications are detailed in *Spurgeon's Sorrows: Realistic Hope for Those Who Suffer from Depression*, by Zack Eswine (2015). Finally, the poems of the 18th-century writer William Cowper trace his constant turning toward God as he dealt with depression and suicidal urges. One particularly poignant poem is "God Moves in a Mysterious Way" (Cowper, 1774):

> God moves in a mysterious way
> His wonders to perform;
> He plants His footsteps in the sea
> And rides upon the storm.
> Deep in unfathomable mines

Of never failing skill
He treasures up His bright designs
And works His sov'reign will.
Ye fearful saints, fresh courage take;
The clouds ye so much dread
Are big with mercy and shall break
In blessings on your head.
Judge not the Lord by feeble sense,
But trust Him for His grace;
Behind a frowning providence
He hides a smiling face.
His purposes will ripen fast,
Unfolding every hour;
The bud may have a bitter taste,
But sweet will be the flow'r.
Blind unbelief is sure to err
And scan His work in vain;
God is His own interpreter,
And He will make it plain.

The Learning Phase

With the support of these and other saints upholding her, Maria may now be open to exploring more of how her false views of self impact her life. She is caught up in seeing herself as depressed because of her failures, even though that is hard to prove in an objective manner. Her therapist may point her to how salvation is all of grace and encourage her to do a Bible study of God's grace in its completeness and independence from our efforts and worthiness. In 2 Corinthians 5:17, Paul taught that Christians (such as Martha) are a new creation in Christ. Her shortcomings and sins are forgiven, and she is to live out of her faith, rather than try to earn it. As to sin, one of Maria's most pressing ones may be the notion that she can earn happiness by obedience. As Philippians repeatedly exhorts us, we are to rejoice in the Lord, but joy is not necessarily free of some sadness. Her helpfulness has ministered to others in a way that has glorified God, even as she struggles to feel good about it.

Consistent with the discussion in Chapter 8 on developing a personal narrative, an exercise her therapist might try in this phase of therapy is as follows:

> Write a several-page narrative of your life, with a paragraph for each era (infancy, elementary school, middle and high school, etc.). Summarize not just a typical event or two, but how this time shaped the story of your life. Now, consider your spiritual values and the ways God has been at work in this story. Rewrite each section to show how

204 Biblical Anthropology, Axiology, Christian Psychotherapy

you grew spiritually, or learned lessons from God, or how these events shaped how you see your calling.

For Maria, the focus would need to be on how she has interpreted her depressed feelings as an "effect" of her failures, rather than as possibly something temperamental. And, as such, her frustrations with herself and guilt only served to deepen the depression. While she may have to accept a degree of melancholy as something she shares with Spurgeon and others, she at least can see the story of how God has worked and is working good out of the depressed feelings—which may just be a tragic way the fall has impacted her life.

The Action Phase

For Maria, in a sense, her life has always been an action phase: trying to chase away her depressed feelings through work. The goal, now, is to act into the lives of others out of love for Christ, who is with her in suffering, rather than in an effort to earn his approval. The focus is more on the motive of love, rather than the motive of trying to live out of a false self. Maria is loved, forgiven, and given grace in Christ—even if her emotions do not always match up. One action might be to help her see her spiritual gifts, taking seriously the comments others have made about her many helpful acts of kindness. Another might be to point her toward the virtue she displays. One way to do this is to have her take the Values in Action (VIA) Character Strengths Survey, which is free at http://www.viacharacter. org/www/Character-Strengths-Survey.

   We hope Maria feels less depressed by reducing her struggle with depression, accepting her identity in Christ even if she has the burden of a propensity for depression. A pivot to focus out of her faith toward others in love, rather than in proving herself, may yield many positive benefits for Maria, her loved ones, and God's kingdom.

Conclusion

In this chapter, we presented a variety of interventions for learning, support, and action in the context of the "biblical anthropology and axiology" pillar of treatment. As a central theme, Christians with emotional disorders can struggle with overly relying on the false self, disconnected from the true self found in Christ. As a result, helping Christian clients to gain a deeper awareness of the voice of the false self, captured in the form of an overreliance on accomplishments, a reputation, or possessions (Pennington, 2000), is key. In turn, Christian clients can learn to shift from the false self to the true self, following Jesus by living out a set of biblical virtues that are modeled by Christ himself. Although the symptoms of emotional disorders may manifest in the form of ruminations, worries, a faulty internal working model of relationships, a negative core schema, or overreliance on the verbal self, we can work with Christian clients to recognize the ways in which these reverberations of the fall can get in the way of responding to Jesus' famous call: "Come, follow me!" (Matthew 4:19).

Note

1 In acceptance and commitment therapy (ACT), fusing with the verbal, conceptualized self (and corresponding "self-story") can undermine psychological flexibility, in that clients may end up distorting reality to preserve this rigid self-narrative, even when presented with evidence to the contrary (Hayes et al., 2012). On the other hand, psychological flexibility involves noticing when the storied self, which can start to develop in childhood based on recurrent messages from caregivers, society, and so forth, is getting in the way of value-based living, then pivoting towards living out a set of well-defined values to enrich life (Hayes et al., 2012). For Christian clients, fusing with the storied self might take the form of holding on to a rigid, problematic story that states they cannot possibly be saved or loved by God because of what they have done or who they believe they are, despite the gospel message in the Bible (e.g., John 3:16; Romans 10:9). In turn, fusing with this inflexible self-narrative, potentially emanating from regular childhood interactions with abusive, neglectful, and shaming caregivers, may get in the way of faithfully following Jesus' teachings and deepening their relationship with him. Ultimately, for Christian clients, well-defined self-narratives can be problematic, rather than helpful, when they (a) are constructed apart from Christ's definition of who they are in him, and (b) get in the way of radically and authentically following Christ wherever he wants them to go.

References

Anderson, R. (2001). *The Shape of Practical Theology: Empowering Ministry with Theological Praxis*. Downers Grove, IL: InterVarsity Press.
Bartholomew, K., & Horowitz, L. (1991). Attachment styles among young adults: A test of a four-factor model. *Journal of Personality and Social Psychology, 61*, 226–244.
Beck, J. (2011). *Cognitive Behavior Therapy: Basics and Beyond* (2nd ed.). New York: The Guildford Press.
Bonhoeffer, D. (1959). *Creation and Fall*. New York: Touchstone.
Boyd, G., & Eddy, P. (2009). *Across the Spectrum: Understanding Issues in Evangelical Theology* (2nd ed.). Grand Rapids, MI: Baker Academic.
Burton-Christie, D. (1993). *The Word in the Desert: Scripture and the Quest for Holiness in Early Christian Monasticism*. New York: Oxford University Press.
Casey, J. (2005). Apatheia. In P. Sheldrake (Ed.), *The Westminster Dictionary of Christian Spirituality* (pp. 114–115). Louisville, KY: Westminster John Knox Press.
Cowper, W. (1774). God moves in a mysterious way. Retrieved from http://library.timelesstruths.org/music/God_Moves_in_a_Mysterious_Way/
Cutler, D. (2003). *Western Mysticism: Augustine, Gregory and Bernard on Contemplation and the Contemplative Life*. New York: Dover Publications.

Doherty, W. (1995). *Soul Searching: Why Psychotherapy Must Promote Moral Responsibility*. New York: Basic Books.

Eswine, J. (2015). *Spurgeon's Sorrows: Realistic Hope for Those Who Suffer from Depression*. Fearn, Scotland: Christian Focus.

Finley, J. (1978). *Merton's Palace of Nowhere*. Notre Dame, IN: Ave Maria Press.

Guthrie, G. (2015). *2 Corinthians*. Grand Rapids, MI: Baker Academic.

Harmless, W. (2008). *Mystics*. New York: Oxford University Press.

Harrington, D., & Keenan, J. (2002). *Jesus and Virtue Ethics: Building Bridges between New Testament Studies and Moral Theology*. Lanham, MD: Rowan & Littlefield.

Harris, R. (2009). *ACT Made Simple: An Easy-to-Read Primer on Acceptance and Commitment Therapy*. Oakland, CA: New Harbinger Publications.

Hayes, S., Strosahl, K., & Wilson, K. (2012). *Acceptance and Commitment Therapy: The Process and Practice of Mindful Change* (2nd ed.). New York: The Guilford Press.

Hoekema, A. (1986). *Created in God's Image*. Grand Rapids, MI: William B. Eerdmans Publishing.

Johnson, C. (2010). *The Globalization of Hesychasm and the Jesus Prayer: Contesting Contemplation*. New York: Continuum.

Johnson, E. L. (2007). *Foundations for Soul Care: A Christian Psychology Proposal*. Downers Grove, IL: InterVarsity Press.

Johnson, E. L. (2017). *God and Soul Care: The Therapeutic Resources of the Christian Faith*. Downers Grove, IL: InterVarsity Press.

Keller, D. (2005). *Oasis of Wisdom: The Worlds of the Desert Fathers and Mothers*. Collegeville, MN: Liturgical Press.

Keller, T. (2010). *Gospel in Life: Grace Changes Everything*. Grand Rapids, MI: Zondervan.

Knabb, J. (2016). *Faith-Based ACT for Christian Clients: An Integrative Treatment Approach*. New York: Routledge.

Kostenberger, A. (2009). *A Theology of John's Gospel and Letters*. Grand Rapids, MI: Zondervan.

Lambert, M. (2013). The efficacy and effectiveness of psychotherapy. In M. Lambert (Ed.), *Bergin and Garfield's Handbook of Psychotherapy and Behavior Change* (pp. 169–218). New York: John Wiley & Sons.

Leahy, R. (2017). *Cognitive Therapy Techniques: A Practitioner's Guide* (2nd ed.). New York: The Guilford Press.

Mathewes-Green, F. (2009). *The Jesus Prayer: The Ancient Desert Prayer that Tunes the Heart of God*. Brewster, MA: Paraclete Press.

McMinn, M. (2008). *Sin and Grace in Christian Counseling: An Integrative Paradigm*. Downers Grove, IL: InterVarsity Press.

McMinn, M., & Campbell, C. (2007). *Integrative Psychotherapy: Toward a Comprehensive Christian Approach*. Downers Grove, IL: InterVarsity Press.

Merton, T. (1961). *New Seeds of Contemplation*. New York: New Directions Books.

Mikulincer, M., Shaver, P., & Pereg, D. (2003). Attachment theory and affect regulation: The dynamics, development, and cognitive consequences of attachment-related strategies. *Motivation and Emotion, 27*, 77–102.

Miles, M. (1983). Detachment. In G. Wakefield (Ed.), *The Westminster Dictionary of Christian Spirituality* (p. 111). Philadelphia, PA: The Westminster Press.

Pennington, B. (2000). *True Self/False Self: Unmasking the Spirit Within*. New York: The Crossroad Publishing Company.

Peterson, C., & Seligman, M. (2004). *Character Strength and Virtues: A Handbook and Classification.* New York: Oxford University Press.

Philippe, J. (2002). *Interior Freedom.* New York: Scepter Publishers.

Pyrne, R. (Ed.). (2015). *The Philokalia.* Philadelphia, PA: The Great Library Collection.

Talbot, J. (2013). *The Jesus Prayer: A Cry for Mercy, a Path of Renewal.* Downers Grove, IL: InterVarsity Press.

Ware, K. (2000). *The Inner Kingdom.* Crestwood, NY: St. Vladimir's Seminary Press.

Welsh, R., & Knabb, J. (2009). Renunciation of the self in psychotherapy. *Mental Health, Religion & Culture, 12,* 401–414.

Wilbourne, R. (2016). *Union with Christ: The Way to Know and Enjoy God.* Colorado Springs, CO: David C. Cook.

CHAPTER 10

Redemption in the Christian Tradition

Introduction

In many ways, this chapter is a summary chapter, a recapitulation or re-heading, as the old rhetoricians called it. It is a summary because any theory of healing requires a sense of wholeness, and to talk about healing and restoration requires some notion of why healing is needed and to what we are restored. Within the Christian tradition, redemption is the source of healing that entails the goal of healing, which has been described as restored communion. To speak of restored communion, then, requires understanding the nature of communion and how it was lost, which is at least touched on in each of the previous sections.

The reason why such a book as this needs to be written is that we encounter many people who struggle with health and wholeness, particularly emotionally and psychologically. We live in a day and age when such struggles are everywhere present. The reasons for such proliferation are many and varied, and are topics for another book. For our purposes, each effort to bring emotional and psychological healing assumes a picture of what health and wellbeing look like. This book is no different. This chapter sets out what health and wholeness look like in the Christian tradition. Like the other chapters, it does not claim to be exhaustive, but to give a sense of how Christianity shapes the psychotherapeutic context. Also like the previous chapters, communion serves as the framing concept. Wellbeing for the Christian tradition can be understood as an ever deepening communion with God, which is both present and progressive. In Christianity, when one entrusts oneself to Christ—trusting that he is who he says he is and has done what he says he has done—this person is a new creation instantaneously (2 Corinthians 5:17). Yet, this is also the beginning of a journey, of becoming a follower of Christ. This journey was introduced in Chapter 7 as sanctification, which is ongoing. It is in many ways the chief task of the Christian life and the path to healing and wholeness. Thus, in Christianity, redemption is both the initiation of communion and its continuation and development throughout life.

The Path of Communion

Healing in the Christian tradition begins with reconciliation of our relationship with God and a deeper understanding of him and his creation, which manifests itself in virtuous human actions and reordered human loves. Through the incarnation of the Son of God, the goodness of creation and humankind are affirmed.[1] The fall broke and fragmented humanity, but it did not eradicate the image of God. Imagine, perhaps, a shattered mirror, where the image is still reflected, but it is disjointed and distorted. To keep with the metaphor, in Jesus, the mirror is repaired. We "see" the truly human life lived as it was intended to be. In redemption, our particular "reflection" of the image is *re*-stored, and through sanctification, our life reflects Jesus more fully.

In the incarnation, Christ serves as mediator—fully God and fully human—and reconciles humankind to God; that is, in Christ, humanity is restored to communion with God. Restored communion starts humankind toward the completeness that was lost in the fall. Though we may continually struggle with inadequacy, and our incompleteness remains problematic, healing starts with Christ, and wholeness is now possible.

In the context of emotional disorders, the Christian view of healing involves strengthening a person's restored relationship with God; that is, learning to turn to God for comfort in the midst of psychological pain. As a result, support in therapy involves helping Christian clients to deepen their intimacy with him; in turn, Christian clients can gain perspective on their inner life, including their psychological suffering, by drawing from the Christian tradition. In these efforts, a Christian view of psychological pain involves acknowledging the tension between surrendering to God and turning away from him, between struggling to trust and yield to his providential care and wanting to trust ourselves and control our circumstances.

As new, reoriented habits are developed, so, too, is the awareness of God's active, loving presence, helping Christian clients to relate differently to their inner life and experiences in the world and strive to find meaning, purpose, and intentionality in even the most difficult circumstances. Through reconciliation *with* God, the ultimate Good, humankind, *through* God, is now enabled to lovingly relate to things properly—to self, others, God, and the world. Accordingly, the development of the virtues reorients a Christian's habits and values toward an ordered and meaningful whole. As Christians are able to relate differently to our inner pain by recognizing that Christ is with us in the midst of these experiences, we can more effectively follow his will, growing in our conformity to his image (Romans 8:29). We can live a life more like Jesus with the help of his Spirit.

Living the Image

When we "look to Jesus," as we discussed in Chapter 7, we see what the truly human life looks like; that is, we see with startling clarity the image of

God in human form living the fully human life—working, eating, relating, and suffering. But the fascinating thing is that, in living the truly human life, he restores humanity. When Christians talk about redemption, our minds almost exclusively focus on the cross and death of Jesus. While this is perfectly true and the "crux" (*cross* in Latin) and center of Christianity, it is the life of Jesus, the perfect Lamb of God, that made him our able substitute. He lived a human life in perfect obedience, succeeding where all other mere humans had failed.[2] The only mediator had to be *fully* human, because it was humankind that failed, but could not be *only* human; because of human frailty and sinfulness, any sacrifice would be for individual sins—both inherited and actual. Jesus alone, as fully God and fully human, could live a life of full obedience in the flesh; in doing so, he could redeem all facets of human life—working, eating, relating, and, yes, even suffering.

Jesus redeems humanity "from the inside," as it were. Irenaeus, a 2nd-century Christian thinker, called this "recapitulation." You might recall this term from the opening sentences of this chapter. Irenaeus borrowed this term from rhetoricians; it literally means to "re-head" something. So, in this book, the main points of redemption discussed in earlier chapters are "re-headed" in this chapter and given more specific treatment. So, too, with humanity. In the Christian tradition, Adam is the first "head" of humankind, and Jesus is the last Adam, a new "head" of humankind (1 Corinthians 15:45–49). So, where Adam failed (and Moses, and David, and so on), Jesus succeeded. In his obedience, Jesus shows us how to live the image.

This is Irenaeus's point. In redeeming humanity "from the inside," Jesus is re-orienting and re-ordering how we live; in doing so, he is re-deeming human life and the created order, re-storing communion. That's a lot of "*re*-ings," but that is why re-capitulation is such an interesting way of approaching Jesus' life. Perhaps an image may help. One of the authors (T.B.) owns a home built in the 1950s. When first moving in, the water line to the refrigerator was made of old copper piping. Every time the refrigerator was moved out, the pipe crimped. Without fail, when trying to "un-crimp" the pipe, it would break and leak. How much easier it would be if one could become small, enter the pipe, and "un-crimp" the line from the inside. Though inadequate, this example provides a way of understanding recapitulation. Jesus enters humanity from the inside and "un-crimps" our disobedient over-reach; in turn, in his death, he overcomes the offense of our sin before our holy God. Jesus' life and death restore us, with his resurrection demonstrating God's acceptance and our restoration.

Now, why does this matter in the clinical context? As noted in Chapter 7, we are told in Hebrews to look to Jesus as our example and motivation. It is easy to assume that, because Jesus was God, his humanity was easy. Yet, Hebrews makes it very clear that Jesus suffered. Though there are many verses that communicate this, one passage will suffice. Hebrews 2:17–18 tells us that Jesus "was made like [us]" and that "he himself suffered when he was tempted." Note that temptation was not a "cake walk" for Jesus, but caused him to suffer. Because of this, "he is able to help those who are being tempted." So, when Jesus redeemed life from the inside, it was not a life shielded from the blows of living in a fallen, broken world. Indeed, because he was God, he felt the brokenness much more fully than we can ever comprehend. Yet, as he did so, he trusted and obeyed, did not sin, and now is able to "empathize with our weaknesses" (Hebrews 4:15). This is why we are told to "approach" God to receive help. The remarkable thing is that Jesus knows fully our pain, why we turn away, and why trusting what we see and feel seems so much easier than trusting God. In the clinical setting, the Christian context consists in helping those who are struggling with fear, anxiety, and other forms of psychological pain see in Jesus a ready partner who really and genuinely knows what they are going through. Certainly, he has the scars to prove it. The rest of the verse just quoted tells us to confidently approach Jesus—the "throne of grace"—so we "may receive mercy and find grace to help us in our time of need." It is in our deepest need that we find the "man of suffering, and familiar with pain" so very near, so very empathic, and so very strong to respond (Isaiah 53:3; Zephaniah 3:17; Hebrews 13:5-6). Our union with Christ in his suffering (Romans 8:17) guarantees that our suffering has divine meaning and has been woven into his story.

Restored Communion and Our Path in the World

A question that often occurs at this point is as follows: how do I live into the image of Christ in my daily life of working, eating, relating, and even suffering? Looking to Jesus is one thing, whereas being conformed to him seems to be another thing entirely. Indeed, participating in the life of Christ is not easy when we consider it involves loving our enemies and doing good to those who spitefully use us (Matthew 5:43-48). To dwell on the point a bit more, consider forgiving one's enemies. When someone steps on our toe, it is easy to forgive. But a more thorough forgiveness is needed when there is a serious offense, for example, when pain and sorrow have been caused. That is not easy, but biblical teaching, confirmed by dozens of studies, indicates that being able to forgive others is a key Christian virtue and essential to human wellbeing in a fallen world.

Fortunately, the Bible presents a two-fold sequence of addressing the injustice that we experience that recognizes the injustice of the aggression, but pivots the victim towards a healing resolution. First, in the Old Testament (e.g., the Psalms), we see followers of God resist the tendency to respond to others with revenge—causing them pain, like they caused us. Instead, they cry to God with great emotion to vindicate them and to address the injustice, since vengeance belongs to God, and not us (Deuteronomy 32:35). This is a healthy first step—to take our heart-felt concerns to the Lord, "drop them off" with him, and allow him to address them—because it takes seriously the meaningfulness of our hearts and shares it with our omnipotent caregiver. That validates our sense of injustice (including the legitimate anger such treatment stirs up), but also prevents us from moving into bitterness and holding on to the anger.

As we internalize God's care for us and learn how to trust him in the core of our being, as a second step, we can move into forgiveness of those who have mistreated us, as Jesus demonstrated on the cross (Luke 23:34) and is taught in the New Testament epistles (Colossians 3:13). Therapists can utilize the REACH model as one way to foster deeper forgiveness of others, recalling the hurt ("R"); emphasizing with the aggressor ("E"); granting forgiveness as an altruistic gift ("A"); committing to forgive the aggressor ("C"); and holding onto the forgiveness over time ("H") (Worthington, 2009).

As Christians progress along the path of communion and live into the form of Christ, this perspective begins to shape how Christians view their experiences, as their mind is being renewed. The mind that was "vain"— attempting to make the self the ultimate good and viewing everything in terms of the self in over-reach—begins to orient things toward God, our true and greatest good. Recall from Chapter 4 that we are embedded knowers, which means we see things through lenses or narratives as finite creatures. In the Christian tradition, walking the path of communion becomes the means by which our narrative is reshaped through redemption, and our mind no longer conforms to the world; rather, it is transformed by the mercy of God (Romans 12:2). The term for "world" used in this verse actually has temporal connotations, literally meaning this "age," or epoch. It is often contrasted in Scripture with the "age to come," when Christ will be Lord of all and creation is restored. So, as we learn to live the image by looking to Jesus, we see the world and live in it as members of the age to come. As we do so, it seems as though we are living in an *un*-natural way, but, in reality, we are living the truly natural life that God created us to live. This is why so many of God's commands seem "counterintuitive"—only by dying do we live, only by giving everything away are we rich, and only through suffering are we made whole. The rest of Romans 12:2 states that, by our transformed mind, we are enabled to "test and approve what God's will is— his good, pleasing and perfect will." We begin to see as God sees, and what is good to God becomes good to us.

Developing the mind of Christ and transforming one's perspective on reality, however, is never simply a human task. It is God intentionally and actively working in us by the Spirit of God. Recall the Trinitarian activity involved in the Christian life. We can see once more how comprehensively the Christian tradition is shaped by the doctrine of the Trinity, and how creation and re-creation are results of thoroughly Trinitarian activity. Indeed, the renewed mind and the work of the Spirit are inescapably related in passages like in 1 Corinthians 2, where the way of seeing the world through Jesus is contrasted with the wisdom imparted through "this age"—which is, again, opposed to the wisdom of the "age to come." We are told that God reveals his wisdom through his Spirit, as revealed in the following verses:

> The Spirit searches all things, even the deep things of God. For who knows a person's thoughts except their own spirit within them? In the same way no one knows the thoughts of God except the Spirit of God. What we have received is not the spirit of the world, but the Sprit who is from God, so that we may understand what God has freely given us... The person without the Spirit does not accept the things that come from the Spirit of God but considers them foolishness, and cannot understand them because they are discerned only through the Spirit... But we have the mind of Christ.
>
> (1 Corinthians 2:10–16)

The Spirit of God, alone, knows the thoughts of God. Yet, it is also the Spirit of God who lives within us. Ultimately, it is the Spirit of God, through Christ, who shapes our mind into the mind of Christ.

It is through the work of the Spirit that we come to see things differently, responding and reacting in reoriented ways that have God as our ultimate trust and our greatest good. By seeing things through Jesus, we relate to them in increasingly transformed ways. In Chapter 4, Esther Meek (2003) communicated this renewed understanding pointedly, noting, "knowing God has unlocked the world for me. In knowing him I engage the world" (p. 144). It is worth considering how knowing God unlocks the world, and, in knowing God, we inescapably engage the world. As mentioned in the fourth chapter, for Christians, knowing God as Father and understanding that this is our Father's world frees us to engage the world with confidence, not fear. Yet, we can extend this understanding even further—it enables us to see the world by way of communion. So, as we engage with the world, we are not simply engaged with objects, but with living expressions of the glory of God. Also quoted in Chapter 4, Meek went on to deepen the reflection, saying:

> But see the tree as a thing made and moved by the utterly faithful words of an infinite person for his own delight, on whose ways we will know better as we explore the tree, and you have unlocked both the wonder of the tree and the majesty of God. Plus, you grasp yourself better, too: you are a knower who images and walks before God among the other things he has made. You are not God. They are not God. But you and they are made by him and thus fraught with significance and value.
>
> (p. 144)

By noticing the triangulation here, we can draw together several things. For Christians, walking the path of communion entails an increasingly closer walk with God, a deeper engagement and perception of the world and our experiences herein, and a deeper understanding of ourselves, which moves us further along the path of communion and deepens our loving dependence and trust of God—the upward spiral, previously mentioned in Chapter 7. In short, for the Christian tradition, the path of communion involves the practice of communion, which makes learning an act of communion and the world, as we encounter it, an occasion of communion. But the starting place of it all is the restored communion with the transcendent personal God, who we can now, through redemption, call our Father.

Restored Communion and Our Life with God

In the Christian tradition, the restored communion of humankind occurs through the person and work of Jesus Christ. In Christ, we have creation redeemed; in turn, in our redemption, we cultivate increasingly transformed lives that look to a future hope. The transformation of our lives through the Spirit is possible through what the Christian tradition calls "union with Christ." For the clinical setting, it is one of the most powerful aspects of the Christian tradition and the practical result of the work of Christ.

In one sense, union with Christ is a way of describing all of salvation and the benefits of the Christian life (Erickson, 1998). It is God's intention that the benefits and transformation of life united with Christ, while fully available to faith, are increasingly experienced in practice. Sometimes this is described as an "already, not yet" distinction. The moment one entrusts oneself to Christ—again, taking him at his word that he is who he says he is and did what he said he did—we are united with Christ and fully accepted before God. It is the work of the Spirit of God in our lives that unites us with Christ, so that our life is intertwined with the life of Christ. So, not only do we look to Jesus in order to live the image, the very Spirit of the living God is working into us the very life of Jesus. Because we could never, by our own strength, live like Jesus, God in his mercy gives us his Spirit as our "helper" (John 14:26). This is what the Bible means in verses such as Galatians 2:20, "I have been crucified with Christ and I no longer live, but Christ who lives in me. The life I now live in the body, I live by faith in the Son of God, who loved me and gave himself for me."

Redemption does not mean that Christians cease being themselves. Rather, God enables Christians to become all he created them to be. We move from being "merely" us, to be "truly" us. Consider the image discussed in John 15:4, "Remain in me [Jesus], as I also remain in you. No branch can bear fruit by itself; it must remain in the vine. Neither can you bear fruit unless you remain in me." Jesus goes on to say, "I am the vine; you are the branches. If you remain in me and I in you, you will bear much fruit; apart from me you can do nothing" (John 15:5). This image is helpful. Think about the grape and its relationship to the vine. The grape cannot exist independently of the vine—the grape's very identity and life is given to it by the vine—but the grape is not the vine, nor the vine the grape. In earlier chapters, creaturely integrity was said to be the result of finitude—we are who we are by our limits, so our creational incompleteness is not a negative, but was only problematized through turning away from God, who was our completeness. In redemption and union with Christ, humankind experiences completeness through restored communion. In this union, we experience the truly human life, life in its fullness through our very uniqueness. Theologian Michael Horton (2011) suggested this with the following:

> [The gospel] announces that all who are in Christ are actually coheirs with him of his estate, members of his body. Grafted by the Spirit onto this Vine, we bear fruit that is not just *like* his own, as if he were merely a model to imitate, but is in fact the fruit that ripens from the sap of his own eschatological life.
>
> (p. 273, italics added)

The point of our union with Christ and our call to "look to Jesus" is so we can become fully who we were intended to be as image bearers. Another theologian, Thomas Torrance (2008), affirmed this reality: "In the full humanity of Jesus, as it is joined eternally to his deity in incarnation and atonement, man's destiny as man is actually assured and restored to its place in God" (p. 186). Perhaps an example might help. We are created uniquely by God. Each human person, in our uniqueness, reflects God's image in unique ways. Recall that God transcends time and space, so his fullness can never be embodied. It requires a multitude of uniquely created humans to even hint at the beauty and wonder of God. It is in restored communion that the shattered image is made whole and we, in our uniqueness, can image forth God as only we can in our creaturely integrity. C. S. Lewis (2001) described this more fully, saying:

> If He had no use for all these differences, I do not see why He should have created more souls than one. Be sure that the ins and outs of your individuality are no mystery to Him; and one day they will no longer be a mystery to you... For it is not humanity in the abstract that is to be saved, but you—you the individual.
>
> (pp. 151–152)

As each person is unique, so, too, will be each person's struggles. God, the great artist, must brush our lives with both bright colors and dark ones if we are to be his masterwork. Again, Lewis (2001) stated the following:

Surely each of the redeemed shall forever know and praise some one aspect of the Divine beauty better than any other creature can. Why else were individuals created, but that God, loving all infinitely, should love each differently. And this difference, so far from impairing, floods with meaning the love of all blessed creatures for one another, the communion of the saints. If all experienced God in the same way and returned Him an identical worship, the song of the Church triumphant would have no symphony, it would be like an orchestra in which all the instruments played the same note.

(pp. 154, 155)

Remember, God is omniscient and personal—he knows each and every one of his children fully and completely because we are his.

This also helps us understand why God takes our sanctification so seriously. God, through Christ and by the Spirit, is at work shaping us more fully into our unique reflection of his image—which is where and when we fully discover our purpose, meaning, and the fullness of life. God, in his good providence, is in control of all our circumstances and experiences—yes, even the painful ones. There is no suffering, no matter how deep or seemingly purposeless, that is not under God's sovereign control. While there is great mystery in this, through the eyes of faith—looking to Jesus by way of our experiences—we can know that God is at work. A biblical image that is helpful is the refiner's fire. Gold, though beautiful and of great worth, contains impurities. To purify gold, the refiner must place it in intense heat. As it is melted, the impurities are broken apart and are separated. Christians have a wide variety of experiences that involve undergoing the "refiner's fire." It is through the heat, yes, in all its intensity, that the impurities in our life are being broken apart. Because the impurities are interweaved with our life, however, it feels as though something of ourselves is being taken away, so we fight it. The irony is that what we are trying to hold on to is the very thing that keeps us from our completeness, the thing that keeps us from living the image and experiencing life in its fullness. This is what the Hebrews 12 passage candidly referred to: "No discipline seems pleasant at the time, but painful. Later on, however, it produces a harvest of righteousness and peace for those who have been trained by it" (Hebrews 12:11). In reference to the "refiner," 1 Peter (1:6–7) said, "Suffering grief in all kinds of trials... [has had to come] so that the proven genuineness of your faith—of greater worth than gold, which perishes even though by fire—may result in praise, glory and honor when Jesus Christ is revealed" (1:7). The unique life that each of us lives is much more precious to God than gold. So precious, in fact, that he will not allow us to be content in impurity. He knows our ultimate good; thus, our ultimate joy is at stake. Though painful, he will only allow us to experience the trials and suffering that will remove the impurities from the gold, which we represent.

It is important to also remember that we do not walk through the refiner's fire alone. The very God who sovereignly brings us to the fire is the same one who will graciously and mercifully carry us through it. It is here where we see the amazing gift that is communion with God. The triune life of God that *perichoresis* refers to is the very life Christians are called to share in our own creaturely way. As mentioned above, the life we now live is lived for God the Father, through union with God the Son, by the empowering of God the Spirit. In John 16:13, the Spirit is said to guide us into all the truth. The Greek term translated as "guide" comes from the root word that means "way" or "road." Interestingly, life is often described in Scripture as a path (or way), and we are called to walk in the "way" of the Lord, the good way, and find rest for our souls (Jeremiah 6:16; Matthew 11:28–30). The guide, then, is one who can lead us on the path because the guide knows the way. The Spirit of God is our guide, who knows the mind of God, lives in us, and guides us in the way. Though the way may be painful at times, we never walk it alone or without purpose, for it is the path of communion. Pain, while very real, cannot "separate us from the love of God that is in Christ Jesus our Lord" (Romans 8:39). To understand the Christian context, then, is to end where we began—with God. To properly understand the life of God is to become aware that all God is—the vibrant inter-Trinitarian life from which all things come and to which all things will return—is personally, powerfully, and providentially for us. Thus, "If God is for us, who can be against us?" (Romans 8:31).

Notes

1 The incarnation is from the Latin *in carne*, "in the flesh," and refers to the doctrine of God becoming human in Jesus.
2 The distinction between "truly human" (Jesus) and "merely human" (fallen humankind) is from Morris (2001). We have found Morris' distinction helpful in showing how Jesus was fully human, yet without the sinfulness of humankind. The obedience and sinlessness of Jesus was, however, as a human committed to obeying the will of the Father. Jesus did not avoid sin by his divinity, but fully obeyed in and through his full humanity. Thus, Jesus is our perfect example and perfect sacrifice. In short, Jesus is our Redeemer.

References

Erickson, M. (1998). *Christian Theology* (2nd ed.). Grand Rapids, MI: Baker Books.

Horton, M. (2011). *Pilgrim Theology*. Grand Rapids, MI: Zondervan.

Lewis, C. S. (2001). *The Problem of Pain*. New York: Harper Collins.

Meek, E. (2003). *Longing to Know*. Grand Rapids, MI: Brazos Press.

Morris, T. (2001). *The Logic of God Incarnate*. Eugene, OR: Wipf and Stock Publishers.

Torrance, T. F. (2008). *Incarnation: The Person and Life of Christ*. Downers Grove, IL: InterVarsity Press.

Worthington, Jr., E. L. (2009). *A Just Forgiveness: Responsible Healing without Excusing Injustice*. Downers Grove, IL: InterVarsity Press.

CHAPTER 11

Redemption in Christian Mental Health

A Theoretical and Empirical Exploration

Introduction

As we saw in the previous chapter, redemption is the restoration of communion with God, based on Christ's perfect life, which alludes to a transition in one's story from a state of bondage to sin and alienation into a new life of grace and freedom. According to Christianity, Christ is the savior or redeemer of the world (1 John 4:14) because he provided a way of reconciliation to God and made possible a new life of greater human flourishing. Christ is "the end of the old world and the beginning of the new world of God" (Bonhoeffer, 1966, p. 67).

So, as we might expect, Christ will be at the center of a Christian psychotherapy model, for it will be based, ultimately, on Christ and his story—his life on earth, yes, as well as the other remarkable events at the end of his life: his crucifixion, resurrection, and ascension—because Christians have been united to Christ and that story. Christian psychotherapy promotes the transformation of Christian clients, in part, by helping them to appropriate, internalize, and participate in the blessings of redemption by the Holy Spirit and faith, so that they recapitulate the story of Christ in their lives, develop a new self-understanding, and reflect more and more the beauty of the Lord (Johnson, 2017). As a result, Christianity is said to be exocentric (Pannenberg, 1985), since it is fundamentally focused outside the self, on to Another; this is, of course, a remarkable distinction of Christian psychotherapy, in comparison with all other forms of psychotherapy.

This is not to say, though, that the self is unimportant in Christianity. On the contrary, Christ laid down his life for his friends (John 15:13), and believers are being drawn into the communion of the Trinity (1 John 1:4), so our wellbeing is important to God; this realization forms part of the redemption of the Christian's self-understanding. However, according to Christianity, the self is situated within a larger context that has an order for which human creatures are rightly fitted. God is the infinitely majestic center of reality, so that human flourishing is characterized, first, by loving God supremely and subordinating everything else to him, including ourselves. Consequently, a key aspect of Christian psychotherapy is helping Christian clients reorganize and recalibrate their values, so that God is supreme and everything else is interpreted in relation to him and his purposes. This God-centeredness would be likely to undermine narcissism and perfectionism (an expectation at least indirectly confirmed; see Watson, Jones, & Morris, 2004; Watson, Morris, & Hood, 1994), since Another, a perfect Other, is the believer's ultimate focus. Such a transfer of perspective, away from ourselves and on to God, can help move Christians towards an objectivity necessary to every kind of effective therapy.

The Therapeutic Value of Experiential Detachment

Over the past couple of decades, many secular models have been converging on a major task of therapy: training clients how to "objectify" their subjective world, without dissociation, so that they are no longer embedded in their disordered subjectivity, and can work through it and, ultimately, reorganize it in more adaptive ways. Cognitive-behavioral therapy (CBT) fosters greater cognitive awareness and regulation (sometimes called meta-cognition), which involve reflecting on and, therefore, objectifying one's internal-relational world. CBT also uses exposure therapy to help people learn how to tolerate subjective and relational distress that they have been avoiding (Abramowitz, Deacon, & Whiteside, 2012; Chawla & Ostafin, 2007). Systematic desensitization is a common kind of exposure therapy. This technique encourages the activation of distress (e.g., fear or anxiety) in a safe setting, where the person is coached in down-regulating the distress through various techniques (e.g., body relaxation, diaphragmatic breathing), often working through a graded hierarchy, in which the distress-inducing focus is first talked about, then brought up in the imagination, then addressed using pictures/role-playing, and, finally, *in vivo* exposure in the real world. Systematic desensitization allows maladaptive emotions to be safely experienced, while engaging in proprioceptive and cognitive activities that help to create some psychological distance from the emotional experience.

Mindfulness models offer another therapeutic pathway that leads to similar psychological outcomes (Brown, Ryan, & Creswell, 2007; Segal, Williams, & Teasdale, 2012). An important technique of mindfulness therapies is training clients to allow themselves to experience distressing emotions while maintaining a non-judgmental, observational stance towards their internal-relational world, allowing negative emotions to come and go without resistance. As a result, the power of difficult, unwanted thoughts and emotions is lessened. Another mindfulness goal is non-attachment, which involves releasing one's desires for objects, people, or the future and maintaining a stance of disinterestedness towards the inner world (Lamis & Dvorak, 2014).

Acceptance and commitment therapy (ACT) encourages clients to become aware of their internal-relational world and develop acceptance towards themselves and their experiences, whether positive or negative, adapting their psychological resources to flexibly address inner distress (Hayes, Strosahl, & Wilson, 2012). Compassion-focused therapy (CFT) similarly encourages the development of a caring, compassionate stance towards oneself and one's internal-relational world (Gilbert, 2010). With slightly different emphases, but similar goals and techniques, these third-wave models of cognitive therapy foster clients' abilities to break free of the hold that negative thoughts and emotions have and develop greater objectivity towards them, as well as themselves.

Psychodynamic therapy has been moving in similar directions over the decades since Freud. Alexander and French (1946) wrote that clients need to "re-experience their story, but with a new ending" (p. 338). Just telling one's story can enable one to gain greater objectivity regarding it, particularly as the narrative continues to unfold, even enlisting the therapy process itself into a story of recovery and growth.

More recently, psychodynamic theorists have identified mentalization as the capacity of being aware of the subjective states and mental processes of ourselves and others (Bateman & Fonagy, 2011; Ekeblad, Falkenstrom, & Hlmqvist, 2016; Fischer-Kern et al., 2008). Mentalization-based therapy encourages clients to reflect on and process their current emotion experiences in the context of strong relational support, while developing greater understanding of the perspective of healthy others towards oneself.

McCullough et al. (2003) combine psychodynamic and cognitive-behavioral approaches to treat "affect phobia" (fear of one's emotion) by helping clients to recognize when inhibiting emotions might be prompting the activation of a defense that enables them to avoid the feared affect, prevent the automatic response, and, instead, pursue healthy emotional experience and expression. By freeing clients from repetitive patterns of emotion avoidance, psychodynamic therapy enables affect to play a constructive role in organizing experience and cultivating an authentic life (Stolorow et al., 1995; Krystal, 1988).

Understanding that maladaptive emotional responses developed in poor relational contexts, relational and attachment therapists concentrate on providing a safe, secure relational context that allows clients to explore their stories and negative emotional experiences (past and present) in the presence of an empathic caregiver with whom clients collaborate to form mutual, healthier relational experiences (DeYoung, 2015; Wallin, 2015).

Emotion-focused and experiential therapy models (Greenberg & Paivio, 1997; Pascual-Leone, 2018) produce analogous results by promoting the activation of negative emotion schemes in session and helping clients explore and process their meaning while they move towards self-understanding and acceptance, enabling more adaptive emotion responses to original or current situations (including one's emotions).

Whether referring to exposure, distress tolerance, objectivity, mindfulness, acceptance, compassion, mentalization, emotion processing, or disidentification, many therapy models aim at cultivating the capacities of clients to relate differently to a disordered psychic element (a belief, emotion scheme, relational perception, defense, or part) by experiencing it, while maintaining it in their consciousness, and then "distancing" themselves from it, regardless of whether or not it is actually modified in and of itself. Over the centuries, Christianity has developed a number of distinctive, theocentric ways that promote these same capacities and processes with Christians by enabling them to disidentify with, or detach from, disordered psychological elements by distinctively Christian means provided by God through Christ and his story.

Christian Teachings that Promote Detachment

One of Jesus Christ's most striking statements points towards a detachment agenda. "Anyone who loves their life will lose it, while anyone who hates their life in this world will keep it for eternal life" (John 12:25). Such drastic-sounding language is intended to promote a radical, gestalt-like reorientation that involves "hating" (that is, reassessing and turning from) our (old) life of autonomy from God, in order to discover a new way of life in communion with God. Recall from the previous chapter that the Apostle Paul adapted this radical orientation in his understanding of the Christian life, tying it to a believer's union with Christ's death: "I have been crucified with Christ and I no longer live, but Christ lives in me" (Galatians 2:20). This suggests that Christians are to develop a new self-understanding that grounds their identity in Christ's presence, love, and activity on their behalf and now within, mysteriously made possible through their being joined by God to Christ's crucifixion.

After teaching about the believer's union with Christ's death and resurrection in Romans 6:1–5, Paul said to Christians in Rome,

> count yourselves dead to sin but alive to God in Christ Jesus… offer yourselves to God as those who have been brought from death to life; and offer every part of yourself to him as an instrument of righteousness. For… you are… under grace… offer yourselves as slaves to righteousness leading to holiness.
>
> (6:11, 13, 14, 19)

In this passage, Paul is encouraging Christ's disciples to reconstruct their self-understanding in relation to Christ and surrender themselves to God, as part of a process of breaking out of their former patterns of thinking, feeling, and living. This suggests that a part of a Christian therapy model involves disidentifying with aspects of one's alienated self ("count yourselves dead to sin") and "offering" oneself, including one's body, by viewing oneself as now "alive" in light of God's righteousness in Christ.

There are many other terms and phrases in the Bible that would seem to imply a kind of detachment: confession (Psalm 32:5; James 5:16; 1 John

1:9), repentance (Job 42:6; Psalm 7:12; Matthew 3:2; Acts 2:38; Romans 2:4; Revelation 2:5), "denying oneself" (Matthew 16:24; Luke 14:23), "taking up one's cross" (Matthew 10:38; Luke 14:23), mortification (Colossians 3:5, 10; Romans 8:13), lament (see Job; Psalm 13; 22; 88; Lamentations), new creation (2 Corinthians 5:17), co-crucifixion and co-resurrection with Christ (Romans 6:1–6; Galatians 2:20, 6:14), and "putting off the old self" and "putting on the new self" (Ephesians 4:22–24). Paul also seemed to exemplify a detachment agenda when he referred to "the flesh" (rather than himself) that fights against the Spirit (Galatians 5:17); and, perhaps most surprisingly, his statement that *he* no longer did the evil he did, but "sin living in me" (Romans 7:17, 20).

Additional practices developed in the coming centuries of Christian soulcare that are also suggestive of detachment include discrimination, dispassion (Evagrios, 1979a), and watchfulness (Evagrios, 1979b); contemplation and renunciation (Merton, 1961); purgation and resignation (John of the Cross, 1935); transparency (Kierkegaard, 1849); recollection (von Hildebrand, 1948); and surrender (De Caussade, 1861).[1]

What especially distinguishes Christian psychotherapy regarding psychological detachment is the believer's union with Christ. Because God the Father has united believers by the Spirit with his Son, our entire existence—our story, body, soul, vocation, and relationships—is to be consistently revisioned and reinterpreted accordingly. All our sinful and disordered desires, emotions, thoughts, and actions have been washed of shame and guilt through union with Christ's death, and all our good, as well as the healing of our alienation and disorderedness, is due to our having been joined to Christ's resurrection and identified with the redemptive purposes of God. Through our union with Christ, believers have received a transcendent transfer, enabling us to pass from the death of our old ways via a mystical resurrection with Christ into a new life, permitting us to enjoy the divine life of communion with God. All that Christ has accomplished in his life, death, resurrection, and ascension to heaven can, thus, be appropriated by "faith" and utilized for therapeutic purposes, on the basis of an authoritative ratification by God—and there is no higher authority, including *oneself* (1 John 3:20). Though "faith" and "believing" are usually rightly understood as directed towards God and eternal realities (John 14:1; Hebrews 11:1), they can also apply to seeing oneself in a new way, that is, according to *Christ* (Romans 6:13; Galatians 2:20; Ephesians 1:3–11; Colossians 3:1–4).

Some Psychotherapeutic Assets of Christian Redemption

Extrapolating from the above Christian teachings, the following are ways in which Christian psychotherapy can promote a unique Christian kind of experiential detachment. To begin with, God's viewpoint of the Christian self is considered transcendent, absolute, and benevolent. The Bible teaches Christians that God loves us and desires our good (Romans 8:31–38). So,

Christian clients are invited to learn to view themselves from the stand-point of the mind of an infinitely loving Caregiver who has always been intimately involved with their story and situation, both providentially and compassionately. Such an orientation adds a theistic dimension to the development of mentalization.

Second, union with Christ is a state in which one is *spiritually* disidentified by God from the rest of reality. The Apostle Paul said, "the world has been crucified to me, and I to the world" (Galatians 6:14); so, one's relationship with one's former idols, faulty attachments, and false self has been severed. "Therefore, if anyone is in Christ, the new creation has come: The old has gone, the new is here!" (2 Corinthians 5:17). Everything in one's life is differ-ent. So, not only is Christ a mediator between us and God, bringing us all together into his communion, but he also is a mediator between each of us and other people, other things, and even from oneself. As Bonhoeffer (1966) put it, a

> boundary lies between me and myself, between the old 'I' and the new 'I.' … At this place I cannot stand alone. Here Christ stands, in the centre, between me and myself, between the old existence and the new.
>
> (p. 61)

Third, believers continue to deal with negative, self-conscious emotions like shame and guilt, and an inner critic that highlights their faults, espe-cially those who were exposed to unhealthy parenting when children. Union with Christ absolves and cleanses believers of their shame and guilt, once and for all, on account of Christ's death on the cross and God's subsequent forgiveness, giving them divine sanction to relinquish their shame and guilt to God and receive the gift of God's perfect righteousness. This gift is not dependent on anything we do, because it is entirely dependent on what God in Christ has done on our behalf (Romans 3:21–26; Ephesians 2:6–10).

Next, Christianity teaches that believers possess two selves, an old self and a new self (Romans 6:6; Ephesians 4:22–24; Colossians 3:9–10), a dis-tinction established by Christ's death and resurrection. The Christian is a new creation (2 Corinthians 5:17), and this divinely established fact allows believers to regard all that is alienated from God and pathological in our current actions and subjectivity as "old," as belonging to our *former* manner of life; so that our psychopathology (our sins and biopsychosocial damage) no longer fully define us (Romans 6:6; Ephesians 4:22; Colossians 3:9). Even more importantly, this divine alteration of our self allows us to identify ourselves with all the fullness and flourishing of Christ, to feel that one is part of the new creation, and to envision or imagine ourselves now as new persons—and established so by God (2 Corinthians 5:17; Galatians 6:15; Ephesians 4:24; Colossians 3:10). We are participants in a new, super-natural order of being and enabled to live a different life that no longer simply repeats the past, but has the possibility of engaging in novel actions that more resemble our exemplar, Christ.

Fifth, union with Christ also allows a personal identification with his story of living perfectly obediently to his Father; suffering unjustly; having one's sin, shame, and guilt removed by God; and being raised from the dead of one's psychopathology and resurrected into the gifted state of perfect acceptance and belovedness, untainted by one's ethical and spiritual limitations. Christ's story provides another's narrative within which one can reconceive one's own narrative: resting in the grace of Christ's goodness, so that the inner demand for perfection and its inevitable shame is resolved; receiving the Gethsemane experience as normative; recognizing that one is not alone in one's unjust suffering—he, too, was forsaken (Matthew 27:46); seeing oneself as just as holy, acceptable, and beloved as Christ; and receiving the Spirit's indwelling presence as a power that makes possible new actions and, therefore, gives a transcendent hope. As a result, Christ's story is being woven into the believer's story, and vice versa.

Sixth, through communion with God in prayer and meditation, believers can learn how to experience, albeit imperfectly, absolute acceptance and love through Christ. As we share our burdens, shame, and frustrations with him, and "hear" him, by faith, respond in kindness and compassion, our sense of shame can be ameliorated, our loneliness can be replaced with his everywhere presence, our traumatic memories can be modified by feeling his grief, and our disabilities can be turned into unique sites of glory.

Finally, knowing that our final state in heaven will be without sin and sorrow—we will be granted the fulfillment of our best desires, when we experience the communion of the triune God in its everlasting fullness—enables us to view our life now through a different lens, permitting greater endurance, tolerance of injustice, forgiveness of others, compassion towards the deficiencies of oneself and others, and hope in this life, bolstered by faith in the life to come.

These therapeutic assets enable Christian clients to disidentify with the challenges of their stories and current troubles, negative emotions, and personal liabilities without denial and dissociation, in order to become increasingly honest with themselves, relinquish shame and defensiveness, challenge the repetition, and imagine and practice new ways of living that are made possible by a holy, loving God. All this occurs in addition to the "common grace" benefits that all human psychotherapies offer their recipients.

So, in addition to the "common factors" that join together all effective psychotherapies, Christian psychotherapy promotes an additional feature common to many contemporary evidence-based models that we are labeling detachment (which is also involved in meta-cognition, mindfulness, acceptance, and mentalization, with subtle variations), but within a unique Christian context and justification: union with Christ and communion with God and others, by faith and the Holy Spirit, to help Christian clients work with their subjectivity and shift from old patterns, chronically reactivated, to new practices, imaginatively realized.

Redemptive Differentiation and Integration

Christians experience an inner conflict between tendencies and desires towards the Good (God, maturation, flourishing, communion, and virtue) and tendencies and desires towards alienation and destruction (unbelief, selfishness, narcissism, aggression, punishment, and evil). As already touched on, the New Testament labels this internal contrast in a few different ways: the law of indwelling sin and the law of the mind (Romans 7:20–23); the flesh and the Spirit (Galatians 5:17–23); and the old self and new self (Ephesians 4:22–24; Colossians 3:9–10). Therefore, we can say that, from its founding, Christianity has promoted a conflict personality theory (Maddi, 1996). An important part of a distinctly Christian psychotherapy agenda, then, is to help Christian clients be able to recognize and differentiate these two aspects. Complicating our ability to discern this fundamental distinction is the created goodness that undergirds all human life, that is, the good dynamic structures that provide the infrastructure of our personal and relational existence and make us unique individuals: our nervous system, cognitive system, emotion/experiential system, overall personality, and so on, each person uniquely fashioned with God's general design plan, including a template for optimal wellbeing. When clients first come in to psychotherapy, they usually present as confused about their internal world and have trouble distinguishing what is valid and healthy from what is destructive and pathological. As a result, part of a distinctly Christian psychotherapy involves helping them gain clarity about what is going on within them in the context of the Christian faith. Figure 11.1 represents the internal conflict that Christians experience in light of redemption (adapted from Johnson, 2017).

Redemptive Differentiation

One way to better understand the unique mechanism of change in a distinctly Christian psychotherapy involves more closely examining the concept of *redemptive differentiation*, or differentiating one's old self (all that pertains to one's sin and disordered goodness) from one's new self (all that pertains to one's created and redeemed goodness) (Johnson, 2017). This process involves a special kind of cognitive restructuring and reorganizing, in addition to significant emotion processing. First, redemptive differentiation requires acknowledging all that pertains to one's subjectivity and assessing whether it is healthy and leads to life or is unhealthy and contributes to one's psychopathology. Because, for Christians, everything that pertains to oneself is united to Christ, the basis of shame and anxiety about one's psychopathology has been addressed and transcendently resolved. However,

	Internal Conflict	
	New Self	Old Self
Structural Features	Created Goodness	Disordered Goodness
Dynamic Features	Redemptive Goodness	Sinfulness

Figure 11.1 Internal conflict and redemption

because Christian clients may present with unresolved shame and anxiety from their past that gets reactivated in the present, an important part of therapy involves talking through aspects of one's story and oneself, of which one is ashamed and about which one worries. Consequently, the therapist has a pivotal role to play by concretely exemplifying God's ultimate reconciliation and acceptance of his children, demonstrating it face to face in session by responding, for example, with empathy, rather than criticism.

On the one hand, redemptive differentiation can be promoted by the recognition of the God-given goodness of one's self: one's unique, created goodness (individual gifts, strengths, and competences common to all kinds of people) and one's redemptive goodness (the blessings all Christians enjoy through union with Christ: being considered by God holy, righteous, reconciled to God, a child of God, and so on). On the other hand, recognizing the Christian's sinfulness (a core tenet within orthodox Christianity) involves identifying personal sins and hostility to God, the self, and others, through confession and repentance. Confession is the verbal acknowledgment to God and oneself (and possibly others) of one's personal sins and sinfulness and taking personal responsibility for them, without minimizing them or blaming others (Job 42:6; Luke 5:8). Repentance is the "turning away" (the New Testament Greek word is *metanoia*, which means "change of mind") from one's previous course of action, a break or disavowal of what one has acknowledged one did. These are two basic *Christian* therapeutic activities of detachment.

The pathology of one's disordered goodness, by contrast, is acknowledged, then reorganized through processes like tolerating the distress of one's traumatic memories and negative emotion schemes and allowing one's defenses and false self to be slowly undermined and relinquished, as they are surrendered to God (Cole & Pargament, 1999; de Caussade, 1861).

Redemptive differentiation can also make use of many standard therapeutic techniques, for example, identifying and challenging maladaptive core beliefs (Beck, 2011), repetitive negative thinking (Ehring & Watkins, 2008), negative meta-cognitive beliefs (Barahmand, Abolghasemi, & Jahanmohammadi, 2008), and intolerance of uncertainty (Mahoney & McEvoy, 2012), all of which contribute to anxiety and depression.

Redemptive Integration

On the road to change, increasingly coming to accept one's entire self and story in Christ involves a corollary process to redemptive differentiation called *redemptive integration*. When paired with differentiation, this subsequent step can help to better understand the change process in a distinctly Christian form of psychotherapy. On the basis of union with Christ's resurrection, the remnants of one's old self, and the internalized record of one's exposure to fallenness (one's negative emotions schemes, difficult memories, faulty thinking, and other biopsychosocial disorder)— one's psychological "weaknesses" (2 Corinthians 12:9–10)—are gradually becoming assimilated into the redeemed foundation of one's created and redeemed goodness, resulting in a more unified and cohesive "new-self" system and narrative (see Johnson, 2017, for a more detailed discussion of this process). Such integration assumes sufficient prior development of the new self to be able to anchor the integrative process. But, as with everything else in our temporal human life, the new self is forming itself while being formed; or, to use a well-worn therapeutic metaphor, we are riding the bicycle while we are building it. Redemptive integration is facilitated by some of the same processes as redemptive differentiation: prayer, meditation, guided imagery, journaling, and working with a therapist, but it is especially consolidated by living out one's faith, that is, practicing increasingly virtuous, embodied ways of thinking, feeling, and living in relation to others, including doing so within the divine laboratory of one's local church (Ephesians 1:11–16).

The integration of one's narrative is an especially important part of biopsychosocial healing (Segal, 2012), and religious conversion has long been recognized as a valuable source of narrative potential, as recorded in the famous hymn "Amazing Grace:" "I once was lost, but now am found; was blind, but now I see." This may be especially apt for those who once lived a dissolute life and have experienced a marked change due to their new relationship with Christ. To promote redemptive integration, as a part of their treatment journey, Christian clients can be encouraged to write out their story in light of God's higher purposes, much like Augustine did in his famous work *Confessions*. As we noted in Chapter 8, McAdams (2006) labeled the story of overcoming obstacles and arriving at a better place as "the redemptive self," which Christians are happy to acknowledge was borrowed from the Christian tradition.

Recollection is a Catholic spiritual discipline especially suited to promote redemptive integration. Von Hildebrand (1948) called it "integration in depth" (p. 137), for it entails getting into a meditative state of mind, letting the secondary "distractions" of life fade away from one's attention, and "gathering together the fragments of one's soul," in order to focus exclusively on God and his ways.

> This concentration of one's attention promotes subjective peace and enables believers to see reality more accurately, including what occurs within, by subordinating all of our other activities to this supreme aim, making it easier to distinguish the superficial from the real and the false from the true, and fostering surrender and release of all the particulars of one's life into God's hands.
>
> (Johnson, 2017, p. 527)

The significance of Christians being in union with Christ for integration can be summarized as, "everything about a Christian now is related to Christ and his redemption by God." As a result, Christian psychotherapy provides a remarkable framework for revisioning everything about oneself in relation to Christ, since our relationship with Christ serves as a transcendent ground by which one can integrate all of one's self and story. The love and favor that one has with God because of Christ's redemption provides a continual, positive basis for the healing and reclamation of one's story, the productive processing of one's negative emotions, and a greater authenticity and openness to the future, enabling the capacity to see reality in light of the new creation.

To conclude the chapter, consistent with Frank and Frank (1993), we have seen that a model of distinctly Christian psychotherapy is able to utilize "common factors" of therapy while incorporating its own "specific ingredients," although by no means operationalized in the same way as mainstream psychotherapy does. While using many of the "building blocks" necessary for all good therapy, when working with Christian clients, a Christian "blueprint" is needed. Redemption is a key feature of the transformative framework that has characterized the Christian tradition and led to its spread over the centuries. In the 21st century, we are better able to understand why Christianity has been such a powerful force for psychological change and refine its therapeutic potential through the application of all the tools now available, but basing them on Christ's redemption and the Christian's union with him.

Note

1 There is obvious similarity with these concepts (which we are calling "detachment") and similar concepts in mindfulness models (which are often labeled "non-attachment"). The two main differences, though, between their approaches to the mental activity of disidentifying with aspects of one's inner reality are that Christian therapy is (a) fundamentally relational (done with God), whereas mindfulness (influenced by Buddhism) is comparatively individualistic; and (b) intrinsically evaluative, reflecting God's assessment, based in the grace of God in Christ, whereas mindfulness explicitly advocates a lack of judgment, since they offer no transcendent basis for resolving it.

References

Abramowitz, J. S., Deacon, B. J., & Whiteside, S. P. H. (2012). *Exposure Therapy for Anxiety: Principles and Practice*. New York: Guilford.

Alexander, F., & French, T. (1946). *Psychoanalytic Therapy: Principles and Application*. New York: Ronald Press.

Barahmand, U., Abolghasemi, A., & Jahanmohammadi, S. (2008). Using metacognitions to identify emotionally vulnerable college students. *American Journal of Health Behavior, 32*, 604–613.

Bateman, A. W., & Fonagy, P. (Eds.) (2011). *Handbook of Mentalizing in Mental Health Practice*. New York: American Psychiatric Publishing.

Beck, J. (2011). *Cognitive Behavior Therapy: Basics and Beyond* (2nd ed.). New York: The Guildford Press.

Bonhoeffer, D. (1966). *Christ the Center*. New York: Harper & Row.

Brown, K., Ryan, R., & Creswell, D. (2007). Mindfulness: Theoretical foundations and evidence for its salutary effects. *Psychological Inquiry, 18*, 211–237.

Chawla, N., & Ostafin, B. (2007). Experiential avoidance as a functional dimensional approach to psychopathology: An empirical review. *Journal of Clinical Psychology, 63*, 871–890.

Cole, B. S., & Pargament, K. I. (1999). Spiritual surrender: A paradoxical path to control. In W. R. Miller (Ed.), *Integrating Spirituality into Treatment: Resources for Practitioners* (pp. 179–198). Washington, DC: American Psychological Association.

de Caussade, J. P. (1986). *The Joy of Full Surrender*. Brewster, MA: Paraclete (original work published 1861).

DeYoung, P. A. (2015). *Relational Psychotherapy: A Primer*. New York: Routledge.

Ekeblad, A., Falkenstrom, F., & Hlmqvist, R. (2016). Reflective functioning as predictor of working alliance and outcome in the treatment of depression. *Journal of Consulting and Clinical Psychology, 84*, 67–78.

Ehring, T., & Watkins, E. (2008). Repetitive negative thinking as a trans-diagnostic process. *International Journal of Cognitive Therapy, 1*, 192–205.

Evagrios (1979a). On discrimination. In *The Philokalia* (Vol. 1, pp. 38–52). Boston: Faber & Faber.

Evagrios. (1979b). Texts on watchfulness. In *The Philokalia* (Vol. 1, pp. 53–54). Boston: Faber & Faber.

Fischer-Kern, M., Tmej, A., Kapusta, N., Naderer, A., Leithner-Dziubas, K., Loffler-Stastka, H., & Springer-Kremser, M. (2008). The capacity for mentalization in depressive patients: A pilot study. *Zeitschrift fur Psychosomatische Medizin und Psychotherapie, 54*, 368–380.

Frank, J., & Frank, J. (1993). *Persuasion and Healing: A Comparative Study of Psychotherapy*. Baltimore, MD: Johns Hopkins University Press.

Gilbert, P. (2010). *Compassion-Focused Therapy: Distinctive Features*. New York: Routledge.

Greenberg, L. S., & Paivio, S. C. (1997). *Working with Emotions in Psychotherapy*. New York: Guilford.

Hayes, S., Strosahl, K., & Wilson, K. (2012). *Acceptance and Commitment Therapy: The Process and Practice of Mindful Change* (2nd ed.). New York: The Guilford Press.

John of the Cross (1935). *The Complete Works of Saint John of the Cross* (E. A. Peers, Trans. and Ed.). Westminster, MD: The Newman Press.

Johnson, E. L. (2007). *Foundations for Soul Care*. Downers Grove, IL: InterVarsity Press.

Johnson, E. L. (2017). *God and Soul Care: The Therapeutic Resources of the Christian Faith*. Downers Grove, IL: InterVarsity Press.

Kierkegaard, S. (1980). *The Sickness unto Death* (H. V. Hong, Trans.). Princeton, NJ: Princeton University Press (original work published 1849).

Knabb, J., Frederick, T., & Cumming, G. (2017). Surrendering to God's providence: A three-part study on providence-focused therapy for recurrent worry (PFT-RW). *Psychology of Religion and Spirituality, 9*, 180–196.

Krystal, H. (1988). *Integration and Self-Healing: Affect, Trauma, Alexithymia*. New York: Routledge.

Lamis, D., & Dvorak, R. (2014). Mindfulness, non-attachment, and suicide rumination in college students: The mediating role of depressive symptoms. *Mindfulness, 5*, 487–496.

Leahy, R. (2017). *Cognitive Therapy Techniques: A Practitioner's Guide* (2nd ed.). New York: The Guilford Press.

Maddi, S. R. (1996). *Personality Theories: A Comparative Analysis* (6th ed.). Pacific Grove, CA: Brooks/Cole.

Mahoney, A., & McEvoy, P. (2012). A transdiagnostic examination of intolerance of uncertainty across anxiety and depressive disorders. *Cognitive Behaviour Therapy, 41*, 212–222.

McCullough, L., Kuhn, N., Andrews, S., Kaplan, A., Wolf, J., & Hurley, C. L. (2003). *Treating Affect Phobia: A Manual for Short-Term Dynamic Psychotherapy*. New York: Guilford.

Merton, T. (1961). *New Seeds of Contemplation*. New York: New Directions.

Metcalf, L. (2017). *Solution-Focused Narrative Therapy*. New York: Springer.

Pannenberg, W. (1985). *Anthropology in Theological Perspective* (M. J. O'Connell, Trans.). Philadelphia: Westminster.

Pascual-Leone, A. (2018). How clients "change emotion with emotion": A programme of research on emotional processing. *Psychotherapy Research, 28*(2), 165–182.

Segal, Z., Williams, M., & Teasdale, J. (2012). *Mindfulness-Based Cognitive Therapy for Depression* (2nd ed.). New York: Guilford.

Stolorow, R., Brandchaft, B., & Atwood, G. (1995). *Psychoanalytic Treatment: An Intersubjective Approach*. New York: Routledge.

von Hildebrand, D. (2001). *Transformation in Christ: On the Christian Attitude*. San Francisco: Ignatius (original work published 1948).

Wallin, D. (2015). *Attachment in Psychotherapy*. New York: Guilford.

Watson, P. J., Morris, R. J., & Hood, R. W. (1994). Religion and rationality: 1. Rational-emotive and religious understandings of perfectionism and other irrationalities. *Journal of Psychology and Christianity, 13*(4),356–372.

Watson, P. J., Jones, N. D., & Morris, R. J. (2004). Religious orientation and attitudes toward money: Relationships with narcissism and the influence of gender. *Mental Health, Religion & Culture, 7*(4), 277–288.

CHAPTER 12

Redemption in Christian Psychotherapy

Introduction

In this final chapter of the book, we present a distinctly Christian psychotherapy within the "redemption" pillar, exploring the ways in which therapists can effectively address reconciliation with God when working with Christian clients. Specifically, we offer a central theme in working with Christian clients with emotional disorders, along with goals for treatment and interventions from a distinctly Christian worldview. Like the third, sixth, and ninth chapters, we turn to a plethora of Christian resources, building on a theological and empirical understanding of emotional disorders from the previous two chapters in the "redemption" section. In concluding the book, our aim is to offer a variety of remaining Christian-sensitive interventions for Christians with depressive and anxiety disorders, strengthening a Christian approach with the "common factors" literature (Lambert, 2013) and other relevant theory and research.

Central Theme

Building on the first two chapters in this section, Christian redemption involves reconciliation with God, leading to the reordering of human loves. From our perspective, it is not the pain of emotional disorders *per se*, but transcendent aloneness in the pain that is the greatest evil in human suffering. Put differently, and as Christians have taught through the centuries, suffering is bad, but sin is worse than suffering. Thus, a restored relationship with our Creator God is an essential step on the way to healing, and growing in this relationship is an intrinsic part of Christian psychotherapy. In this process of redemption, God is now Christians' secure base. As Christian clients venture out into the world to explore, they can call to God when in need of his protection and soothing comfort, confidently reaching for him as a safe haven during instances of uncertainty and distress; this "circle of attachment" (Clinton & Straub, 2010; Knabb & Emerson, 2014) is now in place because of the redemptive work of Christ. Communion with God is the ultimate kind of secure attachment, rooted in Christians' union with Christ, based on Jesus' life, death, and resurrection (Johnson, 2017).

A reordering of loves involves Christian detachment, that is, "correcting one's own anxious grasping in order to free oneself for committed relationship with God" (Miles, 1983, p. 111), and detachment from old patterns of thinking, feeling, and acting, which means Christians can now relate to the self, others, and the world in a healthier manner, deepening an awareness of a self-in-Christ dynamic through divine communion. Rather than being isolated and alone, living out of the false self and unilaterally attempting to somehow "fix" the symptoms that emanate from emotional disorders, Christians can "walk with God through pain and suffering," learning how to "suffer well" (Keller, 2015). Christian virtues are part of this redemptive process, with Christians becoming more like Christ, who modeled humility, kindness, and other Christian virtues for daily living, and who now, through the Spirit, enables believers to participate in his virtue.

As Christian clients experience communion with the triune God, they can relate differently to their inner world, recognizing and distancing themselves from their psychopathology (sin and biopsychosocial damage), which, in turn, allows them to accept themselves more comprehensively in Christ. We believe that a redemptive relationship with Christ can help to cultivate Christian mental health, taking into consideration a wide variety of transdiagnostic conceptualizations of both emotional disorders and healing. Prayer is one of the most important vehicles to help facilitate an awareness of Jesus' already-accomplished redemptive work on the cross and through the resurrection. As we have repeatedly emphasized, *kataphatic* (words and images) and *apophatic* (wordless and imageless) forms of prayer can allow Christians to cultivate a deeper awareness of God's redemptive plan, focusing on sharing in the Trinitarian communion in the process. As a result of a prayerful life, we believe Christians can address several transdiagnostic vulnerabilities to emotional disorders, such as repetitive negative thinking, affect phobia, experiential avoidance, intolerance of uncertainty, meta-cognitive vulnerabilities, reliance on the false self, and struggles with mentalization, mindlessness, and clinging.

Christian clients can use *kataphatic* meditation to reflect upon and internalize the biblical truth of who they are now because of their union with Christ and consider their status with God as justified, holy, and already perfected in Christ. For example, clients can be given a list of biblical verses that highlight various aspects of their union with Christ and be invited to meditate on one of them in their daily prayer and meditation time, throughout the week. This can encourage them to release their guilt, shame, and desire for perfection in this life.

While in a state of prayerful meditation, Christian clients can also process their negative emotions through lament, in which they express their feelings of anxiety, shame, guilt, anger, or sorrow to God in the spirit of Psalms, captured in Lamentations 2:19: "Pour out your heart like water in the presence of the Lord." When Christian clients are struggling with some past or present difficulty, they can spend some time deeply exploring the related negative feelings, then verbalize their experience in words to their heavenly Father; in turn, after a few minutes of such emotional experience and expression, they can surrender the entire situation to God. This offers an additional way for Christian clients to productively experience and express their emotions (McCullough et al., 2003), in contrast to turning to denial or rumination, and further mentalize their negative emotion experiences (Bateman & Fonagy, 2016) and surrender them to God, so that the emotions are resolved by being experientially linked to their union with Christ's death and resurrection (Johnson, 2017). The key is that they experience an emotion shift, so that there is subjective "movement" from the negative emotion state, which is accepted and released, to a positive emotion state, which is a result of calmly receiving God's transcendent resolution of the situation.

In addition, Christian clients can use their imagination in *kataphatic* meditation for the purpose of picturing spiritual metaphors: "The Lord is my shepherd… He makes me lie down in green pastures, he leads me beside quiet waters, he refreshes my soul. He guides me along the right paths for his name's sake" (Psalm 23:1–3), placing themselves in an episode in Scripture (e.g., Jesus washing their feet), or imagining Jesus in the present holding them like a little child and speaking to them words of encouragement and comfort.

As another example, Christian clients can relate differently to repetitive negative thinking (Ehring & Watkins, 2008), including rumination and worry, through *apophatic* meditation, which helps them to rest in God in a wordless, imageless state. In doing so, Christians are learning to relate to the inner world "dispossessively," meaning repeated attempts to pivot from ingrained thinking patterns to God helps Christians relate to their inner world with more flexibility. In the process, Christian clients are developing experiential acceptance (Hayes et al., 2012), which allows them to have more compassion for their depressive and anxiety-related symptoms, rather than trying to avoid them (which leaves them stuck in their ability to follow Jesus).

Apophatic meditation can also help Christian clients to accept uncertainty (Dugas & Robichaud, 2007), given they are cultivating a state of inner surrender, which involves trusting in God's actions, even in the midst of the symptoms of emotional disorders. This reframe is important for healing, in that Christians worship a "suffering servant" (Isaiah 53), who faced the inevitable pain of daily living. As an additional example, metacognitive awareness can be developed (Wells, 2000), which involves being able to notice thinking patterns with a sense of distance and flexibility, rather than getting stuck in deeply embedded thinking patterns.

Finally, Christian mental health involves something analogous to mindfulness and non-attachment, but, instead, is profoundly relational, because it entails communion with God in *kataphatic* and *apophatic* meditation and simultaneous detachment from the created order. With mindfulness, individuals have the ability to observe inner experiences, describe them, relate to them with non-judgmental compassion, and act with non-reactivity and awareness (Baer, Smith, Hopkins, Krietemeyer, & Toney, 2006). By contrast, *kataphatic* and *apophatic* meditation can likewise help Christian clients to observe their inner world, describing inner events with the grace of God in Christ and full acceptance (since *God* is the ultimate judge, and, thus, they are not to lean on their *own* understanding; Proverbs 3:5), an awareness of God's viewpoint, and increasing non-reactivity because God is with them, ministering to them and working within their innermost being. A Christian alternative to non-attachment—*detachment*—is possible because Christian clients know everything about them is united to Christ's life, death, and resurrection, so they are learning to surrender their inner world to God, rather than attempting to hold on to or push away inner experiences. If God is sovereign over Christians' thoughts and feelings, Christians can find rest in him by letting go of the tendency to unilaterally control their inner world.

Goals for Treatment

In applying the "common factors" domains of support, learning, and action (adapted from Lambert, 2013) to redemption, we offer the following over-arching goals within this pillar of treatment (see also Table 12.1):

a) *Support* involves helping Christian clients to walk with Jesus along the path of sanctification, deepening their relationship with him because of his life, death, and resurrection. At times, Christians can focus on his words and use their imagination (*kataphatic* meditation), and at other times they can sit in silence with him (*apophatic* meditation). These methods of Christian meditation are reviewed and practiced in this phase of therapy, with therapists helping Christian clients to cultivate an awareness of Jesus' active, loving presence in the midst of their pain. The ultimate aim is communion with God, made possible by Christian clients' union with Christ, turning to him for comfort and security, and trusting that he is cleansing them of their impurities as they endure the suffering of this world.

b) *Learning* involves gaining an awareness of the reality that Christian clients' sense of aloneness and unilateral efforts to rid themselves of pain may be exacerbating an already difficult psychological experience. As Christians internalize the reality of Christ's redemption, they are less likely to try to calm the storm on their own, and they learn to recognize that God is with them in the proverbial boat of life and is sovereign over the stormy seas of the inner world (Matthew 8:23–27). As Christian clients spend more time with him, they are gaining insight into the inner workings of the mind, reframing and accepting difficult thoughts and feelings because Jesus is there (exemplifying the concepts

Table 12.1 Christian-sensitive common factors in psychotherapy for the "redemption" pillar. Adapted from Lambert (2013)

Support-Related Goals	Learning-Related Goals	Action-Related Goals
Verbalize painful affect in the context of clients' attachment needs with God (i.e., the need for a deeper relationship with Christ)	Verbalize painful feelings via *kataphatic* meditation and sit in silence with God by way of *apophatic* meditation; with both forms of meditation, Christians are moving towards inner acceptance because God is active and present	Face fears because God is present, working to gain a deeper, more flexible awareness of thinking patterns via Christian meditation; in the context of emotional disorders, rumination, worry, and intolerance of uncertainty are often pervasive, overwhelming Christian clients' inner world to the point of keeping them stalled on the roads of life
Reduce isolation by helping Christians to recognize that Jesus is present, functioning as a secure base and safe haven	Through *kataphatic* meditation, Christians are noticing repetitive negative thinking, gently pivoting to God's Word as they pray to him for comfort and encouragement in the midst of pain	Master thinking patterns by recognizing the inner workings of the mind, then shifting to an awareness of Jesus' redemptive presence
Model Jesus' love, mercy, and grace, working with Christians to turn towards an awareness of him for healing	With *apophatic* meditation, Christians are getting to know the inner workings of a busy mind, recognizing their ingrained patterns of repetitive negative thinking and thoughts related to intolerance of uncertainty	Take action with a three-step meditative process on a daily basis—noticing inner experiences, shifting towards an awareness of God, and following Jesus via biblical virtues; in doing so, Christians are practicing the ability to focus on one thing at a time in the present moment with an attitude of compassion and maintaining an awareness of Jesus' redemptive work
Provide a framework for understanding health, dysfunction, and healing (i.e., the grand narrative of Scripture), utilizing *kataphatic* and *apophatic* meditation to help Christian clients deepen their communion with Christ	Help Christians to develop meta-cognitive awareness and detachment, in that they are learning to notice repetitive inner states, before shifting to a focused, sustained awareness of Jesus' redemptive presence	Practice *lectio divina* to focus on Jesus' redemptive work, reconciling Christian clients to God

of detachment, redemptive differentiation, and redemptive integration discussed in Chapter 11).

c) *Action* involves using *kataphatic* and *apophatic* forms of meditation to practice surrendering repetitive negative thinking and a preoccupation with uncertainty to God, accepting (rather than avoiding) difficult inner experiences because God is by Christian clients' side, removing their impurities in the "refiner's fire" and building up in Christians a *new self* composed of God's created and redemptive goodness in Christ. Christians are also able to gain an awareness of when they have an overactive mind, trusting in who they are in Christ, as well as God's providence, rather than clutching or pushing away their thoughts and feelings. As Christian clients adopt the mind of Christ (1 Corinthians 2:16) in meditative prayer, they are better able to see Jesus from the inside out (from the standpoint of the indwelling Holy Spirit, who is drawing them and their inner experience into the Trinitarian communion), as well as see themselves from the outside in (learning to see and feel about themselves and the world the way God does) (Bateman & Fonagy, 2016). Finally, Christians are able to cultivate a more contemplative awareness, learning how to let go of everything (including unrealistic expectations about being completely free from the symptoms of emotional disorders) that does not align with God's will. With emotional disorders, we submit that a major problem involves losing sight of God in the midst of the storm, unilaterally striving to safely swim to shore. Yet, because they are redeemed in Christ, Christian clients can find peace in the middle of sin and suffering, recognizing that he is safely in control of both the storm itself and the boat that will take them where he wants them to go (rather than where they expect to go). Ultimately, taking action involves an ever deepening communion with God, accomplished through spending time with him and made possible because of Christian clients' union with Christ.

Christian Resources

Several Christian sources are useful to develop Christian-sensitive interventions and techniques in the domain of "redemption," including the following (in no particular order):

a) Scriptural references to Jesus' redemptive work on the cross and through his resurrection, placing the client's story in his story of redemption in the context of the grand narrative of Scripture. Psychological pain (especially shame and anxiety) originated from the fall, wherein humankind was estranged from God. Still, because of Jesus' death and resurrection, Christians now have hope. As Christ declared on the cross, "It is finished" (John 19:30). The incompleteness that leads to the pain of emotional disorders (e.g., shame-proneness, repetitive negative thinking about the past and future, intolerance of uncertainty) has been responded to by Immanuel ("God is with us"), the suffering servant who took on and overcame the shame, pain, suffering, and punishment of humankind (Genesis 3:8; Isaiah 53:4–5) and brought in the new creation (2 Corinthians 5:17).

b) The literature on Christian meditative practices for a deeper relationship with God (often referred to as "communion with God" in Protestantism; Owen, 1965, Vol. 2), as well as Orthodox writings on *theosis* (Ware, 2013) and the *Cloud of Unknowing* (Bangley, 2006) on reaching out to God in love. In these works, *apophatic* and *kataphatic* meditation is presented, including specific steps to fellowship with God.

c) Within the Protestant tradition, the Puritan author John Flavel's *The Mystery of Providence* (2015), including his writings on communion with God in the context of God's providence, as well as Puritan prayers in the *Valley of Vision* (Bennett, 1975). Meditating and praying with the help of these *kataphatic* prayers, Christians can gain an awareness of God's trustworthy attributes as they spend time with him.

d) *Lectio divina* (Benner, 2010) as a way to blend *apophatic* and *kataphatic* meditation in order to cultivate a deeper awareness of divine communion, utilizing Scripture on Jesus' redemptive work on the cross.

In each of these writings, which parallel mechanisms of change (the "common factors" as "building blocks") in the modern clinical psychology literature, but also add a meta-understanding of the change process (the Christian "blueprint"), we emphasize the ways in which Christians can gently pivot from the symptoms of emotional disorders to an awareness of God's active, loving presence with them in the new creation. In turn, Christian clients are learning to relate to inner experiences with more tentativeness and acceptance as they follow Jesus into a resurrection life.

The Support Phase: Gaining an Awareness of Being Reconciled to God

In the support phase of therapy, therapists can help Christian clients to verbalize painful affect, entering into the therapeutic alliance as a way to become aware of Jesus' redemptive work. By modeling Jesus' love, mercy, and grace, therapists are embodied signs of God, helping Christians to turn towards an awareness of God's work in Christ for healing. In this process, therapists provide a framework for understanding health, dysfunction, and healing, utilizing *kataphatic* and *apophatic* meditation to help Christian clients deepen their relationship with God. By offering an encouraging, safe, and collaborative relationship, therapists are positioning themselves as the stepping stone towards Christians' experience of God as a secure base and safe haven.

Jesus as the Ultimate Attachment Figure: The "Stronger and Wiser" Other

Building on Chapter 3, Christian clients can map out their "circle of attachment" with Jesus (Clinton & Straub, 2010; Feeney & Collins, 2004; Knabb & Emerson, 2014), emphasizing their emotional experience of venturing out into the world, getting stuck, crying out to Jesus, and returning to him as the ultimate source of soothing comfort and redemptive healing. Returning to the secure base and safe haven dynamic reviewed in the third chapter, Jesus is a perfect secure base, meaning Christians can confidently explore the world because he is a stable, immutable source of support (Feeney & Collins, 2004). As John Bowlby noted about attachment figures, we need a "stronger and wiser" caregiver (Mikulincer & Shaver, 2007) to serve this function.

At a certain point, though, Christian clients experience some sort of stressor in life, leading to the need to reach for Jesus as a source of support; in doing so, Christians are striving to maintain close proximity to him (Feeney & Collins, 2004). In other words, when we are in danger, we naturally gravitate towards a trusted other—in this case, Jesus, our source of redemption—who we long to utilize as a safe haven. Functioning as a safe haven, Jesus is sought after as a source of help and comfort, leading to the amelioration of the stress (and potentially, although by no means inevitably, the stressor) and a sense of contentment, security, wellbeing, and interpersonal satisfaction with him (Feeney & Collins, 2004).

In the context of Jesus' redemptive work, Christians are reconciled to God by way of propitiation (i.e., Jesus has reconciled us to God in his atoning work on the cross by paying the penalty of sin; Romans 3:25), forgiveness (since God has taken away our guilt and shame), and justification (i.e., we are now righteous in God's eyes, rather than viewed by God as estranged sinners) (Norman, 2003). To have hope in this redemption, from a Christian perspective, means we need to understand what we are rescued, ransomed, saved, and freed from, namely, our "great need, misery, and loss" that naturally emanates from the fall of humankind (Jollie, 2015). In other words, we are powerless to help ourselves in our current state (filled with suffering and affliction), must live in an inevitably dangerous world (composed of harmful things, people, and so on), and need a Savior to rescue us from our isolated, broken existence (Jollie, 2015). Looking to the future, moreover, we have hope in a final restoration when Jesus returns again. To be "heavenly-minded," as the Puritans suggested (Jollie, 2015), means we turn from our preoccupations with our pain to Jesus to help us in our struggles, recognizing that he is the final source of hope and healing in a fallen world.

Continuing to build on the discussion in Chapter 3, in applying redemption to the aforementioned "circle of attachment," Jesus is now our secure base and safe haven in a fallen, fragmented world (filled with dangerous things and relationships and suffering and affliction; Jollie, 2015) because of his sacrificial act. What is more, Jesus' work of redemption establishes our unique relationship with our heavenly Father. Because we are reconciled to him through Christ, God is by our side from moment to moment. Moreover, Christ is praying for us in heaven (Romans 8:34), continuously removing our objective guilt and shame, while the Spirit is praying for us subjectively, within the core of our being (John 7:37; Romans 8:26–27), an ever-present calm beneath our emotional conflicts. Unlike human attachments, though, which involve physically leaving an attachment figure to explore (then returning to this person when we are distressed and in need of comfort and safety), the triune God is present in each passing moment.

In helping Christian clients to better understand their need for Jesus' present-moment availability as the ultimate attachment figure, we can move them in the direction of employing him as a secure base, who accompanies them everywhere they go, leading to confident exploration and the utilization of Jesus as a safe haven for soothing comfort in salient times of need. Because emotional disorders can involve low mood, low self-esteem, guilt, rumination, worry, uncertainty, and so forth, turning to Jesus in the midst of pain is paramount for effective affect regulation, especially since he empathizes with our weaknesses, knowing fully what it means to be human (Hebrews 4:15). To gain insight into this dynamic, Christian clients' "circle of attachment" can be mapped out in the context of their struggle with emotional disorders (see Figure 12.1).

Modeling Love, Mercy, and Grace

In the grand narrative of Scripture, Jesus' redemptive work on the cross means Christians are reconciled to God. In Jesus' atonement, God displayed his perfect love, mercy, and grace, sacrificing himself for the brokenness of the world. In the therapy room, therapists working with Christian clients can model (although imperfectly) God's love, mercy, and grace in response to our clients' pain, which can begin to point them to a deeper relationship with Christ. With mercy, we are withholding punishment and judgment, as well as being attuned to our clients' suffering. Reminiscent of the story of the Good Samaritan (Luke 10:25–37), we are responding to the suffering of another person, with our Christian clients presenting to therapy with prior experiences of being ignored, neglected, and so on in their experience of psychological and relational pain. Still, rather than "taking pity on" our wounded clients by "pouring oil and wine" on them, transporting them "to an inn and [taking] care of [them]" (Luke 10:25–37), we are building a therapeutic alliance and responding to their psychological needs by offering understanding, empathy, support, and encouragement as we aid them in restoring their psychological strength so they can get back on the proverbial roads of life.

Certainly, therapists play a unique role in a Christian psychotherapy framework by signifying God's perfect redemption and the removal of clients' sin, shame, and guilt through their listening, acceptance, compassion, and patience. By maintaining a supportive, loving stance towards their

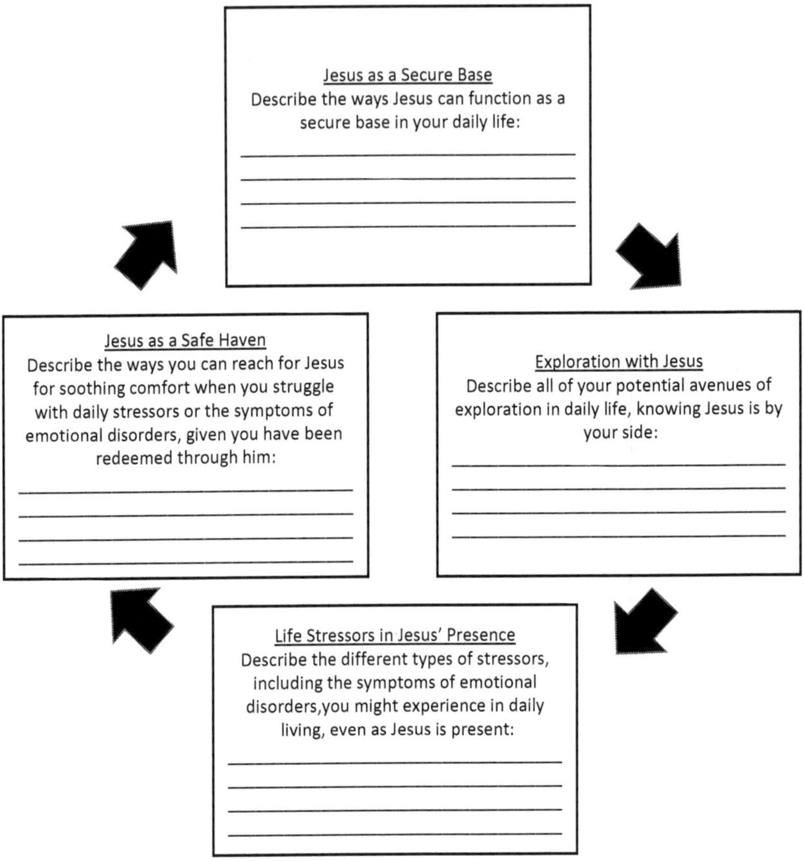

Figure 12.1 Christian clients' "circle of attachment" with Jesus in the context of emotional disorders. Adapted from Clinton & Straub (2010), Feeney & Collins (2004), and Knabb & Emerson (2014)

Christian clients, the latter are enabled to have corrective emotional experiences with a concrete image of God, who more or less resembles their merciful, loving (and invisible) heavenly Father. The therapeutic alliance, then, becomes an imperfect, but palpable, realization of horizontal reconciliation and serves as a mirror of vertical reconciliation.

Grace, moreover, involves bestowing undeserved merit or worth, in that we are affirming the inherent dignity of our clients because they have been created in God's image. Each and every session, to be sure, we are responding to our clients' emotional pain by providing empathy, support, and encouragement, refusing to condemn and offering dignity and merit, which can buffer against the negative effects of emotional disorders. After all, depression often involves low self-esteem and excessive guilt and shame, and anxiety commonly includes themes of uncertainty and future danger. In offering a supportive presence—with love, mercy, and grace as central themes—we are functioning as Christ's body, as Theresa of Avila observed:

> Christ has no body now but yours. No hands, no feet on earth but yours. Yours are the eyes through which he looks compassion on this world. Yours are the feet with which he walks to do good. Yours are the hands through which he blesses all the world.
>
> (as cited in Bowden, 2005, p. 715)

The Grand Narrative of Scripture and Christian Meditation

Returning to the grand narrative of Scripture (reviewed previously in the sixth chapter), humankind was created in God's image, although we are estranged from God because we originally turned away from him. Yet, based on Jesus' work of redemption, we are reconciled to God and patiently await his return to restore all things. As quoted in Chapter 9, because of the believer's union with Christ's death, "The individual's whole being, value system, and behavior are changed... God has now delivered us from the bondage of sin and led us back from the exile of our estrangement from God to a new reconciled relationship" (Garland, 1999, p. 287). One way to help Christian clients maintain an awareness of Jesus' redemptive deliverance—especially when struggling with the symptoms of emotional disorders, such as low self-esteem, rumination, worry, uncertainty, and a preoccupation with danger and future catastrophe—is through the vehicle of Christian meditation.

As considered in the third and ninth chapters, in the Christian tradition, there are *kataphatic* (using words and images) and *apophatic* (without words and images) forms of meditation. An example of the former is Puritan meditation, wherein practitioners meditate on God's attributes, actions, and passages in Scripture so as to focus their mind on him and their salvation in him. With the latter, Christians can employ a single-syllable word (e.g., God, love) to develop a posture of surrendering everything to God and reaching for him in love (an act of the will), rather than knowledge (an act of the intellect) (Beasley-Topliffe, 2017; Johnston, 1970).

In this chapter, we recommend helping Christian clients use both forms of meditation to maintain an awareness of Jesus' redemptive work on the cross, shifting from a preoccupation with the symptoms of emotional disorders to Jesus' mercy, grace, and forgiveness. A condensed version of Puritan meditation (again, a type of *kataphatic* meditation) involves the following (adapted from Beeke & Jones, 2012):

- Shift the focus from inner (e.g., ruminations, worries) and outer (e.g., stressors) concerns to an awareness of God's active, loving presence.

- Gently repeat a short passage in Scripture as a way to focus all of the attention on God. In this case, repeating Jesus' famous saying in John (19:30), "It is finished."

Certainly, the old Christian hymn by James Proctor, "It is Finished," captures the finality of Jesus' redemptive work on the cross:

> Nothing, either great or small—
> Nothing, sinner, no;
> Jesus died and paid it all,
> Long, long ago.
>
> "It is finished!" yes, indeed,
> Finished, ev'ry jot;
> Sinner, this is all you need,
> Tell me, is it not?
>
> When He, from His lofty throne,
> Stooped to do and die,
> Ev'rything was fully done;
> Hearken to His cry!
>
> Weary, working, burdened one,
> Wherefore toil you so?
> Cease your doing; all was done
> Long, long ago.
>
> Till to Jesus' work you cling
> By a simple faith,
> "Doing" is a deadly thing—
> "Doing" ends in death.
>
> Cast your deadly "doing" down—
> Down at Jesus' feet;
> Stand in Him, in Him alone,
> Gloriously complete.

In this famous public-domain hymn from the 1800s, Proctor recommended that we "cease [our] doing" by laying our "doing down at Jesus' feet." In the context of emotional disorders, we can get stuck in unilaterally striving to know why we are struggling with a low mood (Segal et al., 2012) and attempt, on our own, to futilely create a predictable, safe future (Dugas & Robichaud, 2007). Yet, we can shift from these exhausting, unhelpful efforts to simply sitting at Jesus' feet with one of Christianity's most powerful declarations: "It is finished." In the context of the above two-step process, we are first noticing our perseverative, repetitive thinking patterns that are comprised of "earthly-mindedness," before shifting to "heavenly-mindedness" (Jollie, 2015) via meditating on God's plan of redemption, revealed in the pages of the Bible.

To offer one more example, in the Puritan author Richard Allestree's *The Whole Duty of Divine Meditation* (2018), he presents over a dozen topics to meditate on, one of which is especially salient for the purposes of this chapter. With the fourth meditation, "Of Man's Salvation," the author pointed to Titus 2:11: "For the grace of God has appeared that offers salvation to all people." Inspired by this text, Allestree powerfully declared, "He which made me, can renew me," before going on to state, "He created me wonderfully, and redeemed me miraculously; but his love was never so highly expressed, than in his wounds and passion" (p. 55). This Puritan author, writing in the 17th century, concluded with the following: "Have mercy on me, O my physician, my savior, and my righteousness!" (p. 56).

With this 17th-century meditation, we can help our Christian clients consistently turn from their perseverative thinking patterns to an awareness of God's redemptive love, readily poured out to them in Jesus' work on the cross. The following short meditations, thus, can be used to shift the mind from ruminations, worries, and thoughts of uncertainty and catastrophe towards an awareness of the hope and freedom that come from Jesus' atoning, redemptive work some 2,000 years ago:

a. "He which made me, can renew me" (Allestree, 2018, p. 55).
b. "He redeemed me miraculously" (Allestree, 2018, p. 55).
c. "Have mercy on me, O my physician and savior" (Allestree, 2018, p. 55).

Meditations that focus on Jesus' redemptive purposes are especially crucial in the context of ruminations about a past we cannot change and a future we can by no means predict. Rather, God through Christ has forgiven us for our past and holds the future in his hands, guiding our life with his perfect, fatherly care. Since this is the case, we can let go of our own efforts to control, predict, and manage our own life in isolation, repeatedly shifting towards an awareness of his guidance and compassionate presence from moment to moment. Letting go of our need to "do" can also be cultivated with *apophatic* meditation.

The simple meditative instructions from the *Cloud of Unknowing* can be employed in order to help Christian clients focus solely on "[God's] grace through the redemption that came by Christ Jesus" (Romans 3:24), placing everything else beneath a "cloud of forgetting." To summarize this famous work, the *Cloud* author, writing anonymously in the 14th century, suggested that the Christian life involves four stages: "ordinary, extraordinary, unique, and ideal" (Bangley, 2006, p. 3). As we progress in our spiritual growth, we move from being solely focused on worldly endeavors, to being redeemed by God, to longing for a deeper relationship with him (Bangley, 2006).

To cultivate a more intimate relationship with God, the fallen words of this alienated world can be inherently limiting and distracting in our attempts to more fully contemplate God; thus, the *Cloud* author taught that *apophatic* meditation—or "contemplation," as he described it—involves gently placing all our thoughts (other than a simple word that focuses our attention on God) beneath a "cloud of forgetting" (Bangley, 2006). As we do so, we are shifting our mental energy to God by using a single-syllable word (such as "God" or "love"), reaching out to him in a "cloud of unknowing" by prioritizing love, rather than knowledge (Bangley, 2006). To summarize this contemplative process, we read the following in his 14th-century instructional guide:

> The essence of contemplation is a simple and direct reaching out to God. People who pray at this depth do not seek relief from pain nor do they seek increased rewards, but only the fulfillment of God's will. Nothing else shares this simple moment.
>
> (Bangley, 2006, p. 37)

Interestingly, fast-forward to the 21st century, and clinical psychologists point to a "limited capacity channel," meaning that the human mind can only process a limited amount of information at any given time (Segal et al., 2012); for Christian clients who practice *apophatic* contemplation, the mind is filled with Christ, which means their ruminations, worries, and other perseverative cognitions are not prominently displayed in the foreground of mental awareness.

As Christian clients with repetitive thinking learn to shift from their cognitive preoccupations to an awareness of Christ's active, loving presence, they are surrendering to his grace, reminiscent of "a wood in a carpenter's hands, or a house in which someone else lives" (Bangley, 2006, p. 48). As the *Cloud* author conveyed, just like someone shouting for help when in an emergency situation, we are developing the skill of surrendering to his care by keeping our request short and to the point by focusing on a single-syllable word (Bangley, 2006).

In essence, the *Cloud* author's instructions (adapted from Bangley, 2006) involve a two-step process, reminiscent of the one we have mentioned above:

a. First, we are placing all our earthly preoccupations (i.e., all our thoughts that do not involve God himself) beneath a "cloud of forgetting." In this step, we are learning to rest in God's hands, recognizing that his "grace is sufficient" (2 Corinthians 12:9), just like a piece of wood in the hands of a carpenter.

b. Second, we are using a simple word (e.g., "God," "love," "grace") to capture our focused, sustained attention on God, reaching out to him in a "cloud of unknowing" with love, rather than knowledge. In its simplest form, this word dually conveys our need for God's grace and willingness to focus exclusively on him, just like someone shouting for help in a burning building or on a sinking ship.

For the purpose of this chapter, we believe that the word "grace" ("undeserved acceptance and love received from another"; Milliken, 2003, p. 678) helps us to remember Jesus' loving, atoning act on the cross, given God's chief motivation for dying for the sins of the world was love (John 3:16). Certainly, grace is also an ongoing gift of God, which we can experience from moment to moment in the Christian life. In shifting from repetitive, perseverative thoughts, which distract us from God, to repeating this simple word ("grace"), we are learning to simply rest at Jesus' feet, like Mary in Luke's gospel (Luke 10:38–42). Over time, we are letting Jesus' grace be enough (2 Corinthians 12:9) in saving us, redeeming us, and, ultimately, offering us freedom in this world. At the same time, we are recognizing our perseverative thinking patterns, which can get in the way of a deeper, reconciled relationship with Christ. Since Jesus' work is already finished, we are helping our Christian clients to gain a deeper awareness of a relationship that has always been there following their conversion experience.

The Learning Phase: Understanding Redemption in the Context of Emotional Disorders

As Christian clients move from support to learning, they are utilizing daily prayer and meditation to process painful emotions. Whether Christian clients are verbalizing painful feelings via *kataphatic* meditation or sitting in silence with God by way of *apophatic* meditation, they are moving towards inner acceptance because God is active and present. Therefore, difficult inner states are related to in a dispossessive, flexible manner, with Christians working to "find God in all things," as the famous Jesuit motto goes.

Through *kataphatic* meditation, Christian clients are noticing repetitive negative thinking, gently pivoting to God's Word as they pray to him for comfort and encouragement in the midst of pain. With *apophatic* meditation, Christian clients are getting to know the inner workings of a busy mind, recognizing their ingrained patterns of repetitive negative thinking and thoughts related to intolerance of uncertainty. Essentially, Christian clients are developing meta-cognitive awareness, in that they are learning to notice repetitive inner states, before shifting to a focused, sustained awareness of God's presence. Along the way, Christian clients are cultivating a healthy spiritual detachment in that they are letting go of anxious grasping of inner and outer experiences, first focusing on God's active, loving actions in the present moment. Through this learning, Christians can ameliorate unrealistic expectations that lead to experiential avoidance, attaining realistic expectations about the inevitability of pain in a suffering world. Because Jesus is the suffering servant (Isaiah 53), Christian clients, too, will suffer on at least some level in this world. Yet, Jesus provides them with peace and comfort in the midst of inner and outer trials. Overall, they are learning to reframe their view of themselves, others, and God, especially in the context of their expectations about pain. Although Christian clients will continue to struggle because of the fall, they are already redeemed, meaning they can deepen their relationships with God and others in order to blend acceptance and action in the midst of emotional disorders (Knabb, 2016).

Verbalizing and Accepting Pain with Kataphatic Meditation: Focusing on God's Providence

In the Puritan author John Flavel's *Mystery of Providence* (2015), he discussed the importance of viewing "afflictive providences" (also reviewed in the third chapter) through the lens of God's sovereignty, grace, goodness, wisdom, and faithfulness. In other words, for Flavel (who apparently experienced tremendous loss and suffering in his own life), God is sovereign over *both* the positive experiences *and* suffering in this world, meaning that everything has a divine purpose because of God's omnibenevolence, which is consistently directed towards Christians in daily life (Cosby, 2012).

Although reframing suffering as part of God's plan may seem rather controversial in the realm of Christian psychotherapy, "positive cognitive restructuring" in the secular cognitive behavioral literature in response to a variety of traumatic experiences involves viewing "more good than bad in [the] experience," "[finding] positive aspects of [the] experience," and "[finding] a 'silver lining' in [the] event," as measured by the cognitive processing of trauma scale (Williams, Davis, & Millsap, 2002, p. 360). Positive cognitive restructuring of a traumatic event, moreover, is correlated with stress-related growth (Williams et al., 2002). As a result, in Christian psychotherapy, rather than reframing psychological pain as positive solely for pragmatic purposes, Christian clients can work towards cultivating a deeper appreciation for God's providential care in the midst of the struggles of emotional disorders. This reframe is especially salient in consideration of Jesus' redemptive work on the cross—because we are reconciled to God, we are righteous in his eyes, and he has our best interests in mind.

Still, in Flavel's (2015) writings on God's providence, he recommended that we also feel sorrow for the pain we are going through; this sadness, though, should be followed by joy and comfort: "Can the soul be sad, whilst God is with it?" For Flavel, calling out to God is especially important in the midst of pain, given we are reconciled to God, who is with us in each and every step we take: "He will call on me, and I will answer him; I will be with him in trouble, I will deliver him and honor him" (Psalm 91:15; as cited in Flavel, 2015).

As the first exercise in the learning phrase of the "redemption" pillar, we can work with Christian clients to (a) identify an example of recurrent suffering in their life, such as the symptoms of emotional disorders, (b) reframe these "afflictive providences" as emanating from God's perfect plan by viewing them through the lens of God's immutable, trustworthy attributes, (c) express their sadness to God for the pain they are going through, and (d) turn to God for joy and comfort in the midst of this enduring distress. Next, we can help Christian clients to draw inspiration from the 91st Psalm (mentioned in Flavel's *Mystery of Providence*) to dually (e) call out to God, and (f) rest in his perfect comfort because they are reconciled to him through Jesus' compassionate, atoning work on the cross. See Table 12.2 for an organized strategy to slowly walk Christian clients through this six-step exercise. In each step, Christian clients struggling with rumination and worry can write down a brief meditation that they can focus on, thinking deeply within the step by pondering the themes of God's "afflictive providences," God's trustworthy attributes, God as a source of joy and comfort in the midst of suffering, and God as a source of rest. Examples are provided in Table 12.2 for each step to generate ideas for further use.

As a central theme, this exercise can help Christian clients recognize that their perceived aloneness in the pain may actually be what contributes the most to their suffering, rather than the pain *per se*. Consistent with attachment theory, turning to God as a secure base and safe haven means we can reach for him for soothing comfort when we experience the bumps and bruises of life, rather than avoiding the world for fear that our exploration will lead to catastrophic consequences. With God by our side, to be sure, we are able to trust that even the most painful experiences have a divine purpose, which allows us to reframe emotional pain in a more helpful way that leads to resilience and growth, ameliorating the problematic "meta-feeling" (i.e., the "feeling about the feeling," such as sadness or shame about the symptoms of emotional disorders) in the process. By learning to make peace with our painful experiences, we are ameliorating experiential avoidance, which can exacerbate an already difficult experience (Hayes et al., 2012). Worth mentioning, here, we are in no way saying that working with Christian clients with an insecure attachment to God is an easy task or quick fix; rather, this type of therapeutic work takes time and patience. Although by no means exhaustive, we have tried to offer a range of goals, strategies, and perspectives for utilizing attachment theory to impact change within our model (see, e.g., the third, sixth, and ninth chapters, in addition to the current chapter). Still, for a more detailed, workbook-based approach to ameliorating insecure attachments with God via a compassion-based model for Christian shame, see Knabb (2018).

The Valley of Vision and Reconciliation: Imagining Jesus' Smile as a "Ray of Heaven"

In the "Redemption and Reconciliation" section of the *Valley of Vision* (1975), an amalgam of Puritan meditations, a specific meditation simply titled, "Assurance," is especially fitting for the "redemption" pillar of a Christian approach to psychotherapy. The first few lines read as follows:

Table 12.2 A six-step process for verbalizing and accepting pain with *kataphatic* meditation. Adapted from Flavel (2015)

1. Identify an example of recurrent suffering in your life.	"I continue to struggle with rumination and sadness."
2. Reframe this "afflictive providence" as coming from God, viewing it through the lens of God's immutable, trustworthy attributes.	"Although I am experiencing pain, I know that God is with me and has a purpose for my difficult inner experiences" (Genesis 50:20; Romans 8:28).
God's sovereignty	"He is before all things, and in him all things hold together" (Colossians 1:17).
God's grace	"Let us then approach God's throne of grace with confidence, so that we may receive mercy and find grace to help us in our time of need" (Hebrews 4:16).
God's goodness	"God is love" (1 John 4:8). "You are good, and what you do is good" (Psalm 119:68).
God's wisdom	"To God belong wisdom and power; counsel and understanding are his" (Job 12:13).
God's faithfulness	"God is faithful, who has called you into fellowship with his Son, Jesus Christ our Lord" (1 Corinthians 1:9).
3. Express sadness about the "afflictive providence" to God.	"I feel tremendous loss, Lord, and am experiencing a profound sadness because I continue to struggle with rumination, worry, and uncertainty in my life."
4. Turn to God for joy and comfort in the midst of the "afflictive providence."	Like the 119th Psalm, "My comfort in my suffering is this: Your promise preserves my life" (Psalm 119:50).
5. Call out to God to be present in the middle of the "afflictive providence."	"Hear, Lord, and be merciful to me; Lord, be my help" (Psalm 20:10).
6. Conclude by resting in God's perfect comfort because he has responded to the heartfelt cry.	"You turned my wailing into dancing; you removed my sackcloth and clothed me with joy, that my heart may sing your praises and not be silent. Lord my God, I will praise you forever" (Psalm 20:11). "Praise be to the God and Father of our Lord Jesus Christ, the Father of compassion and the God of all comfort" (2 Corinthians 1:3).

Almighty God, I am loved with everlasting love, clothed in eternal righteousness, my peace flowing like a river, my comforts many and large, my joy and triumph unutterable, my soul lively with a knowledge of salvation, my sense of justification unclouded. I have scarce anything to pray for; Jesus smiles upon my soul as a ray of heaven and my supplications are swallowed up in praise. How sweet is the glorious doctrine of election when based upon thy Word and wrought inwardly within the soul!

(p. 51)

In this powerful meditation, the author highlighted the salience of God's love, righteousness, peace, comfort, joy, and, ultimately, salvation, envisioning that Jesus' smile penetrates his soul like a "ray of heaven."

To help Christian clients shift from the symptoms of emotional disorders to an awareness of God's enduring love, peace, joy, and comfort—firmly embedded within Jesus' atoning work on the cross—we can use a simple guided imagery exercise. In this brief exercise, ask your Christian clients to close their eyes, envisioning that Jesus is smiling upon them like a "ray of heaven." Help them to visualize Jesus' penetrating smile, impacting them at the depths of their being and conveying that they are fully accepted by God because of Jesus' sacrifice on the cross. As a result, they can safely rest in his perfect love, peace, joy, and comfort, with nothing else to do or say, other than realizing that they have been reconciled to God. When they experience the symptoms of depression or anxiety (e.g., low mood, guilt, thoughts of worthlessness or unlovability, rumination, worry, themes of uncertainty), they can just notice these inner experiences, before gently shifting to an awareness of Jesus' penetrating smile, which confidently conveys that they no longer need to do anything to receive Jesus' offer of redemption, other than to keep their eyes on his enduring, confident smile.

"Jesus, Save Me!"

In the 14th chapter of Matthew (14:22–33), we read that Jesus was "walking on the lake" in the early morning hours, with Peter attempting to follow him on the water. Yet, Peter took his eyes off Jesus, noticed the wind, experienced intense fear, and started to sink. In the midst of this situation, Peter panicked, "Lord, save me!" In turn, Jesus caught Peter with his hand, escorting him into the boat nearby that was safely floating on the water.

For Christians with emotional disorders, this story can help with the struggle with perseverative thinking. When we get distracted by repetitive thinking patterns, such as rumination, worry, and intolerance of uncertainty, we can frequently take our eyes off Jesus, experiencing the tendency to sink in the waters of life. Yet, when we are able to cultivate meta-cognitive awareness, we can simply notice the winds around us, then shift our focus back to Jesus as we confidently walk towards him.

In the context of emotional disorders, meta-cognition involves "any knowledge or cognitive process that is involved in the appraisal, monitoring or control of cognition" (Wells, 2000, p. 6). We possess a general knowledge of, as well as the ability to regulate, our cognitions. With the former, we may be able to recognize ruminations and worries; on the other hand, the latter can involve monitoring our thinking patterns or shifting our attention (Wells, 2000).

Returning to Peter's struggle to keep his eyes on Jesus when walking to Christ on the water, we can work with our Christian clients to do the following (adapted from Wells, 2000):

a. Monitor their thinking patterns (e.g., "What am I thinking to myself right now as I'm going about my day?"), reminiscent of Peter's awareness of the winds that surrounded him on the lake.
b. Label their unhelpful thinking patterns (e.g., "I'm getting stuck in 'worrying' patterns of thinking"), similar to Peter's awareness of the surrounding winds.
c. Shift their focus from their negative thinking patterns to Jesus when they notice they are beginning to sink (e.g., "These thoughts are just the inevitable 'winds' of life that distract me from walking towards Jesus. I'm going to refocus my attention on him").

In this three-step process, we are helping Christian clients cultivate detachment, which is "the virtue of habitually choosing out of freedom not compulsion, fear, or routine" (Lonsdale, 2004, p. 234). In other words, detachment involves what the Puritans referred to as shifting from "earthly-mindedness" to "heavenly-mindedness" (Jollie, 2015), letting go of earthly preoccupations in order to focus on God. Perseverative, ruminative cognitions can get in the way of walking towards Jesus, especially when we get preoccupied with them, like Peter's struggle with focusing on the wind, not Jesus. Thus, developing the habit of "choosing out of freedom" (Lonsdale, 2004) by fortifying our ability—through meta-cognitive awareness—to notice repetitive negative thinking, then shift our focus to Jesus, is key.

Accepting Pain with Apophatic Meditation

In dialectical behavior therapy (DBT), a third-wave cognitive-behavioral therapy that balances acceptance and change to help clients with affect dysregulation vulnerabilities, "radical acceptance" is promoted (Linehan, 2015). Radical acceptance involves "a complete and total openness to the facts of reality as they are, without fighting the facts or being willful and ineffective," and takes the form of an "all the way, complete and total" attitude in that we are "accepting [reality] in [our] mind, heart, and body" and "[letting] go of bitterness" (Linehan, 2015, pp. 315, 342). Radical acceptance is reminiscent of experiential acceptance (rather than avoidance) in the acceptance and commitment therapy literature (Hayes et al., 2012).

In the Christian tradition, acceptance involves receiving the realization that everything has already been accomplished (finished) ultimately, as far as God is concerned, through Christ's work of redemption, so we cannot do anything to earn our salvation. Instead, we are letting go of control and performance, recognizing that we are loved by God solely because of his enduring grace to us in Christ. Remember, in practicing *apophatic* meditation, we are choosing a simple word to capture our willingness to focus all our attention on God, letting go of all other thoughts and feelings that can distract us from him. In the *Cloud* author's instructions, he recommended using "love" to focus our attention on God, which is certainly fitting for the "redemption" pillar (see John 3:16). In fact, "love" can be used in addition to "grace" (mentioned previously in this chapter), alternating between the two as Christian clients shift from one meditative practice period to the next. As we reach out to God in love—rather than our own self-derived knowledge—we are learning to practice radical acceptance, in that we are ameliorating the tendency to "do" something to earn his favor; rather, we are simply resting in his love by letting go of everything else. For Christian clients with emotional disorders, this involves relinquishing the tendency to search for an answer for why they are experiencing a low mood (Segal et al., 2012) or achieve a unilateral, pseudo-sense of certainty (Dugas & Robichaud, 2007). This two-step process—noticing and letting go of the tendency to control the inner or outer world, and shifting to an awareness of God via gently repeating "love"—can help to cultivate inner acceptance, given we are no longer getting into a "tug-of-war" match with our inner experiences, choosing, instead, to allow God's love to be enough. After all, in his perfect love, God offered his Son to redeem us in our fallen state (John 3:16).

The Action Phase: Noticing, Shifting, and Acting with God

In the action phase of treatment, Christian clients are learning to face their fears because God has redeemed them and working to gain a deeper, more flexible awareness of their thinking patterns. In the context of emotional disorders, rumination, worry, and intolerance of uncertainty are often pervasive, overwhelming Christian clients' inner world to the point of keeping them stalled on the roads of life. Yet, through verbal and nonverbal forms of meditation, Christians are working towards noticing the inner world before gently pivoting towards an awareness of God's protective care in the new creation. As this two-step process happens over and over again—noticing inner experiences, then shifting towards an awareness of God—Christians are practicing the ability to focus on one thing (God) at a time in the present moment with an attitude of compassion towards themselves in Christ. In agreement with mindfulness-based cognitive therapy (MBCT), we believe there is a "limited capacity channel" within the human mind (Segal, Williams, & Teasdale, 2012). Because of this, when Christian clients focus their attention on God, they are unable to simultaneously ruminate, worry, and think about uncertainty. With this indirect strategy, Christians are focusing on what is right and true, consistent with recommendations from the Apostle Paul (Philippians 4:8). As Christian clients focus on God, gently and flexibly pivoting away from repetitive negative thinking, they are able to more effectively follow Jesus, focusing on placing one foot in front of the other as they practice engaging in virtuous behavior. By receiving their new self in Christ, Christians are enabled to rest in Christ's accomplishments on their behalf, rather than their own performance and control, which, in turn, helps them to become more conformed to the image of Christ, learning how to participate in Christ's virtue by grace. Humility, kindness, and love can be practiced, steadily increasing over time, because these virtues organically flow from their life in Christ, rather than because they offer some sort of reward (praise of others) in a utilitarian manner. Action occurs, then, because Christians are turning away from their old self and surrendering it to God and more and more becoming their new self in Christ (Ephesians 4:22–24).

Facing Fears with Christian Meditation: The Jesus Prayer, Communion with God, and Theosis

In the Orthodox Christian tradition, the Jesus Prayer (also reviewed in the third and ninth chapters) is recited in order to practice *theosis*, that is, "participating in the very life of God" (Rakestraw, 1997, p. 257).[1] To put it another way, the Jesus Prayer is the vehicle through which Christians can "share in the mutual indwelling of the three Persons of the Holy Trinity" (Ware, 2013). Biblical support for *theosis*, from an Orthodox perspective, is found in Genesis 1:26, since we were created in God's image (which presumably can increase), as well as Peter's second letter (1:4), which elucidates that we "may participate in the divine nature" (Rakestraw, 1997).

Although this term is not typically familiar to Evangelical Christians, and most Protestants have been historically cautious about *theosis* (or "divinization"), believing it could blur the Creator/creature distinction, a growing number of theologians are engaging in fruitful dialogue on the overlap between the East's emphasis on *theosis* and similar Western notions (e.g., Gama, 2017; Harink, 2009; Rakestraw, 1997). Jonathan Edwards, for example, independently developed a similar doctrine (see McClymond & McDermott, 2011). Elaborating on *theosis*, Rakestraw offered the following:

> Above all, *theosis* is the restoration and reintegration of the "image" or, some prefer, "likeness" of God, seriously distorted by the fall, in the children of God. In this life Christians grow more and more into the very likeness and character of God as God was revealed in the man Jesus Christ.
>
> (p. 261, italics added)

Rakestraw goes on to state that *theosis* resembles sanctification, although more fitting phrases in Western Christianity to capture this term may actually be "conformity to Christ" (Romans 8:29) or "communion with God." Thus, when introducing the Jesus Prayer to promote an awareness of being reconciled to God through Christ, "conformity to Christ" or "communion with God" language may be a better fit so as to avoid misunderstandings or controversies that are currently being worked out in theological circles.

One strategy for promoting internal, Christ-centered transformation that we have advocated throughout the book is the Jesus Prayer (Talbot, 2013). As we suggested in Chapter 3, while breathing in (with the diaphragm) the first part of the Jesus Prayer, "Lord Jesus Christ, Son of God," we place ourselves under his ultimate authority. In this chapter, we highlight that his Lordship has been beautified and intensified by his laying down his life for us as our Redeemer, who has reconciled us to God (Talbot, 2013). As we breathe out, "have mercy on me," we are bringing to mind and relying on Jesus' infinite compassion for us in our predicament (Talbot, 2013), which we are applying to emotional disorders. In other words, we are petitioning Jesus to respond to our pain, given we have been reconciled to God through his life, death, and resurrection. Over and over again, we can breathe in the name of Jesus, then breathe out our request for Jesus to be responsive to our pain and suffering. Not only are we asking Jesus to withhold punishment in our request for mercy on the basis of his atonement, we are also accessing his soothing comfort in the midst of our struggles within the human condition.

In addition, when reciting the Jesus Prayer, we are seeking to face our fears on the roads of life (that is, cultivating experiential acceptance, rather than avoidance; Hayes et al., 2012), as well as noticing with compassion the inner workings of our soul, especially our ruminations, worries, and themes of uncertainty. As we recite this famous prayer, we want to acknowledge when our attention has shifted towards something else, consistent with having an important conversation with a family member at the dinner table. As soon as we notice our mind has drifted "somewhere else," we kindly, gently return to the conversation before us at the dinner table, in this case breathing in the name of Jesus and breathing out our request for his soothing, comforting presence. Over time, we are training our attention to keep increasingly focused on our most loved companion, which takes up all the space in the mind (Segal et al., 2012) that has been previously filled with ruminations, worries, and other distractions.

In light of our union with Christ, there are many ways therapists and clients can adapt the Jesus Prayer to focus on various aspects of their relationship with God and their redeemed status, depending on the needs of the client. For example, in place of "have mercy on me," one could substitute, "abide in me and I in you," "I welcome you into my innermost places," "I am fully accepted in you," "thank you for giving me peace," "fill me with your holy love," or "I release my fear and anxiety." As another variation, clients could tack on a final phrase after "have mercy on me" that reflects some feature of their new self: "your child," "your beloved," "your saint," "your new creation," or "your friend."

Noticing, Shifting, and Following: A Three-Step Meditative Process to Focus on Jesus' Work of Redemption

In continuing this conversation of noticing the tendency of the mind to wander towards unhelpful content and processes, then shifting towards material that is beneficial for psychological and spiritual health, a three-step process that adds action involves the following (a variation of this process was also reviewed in the ninth chapter):

a. Noticing unhelpful thinking patterns as they arise, accepting them momentarily in order to acknowledge their reality with God by our side. In this step, we are being mindful (Segal et al., 2012), rather than mindless.
b. Shifting the focus from unhelpful thinking patterns towards God's presence, whether through *kataphatic* or *apophatic* meditation or some other means (e.g., singing worship music), learning to devote mental energy to what is "true, noble, right, pure, lovely, and admirable" (Philippians 4:8).
c. Resting in Jesus' work of redemption, enabling believers to follow him into a participation in the Christian virtues: humility, kindness, love, the freedom to obey, and so on—that is, life in Christ—first through understanding biblical moral principles, then through the imagination and role-playing, and eventually in everyday life.

In the context of emotional disorders, we are learning to recognize when we are preoccupied with the symptoms of emotional disorders, which can lead to impaired functioning if we dwell on painful thoughts and feelings for too long, then to cry out to God, realizing that his active, loving presence is available to us from moment to moment because of Christ.

For another exercise in the "redemption" pillar, we can have Christian clients with emotional disorders meditate on a number of aspects of who they are in Christ, based on the teaching of the Bible.

> Because of your union with Christ, God has given you the gift of Christ's perfect life, so there is now no condemnation for you (Romans 8:1). In fact, you are now already perfectly righteous (Romans 5:1), holy and beloved (Colossians 3:12), accepted by Christ (Romans 15:7), and a child of God (Romans 8:15–16). Take time each day to read one of these passages and reflect on how they apply to you. Imagine Jesus saying them to you, and practice receiving them into your innermost being.

After clients have practiced the previous exercise as homework for some time, and when they seem ready to move to a more active phase of realizing their union with Christ, the therapist could promote the following exercise.

(a) Bringing to mind your true self in Christ (a beloved, justified, child of God), pick an area of your life where you feel you are falling short in your Christian life and relationships.
(b) Resting in who you are in Christ, write out what is keeping you from growing in Christ in this area.
(c) Resting in who you are in Christ, write out what would it look like to grow in Christ in this area.
(d) Resting in who you are in Christ, imagine doing something that expresses growth in this area (e.g., reaching out to someone in kindness, apologizing for something, or responding in kindness when someone is mean).
(e) Resting in who you are in Christ, finish up by expressing your love and gratitude to God.

Before concluding the chapter, we would like to present one additional strategy for keeping the mind focused on God in response to the "stuckness" that emanates from being distracted by the symptoms of depression and anxiety. In the following four steps, collectively referred to as *lectio divina*, we are combining both *kataphatic* and *apophatic* elements of meditation, which can serve as a fitting conclusion to the "redemption" pillar.

Lectio Divina

Lectio divina (also reviewed in the third chapter) was frequently utilized in monasteries in the Middle Ages and can help practitioners to employ Scripture to focus the mind, then find rest in God. In this next exercise, you will be working with Christian clients to select a passage in Scripture, slowly moving through the four stages of *lectio divina*. Try to help them select a short verse on God's redemptive plan so they can fully absorb it, just like taking a small (not large) bite out of a savory dish of food. After moving with them through each step, you can have them record their reactions in Table 12.3.

In terms of the four steps, Christian clients (a) *read* a short passage in Scripture that emphasizes Jesus' redemptive plan (e.g., John 3:16), (b) *reflect* (or meditate) on the passage by thinking about it on a deeper level, (c) *respond* by praying to God, thanking him for sending his Son to reconcile them to God, and (d) *rest* by sitting in silence and spending time with God in a state of reverence and awe (or contemplation).

Passages to potentially focus on during this four-step process include the following:

a. "It is finished" (John 19:30).
b. "In him we have redemption through his blood, the forgiveness of sins, in accordance with the riches of God's grace that he lavished on us" (Ephesians 1:7).

Table 12.3 Lectio divina within the "redemption" pillar. Adapted from Benner (2010) and Knabb (2016)

	Reactions
Verse in the Bible to focus on:	
Read the verse about God's redemption.	
Reflect on the verse about God's redemption by meditating on it (i.e., thinking deeply about it).	
Respond to the verse about God's redemption by thanking God for his active, loving, compassionate act of redemption and reconciliation.	
Rest in God in silence and stillness, knowing you have already been redeemed and there is nothing further you need to do to receive God's healing love.	

c. "For he has rescued us from the dominion of darkness and brought us into the kingdom of the Son he loves, in whom we have redemption, the forgiveness of sins" (Colossians 1:13).
d. "He did not enter by means of the blood of goats and calves; but he entered the Most Holy Place once for all by his own blood, thus obtaining eternal redemption" (Hebrews 9:12).
e. Clients can imagine Jesus speaking to them, "Peace I leave with you; my peace I give you. I do not give to you as the world gives" (John 14:27). Or, "Come to me, all you who are weary and burdened, and I will give you rest" (Matthew 11:28).

A Case Example

Randy is a 23-year-old seminarian who was referred due to his being convinced he is going to hell. He wrestles incessantly with seeking assurance that he is truly saved and bound for heaven, these thoughts stirring up several years ago when reading a book on assurance of salvation and ramping up since then. He can hardly read his Bible because everywhere he turns there is a verse that cues up his anxious, obsessive thoughts about his eternal fate. He is well informed of doctrine and can debate any reassurance his pastor and professors have offered him. Randy is clearly distraught and miserable as these thoughts hound him day and night. His new wife is struggling, too, as he asks her frequently if she thinks he is saved—even as he realizes she will say "yes," and he will only need to ask her again in a few minutes. Randy deeply believes in God and honors his Word, but despairs of having a relationship with God and being able to serve him in ministry (which has been his goal for years). One of his theology professors finally referred him to a therapist, thinking this goes beyond simply seeking information or understanding.

We offer this challenging case here not only to illustrate interventions in the "redemption" theme, but to introduce a uniquely "religious" pathology: scrupulous obsessive-compulsive disorder (OCD; recognizing that obsessive-compulsive disorder has been moved from the "Anxiety Disorders" to the "Obsessive-Compulsive and Related Disorders" section of the DSM-5). It may be the emotional problem that has the earliest roots in Christian literature as we have documentation of believers struggling with this for centuries; Ciarrocchi (1995) traces evidence for scrupulous OCD in the life of the early Baptist preacher and author John Bunyan (1628–1688). It is a particularly tricky problem for therapists working with Christian clients as it may invite the uninformed therapist to become a compulsion if he or she begins offering reassurance or trying to debate the "logic" of the religious doubt.

Support Phase

Randy will likely feel support when the therapist understands that this is more than a theological issue and, in building the relationship, helps Randy see the emotion underlying the thoughts. One "trick" of OCD is to take anxious feelings and propose a "theory" of why one has them (here, the possibility of not being a Christian), leading to the solution that one must find certainty of salvation prior to relief of the anxiety. This, of course, is futile as it is a matter of faith, and anxious feelings contradict a "feeling" of certainty. The therapist, thus, offers empathy and support for the feelings, defusing them from the thinking processes that will not solve them in the long run.

Also in the support phase, the therapist can exemplify the wisdom of "looking unto Jesus" (Hebrews 12:2). The context, here, makes clear that many of the saints did not enjoy the rewards of their suffering immediately—or even in the present life in some cases. Jesus' strategy for suffering exemplifies the model: hope of eventual joy empowers the bearing of the cross now. Randy—and many other clients with emotional problems—may not get this early in therapy, but the therapist's hope can be contagious over time.

Learning Phase

A risk for many therapists coming from secular training and Western ideology is to see redemption as an individualistic act, rather than as part of a broad narrative. Hebrews 11, as touched on above, shows that Christian faith points beyond personal wellbeing to participation in the metanarrative of God's work in salvation that began by clothing Adam and Eve and ends with his return. Faith does not mean we do not suffer—there is so much teaching on how to suffer in the New Testament, in particular—but, rather, it brings us to suffer with meaning for a cause. Any mother can tell you the pain of childbirth is worth it when she is able to hold the child in her arms. For persons like Randy, the process of accepting the intrusive thoughts about religion and the powerful anxiety of OCD needs to be done in a context of the meaning of the suffering. We have maladaptive emotions because we live in a fallen world, and, while there is suffering here, we have a better hope. Randy may have difficulty seeing this, but the notion that God's plan is bigger than the individual shows his feelings are not the key, but, rather, God's plan and promises that stand, even if we do not feel like they are true.

Here, one helpful technique is defusion, a term that comes from ACT (Hayes et al., 2012). To have a thought is not to believe it or make it true, so with ruminative thoughts of anxiety, depression, or OCD, it is sometimes helpful to move the person "back" from the thoughts to see them as just that—not as "facts" or, in Randy's case, intrusive ideas about what will fix his anxiety. A great biblical illustration of this idea is seen in Matthew 16:13. Peter earns the approval of Jesus and a wonderful promise when he correctly confesses that Jesus is the Son of God, only to be seen as an instrument of Satan a few verses later when he disbelieved Jesus' words about his passion. Peter's mistaken thought did not undermine the truth of his stated faith and the blessing of Jesus. And so it is with us: we cling to our statement of faith and God's approval of it, even when we misunderstand or fear what is happening. Peter's thought did not change the truth of the passion of Christ; it also did not change the fact that he was God's child. Randy will need to act as though this is true of him, even if he logically does not get it due to his intrusive thoughts.

Action Phase

One of the consequences of being preoccupied with negative emotions and obsessive thoughts is that it distracts from the pursuit of following and obeying Jesus. Ironically, by paralyzing the believer, negative emotions can prevent the Christian from doing the things he or she is called to do and finding the joy and fulfillment in so doing. We are not called to feel good, but to obey and love. Consistent with ACT's focus on stepping into values (Hayes et al., 2012), even at the expense of some emotional suffering, Christians can act to obey. ACT therapists sometimes ask a question, "What would the person you want to be do in this situation?" while encouraging them to act in this way even if it is uncomfortable. For Christians, then, we ask, "What would the Christian you want to be do here?" The pivot to acting into values and away from distracting thoughts and emotions frees the person to live the life he or she desires.

For Randy, this will be a key step. If his struggle is placed in the meta-narrative of God's work in redemption and building his kingdom, he can be encouraged to act into his faith by doing the things a Christian does: praying, studying Scripture, being active in his spiritual community, showing love to his family and neighbors, and so forth. Similarly, those with other emotional problems can pivot to living for Christ, seeing their emotions as part of the suffering of service and as helping complete the sufferings of Christ (Colossians 1:24) and live into Paul's value of sharing the fellowship of Christ's suffering (Philippians 3:10).

Conclusion

In this chapter, the "redemption" pillar was focused on, given Jesus' atonement is central to Christians' ability to be reconciled to God. Rather than striving to somehow "fix" their pain on their own and in isolation, the grand narrative of Scripture reveals the hope that is available to Christian clients in Christ's life, death, and resurrection, with Jesus becoming a human to take on the sins of the world and being raised from the dead to bring them into the new creation of communion and joy. Although humans are fallen because we chose to turn away from God, shifting our focus back to him by believing in Christ and following him along the roads of life can help us to ameliorate some (although by no means all) of the suffering that comes from a wandering mind and isolated existence. Because God is our secure base and safe haven, as well as our Redeemer, we can confidently venture out into the world, reaching for him to soothe our inevitable bumps and bruises as we lose our footing during the long treks of life's journeys. Having been reconciled to God through Christ, we can experience a secure attachment with God, maintained by spending time with him in solitude and meditation, enabling us to confidently navigate the beautiful world he created, all the while recognizing that he is firmly planted at the center of existence.

Note

1 See also Knabb and Frederick (2017) for a review of the relationship between *theosis*, the Jesus Prayer, and psychological and spiritual functioning.

References
Allestree, R. (2018). *The Whole Duty of Divine Meditation*. Crossville, TN: Puritan Publications.

Baer, R. A., Smith, G. T., Hopkins, J., Krietemeyer, J., & Toney, L. (2006). Using self-report assessment methods to explore facets of mindfulness. *Assessment, 13*, 27–45.

Bangley, B. (Ed.) (2006). *The Cloud of Unknowing: Contemporary English Edition.* Brewster, MA: Paraclete Press.

Bateman, A., & Fonagy, P. (2016). *Treatment for Personality Disorders: A Practical Guide.* New York: Oxford University Press.

Beasley-Topliffe, K. (2017). *The Upper Room Dictionary of Christian Spiritual Formation.* Nashville, TN: Upper Room Books.

Beeke, J., & Jones, M. (2012). *A Puritan Theology: Doctrine for Life.* Grand Rapids, MI: Reformation Heritage Books.

Benner, D. (2010). *Opening to God: Lectio divina and Life as Prayer.* Downers Grove, IL: InterVarsity Press.

Bennett, A. (Ed.) (1975). *The Valley of Vision: A Collection of Puritan Prayers and Devotions.* Carlisle, PA: The Banner of Truth Trust.

Bowden J. (Ed.) (2005). *Encyclopedia of Christianity.* New York: Oxford University Press.

Ciarrocchi, J. W. (1995). *The Doubting Disease: Help for Scrupulosity and Religious Compulsions.* New York: Integration Books.

Clinton, T., & Straub, J. (2010). *God Attachment: Why You Believe, Act, and Feel the Way You Do about God.* New York: Howard Books.

Cosby, B. (2012). *Suffering and Sovereignty: John Flavel and the Puritans on Afflictive Providence.* Grand Rapids, MI: Reformation Heritage Books.

Dugas, M., & Robichaud, M. (2007). *Cognitive-Behavioral Treatment for Generalized Anxiety Disorder: From Science to Practice.* New York: Routledge.

Ehring, T., & Watkins, E. (2008). Repetitive negative thinking as a transdiagnostic process. *International Journal of Cognitive Therapy, 1,* 192–205.

Feeney, B., & Collins, N. (2004). Interpersonal safe haven and secure base caregiving processes in adulthood. In W. Rholes & J. Simpson (Eds.), *Adult Attachment: Theory, Research, and Clinical Implications* (pp. 300–338). New York: The Guilford Press.

Flavel, J. (2015). *The Mystery of Providence.* Louisville, KY: GLH Publishing.

Gama, M. P. (2017). *Theosis: A Patristic Remedy for Evangelical Yearning at the Close of the Modern Age.* Eugen, OR: Wipf & Stock.

Garland, D. (1999). *2 Corinthians.* Nashville, TN: B&H Publishing Group.

Harink, D. (2009). *1 & 2 Peter.* Grand Rapids, MI: Brazos Press.

Hayes, S., Strosahl, K., & Wilson, K. (2012). *Acceptance and Commitment Therapy: The Process and Practice of Mindful Change* (2nd ed.). New York: The Guilford Press.

Hickman, D. (2016). *Closer than Close: Awakening to the Freedom of Your Union with Christ.* Colorado Springs, CO: NavPress.

Johnson, E. L. (2017). *God and Soul Care: The Therapeutic Resources of the Christian Faith.* Downers Grove, IL: InterVarsity Press.

Johnston, W. (1970). *The Still Point: Reflections on Zen and Christian Mysticism.* New York: Fordham University Press.

Jollie, T. (2015). *A Treatise on Heavenly-Mindedness.* Crossville, TN: Puritan Publications.

Keller, T. (2015). *Walking with God through Pain and Suffering.* New York: Riverhead Books.

Knabb, J. (2016). *Faith-Based ACT for Christian Clients: An Integrative Treatment Approach.* New York: Routledge.

Knabb, J. (2018). *The Compassion-Based Workbook for Christian Clients: Finding Freedom from Shame and Negative Self-Judgments.* New York: Routledge.

Knabb, J., & Emerson, M. (2013). "I will be your God and you will be my people": Attachment theory and the grand narrative of scripture. *Pastoral Psychology, 62,* 827–841.

Knabb, J., & Frederick, T. (2017). *Contemplative Prayer for Christians with Chronic Worry: An Eight-Week Program.* New York: Routledge.

Lambert, M. (2013). The efficacy and effectiveness of psychotherapy. In M. Lambert (Ed.), *Bergin and Garfield's Handbook of Psychotherapy and Behavior Change* (pp. 169–218). New York: John Wiley & Sons.

Linehan, M. (2015). *DBT Skills Training Handouts and Worksheets* (2nd ed.). New York: The Guilford Press.

Lonsdale, D. (2005). Detachment. In P. Sheldrake (Ed.), *The New Westminster Dictionary of Christian Spirituality* (p. 234). Louisville, KY: Westminster John Knox Press.

Manning, B. (1994). *Abba's Child*: Colorado Springs, CO: NavPress.

McClymond, M. J., & McDermott, G. R. (2011). *The Theology of Jonathan Edwards.* New York: Oxford University Press.

McCullough, L., Kuhn, N., Andrews, S., Kaplan, A., Wolf, J., & Hurley, C. L. (2003). *Treating Affect Phobia: A Manual for Short-Term Dynamic Psychotherapy.* New York: Guilford.

Mikulincer, M., & Shaver, P. (2007). *Attachment in Adulthood: Structure, Dynamics, and Change.* New York: The Guilford Press.

Miles, M. (1983). Detachment. In G. Wakefield (Ed.), *The Westminster Dictionary of Christian Spirituality* (p. 111). Philadelphia, PA: The Westminster Press.

Milliken, J. (2003). Grace. In C. Brand, C. Draper, & A. England (Eds.), *Holman Illustrated Bible Dictionary* (p. 678). Nashville, TN: Holman Reference.

Norman, S. (2003). Redemption. In C. Brand, C. Draper, & A. England (Eds.), *Holman Illustrated Bible Dictionary* (pp. 1370–1371). Nashville, TN: Holman Reference.

Owen, J. (1965). *The Works of John Owen* (Vols. 1–16). Edinburgh: Banner of Truth Trust.

Rakestraw, R. (1997). Becoming like God: An evangelical doctrine of theosis. *Journal of the Evangelical Theological Society, 40,* 257–269.

Segal, Z., Williams, M., & Teasdale, J. (2012). *Mindfulness-Based Cognitive Therapy for Depression* (2nd ed.). New York: The Guilford Press.

Smith, J. B. (2013). *Hidden in Christ: Living as God's Beloved.* Downers Grove, IL: InterVarsity Press.

Talbot, J. (2013). *The Jesus Prayer: A Cry for Mercy, a Path of Renewal.* Downers Grove, IL: InterVarsity Press.

Ware, K. (2000). *The Inner Kingdom.* Crestwood, NY: St. Vladimir's Seminary Press.

Ware, K. (2013). *The Power of the Name: The Jesus Prayer in Orthodox Spirituality.* Oxford: SLG Press.

Wells, A. (2000). *Emotional Disorders and Metacognition: Innovative Cognitive Therapy.* New York: John Wiley & Sons.

Wilbourne, R. (2016). *Union with Christ: The Way to Know and Enjoy God.* Colorado Springs, CO: David C. Cook.

Williams, R., Davis, M., & Millsap, R. (2002). Development of the cognitive processing of trauma scale. *Clinical Psychology and Psychotherapy, 9,* 349–360.

Wilson, S. (1998). *Into Abba's Arms.* Nashville, TN: Tyndale House.

Index

Locators in *italic* refer to figures and those in **bold** to tables.